Russia in the European Context 1789–1914

RUSSIA IN THE EUROPEAN CONTEXT 1789–1914

A MEMBER OF THE FAMILY

Edited by

Susan P. McCaffray

and

Michael Melancon

RUSSIA IN THE EUROPEAN CONTEXT 1789–1914
© Susan P. McCaffray and Michael Melancon, 2005.

First published in 2005 by
PALGRAVE MACMILLAN™
175 Fifth Avenue, New York, N.Y. 10010 and
Houndmills, Basingstoke, Hampshire, England RG21 6XS
Companies and representatives throughout the world.

PALGRAVE MACMILLAN is the global academic imprint of the Palgrave Macmillan division of St. Martin's Press, LLC and of Palgrave Macmillan Ltd. Macmillan® is a registered trademark in the United States, United Kingdom and other countries. Palgrave is a registered trademark in the European Union and other countries.

ISBN 1–4039–6855–1

Library of Congress Cataloging-in-Publication Data

Russia in the European context, 1789–1914 : a member of the family / Susan P.
McCaffray and Michael Melancon, eds.
    p. cm.
Includes bibliographical references and index.
ISBN 1–4039–6855–1 (cloth)
    1. Russia—Social conditions—1801–1917. 2. Russia—Economic conditions—1861–1917. 3. Russia—Relations—Europe. 4. Europe—Relations—Russia. I. McCaffray, Susan Purves. II. Melancon, Michael S., 1940–

HN523.R84 2005
306′.0947′0904—dc22   2004057313

A catalogue record for this book is available from the British Library.

Design by Newgen Imaging Systems (P) Ltd., Chennai, India.

First edition: May 2005

10 9 8 7 6 5 4 3 2 1

Printed in the United States of America.

In memory of Reginald Zelnik

TABLE OF CONTENTS

NOTES ON CONTRIBUTORS

Boris V. Anan'ich is a member of the Russian Academy of Sciences in St. Petersburg. He is the author of *Bankirskie doma v Rossii [Banks in Russia] 1860–1914* (Nauka, 1991).

Jonathan Daly is Associate Professor of History at the University of Illinois, Chicago. He is the author of *Autocracy under Siege: Security Police and Opposition in Russia 1866–1905* (Northern Illinois, 1998).

Lee A. Farrow is Assistant Professor of History at Auburn University, Montgomery. She is the author of *Between Clan and Crown: The Struggle to Define Noble Property Rights in Imperial Russia* (University of Delaware, 2004).

Boris B. Gorshkov is Instructor of History at Auburn University. He is the author of "Serfs on the Move: Peasant Seasonal Migration in Pre-Reform Russia, 1800–1861," *Kritika* (Fall 2000).

Lutz Häfner is Adjunct Associate Professor of History at the University of Leipzig. He is the author of *Die Partei der Linken Sozialrevolutionaere in der Russischen Revolution von 1917/1918* (Boehlau, 1994).

Esther Kingston-Mann is Ford Service Professor of History and American Studies at the University of Massachusetts, Boston. She is the author of *In Search of the True West: Culture, Economics and Problems of Russian Development* (Princeton, 1999).

Susan P. McCaffray is Professor of History at the University of North Carolina, Wilmington. She is the author is *The Politics of Industrialization in Tsarist Russia: The Association of Southern Coal and Steel Producers, 1874–1914* (Northern Illinois, 1996).

Michael Melancon is Professor of History at Auburn University. He is the coeditor of *New Labor History: Worker Identity and Experience in Russia 1840–1918* (Slavica, 2002).

Alice K. Pate is Associate Professor of History at Columbia State University. She is the coeditor of *New Labor History: Worker Identity and Experience in Russia 1840–1918* (Slavica, 2002).

Susanna Rabow-Edling is Assistant Professor of East European Studies at Uppsala University. She is the author of *The Politics of Cultural Nationalism* (forthcoming, SUNY Press).

Frank Wcislo is Associate Professor of History at Vanderbilt University. He is the author of *Reforming Rural Russia: State, Local Society and Local Politics, 1855–1914* (Princeton, 1990).

Introduction: A Member of the Family—Russia's Place in Europe, 1789–1914

Susan P. McCaffray and Michael Melancon

A sophisticated Latvian lady, who had immigrated to the United States after World War II, settled first in New York City and later in North Carolina. Here she flourished, presiding over a literary salon and preserving her love of German and Russian literature. In defense of her interests she announced prosaically, "I'm no patriot." One day a friend held forth on the merits of "Eastern European" literature, while she nodded approvingly. When she spoke, however, she gently admonished her companion: "What you say is true; but Latvians do not really consider themselves East Europeans." Her interlocutor, struggling to conceal her surprise, inquired just how Latvians did characterize themselves: Central Europeans, perhaps? Northern Europeans? The lady nodded, wrinkling her brow. "Or," she added, "West Europeans."

In this willful act of geographic imagination lies a reality just as tangible as the treatises of scholars, the treaties of diplomats, and the barbed wire that once passed for an iron curtain. People, both individually and collectively, locate themselves not just physically, but culturally as well. "Western Europe," an imaginary location of prosperity, progress, and peace, not to mention liberty, equality, and fraternity, exists more purely as a cultural symbol than it does as a railway destination. Thus the light of "Western Europe" could shine forth in Riga, Philadelphia, and Sydney, while remaining dim in Clydeside, Belfast, and Andalusia.

It is not difficult to understand why a cultured expatriate would renounce membership in the Eastern Europe of Cold War imagination. The mental and political bifurcation of the world after 1945 gave rise to the useful category "Eastern Europe," which included all the heterogeneous zones from which the Red Army had failed to recede. If "Eastern Europe" was made to bear the weight of all European failures, by default "Western Europe" accumulated more and more luster, toward which even "unpatriotic" Latvians fled, at least in their minds. In fact, the lands that lay east of the iron curtain constituted an imaginary terrain that grew, over 40 years of Soviet–American rivalry, increasingly homogeneous, increasingly lost, and increasingly beyond redemption. One of the saddest consequences of this long contest was the intellectually deceitful homogenization and denigration of so many histories.

Before the twentieth century, the good and the bad Europes had not been identified geographically. To be sure, there were widespread notions among educated Europeans that certain cities, certain universities, even at times certain countries, represented the leading edge of enlightened progress. But eighteenth- and nineteenth-century Europeans were far more open to the possibility that cultural refinement and scientific learning might emanate from any of Europe's far-flung corners. Undoubtedly, a dark and uncultured Europe existed, but it existed within each country, within each great city, and within the hearts of individuals. As the horrors of the twentieth century unfolded, Europe's cultural spokespeople struggled to identify the fatal flaws of a civilization that had once seemed bright with hope of unlimited progress. Their search, unfortunately, was cut short by the post–World War II embrace of ideology and military division as the way to understand and to wall out Europe's heart of darkness. In a deft act of collective sublimation, Stalin's Soviet Union became heir to all of Europe's twentieth-century sins, and all of Russia's subject nations were tainted by association.

Even though this inferior Europe was not entirely contiguous with the lands from which Nazis and Fascists had arisen (not to mention its distance from the bloodied banks of the Somme), it starkly demarcated an un-European Europe—a dark and backward Europe. Of course, more than one generation of Hungarians, Czechs, Poles, and Estonians struggled to escape, at least culturally, from the bloc of lesser Europe. The youth of 1989 reaped their harvest, and in what seemed to a forgetful world like the blink of an eye the imagined fiefdom of "Eastern Europe" melted away. In the years since, the states of the old Soviet bloc have been welcomed into pan-European organizations. With each successive wave of admissions to NATO and the European Union it became clearer that only one people could not escape the stigma of being labeled Eastern Europeans. The Cold War legacy persists in the stark designation of a good and a bad Europe, and Russia's identification with the latter.

Although twentieth-century politicians and publics adopted outright this straightforward characterization, it also influenced historical interpreters. The problem of Russia's place in Europe was not new in the twentieth century, of course. As a frontier land its nature has always seemed disputable to both natives and foreigners. As the easternmost branch of Christendom, in a vocabulary in which "east" meant non-Christian and "Christendom" meant west, Russia's nature has always been open to interpretation. Since the renewal of steady contact between the peoples of westernmost and easternmost Europe during the sixteenth century, interpreters on both sides of Europe have struggled to enumerate their common and distinctive features.

If the interpretive debate is hoary and familiar, the hard edges of Russia's twentieth century imparted to it a new rigidity, not least because many of the interpreters themselves bore the scars of Russia's nightmare years. The Elizabethan adventurer's "rude and barbarous kingdom" becomes Churchill's more ominous "riddle wrapped in a mystery inside an enigma."[1] Ivan the Terrible becomes Stalin, the Third Rome becomes the Third International, Orthodoxy becomes Leninism: the exception becomes the rule, the peculiar becomes the norm. The sense that in Russia a warped Christianity took root and proved unreformable becomes the perception of a warped modernity, which even revolution cannot improve. In an age of intense model building, Russia becomes the model of perversity. Russia's presumed inferiority, backwardness, retarded development, propensity to imitation, and perennial failures become the ubiquitous elements of many, if not most, historical interpretations, and not just foreign ones.

Overlaid as it is with so much obscuring grime, this portrait of Russian exceptionalism may not be susceptible to clarification. It appears that the great debate about Russia's relationship with Europe is not resolvable. The debate itself is a timeless trope, supple and malleable, and no less useful to "the West" than to Russia. Nearly all the greatest Russian historians have weighed in on the matter, several of them explicitly. In his day George Vernadsky was known for his interpretation of Russia's middle ages as lacking the institutions of feudalism. The career-long debate between Richard Pipes and Martin Malia has illuminated Russian political and social history and, at the same time, has forced scholars to ask themselves what, essentially, marks "the West." As Malia's latest volume indicates, even at the culmination of such an illustrious career it will not be possible to settle this debate to everyone's satisfaction.[2]

Although we cannot end the debate, we can shine our own light on it. We can consider the problem from the perspective of our own time, which is especially preoccupied with reflexivity, with frontiers, and with challenges to inherited categories. This is the project that contributors to the present volume have undertaken.[3] Here we consider Russia's long nineteenth century (marked by the universal European hallmarks of 1789 and 1914), the period during which questions of Europe's character and destiny most sharply preoccupied thinkers and statesmen from the Thames to the Volga. The nineteenth century sharpened the question of identity, as Europeans confronted accelerating and earth-shattering changes at home as well as expanding contacts with the worlds beyond Europe. Everywhere people were forced to ponder, for example, what "European" could mean in a world in which Christian pietism was waning; peasant villages were being abandoned; venerable dynasties were falling; and "universal" languages, like the last vestiges of the ancient Roman center, were melting away. Pressure to name the essential elements of European culture came also from encounters in Calcutta, Cairo, Shanghai, Samarkand, and a hundred other places where increasing numbers of European soldiers, missionaries, adventurers, investors, engineers, and reporters found themselves.

For Russia the pressures of the nineteenth century pulled in conflicting directions. On the one hand, as encounters grew with the world that was definitely not Europe, Russians were increasingly assured that they, themselves, belonged to the European world. On the other hand, as industry and constitutionalism slowly extended their reach, new bases of "otherness" within Europe also appeared. The question of Russia's place in Europe sharpened. It preoccupied more and more Russian statesmen, philosophers, businessmen, and writers.[4] The tension in this dual act of self-definition was particularly intense in Russia, but in this area, as in most others, Russia's experience was not atypical of Europe's as a whole. Over the course of the nineteenth century, people living in every corner of the continent risked being relegated to a culturally inferior Europe. This also entailed the possibility of being banished from cultural Europe altogether, if a people did not keep up and make progress along not just some road but *the* road to the luminous future. Philosophers voiced what others believed: the one road led to the one future, at which all of humanity would one day arrive, although Europeans, natural colonizers, would arrive first.[5] The conceptual problem was that Europe was vast and, in truth, diverse. If all Europeans could not squeeze through the portal to the future at the same time, how should the latecomers be perceived? Were they slow (backward, inferior) Europeans? Were they, perhaps, not really Europeans at all? Or, in a society increasingly preoccupied with the labeling of biological categories and miscegenation, were they some sort of a dangerous half-breed, a frontier people of mixed culture and race? The anxiety that we find in Russian writings of this period is also palpable elsewhere. Had the useful category of "Eastern Europe" existed a century earlier than it did, we might have seen a bitter Irishman consign his own country to it in the ruinous 1840s.

What can historians of our own time add to this discussion? Most obviously, we are less explicitly accepting of the image of progress and thus of "the West's" progressive role in history. Many would like to dispense with the notion of progress altogether, but so much is at stake in rejecting this idea that it cannot be abandoned until an appropriate replacement is found. Moreover, a growing number of scholars in our part of the world is willing and able to investigate the indigenous history of people far from Europe. Global history, world history, and postcolonial studies, as well as increasing competence in historical study of the cultures of Africa, the Middle East, and Asia undertaken by Western scholars, cast a reflexive shadow backwards and keep the question of Western identity alive. This only deepens the conundrum about Europe's cultural frontier peoples, including the Russians. The more we learn about various peoples, the less certain we are that our categories are serving us well.

For those who persist in studying the Old World, it becomes increasingly necessary to enter into conversation with newer fields of inquiry. Which of their questions might we ask of our old topic, and how can Russia's experience illuminate new fields of study? The repertoire of analytical tools expands along with the objects of scholarly inquiry. With new tools, and with new uses for old ones, Russian historians are particularly well suited to ask some very important questions, of which, "what is Russia's place in Europe?" is only the most ancient. We might also find ourselves better able to deal with matters such as: is it useful to consider those European cultures undergoing the fastest change as the norm, and those most resistant to change as deviant or backward? According to what premises does the rapid development of industry or revolutionary political change signify success? Similarly, does the durability of old governments, lifestyles, and values signify failure? What is embedded in these notions of success and failure? Any light that Russian historians can shed on these questions may help to illuminate not only historical processes, but also the events of our own time, in which the meaning of the term "Europe" is being contested from Portugal to Turkey.

We might revisit, in addition, the problem of the construction of models and the Enlightenment notion of universal patterns. When similarities between forward and backward parts of Europe appear, should we account for them through recourse to notions of "borrowing" and "imitating"? Or does the existence of these similarities cast doubt on the very notion of forwardness and backwardness? Most profoundly, is it useful and accurate to imagine a progressive, "normal" Europe, a Europe we may as well go ahead and simply identify with nineteenth-century Britain (but only parts of it), from which all other parts deviate to greater or lesser extents? What should we do with the Europe of communal farmers, indolent landowners, and holy wanderers, with the Europe of machine-breakers, fortune-tellers, and reindeer-herders, all of whom existed until at least the twentieth century? If nineteenth-century intellectuals articulated many ways of being European, why, when we look backward, do we see so few? Is it worth the effort to resurrect this nineteenth-century Europe in which it was not yet clear who future generations would crown the winners in the race to the future? Is it even possible to rediscover that nineteenth-century Europe in which many important things were mostly *not* settled? If the answer to either of these last questions is yes, then Russia's nineteenth century is central to the effort.

Each of the scholars contributing to this volume has engaged themes and literature from outside Russian history while pointing to wider applications that might be drawn from the study of Russia. Each essay considers Russians who were either implicitly or explicitly preoccupied with their country's place in Europe during the long nineteenth century. Although these essays do not find unanimity among Russian thinkers and actors, they do reveal an intelligentsia broadly engaged in the effort to identify essential features of modernity and the quest for a definition of European identity. There is strong evidence that throughout the nineteenth century, Russian opinion makers broadly embraced Alexander Herzen's conviction that Russians, as Europeans of a distinct type, had their own contribution to make to the formation of European modernity.

Moreover, these pieces suggest that when Russian thinkers thought the same things as other European thinkers it was because they were participating in a dialogue that engaged all European elites. It may be more fruitful to see Russians as responding to common European experiences than as perennially borrowing and imitating. Altogether these essays invite us to broaden our understanding of Europe and, perhaps, to reject the cultural division of Europe into forward and backward, successful and failed, "Western" and

"Eastern" spheres. They allow us to recognize that self-criticism and debate about the imagined or desired future are, themselves, hallmarks of European civilization. It may be that the sense that the future is theirs to make is the most distinguishing mark of the Europeans.

The subjects under investigation here are statesmen, *intelligenti*, business-men, noblemen and women, jurists, statisticians, and readers of newspapers. They represent the class of Europeans who dreamed aloud about the future, one of the nineteenth century's most characteristic endeavors. We avoid the presumption that whatever the Russians came up with was imitative (but poorly), unsophisticated, late, and doomed. We strive to preserve the sense of rich possibilities that gripped Russian intellectuals, officials, and professionals in the nineteenth century, who were sometimes well informed about other countries, and who enthused about what could be learned from their failures as well as their successes. Several of these essays challenge the chronological assumption that most Russian innovations, and all substantive improvements, post-date their Western counterparts.

The Russia that emerges from this effort is wholly European. Government officials come to see themselves as presiding over an "economy," requiring skilled management of currency, credit institutions, property relations, com-munication networks, labor resources, and statistical information. Educated professionals and businessmen strive to expand their own role in a society over which they believe they should preside and expand their influence over a state that they seek to make their own. In other words, they struggle to extend the public sphere while enhancing their own position within it. Philosophers, social critics, and spokesmen from "the people" master the tools of modern communication in order to raise voices that challenge the elite vision of progress.

If this Russia is European in the nature of most of its challenges and the shape of many of its responses, in the details, the language, the color, and the flavor of its choices, it is a particular place with a culture in some key ways unique. As they responded to many of the similar changes and trends as other Europeans, Russians approached problems from a particular cultural tradition, and operated within a particular geographic environment, which imparted a unique cast to many of their solutions. It is not surprising that a culture rooted in eastern Orthodoxy differed from one colored by Roman Catholicism or radical Calvinism, just as the latter two differed from one another. It is to be expected that institutions that evolved to govern a vast and disparate plain differed from those that arose among inhabitants of a small, maritime island. A people who labor long to prepare for a dark and dangerous winter see life rather differently than the more carefree inhabitants of a bountiful and sunny coast. The particularities of location, climate, history, tradition, language, and religion make Russia different, and impart to Russians a peculiar way of looking at problems common to all. But even in this, Russia is a typical European country. The Europeans are people who have clung to regional as much as "national" distinctions, not to mention languages. No one has resisted the creation of an imperial center better than they have. In nineteenth-century Russia, as elsewhere in Europe, we can see, if we are willing to, the great and varied collision of ancient cultures with the common problems produced by what E.J. Hobsbawm called the "dual revolution" in politics and economy. Thus, when we see Russians reluctant to embrace private property, laissez faire economics, and scientific rationalism we need not read this as evidence of pathological deviance from a universal European norm. Instead, we see the contested possibilities of a nineteenth-century Europe that knew nothing of twentieth-century categories. Ideas that seem strange or doomed in retrospect seemed very much alive 150 years ago, and not just in Russia.

If we can abandon the image of inferiority and deviance, we can more fruitfully analyze some of Russia's special features toward which this volume points. Several of the essays on economic envisioning suggest that officials and entrepreneurs keen to stimulate economic development faced a problem more pronounced in Russia than anywhere else, namely overwhelming distances and the resulting sparseness, not the lack of transportation networks, towns, banks, and capital. The merits of density and the disadvantages of sparseness for industrialization and capitalism are worth a sustained analysis. The question that bridges the line between economic and social thinking is the role of attitudes toward property and work. Several of these essays reveal conscious deliberation by bureaucrats and social critics alike about these two foundational aspects of industrial capitalism. Although the sources of what may well be a distinctive Russian approach to property and work remain debatable, this volume points to several of its consequences, including a comparatively early embrace of state-sponsored welfare legislation. Finally, Russia's long nineteenth century offers a laboratory for characterizing the emergence of a public sphere in the absence of republican institutions. We welcome further investigation into these and other aspects of Russian distinctiveness suggested by our research. We hope, however, that in the future scholars will assert Russian uniqueness more judiciously, and only after testing the claim.

We have organized our collection along two general themes. In the first part, five essays consider Russians inside and outside government who were preoccupied with the quintessentially nineteenth-century European project of envisioning a modern economy. Lee Farrow tackles one of the most fertile areas for comparing and contrasting Russia and the purported model countries in her analysis of Russian inheritance and property law. Through meticulous attention to both law and practice, she is able to illuminate culturally specific practices that address universal questions in ways that differ less than what might be expected from those well-known in the west of Europe. Susan McCaffray examines one prominent bureaucrat/philosopher whose preoccupation with the universal European problems of wartime finance and trade policy led him toward an early prescription for economic development and capital formation. Boris Gorshkov reconsiders Russian labor and social insurance legislation, demonstrating that the response of state, business, and labor elites to the welfare challenges of industrial development were well within the range of European responses and in many ways ahead of the free enterprise giants of westernmost Europe. Frank Wcislo offers a reinterpretation of Sergei Witte, placing him in the context of European railroad builders and technocratic dreamers. Boris Anan'ich demonstrates that at least throughout the nineteenth century, entrepreneurial cultures could be subnational and distinctive, as in the case of Russia's Old Believers and Jews, while still conforming to empire-wide and international standards.

Part II takes up the problem of envisioning a modern, European society. Susanna Rabow-Edling's rich reading of Slavophile thought places them within the tradition of European Romantic nationalists while denying that Romantics (including the Slavophiles) were anti-modern or anti-European. Esther Kingston-Mann examines the views of zemstvo activists and other defenders of peasant agriculture at mid-century. In doing so she explicitly questions the assumption that the English package of enclosure, privatization, and destruction of commons rights represented progress, and that Russia's deviation from these practices represented backwardness. Together Rabow-Edling and Kingston-Mann provide powerful evidence that our conception of "typical European" institutions and ideas has been too narrow. Lutz Häfner's archival study of local clubs and organizations demonstrates the gradual development of a local society that resembled the German or Austrian "Bürgertum" or civil society, while pointing out factors that hindered its full flourishing. Jonathan Daly surveys jurists' efforts to modernize Russia's penal system, offering several surprising comparisons with punishments elsewhere in Europe. Alice Pate takes up the neglected 1912 social insurance legislation that may be seen as a culmination of nineteenth-century Russian thinking about the universal problems of urban welfare in industrialized society. As such it is fascinating to consider the 1912 legislation in light of what had been as well as what was to come. Finally, Michael Melancon interrogates a wide spectrum of the Russian press between 1910 and 1914 and concludes that on the eve of World War I, Russian society, far from being hopelessly at odds with itself, confidently assumed and aimed at integration into the community of modern nations.

The effort to generalize about Russia has undone many fine scholars and writers, although we continue to appreciate those who dare to do so. In this volume the separate contributors have employed careful scrutiny of particular topics in order to reconsider a common generalization about modern Russia: that it was utterly unique, that it deviated fatally from European pathways, and that, implicitly, its twentieth-century problems stemmed from this fatal, permanent exceptionalism. Although we must concede that interpretation is, ultimately, an individual matter, and that the same glass of water may appear half-full and half-empty to different observers, we will be pleased if readers come away from this volume willing, at least, to accept three propositions.

First, in European history, uniqueness is not unique. The peculiar institutions and notions that gradually reveal themselves to long-suffering scholars do not in themselves prove that a given society lies outside an imagined norm.

As José Ortega y Gasset wrote long ago, Europe is a civilization where we find "the same things, but in a different way."

Second, even in the nineteenth century, England ought not to be understood explicitly or implicitly as a universal model, much less synonym, for Europe. Indeed, it may be that if one European country is unique, it is England. At any rate, however successful England's institutions and choices proved to be, historians must help others to understand just how contested many of these institutions and choices were—both at home and abroad. If England's way was widely admired and many efforts were undertaken to emulate it, criticism of England's way was also undoubtedly a typical and widespread phenomenon of nineteenth-century Europe. To put it another way, both the mythical England and the mythical anti-England were hallmarks of the nineteenth-century European (including the Russian) imagination.

Finally, despite its tremendous utility, it may be time to abandon the great interpretive tool of "backwardness." When many different people in many countries are able, thanks to burgeoning media, to carry on long conversations and debate, they will undoubtedly exchange ideas and experiment with practices they learn about in the discussion. When one adopts a practice after another the latter is, technically "behind" (although we note this only if the experiment turns out to be successful). But is the heavy baggage of the term "backward" appropriate to this perpetual, ubiquitous exchange? If General Electric adopts an innovation first embraced by IBM should we characterize GE as a backward corporation? In fact, its board of directors may well consider such ability to extract useful ideas from elsewhere as a sign of managerial prowess. Moreover, if Russia adopted (as it did) a program of universal accident insurance in 1912, but the United States failed to do so until the Depression, should we consider the United States to have borrowed this idea from backward Russia? Is a country backward only if it fails to adopt good ideas? Or just ideas universally accepted as good (if there are any)? Or, perhaps, just if it fails to adopt our ideas? If a country never adopts certain practices, is there any statute of limitations on its designation as backward— a point, perhaps, at which it becomes just different? At the very least, we must interrogate ourselves about this term carefully and explain clearly what we decide we mean by it.

The imagined Europe of nineteenth-century progress, prosperity, and peace remains admirable. That it actually existed, to the extent that it did, is remarkable. That it committed suicide is tragic. There truly is, and always was, a dark and inferior Europe. But it was never contiguous with a polity or even a culture. Like the others, Russians live in both the light and the shadow, and the institutions they have built reflect their mixed record.

NOTES

1. Richard Chancellor traveled to Russia in 1553 and 1555, and his account is available in Lloyd E. Berry and Robert O. Crummey, *Rude and Barbarous Kingdom: Russia in the Accounts of Sixteenth-Century English Voyagers* (Madison: University

of Wisconsin Press, 1968), 9–41. Prime Minister Winston Churchill offered his famous assessment in an October, 1939 radio address in which he declared that he could not predict what Joseph Stalin's Soviet Union was up to.

2. See Martin Malia, *Russia Under Western Eyes* (Cambridge, MA: Belnap Press, 1999). Richard Pipes has authored numerous works that detail his assertion that Russia is better understood as essentially an "Asian" country. For a taste of this view, see his *Russia Observed: Collected Essays on Russia and Soviet History* (Boulder, CO: Westview Press, 1989). George Vernadsky's venerable history is *A History of Russia* 5 vols. (New Haven, CT: Yale University Press, 1969).

3. A few others have begun to consider reinterpreting Russia's relationship to modern Europe. See, e.g., David L. Hoffmann and Yanni Kotsonis, *Russian Modernity: Politics, Knowledge, Practices* (New York: St. Martin's Press, 2000), especially Kotsonis' introduction, 1–16. Other innovative approaches that implicitly address aspects of Russia's place in the wider world include Jane Burbank and David Ransel, *Imperial Russia: New Histories for the Empire* (Bloomington: Indiana University Press, 1998); Esther Kingston-Mann, *In Search of the True West: Culture, Economics, and Problems of Russian Development* (Princeton University Press, 1999); Edith W. Clowes et al., *Between Tsar and People: Educated Society and the Quest for Public Identity in Late Imperial Russia* (Princeton: Princeton University Press, 1991); Laura Engelstein, *The Keys to Happiness: Sex and the Search for Modernity in Fin-de-Siecle Russia* (Ithaca, NY: Cornell University Press, 1992); and Louise McReynolds, *Russia at Play: Leisure Activities at the End of the Tsarist Era* (Ithaca, NY: Cornell University Press, 2003).

4. Well-known participants in the public debate about how much of the Enlightenment legacy to adopt included Westernizers Petr Chaadayev and Vissarion Belinskii, businessmen such as the Riabushinkii brothers or Alexander Fenin, finance ministers from Mikhail Reutern to Sergei Witte and official reformers from Mikhail Speranskii to Petr Stolypin. Countless less well-known figures engaged in these discussions, much of which can be found in print in nineteenth- and early twentieth-century journals.

5. In a recent article, Esther Kingston-Mann quotes John Stuart Mill to the effect that "Whoever knows the political economy of England, or even of Yorkshire, knows that of all nations, actual or possible," and Karl Marx, who observed that "England shows to the less developed nations of the world the image of their future." See her "Deconstructing the Romance of the Bourgeoisie: A Russian Marxist Path not Taken," *Review of International Political Economy*, 10, no.1 (February 2003): 95.

PART I

ENVISIONING AN ECONOMY

2

The Ties that Bind: The Role of the Russian Clan in Inheritance and Property Law

Lee A. Farrow

In *Woe from Wit*, Alexander Griboedov's character Famusov describes the central role of the family in Imperial Russia:

> Very few people work with me who aren't relations
> Most of them are my sister's children,
> Or else my sister-in-law's; there's only one exception—
> Molchalin—that's because he is so capable
> But when it comes to putting up a name
> For a nice post, or some small decoration,
> One has to think of kith and kin![1]

Russia was not unique in this, of course. Aristocratic societies across Europe relied on family ties and patronage for positions at the court, in the church, and in the military. Nepotism was the rule, rather than the exception, and family members were bound together by their successes and failures, politically, economically, and socially.[2]

Family members were also bound together by their interests in landed property. Landownership stood at the center of the European noble's economic, family, and social life, and determined to a large degree his wealth, power, and social status. Exclusive ownership of land (or certain types of land) was, of course, one of the main privileges of the nobility. The Russian nobility certainly fits neatly into the Western picture in this regard: landownership was central to Russian nobles as well, and served as a vehicle for family maintenance and advancement. Moreover, as in Western Europe, many, if not most, of the Russian noble's social relations were dictated by the ownership of land.[3]

Given these commonalities between Russian and European nobilities, one would expect that their laws and customs, as well as their attitudes, about land would be similar. Such is not the case, however. There were some similarities, of course: nobles of all nationalities valued land and wanted more of it. Yet Russian law and custom treated land differently. The most signifi-cant example of this is Russia's long-held practice of redemption, a tradition eventually made law, that permitted extended family members to repurchase sold or mortgaged land during a period of up to 40 years. Furthermore, although it was common in Western Europe for noble families to have very close ties to the land, passing family property from generation to generation more or less intact, and attaching the name of the estate to the family name, in Russia, the situation was somewhat different, with only the wealthiest noble families able to sustain such continuity. Historians have contended that Russian nobles never developed strong attachments to individual estates. Even after the end of compulsory service in 1762, few nobles used this opportunity to invest substantial time and energy in the management and improvement of their estates, a conclusion supported by the limited success of the Free Economic Society in promoting physiocratic ideals and agricul-tural modernization.[4]

There were exceptions, of course. Historians such as Michael Confino and John H. Brown have argued that there were nobles, particularly after 1762, who showed significant interest in and attachment to their estates. Confino argues, for example, that after the abolition of compulsory service in 1762, combined with the opportunities and rights presented by Catherine's reforms of the 1770s and 1780s, noblemen energetically turned to the man-agement of their estates. Brown cites the case of Andrei Bolotov. Famous for his lengthy memoirs and his participation in the Free Economic Society, Bolotov invested significant time and energy into his estate, constructing elaborate gardens and experimenting with new fertilizers. Finally, Priscilla Roosevelt's study of the Russian estate supports the argument that there were many nobles who demonstrated interest in their estates. She describes numerous Russian country estates and the significant time, energy, and money that were invested to create these lavish retreats. Even Roosevelt admits, however, that the Russians were the last of the European nobilities to pursue estate living as a means of social and personal expression.[5]

Historians have tended to regard the nobility's attitudes toward its estates, and practices such as partible inheritance and repeated mortgaging in partic-ular, as examples of irrational and destructive behavior. More recently, how-ever, Valerie Kivelson has suggested that noble inheritance practices should be viewed not as evidence of shortsightedness, but rather as practical strate-gies in a complex social and political system in which nobles were both rulers and ruled. Furthermore, she argues, these practices may suggest how the nobility and crown arrived at a compromise to satisfy the needs and demands of both parties.[6] Kivelson is correct in arguing that noble practices and atti-tudes toward immovable property should be understood within the context of the social and political realities of noble life. Whether these practices were part of a functioning compromise is, however, open to debate. This study argues that the nobility's behavior toward its land emerged less from a sym-biotic relationship between crown and nobility, than from the profound sense of insecurity that members of the nobility felt regarding their persons and property, and that this insecurity derived from the restrictive influences of both the state and the *rod*, or clan.

Throughout the Imperial period, noble property rights were defined and constrained by two overwhelming forces: the state and the clan. The state controlled property in a variety of ways, restricting ownership, establishing inheritance and redemption laws, and confiscating property for crimes and debt. To a large degree, at least for the first half of the Imperial period, Russian nobles possessed land at the pleasure of the monarch. This was particularly true since Russian monarchs used land to reward faithful service and seized land from those who failed to demonstrate sufficient loyalty. Thus, the relationship between tsar, nobility, and landownership was a tightly woven and complex one.

The state, however, was not the only influence at work. Noble property rights were also constrained by the omnipresence of the clan. Though the definition of clan varied depending on the circumstances, one thing is clear— nobles viewed clan membership as important and imbued with certain obligations and rights, particularly with regard to property. In fact, there was a truly familial character to noble landholding in Imperial Russia in which extended family members had a voice in decisions about property that had been in the clan for more than one generation. State laws supported clan influence though inheritance and redemption laws that gave preference to family over nonfamily members and restricted an individual's ability to sell or bequeath land. Though nobles often chafed under the influence of the clan, they simultaneously were quick to assert clan privileges when it offered the potential of personal gain. This strong influence of the extended family over individual desires marks a considerable difference from the situation in Western Europe where, by the eighteenth century, the interests of the smaller family unit predominated.[7] This difference in clan influence accounts, in part, for the differences in land and inheritance laws in Russia as compared with most of those in Western Europe. It also helps to explain the weak, or delayed, development of private property in Imperial Russia.

THE EUROPEAN CONTEXT

The centrality of land in the lives of European nobles naturally meant that inheritance and other methods of land distribution were matters of great importance. Despite this common aristocratic concern, European nobilities employed very different and often complex strategies to oversee land distribution to children and other family members.[8] There were regional differences, of course, both between countries and within countries, and also variations based on wealth within each European nobility. Moreover, practices combined both law and custom and shifted over time. Finally, European nobilities struggled to reconcile the tension between the various interests of family members—between the preservation of the family as a whole and the provision for individual members. This tension was felt not only by the state and its lawmakers, but also by nobles who struggled to strike the right balance. The difficulty of following the correct path helps to explain the complexity of European inheritance law and practices and the many changes that occurred between the thirteenth and nineteenth centuries. In the eternal debate between "lumpers" and "splitters" it might be argued that too many variations preclude the possibility of drawing general conclusions; however, such an argument would be too conveniently dismissive. Even within the varied and complex landscape of European inheritance practices, there are some major tendencies that can be identified, for example, the predominance of male over female heirs and the preservation of the family in general. Perhaps the most significant trend in Western Europe was the adoption of restrictive inheritance practices.

Since land was the central means of wealth and status for most European nobles, the fragmentation of estates was a major concern in inheritance decisions. Thus, by the sixteenth and seventeenth centuries, or in some cases even earlier, most Western European countries had begun to introduce legal devices of various forms to prevent the fragmentation of estates. Primogeniture, for example, existed in both law and custom. The law of primogeniture was strictest in England, but also prevailed in much of Western Europe, though the severity of its application varied from place to place. In many places, for example, primogeniture was used for only a portion of the family's holdings, or was applied only in cases of intestacy. In addition, the custom of primogeniture had a power all its own and influenced testamentary arrangements even where it was not mandated by law. Still, it is important to realize that even where primogeniture was practiced, younger children were usually provided for through a variety of arrangements, including the inheritance of a small family plot or receipt of cash and movable goods.[9] Thus, the restrictiveness of primogeniture depended upon a number of variables.

An alternative strategy to prevent fragmentation was the entail, in which the descent of the land was restricted to a particular line of succession. Entails were adopted in many places in Europe—England, Scotland, France, Italy, parts of Spain and the German regions, and Poland—with, of course, regional variations. The entail was designed to establish a line of heirs beyond the immediate heir, as a series of life tenants who were forbidden from alienating the property. The restrictiveness of this strategy was mitigated somewhat by the fact that in many cases only a part of the family's landed holdings was entailed. Moreover, over time there arose various circumstances under which families could break an entail, usually at some important juncture in the family's life, such as a marriage or death, or for repayment of debts. Nonetheless, the entail was an exclusive strategy that focused on intergenerational land transmission to the exclusion of other non-inheriting family members. The entail was particularly strong in England, where landowners essentially wrested, from Parliament and the courts, the right to restrict alienation and succession to such a degree as to create powerful landowning dynasties.[10]

The desire of English nobles to secure the strength and survival of their families led to the creation of yet another restrictive inheritance strategy, the strict settlement. Strict settlement was a modified version of entail that not only permitted the extension of the line of succession to the unborn, but also added the possibility of alienation as established by the settler. The strict settlement differed from primogeniture and entail in that it clearly focused more on wealth distribution within the family, including rather than excluding daughters, for example. Thus, the focus was still on estate preservation, but the inherited estate was usually burdened with various obligations to other children and the widow.[11] Strict settlement was, thus, an attempt to resolve the tension between overall family preservation and the well-being of individual family members.

There was, of course, one more possibility in the choice of land distribution—partible inheritance. This practice of dividing land more or less equally between sons was far less common among European nobilities than the more restrictive alternatives, but it did occur in some places, particularly in Eastern Europe and Scandinavia. In Poland, for example, though the great magnates began to entail their lands in the late sixteenth century, the middling and lesser nobles adhered to partible inheritance, and in Lithuania and Hungary, estates were divided among sons as well. Similarly, in both Denmark and Sweden, nobles had a tradition of partible inheritance. Rejecting more restrictive practices, nobles in these regions usually suffered the predictable results of continuous division—poor nobles and small plots that were not economically viable. There were methods to mitigate the effects of partible inheritance, such as limiting the number of children who married in each generation, but these could often backfire and result in the extinction of a family.[12]

RUSSIA'S INHERITANCE LAWS

Russia's inheritance customs and laws resembled those of Western Europe in many ways, and exhibited many of the same tendencies. Thus, as one would expect in any society with landed nobility, Russian law favored male heirs over females and showed a concern for preservation of the family. Russian nobles and lawmakers also exhibited the same uncertainty and indecisiveness as their Western counterparts in resolving the tension between the larger, extended family and the more immediate family unit. The Russian solution to this dilemma, however, differed from its resolution in most of Europe. In Russia, nobles believed that partible inheritance best served the needs of the family and Russian property law overwhelmingly favored clan interests well into the nineteenth century to a degree no longer seen in Western Europe.

Prior to the eighteenth century, all privately held land was divided into two distinct categories—*votchina*, or patrimonial land, and *pomest'e*, or service land. In theory, *votchina* was family land, inheritable and free from service obligation, whereas *pomest'e* was tied to service and was not, therefore, eligible for inheritance.[13] In reality, the laws and practices governing these two land types were far more complex and contradictory, blurring the basic distinctions and emphasizing the protection of family members.

Votchina existed in three distinct types: family *votchina*, service *votchina*, and purchased *votchina*. Family, or clan, *votchina* was *votchina* that a person had inherited from another clan member; service *votchina* was that which was granted to an individual for service; and purchased *votchina* was what the individual had acquired himself by purchase or expired mortgage. Family and service *votchina* were governed by the same rules, with an understanding that both were subjugated to the interests of the clan. To some degree, such *votchina* was considered part of the family patrimony, and thus was placed under greater restrictions regarding its disposal.[14] Several characteristics dominated the rules for the inheritance of family and service *votchina* in the pre-Petrine period: an emphasis on familization, the primacy of males, and a preference for partible inheritance.

The *Ulozhenie* of 1649 dedicated one chapter specifically to the disposal of family and service *votchina*, and demanded, whenever possible, the preservation of clan lands. The very first article of this chapter states clearly that hereditary estates are to be inherited by members of the clan. Despite this, during his lifetime a *votchinnik* was allowed to sell or mortgage family and service *votchina*, in which case his children and grandchildren had no claim to it. His brothers and nephews, however, if they had not agreed to the transaction, did have claims to the land and could demand to regain it for the clan by means of redemption. A man was not allowed, however, simply to give away his family or service *votchina* bypassing his children. Similarly, although a man could sell his family or service *votchina* during his lifetime, he could not bypass his children, the legal heirs, when it came to inheritance. This restriction likewise prevented him from leaving it to his childless wife by will. In this case, even if the will was witnessed and signed according to legal specifications, it was considered invalid and the *votchina* was given to his children according to the *Ulozhenie*.[15] These stipulations guaranteed children their right to inheritance.

Male children generally enjoyed preference in the inheritance of *votchina* lands and thus were considered the favored heirs to a man's family and service *votchina*. Upon a man's death, his *votchina*, whether family or service, was to be divided among his sons. Daughters were not to inherit in the presence of living brothers. This preference for male heirs had existed for centuries, and can be found in early law codes such as the *Russkaia Pravda*. Moreover, the rule that daughters could not inherit *votchina* in the presence of living brothers was reaffirmed repeatedly in subsequent legislation, and would often appear in petitions and decisions regarding inheritance. When, out of necessity, a female family member inherited *votchina* lands, she possessed the same rights over this land as a male heir. If the daughters died childless, or if there were no living daughters, however, the order of inheritance reverted to the male line, to those closest to her father within the clan.[16]

Sons usually divided their father's *votchina* among themselves in equal portions, although the *Ulozhenie* itself only specifies equal inheritance among sons under certain circumstances. Regardless, a variety of sources indicates a historical tradition of equal inheritance. The Expanded *Zakon Sudnyi*

Liudem, for example, recommended equal inheritance to assure fairness. Later, the *Russkaia Pravda* called for division into equal portions in cases of intestacy. This historical precedent, along with subsequent legislation and other eighteenth-century sources, suggests that equal inheritance was understood to be the intention of the *Ulozhenie*'s articles on *votchina*.[17]

The *Ulozhenie* also defined specific rules for the disposal of purchased *votchina* with the source of the land dictating the way it would be treated in the law. *Votchina* purchased from another clan member, for example, was still considered family land and thus was not governed by the rules for purchased *votchina*. On the other hand, *votchina* land purchased from another clan was considered purchased *votchina*, as was land that a man purchased as *votchina* out of his own service lands. The law stated that a man could alienate such purchased *votchina* during his lifetime in any way he chose, and his wife, children, and family members had no legal right to challenge his decisions. At the time of the owner's death, purchased estates would be inherited by his sons. Moreover, a wife, even a childless widow, could inherit and have full use of her husband's purchased hereditary estates; upon her death, however, if she had not alienated the purchased estates, they were to be returned to her husband's clan. If a man died with no wife or children, then his purchased estates were to be given to his family.[18] Thus, even purchased *votchina* was, to some extent, responsive to clan interests.

The other type of land that existed in pre-Petrine Russia was *pomest'e*, land that was tied to service and thus, in theory, ineligible for automatic transmission through inheritance in the same fashion as *votchina* lands. The *Ulozhenie* also dedicated an entire chapter to the subject of the disposal of *pomest'e*. The phrasing of many of these articles suggests that by the mid-seventeenth century the normal expectation was that sons would share their father's service lands after his death. Such transference of *pomest'e* from father to sons was addressed in a matter-of-fact manner, focusing on specific problems and disputes that might arise in the process. Moreover, the service record of the son no longer determined his eligibility to receive *pomest'e*. The *Ulozhenie* stated, "If after the death [of servicemen] their service landholdings are granted to their children who have not yet been initiated into a service rank; and those children of theirs die without ever receiving that service rank," thereby recognizing this as a real possibility.[19]

Since *pomest'e* was tied so closely to the obligation of service, one might assume that it could not be retained by those who did not serve. This, however, was not always the case. For example, the *Ulozhenie* ordered that maintenance allotments (*prozhitki*) for wives and children should be taken from the service land of the deceased, which was apparently preferable to parceling out *votchina* to female family members. This *pomest'e* that was left over was to be given into his clan, to those persons who had no service land of their own, or to those who had very little.[20] This rule demonstrates a characteristic of Russian landholding that we have already seen in our examination of *votchina*: the predominance of clan interests. Rather than parcel out *votchina* to female family members, the law favored the preservation of family lands and ordered the distribution of service lands instead. This would seem to contradict the fundamental purpose of *pomest'e*, which was to ensure service to the state. The fact that the law chose to overlook this indicates that clan interests were universally understood to be important, even by lawmakers.

Pre-Petrine inheritance law thus embodied a number of tendencies and assumptions. First, there was a definite interest in the preservation and familization of various types of land. *Votchina*, because it was inheritable and often clan land, was particularly subjected to rules that favored clan interests, but over time, as the distinction between *votchina* and *pomest'e* became blurred, there emerged a tendency to protect clan interests in *pomest'e* as well. Thus, although an individual had some freedom with his land during his lifetime, upon his death the law took over, so much so that even wills could be overridden if necessary. Clan interests were paramount in decisions about land disposal.

A second recurrent pattern that emerges is a distinct preference for male heirs. This proclivity was a strong one, excluding daughters in favor of grandsons, and sisters in favor of nephews. This preference for males even included the inheritance of a widow's *votchina* dowry. The law stated that a deceased widow's *votchina* dowry should be given to her sons and not to her daughters.[21]

The final tendency that dominated pre-Petrine inheritance law is the tradition of partible inheritance. The nobility had practiced partible inheritance as far back as the Kievan period. By the time of the expanded *Russkaia Pravda*, it had been incorporated into law as the required practice in cases of intestacy.[22] This practice persisted into the seventeenth century, and though the *Ulozhenie* does not stipulate partible inheritance in all cases, it was clearly understood to be the recommended, perhaps even required, practice. This long history of partible inheritance set the stage for one of Peter's most famous and controversial laws, the Law of Single Inheritance.

RUSSIAN INHERITANCE LAW IN THE EIGHTEENTH CENTURY AND BEYOND

On March 23, 1714, Peter the Great published the Law of Single Inheritance, establishing new rules for the transmission of family lands and property. The new law required that a father's immovable property must be left to one son, to be determined in advance and, presumably, selected for his ability to manage the family estate. In the absence of a son, the property could be bequeathed to a daughter. If the parents did not designate the single heir, then the law prescribed that the immovable property would pass to the oldest son and movable property would be shared by the other children in equal parts.[23]

Peter explained his opinion in his new law: "the division of immovable estates among children after the father's [death] is of great harm to our government, both to the state interest and to . . . families." He argued that partible inheritance was a harmful practice in three ways. First, Peter believed, it negatively impacted on the state treasury by causing nobles on small plots to overtax their peasants, thereby destroying that group's ability to pay taxes. Second, Peter contended that the division of family lands caused the decline of noble families; in his words, if this practice continued unchecked, "the great family, instead of glory, will be peasants, as there are already many examples in the Russian people." Third, Peter argued that partible inheritance determined the nobility's attitude toward state service, and more broadly toward work itself. Peter maintained that the nobles, "having their free bread, . . . do not serve in any use to the state without force . . . but find any evasion and live in idleness, which . . . is the mother of all evil affairs."[24]

There is disagreement among historians as to whether partible inheritance had the negative effects that Peter perceived. A number of historians have argued that Peter's assessment was correct, presenting evidence of splintering estates to support this theory. More recently, Kivelson has argued that, while partible inheritance did result in the fragmentation of estates, the economic effects of this process were mitigated by the acquisition of new property by each generation. Be that as it may, the testimonies of eighteenth- and nineteenth-century Russians suggest that partible inheritance continued to have detrimental effects on noble families. In his response to a questionnaire of the Free Economic Society, for example, Andrei Bolotov bemoaned the splintering of noble estates and the conflicts that often accompanied such division. Moreover, he was troubled by the agricultural disadvantages of this type of landholding, specifically citing the resulting inefficiency in plowing, sowing, and harvesting. In the next century, Alexander Pushkin condemned partible inheritance even more severely. Pushkin complained about the fragmentation and mortgaging of property, and identified the repeal of the Law of Single Inheritance as a historical mistake, arguing that the progressive splintering of estates had robbed the country of a real nobility and contributed to the Decembrist rebellion of 1825. In any case, Peter believed that partible inheritance was a harmful practice and enacted this law with the hope of ending the erosion of noble family wealth. He was certain that once his law was in effect, "families will not fall, but . . . will be unshakable through glory."[25]

Although Peter's preference may have been for the rational choice of one son as heir, a close reading of the law makes it clear that in lieu of that ideal situation, Peter was not so concerned with which family member received the land, but rather that the estate remain both undivided and within the family. This aspect of the law was in keeping with the legal and popular tradition of favoring the interests of the clan over the individual. Peter had already supported this concept in his law of 1712 that prohibited the last surviving male of a clan from giving or selling his inherited immovable estate to persons outside the clan, either during his lifetime or by means of a will; instead, the last surviving male was required to bequeath it to a female within the clan, but no further removed in degree than granddaughters. In the Single Inheritance Law of 1714, Peter modified his earlier law to provide that in cases when the last surviving member willed the family estate to a female member of the family, her husband and his heirs were obliged in perpetuity to attach her family name to theirs.[26]

Several articles of the Law of Single Inheritance address this problem of keeping land within a family. For example, Article Three provided that a childless landowner should will his immovable property to a family member of his choosing. His movable property could be left either to family members or to persons outside the family. In the absence of a will, his immovable property would go to one person in his family, in the closest line, and his movable property to other family members in equal portions. In the same vein, a later article established that should a childless widow die, remarry, or join a convent, her husband's immovable estate was to be returned to his family, whereas her dowry was to be returned to her family.[27] In all cases, the law specified that the estate was to remain intact.

From the moment Peter enacted the Law of Single Inheritance, the nobility despised it and tried by various means to avoid complying with its letter and intent. For example, fathers would write into their wills a fabricated debt to their non-inheriting children, which would then have to be paid upon the execution of the will. Parents also illicitly sold portions of their land, and divided the money equally among their children; in other cases, the land would be resold to the non-heirs. Peter tried to stop such practices by an ordinance of April 14, 1714 that declared that a cadet who had earned money with which he wanted to buy an estate could do so only after a period of service: seven years in the army, ten in the civil service, fifteen in trade or in a profession. But a cadet who did none of these things could never buy land, "even unto death."[28]

What distinguished the Law of Single Inheritance from most of Peter's other legislations was the scope of its attack on noble family interests. With this law, Peter went into the nobleman's home and dictated to him how he was to provide for his family and bequeath his ancestral lands. Many nobles considered this an infringement on their ability to provide for family members and protect their families' political and social interests, and thus saw Peter's new law as unjust and immoral. Family preservation was critical to eighteenth-century Russian nobles, who still relied heavily on clan and family connections to establish and maintain political and social status. Thus members of the nobility opposed Peter's law because it undermined their ability to develop and sustain these clan and family networks. It also interfered with parents' ability to provide for their children. In a country where trade was not viewed as a suitable option for a non-inheriting noble son, this was no small matter.

A strong sense of familial responsibility, however, does not by itself explain the nobility's opposition to Peter's law: political and social strategies figured as well. It was crucial for noble families to have as many well-connected family members as possible. Partible inheritance allowed more sons to adopt the status of noble landowner and exert influence in the government and society. Sons were not the only protectors of family interest. Daughters and widows also weighed heavily in this equation. Like women of the planter class in the

American Old South, noblewomen in eighteenth-century Russia were status-bearers for their families.[29] Thus it was important for the nobility to provide well for its female members. Well-dowered daughters and widows of substantial means could achieve good matches, which could in turn further a family's political and social interests.

Finally, we must consider one other possible reason for noble discontent with Peter's law. Under Muscovite law, a landowner was restricted in the disposal of his property in many ways, but he was permitted during his lifetime to sell or mortgage his immovable property, so long as he obtained the approval of his fellow clan members. Peter's law attempted to halt the sale and mortgage of immovable property altogether, restricting land transference to a degree usually not seen even in Western Europe where practices like primogeniture, entail, and strict settlement still often included arrangements for younger children to receive small plots of land. Peter's law, then, must have seemed excessively harsh to nobles who had no other real alternatives for acquiring and maintaining social status, wealth, and good marriages for their children. The possession of land, with all its incumbent insecurities, was essential to reaching these goals. Thus Peter's law threatened to thwart the efforts of nobles to attain wealth and status on many levels.

With Empress Anna Ioannovna's accession to the throne in 1730, the nobility's complaints against single inheritance were finally answered. On December 9, 1730 a Senate report argued "it is not only natural but also commanded by divine law that fathers reward each of their children with equal shares," and advised Anna that inheritance decisions should be determined according to the old *Ulozhenie*. The Senate report concluded that the law had merely created "hatred and quarrels among brothers and drawn out litigation involving substantial losses and ruin for both sides," as well as occasional violence where "not only brothers and close relatives but even children beat their fathers to death." Moreover, even when parents technically abided by the law, creative interpretation often produced ruinous results: "Grain, horses and animals are considered as movables and given to the younger brothers and sisters," the report contended, "and just as the heir's village cannot survive without grain and cattle, so the younger brothers' grain and cattle will perish without the villages."[30]

In March 1731, after seventeen years of noncompliance and resistance, Anna repealed Peter's law, calling it "contrary to God's justice" to deprive some children of their inheritance. The new law, for the most part, revived the rules for inheritance rights of sons that had been established by the *Ulozhenie*. There were, however, some important differences. Although Anna's law stated that parents were to divide their property equally among all their children, what this actually meant was the equal division of property among all sons, for daughters were to inherit a different specified portion. Under the new law, daughters were entitled to an inheritance of one-fourteenth of their father's immovable property, or half of the widow's share, in the presence of living brothers. Thus, when a man died, his widow would receive one-seventh of his immovable property, his daughters each one-fourteenth, and his sons would divide the remaining property equally among themselves. In the absence of sons, daughters would inherit the property and divide it equally.[31]

The demise of Peter's Law of Single Inheritance meant that Russian nobles returned to the practice of partible inheritance. The debate over inheritance laws in Russia was far from over, however, and already by the second half of the eighteenth century, some nobles were beginning to question the wisdom of partible inheritance. In February 1763, for example, Catherine set up a commission to examine the question of the nobility's freedom from compulsory state service, granted by Peter III's Manifesto of 1762. The Commission's eventual report to Catherine, however, was far broader in scope and, among other things, requested that the nobility be guaranteed freedom from confiscation except for debt and the right to establish entails.[32]

These thoughts were echoed several years later during the meeting of the Legislative Commission. The noble *nakazy* (instructions to legislators) of 1767 consistently complained about Russia's rules of inheritance and the complex and fragmented nature of landholding in the provinces. The nobilities of Bolkhovskii and Putivlskii districts, for example, bemoaned the fact that generations of partible inheritance had resulted in increasingly numerous and smaller portions. The *nakaz* from the Lukhovskii nobility echoed this complaint, adding that the shares received in inheritance were often too small to support the heirs. Perhaps the most interesting requests on this issue, however, were those that called for the establishment of some form of single inheritance. The nobility of Moscow district, for example, asked that landowners be granted the right not to divide their property in inheritance. There were also calls for the right to establish entails. Thus the nobilities of Ryl'skii and Pereslavskii–Zalesskii districts asked to establish entail in the Western European sense. Such criticisms of estate fragmentation, however, did not mean that all nobles were ready to abandon partible inheritance. The nobility of Maloiaroslavetskii district, for example, asked that fathers and mothers be allowed to divide their immovable property to sons in as equal portions as possible, after granting a share to both their single and married daughters.[33]

It is useful to contemplate why after the vehement opposition Peter's law encountered in the early part of the century some noble factions would now be calling for the establishment of entails. Addressing this question, the historian V.I. Briullov argued that family ties in the upper echelons of Russian society had significantly weakened by the middle of the eighteenth century. As a result, the obligatory distribution of family property among all children was now thought by many to be both restrictive and unreasonable. There is another possible explanation as well. Because they could cope more easily with the changes Peter's law demanded by providing their younger children with cash and other movables, the wealthier members of the nobility had not opposed the law as vehemently as the poorer members.[34] The same distinction might be made about the requests in the noble *nakazy*. Of the hundreds of *nakazy* presented to the Legislative Commission, only a few—primarily those from the Moscow area—called for the establishment of entails. It can be assumed that these nobles could afford to provide for their younger children by other means.

In response to these complaints, in 1774, Catherine permitted the first entail to be created for Count Zakhar Chernyshev. Chernyshev requested that his land remain forever indivisible, passing to his eldest son, then to his eldest son's eldest son, and so on down the line. In the absence of an eligible male, a daughter or other close female relative could inherit. Chernyshev's primary motive was to assure that his land never left the Chernyshev clan. Thus, if a female inherited, she and her heirs were obliged to adopt the family name and the coat of arms of Count Chernyshev. In subsequent years, Catherine created other entails in response to the specific petitions of a few wealthy noblemen, but general guidelines were not established until 1845. Even then, the minimum amount of land required to establish an entail was set at 10,000 *desiatiny*, a number too high for most nobles. As a result, between 1845 and 1905 only 60 entails were established—a statistically insignificant number.[35]

What is interesting about the evolution of inheritance law in Russia is that it tended to move in an almost opposite direction from the path chosen by most European nobilities. Most European nobilities by the eighteenth century were embracing various restrictive inheritance practices such as primogeniture and entail, yet Peter's attempt to import a similar system ended in utter failure. Russian nobles vehemently clung to the practice of partible inheritance and continued to do so through the nineteenth century. By comparison, most European nobilities continued to use various methods to limit the number of inheriting offspring. To be sure, there were efforts in some countries to do away with primogeniture, but only in the nineteenth century and often with minimal effects. Civil entail was abolished in Spain in 1836, but later reformers felt the need to further extend and codify these laws during the Revolution of 1854. In France, the National Convention abolished primogeniture in 1793, but then in 1806 and 1808 Napoleon restored the right of entails, which lasted for another 40 years. Moreover, many French nobles continued to practice de facto primogeniture even after the laws had been changed. Primogeniture dominated inheritance practices in England until the Property Acts of 1925.[36] Thus, though Russian nobles shared many of the same characteristics of European nobilities, they were different from their Western counterparts in the sense that they clung to the practice of partible inheritance and resisted more restrictive patterns that, it has often been argued, created strong nobilities in the West.

RUSSIA'S LAWS OF REDEMPTION

Perhaps the land legislation that distinguishes Russia from the West more than any other was the law of redemption. Redemption was the legal right by which family members could regain family land that had been sold or mortgaged outside of their clan without their permission. Acquired property was not eligible for redemption.[37] Russia's law of redemption was unique in early modern Europe. Though a similar system had existed in medieval Hungary, already by the end of the fourteenth century the rights of the clan were considerably weakened. Moreover, in the Hungarian case, clan rights pertained to the sale or exchange of property, but did not involve the right to demand repurchase. In France, the custom of *retrait lignager* comes closest to the Russian practice, although, it too differs in several significant ways. First, it was a custom, not a law, and it was only practiced in certain regions, mostly in south—southwest France and on a limited scale in the north, but in all cases with strong regional variations. Second, it was practiced across class lines and did not focus on the landowning nobility. Elsewhere in Europe, the nearest comparison to the Russian practice of redemption was the seigneurial right of landlords to claim first right of refusal when tenures on their estates were being sold or to assume the right of inheritance when the holders of the tenure failed to produce a male heir. These rights, however, very specifically dealt with the rights of landlords vis à vis their tenants and (with the exception of France) did not apply to the property of nobles and their families.[38] Thus, Russia's redemption laws serve as another important distinction between the experiences of European and Russian nobilities with regard to landownership and property rights.

The principle of redemption was first legally established in Russia by the Sudebnik of 1550, which ordered that if a man sold or mortgaged his ancestral lands, certain members of his family had the right to redeem, or repurchase, that land from the new holder. Specifically, any of the original owner's brothers or nephews who had not agreed to the transaction could redeem the alienated land, provided that the claim was made within the 40-year time limit set by the Sudebnik. Other family members were excluded from redemption by virtue of their participation in the transaction or their relation to the owner. Thus, none of the owner's brothers or nephews who had witnessed and agreed to the transaction could claim the right of redemption. Direct offspring of the owner also were denied the privilege of redemption since it was assumed that, being under their parents' control, they were not in a position to disagree. In 1649, the *Ulozhenie* reaffirmed the principle of redemption and the time limit of 40 years.[39]

The redemption procedure worked as follows. When immovable property was sold or lost through an expired mortgage into another clan, a family member could petition the Votchina College to reclaim that land by redemption. As with the rules of inheritance, the preferred redeemer was the male relative closest to the owner. The Votchina College investigated these claims, simultaneously seeking out testimony from any relatives who were closer in relationship than the petitioner that they had no objections to the redemption by their clansman. When Osip Kudriavov petitioned in 1741 to redeem the land in Rzhevskii district that had been sold by his distant cousin, Lavrentii Kudriavov, the Votchina College ordered that Lavrentii's first cousins be questioned to be certain that they did not want to redeem this property. Once this was ascertained, the property could be given to Osip in redemption. This was not the end of the process, however. Once a petition was accepted and approved, the Votchina College would order that the land in question be appraised, taking into account any improvements or structures that had been added to the property.[40] The redeemer would then pay the "redemption money," the assessed value of the land, along with a required fee.

The problems that this legal principle presented for a noble landowner can be easily imagined. For a period of four decades, the new owner could never be sure that the property was truly his to develop, since he was always threatened by the possibility of clan redemption. Furthermore, he could not be sure that at the time of redemption he would be adequately compensated for the money and materials he had invested in the property. In this way, for as long as 40 years, a noble landowner could live with the legitimate fear that at any moment he might be forced to resell his land to the family from which he had bought it. The practice of redemption posed certain threats to the redeemer as well. The new owner of a piece of property might decide to thwart the redeemer's intended goal of repurchase, and there were several ways in which this might be done. The current owner might, for example, quickly resell the land at a higher price, thereby leaving the redeemer to pay a higher redemption price. On other occasions, angry landowners stripped the property of all its valuable assets so that the redeemer bought back a ruined piece of property.[41]

Finally, in 1737, a new law on redemption shortened the time limit for redemption to three years. The law detailed the previously discussed abuses and determined that the new term for redemption of family and service *votchina* should be much shorter. After the three-year term, no redemptions were to be approved. Only seven years later, Elizabeth found it necessary to augment and elucidate the existing laws on redemption. In an *ukaz* of May 11, 1744, Elizabeth ordered that the recipient of expired mortgaged property had to wait one year before selling, mortgaging, or including that newly acquired property in a dowry. At the end of a year, he was free to alienate it in any manner he chose, and anyone desiring to redeem it would have to do so according to the most recent transaction price.[42]

Despite these attempts by the crown to clarify and reform the laws of redemption, the nobility continued to be troubled by abuses of the system. The complaints about redemption that arose during the Legislative Commission of 1767 give some indication of the problems the nobility faced. The nobles of Orel province, for example, complained in their *nakazy* that wealthier nobles lent money to poorer nobles at usurious rates, being certain to take a mortgage on the borrower's property and foreclosing as soon as the mortgage expired. Often, this foreclosing thoroughly ruined the property, so that if the borrower's family managed to scrape together the money to redeem it, they would find it ravaged and serfless.[43]

Thus, the policy of redemption was inherently flawed in that it contributed to the nobility's insecurity about its property, thereby discouraging investment and encouraging what under other circumstances would have been considered self-destructive behavior. In fact, the policy of redemption continued to threaten the security of landholding well into the next century. As late as 1875, critics of the institution of patrimonial property argued at the First Congress of Russian Jurists that the policy of redemption prevented new owners from trying to improve their property.[44]

CONCLUSION

Though the Russian nobility shared much in common with nobilities in Europe, particularly those in Eastern Europe and Scandinavia, with regard to landholding and property law, some important distinctions can be drawn. Regarding inheritance, Russian practices differed from those in Western Europe in that Russians clung to partible inheritance whereas their Western contemporaries began to devise strategies to keep landed estates together from generation to generation. But more than any other policy, it was Russia's law of redemption that set her apart from her Western, and even her Eastern, European counterparts. Ironically, Russia's combination of partible inheritance and redemption laws resulted in a far more restrictive system of ownership than those that existed in Western Europe. In Russia, families may have had more freedom in dividing their lands by means of inheritance, but this greater freedom was essentially an illusion since it was restricted by clan interests and undermined by the laws of redemption. The result was a system where family control was present on both ends—both at the time of inheritance or sale decisions, and after the fact, in being able to undo a sale or mortgage. The clan was given such a voice in the management of land that in many ways it served as a choke-hold on the development of truly individual property ownership. The insecurity of Russian nobles with regards to their property served to further weaken their ties and commitment to any one piece of land and helps to explain why, when other nobilities were advocating restrictive inheritance practices, Russian nobles continued to divide their property.[45] This pragmatic attitude toward land was only further enhanced by the various repressive measures of the regime such as confiscation. If land was simply a commodity to be held tenuously and briefly, why invest in it emotionally or financially? Thus, in Russia, the restrictions created by state and clan interests in landownership combined to create a mercenary view toward landed property in particular and a very weak system of private property in general.

NOTES

1. Alexander Griboedov, "Woe from Wit," in *The Government Inspector and Other Russian Plays*, trans. with an introduction by Joshua Cooper (London: Penguin, 1972; reprint, 1990), 152; Meehan-Waters' research confirms this impression, revealing that the large majority of those in the top four military and civil ranks in 1730 were related to someone else in the top ranks; see Brenda Meehan-Waters, *Autocracy and Aristocracy, The Russian Service Elite of 1730* (New Brunswick: Rutgers

University Press, 1982), 170–203. Other historians have also stressed the importance of clan ties in noble political and social life; see Nancy Shields Kollman, *Kinship and Politics* (Stanford: Stanford University Press, 1987); Gustave Alef, "The Origins of Muscovite Autocracy: the Age of Ivan III," *Forschungen zur osteuropaischen Geschichte* 39 (Berlin, 1986); Robert O. Crummey, *Aristocrats and Servitors* (Princeton: Princeton University Press, 1983); John Le Donne, "Ruling Families in the Russian Political Order, 1689–1825," *Cahiers du monde russe et sovietique*, 18 (July–December, 1987): 233–322.

2. Jonathan Powis, *Aristocracy* (Oxford: Basil Blackwell, 1984), 1–15.

3. Ralph Gibson and Martin Blinkhorn, eds., *Landownership and Power in Modern Europe* (London: HarperCollins, 1991), 3–16; Powis, 24–25; M.L. Bush, *Noble Privilege* (New York: Holmes and Meier, 1983, 2–3, 21); Dominic Lieven, *The Aristocracy in Europe, 1815–1914* (New York: Columbia University Press, 1992), 74–100.

4. Marc Raeff, *Origins of the Russian Intelligentsia* (New York: Harcourt Brace, 1966), 46; Seymour Becker, *Nobility and Privilege in Late Imperial Russia* (DeKalb: Northern Illinois University Press, 1985), 29–31; A. Romanovich-Slavatinskii, *Dvorianstvo v Rossii ot nachala XVIII veka do otmeny krepostnago prava* (St. Petersburg: Tip. Ministerstva Vnutrennykh Del, 1870), 165–167; Colum Leckey, "Provincial Readers and Agrarian Reform, 1760s–70s: The Case of Sloboda Ukraine," *Russian Review* 61, no.4 (October 2002), 538–539.

5. Michel Confino, *Domaines et seigneurs en Russie vers la fin du XVIIIe siecle. Étude de structures agraires et de mentalités économiques* (Paris: Institut d'études slaves de l'Université de Paris, 1963). This idea is also supported by S.A. Korf, *Dvorianstvo i ego soslovnoe upravlenie za stoletie 1762–1855 godov* (St. Petersburg: Tip. Trenke Fiusno, 1906), 13–14, and Romanovich-Slavatinskii, 198; John Halit Brown, "A Provincial Landowner: A. T. Bolotov (1738–1833)" Ph.D. diss. (Princeton University, 1977), 59, 72, 83. See, also, Edgar Melton, "Enlightened Seigniorialism and Its Dilemma in Serf Russia, 1750–1830." *Journal of Modern History* 62, no.94 (December 1990): 675–708; Priscilla Roosevelt, *Life on the Russian Country Estate* (New Haven and London: Yale University Press, 1995), 3.

6. Valerie Kivelson, "The Effects of Partible Inheritance: Gentry Families and the State in Muscovy," *Russian Review* 53 (April 1994): 199.

7. Lawrence Stone, *Family, Sex and Marriage in England, 1500–1800* (New York: Harper and Row, 1977), 411–412; Martyn Rady, *Nobility, Land and Service in Medieval Hungary* (New York: Palgrave, 2000), 109.

8. There is a vast literature that deals in whole, or in part, with the subject of European inheritance practices. See, e.g., Janos M. Bak, ed., *History and Society in Central Europe, Nobilities in Central and Eastern Europe: Kinship, Property and Privilege* (Budapest: Hajnal István Alapítvány, 1994); John Brewer and Susan Staves, eds., *Early Modern Conceptions of Property* (London: Routledge, 1995); Amy Louise Erickson, *Women and Property in Early Modern England* (London: Routledge, 1993); Robert Forster, *The Nobility of Toulouse in the Eighteenth Century: A Social and Economic Study* (Baltimore: Johns Hopkins University Press, 1960); Rebecca Gates-Coon, *The Landed Estates of the Esterházy Princes: Hungary During the Reforms of Maria Theresa and Joseph II* (Baltimore: Johns Hopkins University Press, 1994); John Habbakkuk, *Marriage, Debt and the Estates System: English Landownership, 1650–1950* (Oxford: Oxford University Press, 1994); David Herlihy, "Land, Family and Women in Continental Europe, 701–1200," Tradition 18 (1962): 89–120; Thomas Kuehn, "Some Ambiguities of

Female Inheritance Ideology in the Renaissance," *Continuity and Change* 2, no.1 (May 1987): 11–36; Gregory Pedlow, "Marriage, Family Size and Inheritance among Hessian Nobles, 1650–1900": *Journal of Family History* 7, no.4 (Winter 1982): 333–352; David Warren Sabean, *Property, Production, and Family in Neckerhausen, 1700–1870* (New York: Cambridge University Press, 1990); Eileen Spring, *Law, Land and Family: Aristocratic Inheritance in England, 1300–1800* (Chapel Hill: University of North Carolina Press, 1993).

9. Bush, *Noble Privilege*, 192, 198; Barbara English and John Saville, *Strict Settlement, A Guide for Historians* (Hull: University of Hull Press, 1983), 13–24; Robert Wheaton, "Affinity and Descent in Seventeenth-Century Bordeaux," 119, and "Introduction: Recent Trends in the Historical Study of the French Family," 15, in *Family and Sexuality in French History*, ed. Robert Wheaton and Tamara K. Hareven (Philadelphia: University of Pennsylvania Press, 1980); Andrés Barrera-González, "Eldest and Younger Siblings in a Stem-Family System: The Case of Rural Catalonia," *Continuity and Change* 7, no.3 (1992); 335–336; José Manuel Pérez García, "Rural Family Life in La Huerta de Valencia During the Eighteenth Century," *Continuity and Change* 7, no.1 (1992); 81–82, 85; Judith J. Hurwich, "Inheritance Practices in Early Modern Germany," *Journal of Interdisciplinary History* 23, no.4 (Spring 1993): 711–718.

10. Joan Thirsk, "The European Debate on Customs of Inheritance, 1500–1700," 177–191 and J.P. Cooper, "Patterns of Inheritance and Settlement by Great Landowners from the Fifteenth to the Eighteenth Centuries," 192–327 in *Family and Inheritance, Rural Society in Western Europe, 1200–1800*, ed. Jack Goody, Joan Thirsk, and E.P. Thompson (New York: Cambridge University Press, 1976); English and Saville, 13–24; Lloyd Bonfield, " 'Affective Families', 'Open Elites' and Family Settlements in Early Modern England," *Economic History Review*, 2nd ser., 39, no.3 (August 1986): 346–347; Forster, 124; J.V. Becket, *The Aristocracy in England, 1660–1914* (Oxford: Oxford University Press, 1986), 58.

11. English and Saville, 13–24; Bonfield, 346–347.

12. Cooper, 199, 294; Bush, *Rich Noble*, 111–125; Rady, 29; Powis, 19.

13. V.O. Kliuchevskii, *Kurs russkoi istorii, Sochineniia v deviati tomakh* 4 (Moscow: Mysl', 1989), 78–80; Nikolai P. Pavlov-Silvanskii, *Feodalizm v Rossii* (Moscow: Nauka, 1988), 109–116, 450–471; Jerome Blum, *Lord and Peasant in Russia from the Ninth to the Nineteenth Century* (Princeton: Princeton University Press, 1961), 84–85, 168–188; Robert O. Crummey, *The Formation of Muscovy 1304–1613* (London: Longman, 1987), 108–109.

14. Laws in many countries distinguished between family-inherited land and land acquired by other means; Erik Fügedi, "Kinship and Privilege: The Social System of Medieval Hungarian Nobility as Defined in Customary Law," in *History and Society in Central Europe, Nobilties in Central and Eastern Europe: Kinship, Property and Privilege*, ed. Janos M. Bak (Budapest: Hajnal István Alapítvány, 1994), 60; Blum, 81.

15. Chapter 17, Article 1 in Richard Hellie, trans. and ed., *The Muscovite Law Code (Ulozhenie) of 1649. Part I: Text and Translation* (Irvine, CA: C. Schlacks, 1988); *Polnoe sobranie zakonov* (Moscow: Gos. Tip., 1830), 2: 765; 1: 34; 2: 764.

16. *PSZ* 2: 634, art. 6; *Russkaia Pravda*, art. 95, in George Vernadsky, trans., *Medieval Russian Laws* (New York: Octagon Books, 1965); Nikolai Rozhdestvenskii, *Istoricheskoe izlozhenie russkago zakonodatel'stva o nasledstve* (St. Petersburg, 1839), 34; *PSZ* 1: 32; *Ulozhenie* 17: 4; *PSZ* 2: 860, sec. 2, art. 1.

17. *Ulozhenie* 17: 15. Sons could also receive their father's *votchina* jointly, in which case neither of them could carry out transactions on the land without the knowledge and consent of the others; *Ulozhenie* 17: 13; Eve Levin, "The Role and Status of Women in Medieval Novgorod," Ph.D. diss. (Indiana University, 1983), 11; Russkaia Pravda, art. 92; Rozhdestvenskii, 35; *PSZ* 2: 634, art. 4; Rossiiskii gosudarstvennyi arkhiv drevnikh aktov (RGADA), f. 22, op. 1, d. 156; The 1731 statute repealing Peter's law says that land would henceforth be divided equally among children "according to the *Ulozhenie*."

18. *Ulozhenie* 17: 5. So long as the land was purchased, and not redeemed back into the clan, it was considered purchased; *PSZ* 2: 814; *PSZ* 2: 764; *Ulozhenie* 17: 1, 2, 6; *PSZ* 2: 634, art. 1; 1: 46.

19. *Ulozhenie* 16: 33.

20. *Ulozhenie* 16: 13. If there were no clan members who fit this description, then the *pomest'e* was to be given to members of other clans; *Ulozhenie* 16: 13. Subsequent legislation, however, would mandate that escheated *pomest'e* be given only to clan members; *PSZ* 2: 949.

21. Rozhdestvenskii, 39, 43; *PSZ* 2: 674.

22. Russkaia Pravda, art. 92.

23. For a thorough discussion of this law, see Lee Farrow, *Between Crown and Clan: The Struggle to Define Noble Property Rights in Imperial Russia* (University of Delaware Press, 2004).

24. O.I. Chistiakov, ed. *Rossiiskoe zakonodatelstvo X–XX vekov v deviati tomakh* 4 (Moscow: Iurid. Lit-ra, 1986), 295–296. Peter's law applied not only to noble estates, but also to shops and other forms of immovable property. Clearly, however, the law was aimed primarily at the nobility.

25. Jerome Blum has presented data from the cadastral survey of Tver', which in 1540 listed 318 *votchiny* as belonging to 659 owners. Eight years later the same votchiny were held by 771 owners. Over the same period of time, the average holding decreased in size as well, in one district from 970 *chetverts* per individual to 176 *chetverts*; Blum, 172; Kivelson, "The Effects of Partible Inheritance," 205–206; Paul Dukes, *Catherine the Great and the Russian Nobility* (London: Cambridge University Press, 1967), 100; A.B. Anikin, *Muza i mamona: sotsial'no-ekonomicheskie motivy u Pushkina* (Moscow: Mysl', 1989), 196–197; *Rossiiskoe zakonodatel'stvo* 4: 296.

26. *PSZ* 4: 2471. Beyond this degree, the land would be considered escheated and would revert to the state. Later, after Peter's death, the supplemental law of 1725 strengthened this point, adding that if no eligible parties would consent to the addition of the family name, then the property would be considered escheated and written to Her Majesty; *PSZ* 7: 4722, art. 7.

27. *Rossiiskoe zakonodatel'stvo* 4: 298, art. 9.

28. Romanovich Slavatinskii, 251–252; L.R. Lewitter, "Commentary," in *The Book of Poverty and Wealth*, by Ivan Pososhkov (London: Athlone, 1987), 132; *PSZ* 8: 5653; *PSZ* 4: 2796.

29. Robin Bisha, "The Promise of Patriarchy: Marriage in Eighteenth-Century Russia," Ph.D. diss. (Indiana University, 1993), 143–144; Elizabeth Fox-Genovese, *Within the Plantation Household: Black and White Women of the Old South* (Chapel Hill: University of North Carolina Press, 1988).

30. *PSZ* 8: 5653.

31. *PSZ* 8: 5717.

32. Isabel de Madariaga, *Russia in the Age of Catherine the Great* (New Haven: Yale University Press, 1981), 83–87.

33. *Sbornik Imperatorskago russkago istoricheskago obshchestva (SIRIO),* 136 v. (St. Petersburg, 1874–1916), 68: 496–497 (Bolkhovskoe nobility); 589 (Putivl'skii uezd); *SIRIO* 8: 481 (Lukhovskoe nobility); 4: 228–229 (Moskovskii uezd); 68: 623–625 (Ryl'skii uezd); 8: 496 (Pereslavskii-Zalesskii uezd); 4: 326 (Maloiaroslavetskii uezd).

34. Dukes, 161; Romanovich Slavatinskii, 251–252; Soloviev, Sergei, *Istoriia Rossii s drevneishikh vremen: v piatnadtsati knigakh* (Moscow, 1959–63), X, vol. 19, 225; and Dukes, 8.

35. *PSZ* 19: 14117; Becker, 70–71; A.M. Anfimov, "Maioratnoe zemlevladenie v tsarskoi Rossii," *Istoriia SSSR,* 5 (1962): 151–159. One *desiatina* equals 2.7 acres.

36. Raymond Carr, *Spain, 1808–1939* (Oxford: Oxford University Press, 1966), 176, 255; J.P. Cooper, "Patterns of Inheritance and Settlement by Great Landowners from the Fifteenth to the Eighteenth Centuries," in *Family and Inheritance,* 276; Margaret H. Darrow, *Revolution in the House: Family, Class, and Inheritance in Southern France, 1775–1825* (Princeton: Princeton University Press, 1989), 16, 70; A.W. Simpson, *A History of the Land Law,* 2nd. ed. (Oxford: Oxford University Press, 1996), 276.

37. *Ulozhenie* 17: 31; *PSZ* 26: 19243.

38. Rady, 97; Paul Ourliac, "Le Retrait Lignager dans le Sud-Ouest de la France," *Revue historique de droit français et létranger* 30, no.4 (1952): 328–355. The right of first refusal was called *retrait lignager* in France, *prawo retraktu* in the Poland, *recht van naasting* in the Netherlands, *Losungsrecht, Vorkaufsrecht* or *Näherrecht* in the German states or *resumption* in England. The right to take land in the absence of a male heir was called *mainmorte* in France. See, Bush, *Noble Privilege,* 167.

39. 1550 Sudebnik, art. 85, in Michigan Slavic materials, no.7. *Muscovite Judicial Texts 1488–1556,* compiled, trans., and ed., with annotation and selected glossary by H.W. Dewey (Ann Arbor: Department of Slavic Languages and Literatures, 1966); In the *Ulozhenie* 22: 6, it was established that children were under the full control of their parents and this rule was upheld in subsequent legislation and in the courts; see, RGADA, f. 22, op. 1, d. 130, l. 3; *Ulozhenie* 17: 30.

40. RGADA, f. 1209, op. 83, d. 298. See, also, RGADA, f. 1209, op. 83, d. 232 and op. 84, ch. 14, d. 223.

41. RGADA, f. 1209, op. 84, ch. 14, d. 251 and d. 69; f. 1209, op. 83, d. 206.

42. *PSZ* 10: 7339; 12: 8936.

43. Wilson Robert Augustine, "The Economic Attitudes and Opinions Expressed by the Russian Nobility in the Great Commission of 1767," Ph.D. diss. (Columbia University, 1969), 102.

44. William Wagner, *Marriage, Property and Law in Late Imperial Russia* (Oxford: Clarendon Press, 1994), 258.

45. For a full discussion of confiscation practices see, Farrow, *Between Clan and Crown.*

3

Capital, Industriousness, and Private Banks in the Economic Imagination of a Nineteenth-Century Statesman

Susan P. McCaffray

Between 1793 and 1815 the leading states of Europe found themselves almost constantly at war. Statesmen charged with keeping treasuries full confronted crushing challenges. Their task was complicated by a growing sensitivity to the importance of foreign trade in general, and the boom in British cotton exports, in particular. To such traditional government concerns as protecting the nation's money and filling its treasury the emergence of political economy now added additional "economic" duties, which included encouraging commerce and the growth of capital. At the intersection of theoretical political economy and state policy, and the intersection of credit, money, and budgets, was the effort to understand and organize banking. The years of warfare straddling the eighteenth and nineteenth centuries witnessed banking innovation throughout Europe and produced fundamental economic works on the subject. English economist David Ricardo became famous by criticizing the Bank of England and demanding a return to the gold standard. Less well known, but occupied by similar concerns, was the Russian official and political economist, N.S. Mordvinov. A review of Ricardo's and Mordvinov's ideas from this period illuminates the ways in which Russian banking resembled and differed from the English system and demonstrates the common nature of the problems Russian and English political economists perceived.[1]

Once upon a time, and not so long ago, even the most fundamental economic questions seemed debatable. For example, what is money? Should it be a government monopoly? What makes different monies more or less valuable over time and space? Do money and credit promote manufactures and trade, or do manufactures and trade promote money and credit? Should credit operations be public or private? Of all the clever ways that people have discovered to get rich on these operations, which are moral? Which are most likely to enrich the state? Which promote the public good? How do the government's monetary and fiscal needs mesh with the credit and financial needs of merchants, manufacturers, and farmers? Resolving such questions was a lengthy and circuitous process involving wrong turns, dead ends, painful experiences, considerable insight, and flashes of real brilliance. However dry the subject of money, credit, and banking may appear at first glance, eavesdropping on its early practitioners reveals some important truths about the growth, and even the nature, of a system we all but take for granted today.

A brief review of Europe's monetary history reveals that banks and bank-like businesses arose to perform three overlapping functions: to accept deposits for safekeeping; to lend money; and, in the process of lending, to create money substitutes, such as bills of exchange or bank notes.[2] Deposit banking was originally separate from lending operations, and at first was undertaken almost exclusively by governments.[3] Following Italian precedents from the late Middle Ages, in 1609, the City of Amsterdam established its famous public deposit bank in response to the tremendous confusion created by the circulation of a multitude of competing Dutch and foreign coins. In creating this public bank, the City of Amsterdam required depositors to accept "bank money," a credit on the bank's books, in place of coin, granting the bank a monopoly on discounting bills of exchange of a certain value. Adam Smith, himself, later commended this Bank's utility in providing a medium of universal and durable value for merchants.[4] Later in the seventeenth century, governments in Italy, Germany, and Holland followed Amsterdam's lead, establishing deposit banks to stabilize the currency and assist foreign trade.

Lending and creating money substitutes, on the other hand, tended to be private businesses. They developed in busy commercial centers, where merchants offered such auxiliary services as pawn-broking, money changing, and issuing bills of exchange, which Italians pioneered by the thirteenth century.[5] By the sixteenth century, the center of merchant banking had shifted to the south German towns. In the eighteenth century, Scottish and English merchants supplemented their incomes by accepting deposits and discounting bills of exchange. In the process they created the most decentralized banking system in Europe.

At the turn of the nineteenth century, Russia's banking system was unique, just like everyone else's. Despite basic similarities that grew out of the missions banks, money, and credit were meant to perform, the various countries of Europe developed home-grown and idiosyncratic practices that fit the particularities of their political, geographical, commercial, and monetary situations. Although Russia lacked the commercial density that had created banking pioneers, in fundamental ways the history of Russian banking resembles that of other continental countries.

Throughout the sixteenth and seventeenth centuries the chief constraints on commerce in Russia were distance from the Atlantic, source of goods and silver; sparseness of population and towns; difficulty of transportation and communication; and a tradition of government confiscation. Although European and American silver found its way to Russia, until the 1730s the country remained outside the zone in which bills of exchange circulated.[6] By the late 1730s, however, Russia's commercial integration with the rest of Europe was sufficient that bills of exchange had become the primary means for conducting foreign trade.

Within the country, merchants created a system of private credit appropriate to local conditions, some of which were unique to Russia. They occupied a vulnerable and ambiguous legal position. It was not unusual for the government to confiscate the property of a prosperous merchant. In such a climate, it was rational for merchants to keep their credit operations small and informal. On the other hand, just as merchants sometimes suffered at the hands of an overbearing state, they also benefited from frequent state grants of land and resources. George Munro has argued that Russian merchants did not need to borrow capital to the same extent as foreigners because of the tsarist government's propensity to invest its vast land and material resources in favored enterprises.[7] More analysis of this question is needed, but it seems possible that such nonliquid investment obviated, and thus retarded, the development of financial credit and money substitutes.

Nonetheless, a system did evolve in the eighteenth century to meet existing credit needs. Wealthy landowners, officials, and officers lent to merchants, generally via letters of credit or promissory notes [*veksel*]. Although a 1729 statute governed the use of promissory notes, courts did not effectively protect lenders, contributing to the extremely high interest rates, which ran as high as 30 percent at mid-century.[8] Writing in 1748, V.N. Tatishchev bemoaned the inconvenience of pursuing debtors all the way to the Senate. He lamented that local magistrates considered only the interests of merchants, creating a situation in which, "no one wants any longer to place trust in merchants or lend them money, even though many people have money— and a lot of it—lying idle, or else they make use of it in ways not beneficial for the state."[9] Despite their high cost, promissory notes did gain wide currency as a form of short-term credit and circulated as a kind of paper money. Munro demonstrates that the use of notes was quite widespread by the 1770s. It was also fairly contentious. In 1773, notes from 114 different towns were protested in St. Petersburg.[10]

By the middle of the eighteenth century, then, Russian merchants and noble landowners sought significant quantities of credit. Empress Elizabeth responded to the situation, as the city of Amsterdam and its imitators had done previously, by launching the State Loan Bank in 1754. The bank aimed to standardize an informal system by which various government departments made loans that often amounted to raids on public monies by highly placed officials. In its first incarnation, this institution consisted of two virtually independent banks, the Bank for the Improvement of Commerce at the Port of St. Petersburg and the Bank for the Nobility, with offices in both St. Petersburg and Moscow. The same law that established these banks also established a maximum interest rate for private loans of 6 percent.[11]

The Bank for Commerce did not flourish, thanks in part to flawed policies and in part to the propensity of merchant borrowers to consider government loans as grants. In 1780, the bank was merged with the Bank for the Nobility, a group the state considered more reliable and worthy of government loans.[12]

By 1817, the various Russian state banks were accepting unlimited private deposits and paying compound interest at four percent per annum. In payment of this interest, the banks issued notes of deposit (*vkladnye bileti*), which circulated as money. The bearers of these notes, generally noble landowners and officials, in turn lent them to merchants for at least another four percent. According to I.F. Gindin, Russia was "the only government in the world that accepted unlimited deposits in its banks."[13]

Although it is often argued that the growth of private banking lagged in Russia because of the prohibition against private joint stock banks, this is only partly true.[14] For one thing, at the turn of the nineteenth century, joint stock banks did not exist anywhere in Europe. Joint stock banks, or private banks of deposit, and the paper notes they issued, had a bad reputation everywhere, and governments saw it as their duty to protect investors from such enterprises. Banks such as the English Sword Blade Bank and John Law's French bank had succumbed to disasters associated with stock speculation in the Mississippi and South Seas Bubbles in the 1710s and 1720s. Thereafter formal banking all but ceased in France, and joint stock banks were not permitted again in Britain until the 1830s, in France in the 1840s, in Germany in the 1850s, and in Russia in the 1860s.[15] Thus, early in the century, most formal banks of deposit throughout Europe were public entities, as was the case in Russia.

Moreover, in Gindin's view it was the attractiveness of depositing savings in the various state banks on highly favorable terms that prevented the establishment of private banks of deposit in Russia through the middle of the nineteenth century.[16] Government banks preserved their monopoly not through statutory prohibitions against the creation of private deposit banks, but by offering terms with which would-be private banks could not compete.[17] It is beyond the scope of this chapter to determine whether the supply of credit available to Russian merchants and landowners at the beginning of the nineteenth century was adequate. However, the private promissory notes and the State Bank notes supplied significant quantities of money in excess of the imperial currency. To these instruments a third type of paper money had been added in Russia in 1768, when Catherine II created the Assignat Bank at the start of her first Turkish War, thus creating a government-backed paper currency. In 1786, the Assignat Bank became a new State Loan Bank combining the issuing and lending functions for the first time.[18] In the combination of private merchant credit and paper, public deposit banks and notes, and experimentation with paper currency, Russia's monetary and credit system resembled that of many continental countries around 1800. The great difference between Russia and her smaller neighbors to the West was the lack of commercial density. Far from the innovation-spawning currents of the Atlantic, cursed by the inhibiting distances between towns, and hampered by weak property rights and few constitutional limits, the pace and volume of trade lagged.

One of those who worried about how to quicken the tempo of Russia's economic life, and to realize the country's vast potential, was state official and political economist Nikolai Semenovich Mordvinov (1754–1845). The most prolific Russian political economist of the late eighteenth and early nineteenth centuries, Mordvinov chaired the Department of State Economy under Alexander I, and later the Department of Civic and Spiritual Affairs under Alexander and his successor. In the early part of Alexander's reign, Mordvinov worked closely with noted reformer M.M. Speranskii, particularly on the Financial Plan of 1810, which aimed at a thorough reform of all aspects of government economic policy. Thus, Mordvinov often had an official platform to launch his many schemes for improving Russia's economic condition. Even during the frequent periods in which Mordvinov was out of favor and out of government service, his written opinions circulated widely in court circles. The ten volumes of his collected works comprise, in effect, a consistent and often prescient assessment of Russia's economic potential and problems.[19]

Mordvinov was part of that first generation of European thinkers and statesmen to embrace the political economy of Adam Smith and was conversant with the work of the small, cosmopolitan club of continental Smithians, which included the Frenchman J.-B. Say, the German George Sartorius, and the Baltic-born Russian Heinrich Storch. Mordvinov took Smith as a point of departure, fully embracing his fundamental idea that land and labor were the sources of a nation's wealth and that economic freedom was the catalyst for its growth. Mordvinov sought to stimulate Russian manufactures, to encourage agricultural improvement, to promote trade and exports. As an economic official during the years of the Napoleonic wars, he was compelled to devote more time than he might have wished to technical monetary and budgetary questions. Here he demonstrated a preference for bullion and strove to limit assignat emissions, but acknowledged that paper money of some kind was needed to facilitate commerce and fulfillment of government obligations. He produced no end of schemes to ease military and other state expenditures. A theme that knitted all of these concerns together was Mordvinov's interest in bank reform, particularly his scheme to promote private provincial banks.

In Russia, the first decade of the nineteenth century marked a departure from the sense of satisfaction and prosperity that had characterized the age of Catherine the Great. War, budgetary distress, and a gradual downturn in the country's relative economic position led many to contemplate reform.[20] The most eloquent of these was Mordvinov. Like Smith, Mordvinov was convinced that ending government restrictions on individual economic initiative was fundamental to expanding national wealth. However, Mordvinov was looking at a very different country than Smith's. Interpreting the lag in commercial activity of all kinds as a problem of stimulating initiative, Mordvinov became convinced that the government must find a way to encourage capital formation and to make capital available to innovators. This led him to a lifelong preoccupation with banking.

As early as 1803 he had submitted to the new tsar a proposal for a state "labor-enhancing [*trudopooshchritel'nago*]" bank. His idea was to separate the lending function from the assignat-issuing function of the State Loan Bank and to appoint a purposeful board of directors for the loan bank comprised of experts in various arts and sciences. The directors would be authorized to underwrite ventures of all kinds, whether in agriculture, industry, livestock production, or fisheries, discriminating among proposals as to their general utility to the state. Those most worthy would be funded at the lowest rates of interest for the longest period, with a sliding scale for projects judged less worthy. Proposals of exclusively private utility would not be underwritten at all.[21] Although this proposal did reach the State Council in 1803, as of September 1812, Mordvinov was complaining that nothing had come of it.[22] In proposing a separation of the money creation and the lending functions, Mordvinov anticipated English political economist David Ricardo by over a decade. Ricardo first proposed separating the functions of the Bank of England in a letter to Thomas Malthus in 1815, and first published the idea in the *Principles* in 1817.[23] Ricardo sought to separate the two functions of the quasi-private Bank of England in order to gain exclusive public control over the country's currency, leaving the lending operations to the private owners of the Bank of England. Presumably Mordvinov had in mind that both of the Russian banks created by separating the functions would continue to be state-controlled. Like virtually all Russian economists in all eras, Mordvinov did not think the government should relinquish control over such powerful instruments of economic development.

The year 1813 found Mordvinov temporarily out of government service, having resigned in protest over Speranskii's firing. As head of the Department of State Economy from 1810 to 1812 Mordvinov had overseen the monetary aspects of the Financial Plan, and had been consumed by the problem of financing the government in time of war and of the falling value of the assignats.[24] It was in this atmosphere that he penned an essay entitled "A Consideration of the Strong Public Benefits that Would Follow the Establishment of Private Provincial Banks," in February 1813.[25] This essay reveals several of his main preoccupations and themes: his commitment to sound money and balanced budgets; Russia's opportunity to learn from a critical analysis of the experience of other countries; the need for capital, which enhances the productivity of labor and resources and which might, specifically, improve agriculture and stimulate manufactures; the need for a reformed tax system based on equal and universal liability; and a patriotic conviction that Russia's potential for economic development and prosperity was vast, though the country's great size presented difficulties as well as advantages.

Mordvinov began his proposal for private provincial banks with a summary of lessons presented by England and France based on a 23-page study of their economic history that he wrote in 1810.[26] France, he argued, had been blessed by nature with many advantages. It was bordered both by the Atlantic Ocean and the Mediterranean Sea. Useful rivers traversed its northern agricultural lands, while it also enjoyed the fruits of a southern climate. On its eastern flank France was in a position to influence the peoples of Europe politically, while its border with Spain had permitted the influx of American silver.[27] Despite these advantages, the French government was perennially in danger of defaulting on its debts, and had done so three times. The French government had done too little to build up the true source of national wealth, that is the labor and productivity of the people. Even worse, it had generally resorted to taxing capital, which limited its growth and caused great harm.[28]

The example of England was completely different: it had received little from nature, but had learned to increase its wealth through labor and technique. Despite its open access to the sea, England suffered from terrible weather and poor soil. Still, the English people and the English state had grown rich. The basis for English prosperity was English agriculturalists, who had mastered the art of improving the soil and of livestock breeding, and who were encouraged by a government that had created good roads and waterways for free and rapid transportation of goods throughout the whole country. England was a place where, "intelligence, artfulness, activity, private efforts acting in concert . . . lead science and work to perfection, and where each laborer contributes to the growth of the general national wealth."[29] From this basis in agriculture, England had proceeded to establish a worldwide commerce, to settle many lands and extract resources from them, to produce manufactures and tools. It was from a correct understanding of the power of capital and the ways of encouraging its growth that England had grown so prosperous. Through the creation of banks, money that once had lain idle could be put to use, quickening exchange and serving the needs of the people.[30] The national wealth of England had led to such ample reserves that England had been able to sustain 20 years of warfare without endangering the state budget or public welfare, a feat that much impressed Mordvinov, who had labored so diligently to shore up Russia's beleaguered budget in the recent interval between campaigns.[31]

Mordvinov's efforts in comparative history led him to conclude that money was only a small part of national wealth. Moreover, it was not its amount, but its free and rapid circulation that enhanced both public and private endeavors. Improving the monetary system did not entail adding to the supply of money, but rather directing that money toward useful and productive activity. Thrift and moderate expenditure were the basis of increasing income, and to encourage such thrift, institutions must exist that always stood ready to accept and quickly augment savings deposits. This money would be the main tool in directing human activity toward the achievement of the highest degree of enlightenment, grandeur, and greatness. Moreover, it was necessary that such banks exist in each province, where they would be more familiar with local needs and possibilities. Through taxes, public income must be extracted from this growing social wealth, but the more money that was left in the hands of the industrious segments of the population, the more quickly social wealth would grow.[32]

It was clear to Mordvinov that each segment of the population could benefit from having more capital at its disposal. In the countryside, it was desirable that the capital currently stored as grain be converted into monetary capital. The former was a kind of capital subject to destruction by insects and time; monetary capital, on the other hand, could be invested in socially useful things such as churches, schools, hospitals, roads, as well as improvements to fields and gardens.[33] Artisans would benefit from investing their savings in two ways: by saving, they would guard themselves against wasting their money on the temptations and vices of urban life, and also earn interest that would provide for them in old age and illness. Best of all, they would be able to confer property upon their heirs.[34]

It was for noblemen, however, that Mordvinov foresaw the greatest advantages. He was concerned about the gradual decline in the wealth of noble families as it was divided among the heirs in each generation. He outlined a scheme by which noblemen could make deposits that would create a substantial fund of capital for their heirs over the course of several generations.[35] As the first support of the throne, it was important that the nobility be established on a firm financial foundation, and their savings would not only secure their own families, but also provide a basic fund of working capital for the new banks to lend to all sorts of borrowers. Thus, invested savings could provide security for individuals and families, build up institutions of social welfare throughout the entire country, and, in countless ways, increase activity, stimulate industriousness, make work more productive, and generally increase every kind of national construction, welfare, and enlightenment.

If Mordvinov's bank proposal aimed to unleash the country's productive forces, it also addressed the overwhelming state financial dilemma of his time, namely, the related problem of paper money (assignats) and the state budget. Ever since their original issue the assignats had slowly fallen in value compared to the silver ruble, but the large emissions during the years of the Napoleonic wars had exacerbated their decline. Like most of his contemporaries, Mordvinov believed that the most critical task of state officials was to raise the value of the assignats and gradually redeem them at full value. The monetary sections of the Financial Plan of 1810 had called for an assignat redemption fund to be created from the gradual sale of state lands. To raise the value of the assignats, the Plan called for reducing their emission, which would be made possible through budgetary discipline.[36] Mordvinov acknowledged the utility of paper money as a means to increase the money supply and expand trade. However, he believed that the growing divergence in value between the paper and metallic money was harmful, and not only because it was inflationary.

Mordvinov believed that in a country as large as Russia the existence of moneys of different values exacerbated the difficulty that already existed in maintaining a unified monetary system. One of the more complex and vexing problems posed by the assignats was that their value both differed from that of the silver ruble and, worse, varied from one part of the country to another.[37] In some areas, silver rubles were easier to get hold of, while in others they were more rare. The differential demand for assignats from region to region based on the volume of commercial activity and the availability of silver rubles, produced complex monetary dealings and money whose value fluctuated from place to place. While one might admire ordinary Russians' enduring ability to operate complicated monetary systems, from a state standpoint, such a situation was unacceptable. Mordvinov argued that the only way for such a large country to preserve a unified currency was by tying any paper money strictly to one national standard, the silver ruble.

Thus, the private provincial banks in Mordvinov's view, should be authorized to issue their own bank notes, but the law must require them to be fully backed by silver. He would require that banks preserve the value of their paper by withdrawing notes from circulation whenever their value fell 0.5 percent below the nominal silver value.[38] Thus, Mordvinov was aiming for flexibility and expansion in the money supply while unifying the system through the silver standard. He argued that such a system would promote public confidence in all forms of money: bank notes, assignats, and silver.[39] The quickening of commerce would enhance the value of the assignats by increasing demand for them, and raise the respectability of silver by preventing hoarding and keeping its circulation regular.

It is remarkable that Mordvinov's concerns resemble those of David Ricardo at precisely the same time. Although the utterly unique English banking system differed profoundly from the more typically continental Russian system, both Ricardo and Mordvinov found themselves pressed by extraordinary events to seek the ideal balance between centralization and local flexibility.

In Britain the private country banks began to accept deposits in the eighteenth century. Scottish law permitted bankers to create cash accounts, or lines of credit, before the English, but English bankers did a brisk business in discounting bills of exchange.[40] In the early years of the nineteenth century, British bankers began to realize that they need not keep a cash reserve to cover the full amount of deposits. The next step was to ask themselves what "prevented them from extending their clientele, and increasing the circulation by discounting bills not in cash but in their own notes, in their own paper money, payable by them on demand?"[41] Thus began the process by which English private country banks issued bank notes, or paper money. Elie Halévy characterizes this system as highly speculative and shaken by repeated crises. Nonetheless, there were as many as 353 private country banks in England by 1797, which issued 20 million pounds of bank notes between 1810 and 1815.[42]

Although the British banking system was distinguished by the preponderance of private country banks, it gradually became centralized, as country banks in agricultural districts found themselves holding more deposits than they could lend locally. Money found its way to London, which, "served as a sort of natural balance to establish an equilibrium of supply and demand between the banks of the agricultural and those of the manufacturing districts."[43] It was London's central role in clearing that made this apparently decentralized system work. The final act in the centralization of the British credit system was the London banks' use of the Bank of England as a bank of deposit.

The Bank of England, founded in 1694 as a private entity with a public mission, was not originally envisioned as a central clearing bank for private depositors. Rather, its purpose was to cover government debt in time of war. Coincident with the Glorious Revolution of 1688, the Bank of England was established by a group of English and foreign merchants. The bank lent the government money in exchange for perpetual annual payments and acquired monopoly rights in its operations in 1713, which included the right to issue bank notes in London.[44] In time, the Bank of England performed more and more services for the government, such as discounting its treasury bills, and the government deposited all of its funds in the bank. As Charles Kindleberger writes, the special relationship between the Bank of England and the government could exist only in a state where a powerful representative assembly had committed to voting on annual budgets and had exerted the right to examine the bank's books. Thus this apparently decentralized system did, in fact, have a center, and that center was linked closely to the government. It was through the Bank of England that Parliament gradually gained control over the country's money supply.

Despite long experience, the English banking system was not immune from frequent banking crises, such as the one that occurred in 1797 when holders of bank notes suddenly demanded cash payments en masse. This panic led the Bank of England to suspend cash payments indefinitely.[45] Thus, Britain got through the rest of the war years on its own version of paper money (private bank notes not convertible to cash) just as France and Russia survived on theirs (state paper money, or assignats). Although significant differences existed between Russia's assignats and the Bank of England's banknotes, the problem that presented itself around 1809–10 in each country was how to raise the value of the paper money, which was falling relative to bullion. It was at this point that Ricardo famously entered the ranks of the "bullionists," arguing that the high price of gold was related to the excessive issue of bank notes. Ricardo's pamphlets succeeded, over several years, in convincing the British public that there was a crucial connection between monetary policy and the general state of the country's economy and individuals' businesses.[46] Gradually it became clear that the public had a compelling interest in the policies of the ostensibly private Bank of England, which was now serving essentially as a bank of issue for the British government. Although anti-bullionists forestalled a return to convertibility for 10 years, in 1819 the Bank of England restored cash payments, launching the era of the gold standard.

Mordvinov and Ricardo shared several key insights and convictions. They thought it useful to separate the money issuing and lending functions of the central bank, although they emphasized different benefits. They embraced a decentralized banking system (albeit the Russian one existed only in Mordvinov's imagination) tied together loosely at the center through a currency (whether private or public) backed by bullion (silver or gold). As public officials, each was keenly aware of the central bankers' (and the government's) propensity toward an inflationary issuing of excess money under the budgetary pressures existing in time of war. Considering the profound differences between the economic and political situations of their respective countries, such common insights are impressive. They are attributable to the common economic pressures of the war years as expressed in the new language of political economy, a language that did not need to be translated from English to Russian precisely because it was being learned in both places at the same time.

Mordvinov also argued that private provincial banks would not only improve the country's monetary system but also generate more income for the treasury, by augmenting the wealth of taxpayers. Mordvinov concluded from his study of English and French taxation that it was harmful and unjust to tax the idle classes less than the productive ones, and that any fees or taxes that undermined the production of capital or penalized industriousness were counterproductive.[47] The government had an obligation to protect all of its subjects equally, and it was wrong for it to burden them unequally. Moreover, it was detrimental to private interests for the government to increase taxes sharply in troubled times. And what was harmful to private interests was always harmful to state interests. The answer to all of these concerns, Mordvinov argued, was an income tax to which all *sosloviia* would be equally liable. This tax was to replace all the various guild fees and special agricultural imposts that burdened particular groups.[48] Mordvinov envisioned that the government would in turn invest these receipts and build up a tremendous reservoir of reserved funds, which would become the "guardian of the empire's well-being."[49] He further proposed a special military tax. Mindful of the teachings of political economists who considered it shortsighted to lock away resources for future wars, Mordvinov proposed to impose a surcharge of one kopek per ruble of taxes paid to establish a military fund that would be duly invested. For 48 years neither the capital nor the interest could be disturbed, but after that time the interest might be spent on socially useful projects. Writing in 1813, Mordvinov clearly was preoccupied with the disturbing ability of emergency military expenditures to upset the best-laid plans of responsible finance officers, and he sought to plan for such expenditures in advance without undue harm to the capital formation.[50]

In this essay, Mordvinov demonstrated his complete immersion in the new economic worldview. On each page of his essay Mordvinov argued that the source of all public wealth and well-being was the industriousness, effort, enrichment, and thrift of individual people of all ranks. Private property, he asserted, was better cared for and more wisely used than state property. The state's role in creating national prosperity was to devise means of magnifying the efforts of its subjects: by encouraging the creation of wealth-creating banks, by establishing a sound and unified monetary system, by planning for extraordinary state expenditures ahead of time, and by extracting income from the people in the least harmful ways. He clearly saw capital as stored labor, and therefore as something almost sacred: to waste capital was to insult the work of those who had created it. For Mordvinov, the acceptable means of preserving this precious capital was to employ it in the enhancement of public well-being, either by building useful things or by investing it where it would grow. His grasp of political economy was complete and nuanced. Like all political economists, Mordvinov was in Smith's debt, but he had not "borrowed" these ideas from the West anymore than had his contemporaries, Ricardo and Say.

In fact, Mordvinov himself contributed original ideas to the field of political economy. One preoccupation of his that had not figured prominently in the works of Adam Smith was his interest in the particular problems of large countries, and he often compared the experiences of larger and smaller countries. As an avid patriot, Mordvinov always sang the praises of the vast Russian land, often waxing poetic about its expanse and variety. He outlined several advantages of Russia's immense size: such variety of climates and peoples naturally gave rise to a great diversity of talents; it predisposed the Russian state to prosperity and greatness because the peoples of the Russian Empire could engage in agriculture, commerce, and industry. Such diversity promoted internal competition. But size was not an unmitigated blessing, and it would not overcome a lack of industriousness or capital. "A large state with little monetary capital will always be weak, wild, without manufactures, industry or trade," he wrote. "A small one, with great monetary capital, is abundant in everything, in all kinds of amenities, and joins the ranks of the great powers."[51] It was Peter I who had begun the transformation of Russia, which before that time had been a vast but wild land, by "opening the path to enrichment with the financial capital of Holland and England."[52]

Because of the empire's size, Mordvinov thought it especially desirable that banks exist outside the Empire's biggest cities. In the great cities too much accumulated wealth was wasted on luxuries and unproductive expenditure, but in the provinces banks would make loans to producers based on a close understanding of local needs.[53] Russia was a huge country, but if capital could only be accumulated and dispersed in the two major cities, it was hardly as big as an average European country. Much needed to be done in Russia to build up the country's infrastructure, and the government could not do all this by itself. Particularly a country so large as Russia needed the efforts of all its citizens. "No government of any type," wrote Mordvinov, "has sufficient income itself to construct everything that is needed for the private and the public good throughout its whole expanse."[54] A large country needed many banks in order to unlock its great potential; its investment capital could not be accumulated in a handful of cities, where bankers and entrepreneurs were unfamiliar with the needs and opportunities of more distant provinces.

Although Mordvinov's proposal was not adopted in his time, his essay demonstrates two important points. First, Russia did not lack sophisticated political economists who were writing at the same time as the important political economists of England, France, and Germany. Some of these Russians, including Mordvinov, had completely mastered the principles of the new science of public wealth, and had advanced to the point of investigating how they might apply differently to countries of different sizes or situations. Second, it is interesting to consider that, though Mordvinov did not always succeed in influencing state policy, he did bequeath an important philosophical legacy to later generations. From the 1860s on, Russian economic thought was increasingly rooted in the soil of political economy. Classical political economy became the philosophical point of departure for Russian officials as well as its liberal and even Marxist critics. Anticipating German economist Friedrich List, Mordvinov had identified national distinctions that would require modification of a general theory produced in Britain.

Finally, the early history of Russian banking and early proposals to improve it demonstrate that, although Russian banking practice had its unique features, even in this it was not outside the mainstream of European economic practice. The early history of banking was everywhere idiosyncratic and specific to a country's commercial position and political culture. Like that of other countries, Russia's banking system evolved through trial and error as well as by observing and adapting the example of other states. When Mordvinov died in 1845 those who thought about banks and economic development were grappling with the problem that most distinguished Russia, its size. Despite Russian distinctiveness, marked similarities existed between the preoccupations of its economists and businessmen and those abroad. Russia's banking system developed through a combination of private credit and public institutions common to other European states, and did not develop significantly later than that of other continental powers. Although state banks developed in Russia, they were not originally conceived as a substitute for private lending, and neither they, nor government anxiety about private joint stock banks, were unique in Europe. We do well to remember here what Jose Ortega y Gasset claimed as the key to European history: "*Eadem sed aliter*: the same things, but in another way."[55]

NOTES

1. The research for this paper was supported by the College of Arts and Sciences at The University of North Carolina at Wilmington and the Department of History's Moseley Fund at the university. I am grateful for the critique of colleagues in the departmental research forum, especially Paul Townend and Michael Seidman.

2. Charles F. Dunbar, *The Theory and History of Banking* (New York and London: G. P. Putnam's Sons, 1929), 9.

3. Charles P. Kindleberger, *A Financial History of Western Europe* (New York: Oxford University Press, 1993), 49.

4. Ibid., 49–50; Adam Smith, *An Inquiry into the Nature and Causes of the Wealth of Nations*, R.H. Campbell and A.S. Skinner, eds. (Indianapolis: Liberty Fund, 1981), vol. 1, Book 4, 480–481.

5. Kindleberger, *A Financial History*, 41–45.
6. Ian Blanchard, *Russia's "Age of Silver": Precious Metal Production and Economic Growth in the Eighteenth Century* (London: Routledge, 1989), 163–172.
7. George E. Munro, "Finance and Credit in the Eighteenth-century Russian Economy," *Jahrbücher für Geschichte Osteuropas*, Band 45, Heft 4 (1997): 552–560.
8. Ibid., 553.
9. Ibid., 556.
10. Ibid., 560.
11. S.Ia. Borovoi, *Kredit i banki Rossii* (Moscow: Gosfinizdat, 1958), 36–38; 44–45. A recent article that provides very rich detail about Russian banking practice is Sergei K. Lebedev, "European Business Culture and St. Petersburg Banks," William Craft Brumfield et al., eds., *Commerce in Russian Urban Culture, 1861–1914* (Washington, D. C.: Woodrow Wilson Center Press, 2001), 21–38.
12. Munro, "Finance and Credit," 556–557.
13. I.F. Gindin, *Gosudarstvennyi bank i ekonomicheskaia politika tsar'skogo pravitel'stva (1861–1892gg.)* (Moscow: Gosfinizdat, 1960), 81.
14. A detailed discussion of the development of Russian corporate law, with its continued emphasis on government tutelage, is found in Thomas C. Owen, *The Corporation Under Russian Law, 1800–1917* (Cambridge: Cambridge University Press, 1991). See pp. 97–111 for details on joint stock banking at mid-century.
15. The first German joint stock bank appeared in Cologne in 1841. France also adopted joint stock banking in the wake of the 1848 financial crisis, the first such enterprises being chartered in the mid-1850s. See Rondo Cameron, *Banking in the Early Stages of Industrialization: A Study in Comparative Economic History* (New York: Oxford University Press, 1967), 162 and 107.
16. The main state lending institutions in the early nineteenth century were the State Loan Bank, the State Commerce Bank, and the Welfare Funds of St. Petersburg and Moscow. See Gindin, *Gosudarstvennyi bank*, 80.
17. Ibid.
18. See Borovoi, *Kredit i banki*, 62–63.
19. Mordvinov's writings fill over nine of the ten volumes of V.A. Bil'basov, *Arkhiv Grafov Mordvinovykh* (St. Petersburg: Skorokhodova, 1901–1903); his *lichnyi fond* at RGIA is f. 994.
20. Ian Blanchard summarizes Russia's relative decline in the first half of the nineteenth century, noting that by 1788 "the average Russian was as rich as his English counterpart and only 15 per cent poorer than the average Frenchman," placing the Russian "at the very top of the international national income league table." However, thanks primarily to unfavorable climate conditions and harmful agricultural practices, Russian national income began a rapid and precipitous decline around 1807 that lasted until the early 1850s, so that per capita income fell to lower than it had been in the time of Peter the Great, and far lower than that of contemporary Britain. See Ian Blanchard, "Eighteenth-century Russian Economic Growth: State Enterprise or Peasant Endeavor?" *Jahrbücher für Geschichte Osteuropas*, Band 45, Heft 4 (1997): 543–544.
21. N.S. Mordvinov, "Proekt trudopooshchritel'nago banka," in *Arkhiv Grafov Mordvinovykh*, vol. 3, 147–178.
22. Ibid. 147–148.
23. See "Note on 'A Plan for a National Bank' " in David Ricardo, *Works of David Ricardo*, Piero Sraffa, ed. (Cambridge: Cambridge University Press, 1966) vol. 4,

272. Ricardo's "Plan" was not published until after his death, in 1824. It opened with the observation that the Bank of England performed two utterly distinct functions, issuing paper currency and advancing loans, and that these functions could be carried on by separate bodies without disadvantage to anyone.

24. An abbreviated version of the Plan appears as "Plan finansov M. M. Speranskogo (1809 g.)," *Sbornik IRIO* XLV (St. Petersburg, 1885), 1–73.

25. N.S. Mordvinov, "Razsuzhdenie o mogushchikh posledovat' pol'zakh ot uchrezhdeniia chastnykh po guberniiam bankov," *Arkhiv Grafov Mordvinovykh*, vol. 5, 236–288. Editor Bil'basov says this essay was first published by a decision of Tsar Alexander in 1816, though it did not have a very wide distribution at that time. A second edition came out in 1817, and a third in 1829.

26. "Rabota N. S. Mordvinova o chrezvychainykh raskhodakh v Anglii i Frantsii," 1810, RGIA, f. 994, op. 2 d. 899, listy 1–23. This document is not found in his published papers, but Mordvinov draws heavily from it both for this study of provincial banks and for his 1810 work, "O monetnoi sisteme," May 1810, f. 1148 op. 1 d. 1 (vol. II), listy 125–151 (an unsigned work produced by the Department of Economy, clearly the work of Mordvinov himself).

27. Mordvinov, "Razsuzhdenie," 240.

28. Ibid., 245.

29. Ibid., 242.

30. Ibid., 243.

31. Ibid., 244.

32. Ibid., 246–247.

33. Ibid., 265–266. Mordvinov is the most vague and brief in describing how "rural capital" can be created. In general, his position on serfdom was highly conflicted. He never successfully reconciled his idea that free labor was the most productive use of human talent and his considerable respect for the work of Russian peasants with his profound unwillingness to undermine the legal security of noble property, which he often used as an example of the kind of secure property rights that should be extended to all segments of the population. Here he compares the situation of the Russian peasants favorably with that of landless English farm workers because Russians did not work as hired laborers subsisting on a daily wage, but rather as owners of their homes, tools, and cattle. He also advances the positive assessment of the peasant *obshchestvo* found among later nineteenth-century *intelligenti*.

34. Ibid., 267–268.

35. Ibid., 269–271. Mordvinov called for volunteer noble depositors who would leave their initial investment and all of the accrued interest undisturbed for 45 years, after which the heirs would begin to receive two-third of the going interest rate, with the remaining one-third accruing to the account; the annual payment would remain fixed for 30 years at the rate pertaining when the payment began. After 30 years, the payments to the heirs would be recalculated based on the accrued capital and the current interest rate. After 105 years, the bank would transfer all the accrued interest to the account and pay the heirs the full prevailing rate.

36. *Vysochaishii manifest o sostave zaimov*, May 27, 1810, RGIA, f. 1152 op. 1 d. 1, listy 170–172; a good discussion of the problem of redeeming the assignats is in Helma Repczuk, "Nicholas Mordvinov (1754–1845): Russia's Would-be Reformer" Ph.D. diss. (Columbia University, 1962), 232–233, and in Walter Pintner, *Russian Economic Policy under Nicholas I* (Ithaca, NY: Cornell University Press, 1967), 185.

37. Mordvinov, *Razsuzhdenie*, 277; the matter of differential rates is addressed by Blanchard, *Russia's Age of Silver*, 209–210. A study of the value of promissory notes and deposit notes throughout the country might well reveal a similar situation.
38. Mordvinov, *Razsuzhdenie*, 278.
39. Ibid., 279.
40. Elie Halévy, *A History of the English People in the Nineteenth Century*, vol. 1, *England in 1815* (New York: Barnes and Noble, Inc., 1961), 338–339.
41. Ibid., 340.
42. Ibid., 339–341.
43. Ibid., 341.
44. Kindleberger, *Financial History*, 55–56 and Halévy, *History*, 344–345.
45. Halévy observes that, "Despite the crises which compelled periodically the liquidation of a large number of banking houses, banks continued to multiply." He counts 89 bank failures between 1814 and 1817. See *History*, 339.
46. Ibid., 348; David Ricardo, "High Price of Bullion, A Proof of the Depreciation of Bank Notes" (1810), in Sraffa, ed., *Works*, vol. 3, 51–127; on the politics of the debate between bullionists and anti-bullionists, see Boyd Hilton, *Corn, Cash and Commerce: The Economic Policies of the Tory Governments, 1815–1830* (Oxford: Oxford University Press, 1977), 31–66.
47. Mordvinov, *Razsuzhdenie*, 253–254. In his "Rabota o chrezvychainykh raskhodakh v Anglii i Frantsii" Mordvinov approved of the English practice of taxing nobles as well as peasants and considered the evolution of the all-class "land tax" to be the cornerstone of English fiscal security.
48. Ibid., 255. Mordvinov suggested that at first the income tax rate would require those receiving 1,000 to 9,999R per year to pay one ruble; those receiving over 10,000R would pay 1% per year.
49. Mordvinov, *Razsuzhdenie*, 257.
50. Ibid., 258–259.
51. Ibid., 272.
52. Ibid.
53. Ibid., 248.
54. Ibid., 250.
55. Cited in Robert Wohl, *The Generation of 1914* (Cambridge: Harvard University Press, 1979), 3.

4

TOWARD A COMPREHENSIVE LAW: TSARIST FACTORY LABOR LEGISLATION IN EUROPEAN CONTEXT, 1830–1914

Boris B. Gorshkov

Factory labor legislation in tsarist Russia is almost a blank page in our understanding of the era. This article seeks to fill this page by chronicling the introduction of laws on factory labor in tsarist Russia and by situating this legislative process into the general context of labor legislation in Europe during the nineteenth and early twentieth centuries. Throughout the nineteenth-century, Russia's industrial labor force was undergoing constant change. Unfree labor, that is the labor of individuals juridically attached to state or manorial factories, was already declining sharply by the mid-nineteenth century in favor of a free, hired industrial labor force based upon the employment of peasant-migrants. With the rapid development of the capitalist economy during the second half of the nineteenth century, the number of industrial workers grew dramatically. In order to accommodate the needs of capitalist development, regulate labor relations, and spur the growth of a reliable labor force, the tsarist government introduced numerous decrees and laws beginning in the 1830s and continuing into the early twentieth century. These acts, introduced over many decades, took the form of regulations regarding the terms of employment, work hours for women and children, health insurance, worker's compensation, and old age pensions, as well as requirements about children's education.

Labor protective legislation in Western Europe and North America has inspired a rich body of scholarly literature. Leftist historians have taken a special interest in the subject, the historiography of which has therefore been dominated by Marxist methodological approaches. The very rich leftist scholarship focused on class relations and stressed class division in its analysis of labor laws. Leftist studies displayed no interest in social divisions along lines other than class. Non-class divisions only recently came to scholarly attention. Gender divisions became a particularly important methodological basis for feminist analysis. Feminist historiography broadened our views of labor protective laws by examining gender politics and relations.[1] Inspired by the ideas of postmodernism, in particular its notion of fragmented society, recent historians have explored relations among various social and cultural groups even beyond class and gender.[2]

By definition, the topic of Russian labor legislation has not benefited from the above-mentioned intellectual tendencies. Late imperial scholars first showed an interest in labor legislation when industrial labor came to the attention of legislators and social reformers. As regards the Soviet era, Vladimir Gessen's two 1927 monographs about child labor and the corresponding legislation remain to this day the major studies of factory legislation.[3] To the extent that late imperial and early Soviet scholars explored and explained the issue, they did so within the constraints of contemporary methodologies and approaches. In any case, these studies, especially on the issue of labor legislation, have fallen into obscurity. Since the late 1920s, Soviet historiography revealed little serious interest in studying tsarist labor protection laws and no specific study of the subject appeared in the Soviet Union. The abundant literature on the workers' movement and labor unrest tended to assume, despite the absence of systematic research, that tsarist labor laws were ineffective. Many studies simply did not mention these laws. Non-Russian language histories have devoted even less attention to tsarist factory legislation. A number of economic studies and several monographs on workers and other topics addressed labor laws in passing. The authors typically mention the existence of some labor laws and then move on to other matters.[4] The early-twentieth-century factory and social welfare legislation, as well as its implementation and dynamics, remain largely unexplored to this day.[5] As a consequence, no coherent picture of tsarist labor legislation, much less its placement among that of other industrializing countries, exists in current historiography. This sporadic attention to Russian factory labor laws encourages a misleading impression that such laws were simply absent in tsarist Russia or that they had no effect.

This study utilizes archival documents, tsarist law codes, government publications, ministerial reports, and statistics, as well as existing Russian language literature to explore the attempts of governmental and nongovernmental reformers to regulate factory labor, and introduce welfare and education for working people. It situates the analysis within the context of a similar process occurring outside Russia, focusing on the timing, pace, and the degree of effectiveness of labor laws. It will also note the emergence of a labor reform movement that transformed contemporary attitudes toward factory labor and social welfare, and facilitated the introduction of labor legislation. To be sure, the absence of systematic study precludes the possibility of a full-fledged comparative article. Still, this article will make comparisons when possible, and trace basic similarities and differences between Russia and other European nations. The major thesis of this study is that during the course of the nineteenth and early twentieth centuries, factory legislation underwent a change from fragmented laws focused only on employment into a comprehensive and universal law on employment, work, and welfare. Although Russian factory laws reflected the country's national specificity within various discursive, political, and economic contexts, the Russian laws displayed patterns quite similar to other countries. The introduction of factory laws was a process common to virtually all industrializing countries of the late nineteenth century.

DYNAMICS OF THE LABOR FORCE: INSTITUTIONAL AND HUMAN FRAMEWORK

During the first half of the nineteenth century, Imperial Russia's industrial labor force experienced a notable change. Hired, contracted labor began to replace the labor of hereditary serfs, unfree workers juridically attached to an enterprise. Hereditary serf labor was largely practiced in the noble (manorial) and state-owned factories that dominated Russian industry in the seventeenth and the eighteenth centuries. Although historians debate the total number of unfree workers employed in state and manorial factories, it is clear that from the beginning of the nineteenth century, because of the growing number of factories owned by non-gentry individuals, the total number of those workers began to decline rapidly, as did the number of manorial and state-owned factories. The expansion of the commercial activities of the peasantry also further accelerated this tendency. From the late 1790s on, non-gentry individuals, according to the imperial legislation, could not possess serfs and therefore could not use this form of labor. Their factories relied on the labor of hired workers. In 1825, the work forces in the Russian cotton and silk industries—owned predominantly by non-noble persons—consisted of, respectively, 83.1 and 94.8 percent free labor and, in 1857, approached 100 and 97 percent free labor. From 1800 on, the state introduced laws that gradually emancipated state factory workers. The legislation of 1861–64 finally brought unfree labor in Russia to an end.[6]

Free-hired workers were usually recruited from peasant–migrants. From the late eighteenth century, peasant–migrants—men and women, adults and children—gradually began to dominate the factory labor force.[7] For example, in 1848 in Moscow city, they constituted between 80 and 90 percent of the city's total industrial labor force. In 1853, Moscow had 436 large enterprises with a total of 45,359 workers. About 1.4 percent (645) laborers of these enterprises were hereditary serfs, between 10 and 20 percent were workers of urban estates, and the remainder were peasant-migrants.[8] After the abolition of serfdom in 1861 and the reforms of 1861–1864, the entire factory work force became contract labor. With intensified industrialization during the late nineteenth century, workers increasingly became a notable group in Russia's social scenery. According to the 1896 census, the number of factory workers reached nine million.[9]

A notable, perhaps the most distinctive, feature of Russian industrial labor is that the majority of workers maintained close ties with the countryside, whether they wished to or not. Having migrated to a city, the peasant-migrant usually retained all legal, economic, and social ties with the village.

Before the emancipation act of 1861, serf peasant-migrants were still legally subject to the landowner and therefore had to return to the home village after the period stated in their leave documents (passport or ticket) had ended.[10] Most migrants owned a certain amount of land and, during the months of spring and summer, many returned to the countryside. According to an 1846 account, in Moscow factories, the typical working year lasted nine months. From June through September factories dramatically decreased their production because most workers left for the village.[11] Peasants also regularly returned to their villages to observe religious holidays or communal festivals. Because of special fiscal arrangements, these legal, economic, and cultural ties to the countryside persisted even after the 1861 emancipation. In the late nineteenth century, the average number of workers who periodically returned to the countryside equaled 14.1 percent of the entire workforce. Depending on the industry, it ranged from 1.7 to 83.1 percent.[12] The ties with the village sometimes provided peasants with a refuge. When repelled by harsh working and living conditions in polluted industrial areas, some workers abandoned their contracts and returned home.[13]

The migrants' ties with the village had an important impact on the gender–age composition of industrial workers. Throughout the nineteenth century, adult males predominated within the factory labor force, which suggests the high degree of peasant women's involvement in the rural economy and society: they maintained the household and actively engaged in cottage industries and agricultural production.[14] Rapid industrialization and changes in the post-1861 rural economy led more and more women to seek labor in factories. In 1901, out of 1.7 million industrial workers in Russia recorded by factory inspectors, 450,000 (27 percent) were women; by the end of 1913, this figure approached 723,913 (31.2 percent).[15]

The nineteenth-century Russian industrial labor force, like industrial labor forces in industrializing Europe and North America, also included children. Most working children came from the countryside, where the majority of children lived, while a few were the cities' poor and inmates of foundling homes. The employment of children was an established practice aimed at educating and apprenticing. During the eighteenth and the earlier years of the nineteenth century, the state sanctioned the sending of children to factories with the purpose of having children "learn an industry" and "gain an education."[16] In other countries, the use of children in production was also widely accepted by most lower social classes as a form of preparation for adulthood. In addition, children's employment was meaningful for the economic survival of their families, which often depended on the labor contribution of all family members.[17] Industries usually employed children in unskilled auxiliary operations and paid at the lowest rate. Although evidence about the numbers of children employed in industries is incomplete, according to some reports, during the 1850s about 12 percent of Russia's industrial workers were children, ranging from 0 to 40 percent in individual factories. With the industrial expansion of late-nineteenth-century Russia, the number of child factory workers increased considerably. For example, at the end of the 1850s, the number of Moscow province factory children reached 10,184 (15.2 percent). By 1871, it had increased to 29,144 and continued to grow during the following decades.[18] As noted, child factory work occurred in all industrializing countries of the period. For example, in mid-nineteenth-century France (ca. 1845), industries employed 143,665 children under 16 (about 12 percent of the entire industrial work force), ranging from 4.7 to 25 percent in individual departments of France. In 1874, child laborers constituted 12.5 percent of industrial workers in England. As elsewhere, in Russia the majority of factory children worked in textile (mostly cotton) production.[19]

In Russia, the novelty and uncertainty of the industrial environment, along with feelings of regional identity, prompted peasants to organize themselves into informal extra-legal fraternal associations, *zemliachestva* and *arteli*.[20] Similar regional workers' associations existed in nineteenth-century France, Germany, and other industrializing countries throughout Europe. In Russia, most *zemliachestva* and *arteli* associations included both sexes and various ages, although some associations consisted only of one sex or included only children (the latter were particularly true for *arteli*). Throughout the nineteenth century, these associations functioned as important social agencies, providing crucial social, economic, and cultural services for their members employed away from the native village. The associations offered financial and mutual assistance, helped to find employment, and served as the means of mitigating the harshness of workers' lives. Through the informal regional ties of their associations, workers from the same locale could maintain common customs, traditions, and practices of their native region. These ties were essential to most workers since industrial work involved high risk-taking—in cases of unemployment or labor protest, the *zemliachestva* could act as a safety net by providing their members with necessary support. In the process of adaptation and adjustment to the new industrial environment, during the late nineteenth and early twentieth centuries, peasant-migrants gradually turned their *zemliachestva* and *arteli* into worker's unions, cooperatives, and other modern labor organizations. In Russia, these remained voluntary, informal, and extra-legal until the 1905 legislation provided a legal basis for the establishment of formal workers' associations. In this case, Russian legislative reality sanctioned workers' practice retroactively. It is against this background that Russian factory legislation developed.

EARLY FACTORY ACTS

The earliest Russian statutes about freely hired factory labor date back to the 1830s and 1840s, and aimed at meeting the challenges of a rapidly expanding free market economy and securing a free labor force within the context of existing serfdom. For the most part, these laws focused on employment and addressed neither labor protection nor working conditions. The initiators and patrons of the early legislation were mainly local bureaucrats and members of the entrepreneurial class, who sought to provide a stable labor force for developing industries. In this connection, from the 1830s on, the government also introduced new legislative acts aimed at facilitating peasant mobility. During the 1830s–1840s, the Moscow Section of the Manufacturing Council influenced the approval of a number of decrees that loosened the policies for issuing and extending passports for peasant-migrants. The 1835 decree withheld the right of landowners and local authorities to recall employed peasant-migrants from employment until the expiration date of the passport for temporary leave. Initially limited to the Moscow and St. Petersburg districts, by the early 1840s the decree was extended to most Russian industrial provinces.[21]

The 1835 legislation was one of the earliest attempts in Russia to demarcate the relationship between the employer and the employee. The act specified that the employment of all workers rested upon the conclusion of a written personal contract between employer and employee that indicated the responsibilities of both sides; minors could not be employed without the agreement of their parents or guardians. The decree's provisions required factory owners to inform workers about factory rules and the respective responsibilities of workers and managers, and to post factory rules so that workers could read them. The law introduced workbooks that prescribed the conditions of employment as regards responsibilities, wages, and worker's productivity. Employers were obliged to pay their workers in a regular manner and according to the contractual terms. Arbitrary wage reductions or substitutions of money for commodities subjected employers to penalties. Simultaneously, the decree penalized workers for striking or stopping work in order to "force the owner to fulfill" the contract's terms and for divulging manufacturing secrets. Since most workers were peasant-migrants whose period of stay outside the village was set by their passports, the period of the contract's validity was usually limited by the terms of the passport. The decree prohibited workers from leaving their employers until the expiration of the contracted employment period.[22] This regulation was, however, difficult to enforce. Peasants' close ties to the rural economy caused high labor fluidity and in turn hindered capitalist labor organization and labor supervision. Many entrepreneurs and managers complained that workers left their enterprises before the contracted time in order to return to the countryside or to seek better employment opportunities.[23] According to contemporary accounts, most employment agreements were oral and only "a few" workers, usually the most skilled, had written contracts. Oral contracts predominated during the 1850s and following decades as well.[24]

Initially intended only to regulate the relations between the worker and the entrepreneur, the 1835 decree in fact challenged the basis of serfdom by limiting landlords' rights over their subjects, especially as regards recalling them back to the estate. Further legislation of 1848–49 entirely abolished written permits for temporary migration of serfs within 30 *versts* (about 32 kilometers) of the village.[25] These laws were of tremendous historical importance, providing an important legal foundation for the abolition of serfdom during 1861–64 by undermining the legal bonds that tied millions of serfs and state peasants to their landlords or home villages.

Another early Russian factory legislative act that merits discussion was the 1845 decree on factory employment of children. The need for the introduction of a basic law regulating child labor became evident as government officials learned about the widespread abuses of child labor in industry. The introduction of this legislation was actually provoked by the workers' uprising at the Voskresensk cotton mill (Dmitrov district of Moscow province) in 1844. The mill employed serfs of the landlord Dubrovin in the Massal'sk district of Kaluga province, ostensibly sent by their landlord "to learn the spinning industry." The majority of these serfs were in fact children. The workers testified that the employer used them as auxiliary workers.[26] The landlord stated that, "the children live [in the factory] in a quiet building, have healthy food, and perform work suitable to their age." To the contrary, provincial officials found that the children, most of whom "still needed parental care," were toiling day and night from 14 to 16 hours a day. This fact motivated the Moscow province civil governor to inspect the large factories of the province. In his report, he wrote that "although the machines make labor easier, night work is difficult for workers, and for children in particular, because of the character of the industry." Concerned government officials soon found out that child labor was a common practice in most Russian industries and particularly in cotton spinning factories. In August 1845, the government restricted child labor in factories by prohibiting work between midnight and 6 a.m. for children below 12 years of age. The legislators placed the responsibility for the implementation of this law upon local officials and, unfortunately, did not introduce any penalty for its violation.[27] According to historian M.I. Tugan-Baranovskii, employers continued to evade the law, especially because the legislators and local officials refused to establish an effective inspection system.[28] Nevertheless, this law marks the first attempt on the part of tsarist legislators to place labor under its direct regulative control.

The 1845 law also signified the beginnings of a transformation of Russian government officials' attitudes toward child labor. During the early nineteenth century, the state officials largely responsible for imperial law making viewed the use of child labor as normal. This resulted in the practice of sending orphans in foundling homes to factories, as mentioned above. Another interesting example of this attitude comes from a law that obliged children of manorial factory workers to work. In 1811, a state official inspecting the Krasnosel'skaia mill found it unacceptable that boys below 15 years of age did not work at all and that the workday for the other teenagers lasted only 10 hours. Within a few months, the Imperial Senate issued a special decree for this mill that stated that the workers' children had to go to work at age 12.[29] In sharp contrast, by 1845 many state officials began to view child labor as immoral, a turnaround that provoked and deepened governmental concern about this issue.[30]

Elsewhere in Europe, the first laws that regulated children's employment were introduced in Zurich in 1815, in England in 1833, in Prussia in 1839, in France in 1841, and in northern parts of Italy in 1843. In 1852 and 1859, Sweden and Austria introduced similar legislation. These laws set the minimum employment age (usually eight or nine, as in the English, French, and Prussian statutes), banned children of various ages from night work, limited their daily work hours, and introduced factory inspectors to supervise the laws' implementation. The English act of 1833, which limited the employment age to nine and introduced factory inspectors, originally concerned only children employed in the textile industry. In 1867, the statutes were extended toward all other industries. By the 1870s, child labor laws became common for most of industrializing Europe. Like the 1845 Russian law, most of these early European laws lacked sufficient provisions for their enforcement and were evaded by employers, as confirmed by historians of labor legislation.[31]

Throughout Europe, the early labor laws dealt primarily with child factory labor, while at first ignoring other categories of workers. With the exception of England, where the 1842 and 1844 laws restricted night work for women, the employment of women did not yet become a subject of a specific concern. The early Russian decrees also did not address employment of women. Thus, the 1844 law and certain earlier measures align Russia with the general European tendency to protect working children as a first step in labor-oriented legislation.[32] The 1835 Russian statute, which introduced the employment contract and addressed other labor questions, reflected Russia's socioeconomic uniqueness in that its provisions mediated between an emerging free market and serfdom.

Overall, in Russia, as elsewhere in Europe, early factory legislation did not even approach establishing uniformity in industrial labor legislation. For the most part, the laws were fragmented and specific, addressing particular industries or social categories of workers. Nor did these laws concern education and social welfare for all workers, except as regards certain unenforced statutes on child labor. Despite obvious shortcomings, the earliest legislation in Russia and in the rest of Europe had an important side. First, it signified the readiness of politically diverse states to intervene in labor relations. Second, beginning with the child labor protection acts, industrial labor in general became an issue of discussion for state authorities and concerned social reformers during the following decades. Both in Russia and elsewhere, the issue of workers' education and welfare persisted as a special topic in these debates.

PUBLIC DEBATES IN RUSSIA DURING THE 1860S AND 1870S

By the late 1850s, the 1835 decree on labor relations was no longer adequate to the case. The expanding free market, which was accompanied by a growing number of labor disputes, demanded more effective legislation. During the 1860s and 1870s, under the influence of the advocates of labor reform, who demanded attention to the conditions of workers, the tsarist government undertook several new initiatives. It set up a number of commissions to inspect labor conditions in industries. These had the goal of reviewing existing factory statutes, working out legislative propositions, and bringing them to public discussion among employers, state and local bureaucrats, and members of the juridical, medical, and educational professions.

The first comprehensive legislative proposal came out in 1862. This was a collective effort of a commission organized in 1859 by the ministries of finance and the interior. The commission included government officials, lawyers, physicians, educators, and employers. Although it retained the basic provisions of the 1835 legislation, especially as regards the contract of employment framework, the legislative draft proposed further restricting child labor, introducing financial compensation for work-related accidents, and instituting an office of factory inspectors to supervise the implementation of factory regulations. Other new provisions addressed worker–employer relations and disputes. The draft also suggested a minimum employment age of 12 and a 10-hour workday between 5 a.m. and 8 p.m. for persons of 18 and under, thus disallowing night work for children. This proposal was passed down to provincial governments and industrialists' associations for review and discussion.[33]

The opinion of state and local officials, public activists, and industrialists on the proposed regulations was divided. In general, most statesmen at the state and local level supported state intervention in general, and the legislative measures in particular.[34] State and particularly local officials were the first ones to observe and mediate workers' complaints. As members of the ruling class, they believed that it was their natural, paternalistic duty to protect workers. According to various state and local police reports, the incidence of labor disputes intensified during the 1850s. State and local bureaucrats hoped that the new legislative measures would facilitate containment and adjudication of workers' complaints.[35] In contrast, as attested to by the outlooks of local entrepreneurial associations, most industrialists opposed the proposed regulations, and viewed them as an attack on the freedom of industry and the employment contract.[36]

The most contentious issue of the proposal was child labor. Although the provision to limit the employment age to a minimum of 12 years received general approval, the questions of the workday and night work did not achieve any consensus. During the 1860s, many contemporaries still viewed children's industrial employment as a necessity because of the impoverished economic conditions of working families. The members of the entrepreneurial class argued that restrictions on child labor would have an unfavorable impact on both industry and children. Entrepreneurs stated that children usually received work "appropriate to their ages." Many argued that having lost the opportunity to work and earn money in industries, children would not be able to contribute to their families' incomes, a situation that would make it difficult for most families to give their children a proper education.[37]

The debates of the Moscow Section of the Manufacturing Council reveal that most entrepreneurs from the central industrial provinces complained that any restriction on the labor of children from 12 to 16 years of age would have a dire impact on the industry and argued that without the help of children, adult workers could not operate factory machinery. They supported a minimum age for employment of 11 years, a 13-hour maximum workday, and the elimination of all restrictions on night work.[38]

Although statesmen and bureaucrats advocated the general employment provisions of the draft, many did not want any decisive restrictions on children's employment. They argued that the law should require employers not to exhaust working children and to assign them tasks appropriate to their strength. Some believed that children's employment could benefit both industry and children's parents. For example, the prominent conservative public activist Admiral N.S. Mordvinov remarked that the children of parents living in hardship "can be of a solid use for the development of industry."[39] Moscow Governor-General Count A.A. Zakrevskii wrote in his report to Nicholas I that the condition of many working families was miserable and that the work of their children would bring some alleviation.[40] The governor of Vladimir province suggested that proposed restrictive measures would not prevent child labor at home. "Immaturity of the child cannot be a significant basis for the restricting of children's employment." He argued that "it is more humane for children and juveniles to work in factories than at home."[41] Obviously, both governors used this language as a rhetorical ploy and in reality were chiefly concerned about the provinces' industries. At that time, both Moscow and Vladimir provinces were important centers of Russian textile production, which heavily relied on child labor. Other statesmen, however, strongly criticized the industrialists' hostility toward employment regulations and asserted that "employers were concerned only about their own pockets and did not care about people's welfare."[42]

In 1866, these debates and legislative initiatives culminated in the introduction of the new factory code. The new law yielded to the industrialists' attitudes. All progressive proposals to further restrict children's employment and to establish a factory inspectorate remained largely in abeyance. The law left in place most basic employment provisions of the 1835 law and introduced the employers' liability provisions. It obliged employers to provide free medical care for work-related accidents and some paid medical services for their workers in all industries (similar measures were introduced in the mining industry in 1861). The law required all manufacturing establishments with 100 employees or more to hire a medical doctor and to maintain hospital beds at the rate of 5 beds for every 1,000 workers. With the absence of a system of factory inspection and clear provisions for implementation, however, most enterprises evaded the new regulations.[43] In 1884, when newly introduced factory inspectors examined factories, they reported that most enterprises neither maintained medical facilities nor hired doctors.[44] Nonetheless, the appeal for labor reform brought about an important discussion of industrial labor education and workers' welfare.

Legislative initiatives and the debates about labor protection and workers' welfare legislation continued during the 1870s. In 1870, the state set up a new commission to review workers and domestic servants legislation.[45] Legislators and reformers were concerned not only with employment and work, but also with workers' education and welfare. The records of the first congress of industrialists, which met in 1870, provide insights into the debates about workers' welfare and education. In general, delegates favored compulsory education for working children. The issue of funding it, however, was controversial. The members of the Russian academic community, who participated in these debates, were strong advocates of compulsory education. This is well reflected in statements by some reform-minded intellectuals that if industrialists employed workers in a way "that brings them significant profits," they must spend money on workers' welfare and schooling. Regardless, most industrialists were unwilling to take responsibility for funding education. They argued that education in factory schools must be paid for other than by the employers, who had high expenses for other needs.[46]

The issue of compulsory education was debated in local governments (rural zemstvos and city dumas). An important proposal came from the government of Vladimir province, Russia's major textile producer. It suggested that the owners of enterprises with 100 or more workers should organize schools for children of their workers, not only for employed children.[47] In 1874, specific suggestions about schooling for working children came from the commission for technical education of the Imperial Russian Technical Society. It proposed that factory schools should be set up no more than four miles apart in all locales where the number of factory and shop workers approached 500 people. Additionally, the commission suggested introducing a small tax on all businesses in order to organize these schools and a low tax on workers' wages in order to provide free education.[48]

The ongoing debates during the 1870s indicate that concerned reformers and industrialists also displayed an interest in improving the morals of workers and in the development of workers' culture. Some emphasized the importance of Christian morality and religious values. Regarding the curriculum for factory schools, they suggested that the subjects should be limited to theology and Christian morals, which "form a necessary foundation for a disciplined worker." In contrast, other delegates stated that the moral health of workers lay in "the improvement of [their] material and physical well-being," the necessary basis for workers' culture. They argued that rather than teaching theology, factory schools should educate young workers in natural sciences, factory legislation, hygiene, history, and so on.[49]

Questions about limiting the workday and about children's employment continued to attract attention during the 1870s. Some entrepreneurs still viewed these ideas as an attack on the freedom of industry and labor. Others even argued that restrictions of children's and women's employment would demoralize workers: "what would working families do if children could not work until seventeen? What would women do? It is clear what they would do.

These families would fall into drunkenness and poverty." A few entrepreneurs, however, suggested that children under the age of 14 years should not be employed in industry at all, while children from 14 to 16 should be provided with work according to their strength and with the possibility of getting an education. They suggested banning the employment of all juveniles and women in "perilous" industries including rubber, tobacco, and others. Members of the reform-minded intelligentsia continued to argue that the material benefits from child labor was problematic even for working families because it reduced workers' monthly wages to minimal rates.[50] During the 1870s, the opinion of most local officials was in favor of restricting but not eliminating children's employment.

Once again, these debates were similar to those in almost all European countries. Wide public discussion of the employment of children and women and of industrial workers' education and welfare took place in all industrializing countries, including England, France, and Germany, and reached its most intensive phase during the late nineteenth century. Initially, this discussion concerned child labor, but it soon extended to working women and to the issues of workers' education and welfare. To one extent or another, factory owners and employers everywhere opposed decisive factory labor regulation. Among those who staunchly advocated labor protective laws were usually male middle-class reformers—enlightened members of legal, medical, and educational professions, and statesmen. In general, almost everywhere in Europe, strong opposition to female labor laws came from the feminist movements, whose members mostly belonged to the middle class and spoke out for legal equality between men and women.[51]

In Russia, the ongoing discourse about industrial labor broadened the lawmakers' attitudes toward the issue and created a favorable climate for further social legislation. The new legislative approaches were more coherent than the earlier acts. They concerned factory employment, education, welfare, and the health of workers.[52] This broadening of the discussion about labor legislation provided an important basis for new legislative initiatives during the 1880s. The public discussion continued into the late imperial decades and accompanied the introduction of new labor protection and workers' welfare laws.

TOWARD A COMPREHENSIVE LAW: LATE IMPERIAL RUSSIAN LEGISLATION

The debates about industrial work among concerned bureaucrats, industrialists, and academics that emerged during the 1860s and 1870s provided an important foundation for and facilitated the introduction of new factory laws during the late imperial period. In June 1882, the State Council approved a law on children's industrial employment and work. The law prohibited the industrial employment of children below 12 years of age. The law's provisions limited the workday to 8 hours and banned night and Sunday work and work in industries perilous to the health of 12–15-year-old children. The law obliged employers to provide their juvenile workers with 3 hours a day or 18 hours a week free time in order to attend public schools (or their equivalent). The law divided all industrial areas of Russia into districts. It introduced in each district an office of inspectors "in order to supervise the implementation of laws which regulated factory employment and work, education of juvenile workers, help workers file complaints, and consider with members of the local police office transgressions of this legislation." The law's provisions were enacted on May 1, 1883.[53] The introduction of the 1882 law marked the beginning of a coherent process of social legislation in Russia during the following years and decades.

On June 12, 1884, the government introduced the law on compulsory schooling for children who worked in factories. Further legislation in 1885 prohibited night work for women and children under the age of 17 in the textile industry. The law reserved the right for the minister of finance, with the agreement of the minister of the interior, to extend its provisions.[54] The factory law of 1886 extended the area of responsibility of factory inspectors toward all workers employed in private industries, not only minors. (State factories and mines introduced factory inspectors earlier, in the 1830s and 1840s.) In 1892, the government issued a decree that introduced restrictions on women's and children's employment in the mining industry. Women and juveniles below 15 years of age were prohibited from night work as well as from work underground. The workday in the mining industry for juveniles was limited to 8 hours. Supervision for the implementation of this decree was laid upon district inspectors and their assistants.[55] The law of June 2, 1897, limited the workday to 11.5 hours a day and to 10 hours for night work in all industries. It must be noted that the enactment of these laws, like laws elsewhere in Europe, reflected labor protest and the growing awareness of hardships that workers endured. This, however, should not obscure the significance of the legislative process and discussion that had been under way long before the outbreaks of labor protest.

To be sure, the Russian law about child labor was difficult to enforce because children themselves often resisted its provisions. Children from economically impoverished worker and peasant families tried to hire themselves out in order to sustain their own lives and to provide some support to their parents as well. In order to get employment, underaged children exaggerated their real ages by several years. One contemporary noted that small boys working underground in mines, when asked how old they were, "to your astonishment, would answer: 'fifteen.' It [was] not in the interest of the boy himself to reveal the truth about his age—he can lose his job." The contemporary argued that the mine administration was well aware of this but never tried to comply with the minimum employment regulation.[56] For similar reasons, other European countries also had difficulty with the implementation of child labor laws.[57]

Regardless of violations, the labor laws had significant implications. The introduction of the factory inspectorate, whose supervising activity during the late 1880s and 1890s proved itself quite efficient, had a tremendous impact. Factory inspectors began to collect data on industrial labor and published regular reports. In Russia, starting in 1885, factory inspectors' reports appeared annually until the 1917 revolution. They addressed the implementation of labor laws, the number of workers, their age and gender, working and living conditions, and education and medical care. The effectiveness of the inspection system is illustrated by the inspectors' frequent conflicts with employers. In 1887, the Moscow Association for the Support of Russian Industry complained to the Finance Minister I.A. Vyshnegradskii that with the introduction of factory inspection there occurred many "disagreements and conflicts" between inspectors and employers. Industrialists stated that "the law placed factories at the mercy of persons [inspectors] who do not know the industry and its needs."[58] By 1913, factory inspectors supervised 19,292 enterprises with 2,231,522 workers.[59]

From 1885 on, the records of the district factory inspectors provide systematic reports on working conditions and in particular, on children's employment and welfare. The reports suggest that the number of children working in industries, and particularly very young ones, had dramatically decreased. For example, before 1883, children accounted for 10.38 percent of industrial workers throughout Vladimir province, an area of heavy textile production; by 1885, the number of children fell to 3.8 percent. According to the Vladimir province district factory inspector, "with the introduction of the [1882] law the owners dismissed children from their factories."[60] In Kostroma province, famous for its linen production, before 1883 there were 1,735 children under 15 years of age working in the province's industries, whereas after the law was introduced, the number fell to 695 children of that age. Overall, in 1884 working children accounted for 15 percent (132,000) of Russia's industrial workers. In 1913, only 1.6 percent of industrial workers were children aged 12–14, whereas 8.9 percent were aged 15–17. The law also affected the actual workday for children. Before its introduction, the regular workday lasted 12–13 hours. After it was introduced, the day approached the norm specified by the law.[61] All of these changes signify the effectiveness of the new legislation and of the inspection system it created.

Although heavy Russian industrialization came somewhat later than in other countries of Northern Europe, the pace and timing of the labor laws' introduction in Russia conformed to the general European pattern. In most industrializing countries, the most decisive laws regarding children's and women's labor, the workday, and the institution of factory inspectors appeared during the later decades of the nineteenth century. For example, as already mentioned, in England the earlier legislation, which forbade the employment of children under 9 and introduced factory inspectors in the textile industry was extended to all industries in 1867. France banned the full-time industrial employment of children below 12 and instituted factory inspectors in 1874. (The law allowed part-time employment for children between 10 and 12 in some exceptional cases.) Belgium introduced her first child labor and factory inspector law in 1889. (A Belgian law of 1884

prohibited boys below the age of 12 and girls below 14 from work underground in the mining industry.) An 1889 law restricted children's and
women's employment and established factory inspectors in the Netherlands.[62]
   Historians still debate the significance of these laws. Most recent studies
argue that labor protection laws appeared at a time when most of their provisions had already lost their importance. One historian of child labor in
Britain pointed out that the restrictions on children's employment were
introduced in the textile industry (in 1833) when the number of child
workers had already declined.[63] Other scholars emphasize that female labor
protective laws were ineffective and gender biased—they were primarily concerned with the protection of women as mothers, not as workers, and, for the
most part, aimed at eliminating women from production and confining them
to the domestic sphere.[64]
   An important period in the development of Russia's legislation regulating
factory employment and labor came after the 1905 revolution, which served
as a final impetus to introduce and implement new labor laws. Concerned
about the wave of worker protest, the government acknowledged that economic hardship caused the strikes and disturbances among workers. The
finance minister, the liberal paternalist V.N. Kokovtsov, supported the further
development of labor legislation in order to alleviate the workers' plight and
put limits on employers' arbitrariness. In 1905, the government, prompted
by the revolutionary outbreak, created a commission to speed up the ongoing legislative activities to revise labor legislation that had started in 1903.
The government appointed Kokovtsov as chairman. The commission consisted of prominent state officials and representatives of various business
groups. Minister Kokovtsov allowed the representatives of local governments
(zemstvos and dumas), the working class, members of the factory inspectorate, and university professors to discuss various points of the commission's
new legislative proposals, which were published in *Torgovo-promyshlennaia
Gazeta (Trade and Industry Newspaper)*.[65] Although it is not clear that workers
participated in the resulting discussion, business and scholarly groups sent in
suggestions to the commission.
   The commission revised the existing factory acts and worked out five new
legislative propositions: these included legislative drafts on the workday and
its divisions, on medical care for industrial workers, on state health insurance
funds, on reconsideration of existing laws that outlawed strikes, and on
workers' associations. The commission suggested limiting the workday to
8–10 hours, depending on the industry and the character of work. Most
entrepreneurs, however, objected that many Russian industries already had a
10-hour workday and that other countries had no such universal regulations
of the workday. The French legislation of 1892, for instance, imposed the
10-hour day only for juvenile workers and women and extended this provision to all workers in 1900. The 1901 British act limited the working week to
55.5 hours only for women in the textile industry and to 60 hours in other
industries. Consequently, the Kokovtsov commission's proposition was not
enacted and the workday remained 11.5 hours, the norm introduced by the

1897 law.[66] The propositions on strikes and workers' unions, however, were actually formulated as laws. With some restrictions, the laws of 1905–06 legalized strikes and provided a basis for the organization of workers' unions and cooperatives "aimed at pursuing economic interests and improving labor conditions of their members."[67] Restrictions on strikes applied to industries and businesses defined as those of "national vital importance," such as transportation, telegraph, postal service, banking, and so on. The last statutes also allowed for the expansion of the legal workers' movement often noted in histories of the post-1905 era. Although strikes were legalized in 1906, it must be noted that workers actively utilized this form of labor protest well before the 1906 legislation. With a few exceptions, strikes were resolved peacefully, by means of negotiation and compromise between the involved parties.[68]

Although the commission's proposal about insurance did not come into force at once, it provided a foundation for the 1912 insurance law. This law, with its over 500 articles, established compulsory medical insurance and medical funds for all industrial workers and financial compensation for workers and members of their families for work-related accidents, injury, or death. The law instituted elected insurance boards, which administered funds collected from compulsory contributions made by employers and workers. By mid-1914, over 340 insurance boards with a membership of over 370,000 workers had arisen in Moscow Province alone; by the end of 1915, fully 77 percent of Moscow factory workers belonged to insurance funds. Similar results occurred in other major industrial centers of Russia. According to Arutiunov, by June 1914, over 2,800 insurance boards representing over two million workers had been established throughout Russia.[69] All of this activity was capped in 1913 when for the first time and entirely unnoticed in the historical literature, all existing labor laws were collected into a single volume— the Factory Law Code—Russia's first uniform and comprehensive legislation on industrial labor.[70]

Elsewhere in Europe, the timing of laws permitting strikes and labor unions and introducing social insurance laws varied, but, in general, such legislation, as in Russia, occurred during the late nineteenth and early twentieth centuries. Although Britain had a long history of workers' unions, the first law that fully protected the country's trade unions from illegality appeared only in 1871. Germany pioneered in the introduction of work-related illness and accident compensation laws in 1883 and 1884, partly as a response to the growing socialist movement. Regardless, in 1886 Prussian police restricted and in 1901 prohibited strikes. In 1897, Britain introduced the workmen compensation act. In 1916, Denmark established industrial accident compensation for workers. Although well before the outbreak of World War I most European nations had abolished penal sanctions against strikes and trade unions, during the war some countries such as Britain outlawed strikes and hardened its policy toward the workers' movement. After the war, as a response to the rise of the socialist movement among workers, almost all European nations introduced the eight-hour workday and unemployment compensations on their way to the creation of modern welfare states.[71]

Conclusion

In summary, this article reveals that during the nineteenth and early twentieth centuries Imperial Russia's factory legislation progressed from fragmentary statutes to the full coherent factory labor code of 1913. During the 1830s and 1840s, in order to meet the challenges of free enterprise, the government undertook some fragmentary attempts to regulate the employment of freely hired workers. The 1835 statute, Russia's first labor law, introduced the personal contract as the principal basis for employment. In 1845, the government issued the first law against night work for children. These first factory laws promoted further discussion of industrial labor and workers' welfare. During the 1860s and 1870s, debates about labor legislation accompanied the development of a new concept of labor and workers' welfare and facilitated the subsequent introduction of more effective and far reaching labor regulations. For example, the legislation of 1866 obliged employers to provide health care and free medical services. The laws of the 1880s and the following decades were much more systematic and comprehensive. They expanded the scope of the earlier legislation by addressing in detail work conditions, education, and medical care, as well as implementing enforcement by the creation of the factory inspectorate. These laws marked a turning point that laid the groundwork for social legislation in Russia during the early twentieth century. The laws of 1905–06 legalized strikes, labor unions and other worker-oriented associations, whereas the 1912 law institutionalized systematic state-sponsored medical insurance for industrial workers. These developments in Russia occurred at a time when similar processes were under way in other industrializing countries of Europe. Russia's labor protective legislation and the debates about it indicate a certain willingness on the part of the tsarist state to seek juridical measures to ameliorate the problems of workers' poverty, ignorance, and material deprivation. Lastly, I would like to argue, as I have elsewhere, that the Russian labor and welfare laws had the potential to considerably ease the workers' plight had World War I not frustrated all such efforts.

Notes

1. For discussion, see these essay collections by prominent feminist and gender-study scholars: Linda Gordon, ed., *Women, the State, and Welfare* (Madison: University of Wisconsin Press, 1990); Ava Baron, *Work Engendered: Toward a New History of American Labor* (Ithaca and London: Cornell University Press, 1991) and Ulla Wikander et al., *Protecting Women: Labor Legislation in Europe, the United States and Australia, 1800–1920* (Urbana and Chicago: University of Illinois Press, 1995).

2. See, e.g., Linda Gordon, "Black and White Visions of Welfare: Women's Welfare Activism, 1890–1945," *Journal of American History* 78 (September 1991): 559–590.

3. For examples of imperial scholarship, see E.N. Andreev, *Rabota maloletnikh v Rossii i v Zapadnoi Evrope* (St. Petersburg, 1884); E.M. Dement'ev, *Fabrika, chto ona daet naseleniiu i chto ona u nego beret*, 2nd ed. (Moscow: Tip. I. D. Sytina, 1897); V.I. Smevskii, *Rabochie na sibirskikh zolotykh promyslakh: Istoricheskoe issledovanie* (St. Petersburg: Tip. Stsiulevicha, 1898); M.I. Tugan-Baranovskii, *Russkaia fabrika v proshlom i nastoiashchem: Istoricheskoe razvitie russkoi fabriki v XIX veke* (St. Petersburg: Izd. O. N. Popovoi, 1898); V.P. Litvinov-Falinskii, *Fabrichnoe zakonodatel'stvo i fabrichnaia inspektsiia v Rossii* (St. Petersburg: Suvorin, 1890); and A.N. Bykov, *Fabrichnoe zakonodatel'stvo i razvitie ego v Rossii* (St. Petersburg: Tip. Pravda, 1909). For examples of Soviet historiography, see V. I. Gessen, *Trud detei i podrostkov v Rossii. Ot XVII veka do Oktiabr'skoi Revoliutsii* (Moscow and Leningrad: Gosizdat, 1927) and idem, *Istoriia zakonodatel'stva o trude rabochei molodezhi v Rossii* (Leningrad: Izdat. Leningradskogo Gubprofsoveta, 1927).

4. Labor legislation in the 1830s and 1850s receives attention in Reginald E. Zelnik, *Labor and Society in Tsarist Russia: The Factory Workers of St. Petersburg* (Stanford: Stanford University Press, 1971), 30–40 and James H. Bater, "Industrialization of Moscow," in James H. Bater and R.A. French, eds., *Studies in Russian Historical Geography*, 2 vols. (London, New York: Academic Press, 1983), 2: 281–282. Labor laws in the 1880s and 1890s are analyzed in Gaston V. Rimlinger, "Autocracy and the Factory Order in Early Russian Industrialization," *Journal of Economic History* 20 (1960): 67–92; idem, "The Management of Labor Protest in Tsarist Russia, 1870–1905," *International Review of Social History* 5, pt. 2 (1960): 226–248; Frederic C. Giffen, "The Formative years of the Russian Factory Inspectorate, 1882–1885," *Slavic Review* 25 (1966): 641–650; idem, "The 'First Russian Labor Code': The Law of June 3, 1886," *Russian History* 2 (1975): 83–102; Robert R. Johnson, *Peasant and Proletarian: The Working Class of Moscow in the Late Nineteenth Century* (New Brunswick, NJ: Rutgers University Press, 1979) and Rose L. Glickman, *Russian Factory Women: Workplace and Society, 1880–1914* (Berkeley: University of California Press, 1984). Examination of all these sources provides a very fragmentary picture of the overall legislative process.

5. The most recent research on the social welfare legislation and its implementation is summarized in Alice K. Pate, "The Implementation of the Social Insurance Law in 1912," a paper delivered at the American Association for the Advancement of Slavic Studies national convention on November 21, 1999 in St. Louis, Missouri. For a fuller discussion, see her article "The 1912 Insurance Law" in this collection.

6. On the topic of hereditary serf workers, see Boris B. Gorshkov, "Serfs on the Move: Peasant Seasonal Migration in Pre-Reform Russia, 1800–61," *Kritika* 1 (Fall 2000): 627–656, 635, n. 32; Tugan-Baranovskii, *Russkaia fabrika*, 82–131, and Jerome Blum, *Lord and Peasant from the Ninth to the Nineteenth Century* (Princeton: Princeton University Press, 1961), 308–325. See also A.M. Pankratova, ed., *Rabochee dvizhenie v Rossii v XIX veke*. vol. 1, *1800–1860: Volneniia krepostnykh i vol'nonaemnykh rabochikh* (Moscow: Nauka, 1950), 7–107.

7. For discussion of peasant-migrants, see Gorshkov, "Serfs on the Move," 635–640. About children's industrial employment, see idem, "Factory Children: An Overview of Child Industrial Labor and Laws in Imperial Russia, 1840–1914," in

Michael Melancon and Alice K. Pate, eds., *New Labor History: Worker Identity and Experience in Late Tsarist Russia* (Bloomington: Slavica Publishers, 2002), 9–33.

8. Gorshkov, "Serfs on the Move," 639; B.N. Kazantsev, *Rabochie Moskvy i Moskovskoi gubernii v seredine XIX veka* (Moscow: Nauka, 1976), 54–76.

9. Historians usually cite the figure of 1,710,735 for the late 1890s. This figure includes workers only of enterprises examined and reported by factory inspectors. Millions of workers of many businesses, in particular, large state enterprises and small private ones, did not enter into these reports. The data of the 1896 census is more representative. *Svod otchetov fabrichnykh inspektorov za 1901* (St. Petersburg: Tip. V. Kirshbauma Departamenta Ministerstva Finansov, 1902), iii; A.G. Rashin, *Formirovanie rabochego klassa Rossii. Istoriko-Ekonomicheskie ocherki* (Moscow: Izd. sotsial'no-ekonomicheskoi literatury, 1958); and P.I. Kabanov et al., eds., *Ocherki istorii Rossiiskogo proletariata* (Moscow: Izd. Sotsial'no-ekonomicheskoi literatury, 1963), 21.

10. Gorshkov, "Serfs on the Move," 634, 640.

11. *Moskovskie vedomosti* (December 7, 1846).

12. Dement'ev, *Fabrika*, 4–11.

13. Rossiiskii gosudarstvennyi istoricheskii arkhiv (hereafter RGIA) f. 18, op. 2, d. 1927, ll. 212, 213; Tsentral'nyi istoricheskii arkhiv Moskvy (hereafter TsIAM) f. 14, op. 1, d. 3266, ll. 2–38 and f. 2354, op. 1, d. 41, ll. 197a–199, 228.

14. For discussion of women's cottage industries in the late nineteenth century, see Judith Pallot, "Women's Domestic Industries in Moscow Province, 1880–1890" in Barbara Evans Clements, Barbara Alpern Engel, and Christine D. Worobec, eds., *Russia's Women: Accommodation, Resistance, Transformation* (Berkeley: University of California Press, 1991), 163–184.

15. *Svod otchetov fabrichnykh inspektorov za 1901*, iii and ibid. for 1913, xliii.

16. For example, the 1804 Senate decree sent 12–15-year-old orphans and poor children to the Aleksandrovskaia textile mill for six years "to learn textile making." See *Polnoe sobranie zakonov Rossiiskoi Imperii* 1st series, 1649–1824 [hereafter PSZ 1] (St. Petersburg: Tip. 2-go Otdeleniia Ego Imperatorskago Velichestva Kantseliarii, 1830), no.21368. Similarly, the government provided state factories with a legal basis for using the labor of the children of workers ascribed to these enterprises. The decree "On the improvement of Pavlovskaia wool and Ekaterinoslav leather mills" stated that all children of the mill workers above ten years of age were supposed to work in these factories. See PSZ 1, nos.22099 and 27438, and Gorshkov, "Factory Children," 9–10. About child labor in other parts of Europe, see Pamela Horn, ed., *Children's Work and Welfare, 1780–1890* (Cambridge, UK and New York: Cambridge University Press, 1995) and Colin Heywood, *Childhood in Nineteenth-Century France: Work, Health and Education among the Classes Populaires* (Cambridge, UK and New York: Cambridge University Press, 1988) and Peter Kirby, *Child Labor in Britain, 1750–1870* (New York: Palgrave Macmillan, 2003).

17. Gorshkov, "Factory Children," 10.

18. Ibid., 13–15.

19. French data cited from Lee Shai Weissbach, *Child Labor Reform in Nineteenth Century France: Assuring the Future Harvest* (Baton Rouge: Louisiana State University Press, 1989), 16–19. English data are from Clark Nardinelli, *Child Labor and the Industrial Revolution* (Bloomington and Indianapolis: Indiana University Press, 1990), 106, Table 5.2. For discussion of Russia, see Gorshkov, "Factory Children," 14–15.

20. There are major differences between *zemliachestva* and *arteli: zemliachestva* were organized in urban areas or at large enterprises, and usually were stationary and large in membership. *Arteli* were often small groups of peasant-migrants who jointly sought temporary or seasonal work. For discussion of *zemliachestva* and *arteli*, see Gorshkov, "Serfs on the Move," 645–646; Christine D. Worobec, *Peasant Russia: Family and Community in the Post-Emancipation Period* (Princeton: Princeton University Press, 1991); Jeffrey Burds, "The Social Control of Peasant Labor in Russia: The Response of Village Communities to Labor Migration in the Central Industrial Region, 1861–1905," in Esther Kingston-Mann and Timothy Mixter, eds., *Peasant Economy, Culture, and Politics of European Russia, 1800–1921* (Princeton: Princeton University Press, 1991), 52–100; Johnson, *Peasant and Proletarian;* and Zelnik, *Labor and Society.*

21. Analysis of the earlier decrees is in Gorshkov, "Serfs on the Move," 641; Zelnik, 30–40; Bater, 281–282; B.N. Kazantsev, "Zakonodatel'stvo russkogo tsarizma po regulirovaniiu krest'ianskogo otkhoda v XVII-XIX vv," *Voprosy istorii* 6 (Moscow, 1970): 20–31; *idem, Rabochie Moskvy*, 98; N.S. Kiniapina, " 'Rabochii vopros' v politike tsarizma vtoroi chetverti XIX veka," *Istoriia SSSR* 1 (1967): 39–40 and Tugan-Baranovskii, *Russkaia fabrika*, 132–146.

22. *Polnoe sobranie zakonov Rossiiskoi Imperii*, 2nd series, 1825–1879 [hereafter PSZ 2] (St. Petersburg: Tip. 2-go Otdeleniia Ego Imperatorskago Velichestva Kantseliarii, 1885), vol. 10 (1835), no.8157. Also see Kiniapina, "Rabochii vopros," 39–40; Kazantsev, *Rabochie Moskvy*, 109–133 and Tugan-Baranovskii, *Russkaia fabrika*, 132–146.

23. RGIA f. 18, op. 2, d. 1927, ll. 212–213; TsIAM f. 14, op. 1, d. 3266, ll. 2–38 and f. 2354, op. 1, d. 41, ll. 197a–199, 228.

24. RGIA f. 18, op. 2, d. 1927, ll. 1–2.

25. For discussion of the legislation on temporary migration, see Gorshkov, "Serfs on the Move," 633–634, 638; and David Moon, "Peasant Migration, the Abolition of Serfdom, and the Internal Passport System in the Russian Empire, c. 1800–1914," David Eltis, ed., *Coerced and Free Migration: Global Perspectives* (Stanford: Stanford University Press, 2002), 324–357.

26. Gessen, *Istoriia zakonodatel'stva*, 50.

27. PSZ 1, no.19262.

28. Tugan-Baranovskii, *Russkaia fabrika*, 139.

29. Ibid., 138.

30. About state officials' changing views about child labor, see Gorshkov, "Factory Children," 22–29.

31. Child labor legislation is discussed in Bob Hepple, ed., *The Making of Labour Law in Europe: A Comparative Study of Nine Countries up to 1945* (London and New York: Mansell Publishing Ltd., 1986), 81, 89–94; Weissbach, *Child Labor Reform*, 123; Nardinelli, *Child Labor;* and Jane Lewis and Sonya Rose "Let England Blush," in *Protecting Women*, 91–124.

32. Hepple, *The Making of Labour Law* 82, 94–95.

33. Gosudarstvennyi arkhiv Rossiiskoi Federatsii (hereafter GARF) f. 102, op. 42, d. 34 (1), ll. 76–77; *Trudy komissii uchrezhdennoi dlia peresmotra ustavov fabrichnogo i remeslennogo*, 2 vols. (St. Petersburg, 1863), 2: *Prilozhenie XV*, 274–278; and Andreev, *Rabota maloletnikh*, 5, 12.

34. *Trudy komissii*, 2: *Prilozhenie XV*, 274–278.

35. TsIAM f. 2354, op. 1, dd. 40, 41, 42, especially d. 41, ll. 108–109; GARF f. 102, op. 42, d. 34(1), ll. 74–86.

36. *Trudy komissii*, 2: *Prilozhenie XV*, 276–278; Andreev, *Rabota maloletnykh*, 6, 12, 16.
37. *Trudy komissii*, 2: *Prilozhenie XV*, 274–278.
38. TsIAM f. 2354, op. 1, d. 49, l. 38.
39. M. Balabanov, *Ocherki po istorii rabochego klassa v Rossii*, 2 pts. (Kiev: Sorabkopa, 1924), 1:58.
40. Ibid., 1:108.
41. *Trudy komissii, Prilozhenie XV*, 287.
42. *Trudy komissii, Prilozhenie XV*, 274–275, 290–292.
43. See Zelnik, *Labor and Society*, 35–37; Theodore H. Freidgut, *Iuzovka and Revolution*, vol. 1, *Life and Work in Russia's Donbass, 1869–1924* (Princeton: Princeton University Press, 1989), 137–140; V.Ia. Laverychev, *Tsarizm i rabochii vopros v Rossii (1861–1917)* (Moscow: Mysl' 1972), 30–31, Tugan-Baranovskii, *Russkaia fabrika*, ch. 5, PSZ 2 (1861), no.36719; Litvinov-Falinskii, *Fabrichnoe zakonodatel'stvo*, 219–224.
44. P.A. Peskov, *Fabrichnyi byt Vladimirskoi gubernii: Otchet za 1882–1883 fabrichnogo inspektora nad zaniatiiami maloletnikh rabochikh Vladimirskogo okruga P. A. Peskova* (St. Petersburg: Tip. V. Kirshbauma Departament Ministerstva Finansov, 1884), 115.
45. Gorshkov, "Factory Children," 19.
46. Gorshkov, "Factory Children," 20; *Protokoly i stenograficheskie otchety 1-go Vserossiiskogo S"ezda fabrikantov, zavodchikov i lits interesuiushchikhsia otechestvennoi promyshlennost'iu v 1870 g.* (St. Petersburg, 1872).
47. Gorshkov, "Factory Children," 21; Andreev, *Rabota maloletnikh*, 42–43.
48. Gorshkov, "Factory Children," 22.
49. Gessen, *Istoriia zakonodatel'stva*, 70–71.
50. Ibid.
51. The German case stands somewhat apart. In Germany, the initiatives to protect and restrict female industrial labor were welcomed by most social groups, including feminists. For discussion, see Alice Kessler-Harris, Jane Lewis, and Ulla Wikander, "Introduction" in *Protecting Women*, 1–27; and Hepple, *The Making of Labor Law*, ch. 2.
52. Gorshkov, "Factory Children," 20–21.
53. *Sbornik postanovlenii o maloletnikh rabochikh na zavodakh, fabrikakh i v drugikh promyshlennykh zavedeniiakh* [Collection of laws about child industrial labor] (St. Petersburg: Izdanie Khruleva i Zhivotovskago, 1885), 1–43.
54. *Sbornik postanovlenii*, 1–43; *Polnoe sobranie zakonov Rossiiskoi Imperii 3rd series* [hereafter PSZ 3] (St. Petersburg: Tip. 2-go Otdelenia Ego Imperatorskago Velichestva Kantseliarii, 1885), no.3013.
55. PSZ 3, nos.8402 and 11391. Also see *Svod zakonov Rossiiskoi Imperii*. (hereafter SZ), vol. VII, *Ustav Gornyi* (St. Petersburg: Tip. 2-go Otdelenia Ego Imperatorskago Velichestva Kantseliarii, 1893), no.655.
56. Cited in K.A. Pazhitnov, *Polozhenie rabochego klassa v Rossii*, vol. 2 (Petrograd: Izd. Byloe, 1923), 28.
57. See, e.g., Weissbach, *Child Labor Reform*, 206–226.
58. Litvinov-Falinskii, *Fabrichnoe zakonodatel'stvo*, 314–318.
59. GARF f. 4100, op. 1, d. 96, l. 6.
60. Peskov, *Fabrichnyi byt Vladimirskoi gubernii;* and idem, *Otchet fabrichnogo inspektora Vladimirskogo okruga P. A. Peskova za 1885 g.* (St. Petersburg: Tip. V. Kirshbauma Departamenta Ministerstva Finansov, 1886), 25–26.

61. Gessen, *Istoriia zakonodatel'stva*, 100.
62. Hepple, *The Making of Labor Law*, ch. 2.
63. For discussion see Nardinelli, *Child Labor*, 144.
64. See, e.g., Jane Jenson, "Representation of Gender: Policies to 'Protect' Women Workers and Infants in France and the United States before 1914," in Gordon, *Women, the State and Welfare*, 152–198; and Lewis and Rose, "Let England Blush," 91–124. Also see Kessler-Harris, Lewis, and Wikander, "Introduction" in *Protecting Women*.
65. *Rabochii vopros v komissii V. N. Kokovtsova v 1905 g.* (Moscow: Voprosy truda, 1926), 41, no.5.
66. SZ (1913), vol. XXI, part 2, *Ustav o promyshlennom trude*.
67. *Rabochii vopros v komissii V. N. Kokovtsova*, nos.15, 25, and 27; and PSZ 3 (1905), no. 26987, see section II, p. 852; and SZ (1913), vol. XXI, part 2, *Ustav o promyshlennom trude*, no.230.
68. See Freidgut, *Iuzovka and Revolution*, vol. 1 and vol. 2, *Politics and Revolution in Russia's Donbass, 1869–1924* (Princeton: Princeton University Press, 1994).
69. Pazhitnov, *Polozhenie rabochego klassa*, vol. 2, 146–148; Elise Kimerling Wirtschafter, *Social Identity In Imperial Russia* (DeKalb: Northern Illinois University Press, 1997), 148; G.A. Arutiunov, *Rabochee dvizhenie v Rossii v period novogo revoliutsionnogo pod"ema, 1910–1914* (Moscow: Nauka, 1975), 258.
70. SZ (1913), vol. XXI, part 2, *Ustav o promyshlennom trude*.
71. Hepple, *The Making of Labor Law*, ch. 2.

5

Rereading Old Texts: Sergei Witte and the Industrialization of Russia

Frank Wcislo

Few personalities loom larger in the historical literature studying late imperial Russia than Sergei Witte, and few of those texts have withstood the vicissitudes of time and fashion more successfully than Theodore Von Laue's portrayal of the *ancien regime*'s great industrial modernizer. While the interpretive concerns of historians of Russia have moved beyond the framework of backwardness and industrialization within which Von Laue portrayed the tsarist statesman, among nonspecialist European historians Witte's name often still remains synonymous with what Von Laue termed the efforts of the autocratic state to industrialize, modernize, and thus overcome the "penalties of backwardness" that rendered the Russian *ancien regime* archaic in the modern Western world.[1] One need only consider introductory undergraduate surveys of European history and the degree to which Von Laue's Witte, either directly or implicitly, still occupies a central place in narratives of the Empire's last decades. When generalists survey early-twentieth-century Europe, Witte, the great industrializer, and more broadly the "Witte system" of state-sponsored industrialization that Von Laue elaborated, remain historiographical fixtures in explaining the revolutionary end-time of the tsarist Empire and the emergence of its Soviet, communist successor. More than three decades after its appearance, Von Laue's portrayal of Witte and his Russia remains a touchstone in interpreting Russia's place in European history.

All historians, to some degree, suffer the influence of their times. Writing in the 1960s, Von Laue can hardly be faulted for a preoccupation with third-world backwardness, the imperatives of industrialization and modernization that he believed it imposed upon both the tsarist and the soviet states, and, finally in his view, the systemic crisis that the drive to "industrialize" and thus compete with a more developed European first world provoked in Russia both before and after the 1917 Revolution. Nor, given the sociological concerns of a Cold War era that compared capitalist and communist systems, is it surprising to find Von Laue modeling modernity in terms of autonomous private initiative, liberal constitutionalism, sovereign nation-states, and mature, postindustrial societies—all set against the antitheses of the post-Stalinist social and political order. With such assumptions about the modern governing his research, Von Laue read them back onto imperial history, and emphasized the degree to which Russia's historical development had diverged from this "first world" path toward modernity. Emphasizing Russia's exceptionalism, Von Laue privileged statist intervention and societal backwardness as the preeminent features of late imperial history. A backward Russian society of agrarian elites, peasant masses, and a semi-medieval merchantry (*kupechestvo*, not bourgeoisie) was incapable of shouldering the required task of industrial modernization, and itself necessitated a Witte "system" of state intervention in the national economy. Such industrialization from above limited and constrained entrepreneurial initiative, valued economic power over constitutional liberty, and amplified the statist, authoritarian, and ultimately totalitarian tendencies of modern Russian history. "Industrialization," Von Laue wrote in his conclusion,

> called for an all-out effort by the government to enlist the energies of its subjects, to arouse their enthusiasm for a new way of life, and, most basically, to mold their habits and values so as to make them conform, voluntarily or involuntarily, to its discipline. . . . In other words, the new autocracy toward which Witte groped was to rally both government and people to one common, almost superhuman effort. This was the lesson which linked the Witte system with the Soviet regime. . . .[2]

Witte, and the program of state-sponsored industrialization that Von Laue portrayed more than thirty years ago, focus attention on a Russia found at the periphery of European life, and a history distinct from that which occurred in "the West."

If ultimately Von Laue represented state-sponsored industrialization as an almost super—if not supra—human process, no less Nietzschean, in the final analysis, was his portrayal of the man who had undertaken the "industrialization of Russia." Here, too, theoretical preconceptions informed Von Laue's thinking, in particular his interest in a "native" intelligentsia exposed to the influences and cultural challenge of "Western" life. Witte "was trapped," Von Laue wrote, "in the 'contradictions' (to use a Marxist term so appropriate to Russian conditions in this age) which stemmed from the disparate combination of western and native elements in his parentage, in his career, and in the Russia in which he rose to power."[3] In his generally sympathetic biographical treatment of Witte, Von Laue always was concerned to reveal the ways in which Witte's life, much like tsarist society itself, had been subject to the dual influences of Russia and the West. Hence, it was important that his youth was shaped during the 1850s and early 1860s not only by a family "united in their deep loyalty to the Tsar and the Orthodox Church," but also by an upbringing in the recently colonized Caucasus, where Witte could experience "the freedom of the frontier." Of equal import were the first years of his career as a railway administrator during the 1870s, when, especially in Odessa, that "entrepot for Western ideas and institutions," an "ambitious young official could be well apprenticed to the ways of modern capitalist society." He was part business "magnate" and "tycoon," part "fanatical" adherent of autocracy; part author conversant with major works of European political economy, and part romantic Slavophile suspicious of Western capitalism.[4] Witte in Von Laue's treatment was a totem: an amalgam of an old patriarchal and new Westernized Russia, both the man and the country entrapped in an unstable separation from a more advanced, European first world.

Historians also cannot be blamed for their primary sources, particularly materials as rich as those available to the biographer of Witte. Much of what we know of Witte's life, especially in the late nineteenth century, derives from the copious memoirs that he wrote after 1906. No better source could be found to represent Witte as a supra-human personality, since that was the self-image that the former premier cultivated at every opportunity in his writing. Nor would it be easy to miss there his bitter personal disillusionment following the upheavals of 1904–06, and the wreckage of his own aspirations to salvage a reformed autocracy, factors that in turn fed premonitions of systemic disaster for both a dynasty and an existing social order whose peculiarities his personal despondency only led him to emphasize ever more darkly.[5] Writing in the early 1920s, Witte's adopted daughter, Vera Naryshkina, remembered him as a "stern giant (*surovyi velikan*),"[6] an image fitting for the brooding, mercurial, rejected figure who spent his last years, when not questing to return to power, crafting a reputation for posterity. Prior to these memoirs, a ministerial career had produced scribbled marginalia and ghost-written memoranda that now litter the imperial archives of St. Petersburg. Those bureaucratic documents, too, have left their impression on scholars all too often ready to see a distant, Herculean, yet doomed Witte, sometimes seemingly an Alexei Karenin, at the heights of tsarist power. Yet, especially set against this background, writing that Witte authored before he entered the Ministry of Finances in 1888, is strikingly different in tone and authorial perspective from those mentioned previously.[7] They reflect a Witte who regarded both himself and his world with an air of confidence, optimism, and unprecedented possibility—a mood reminiscent of what Eric Hobsbawm has called the Age of Empire.

In the third volume of his magisterial examination of Europe's long nine-teenth century, Hobsbawm reminds his late-twentieth-century contemporaries that the years 1875–1914 constituted an era of paradox: peace led to unprecedented war; triumphant imperial states created the conditions for anticolonial revolutions that would eventually disintegrate them; militant organized labor explicitly demanded the overthrow of a capitalism that was so flourishing it was beginning to improve even the socioeconomic position of the proletariat; liberal bourgeois democracies were laying the foundation for a mass politics that would render the bourgeoisie peripheral; avant gardes were repudiating nineteenth-century culture and intellectual life even as ever greater masses of people, exposed to both via a variety of media, looked with hope and optimism to a future much like their present. The "basic pattern" of the Age of Empire, Hobsbawm writes, "is of the society and world of bourgeois liberalism advancing towards what has been called its 'strange death' as it reaches its apogee, victim of the very contradictions inherent in its advance." Quite elegantly, Hobsbawm notes that, "there is nothing about the historical pattern of reversal, of development undermining its own foundations, which is novel or peculiar to this period as distinct from any other." Yet, aware that all too often these last decades of the "long nineteenth century" serve other purposes—either to anchor a sentimental longing for a bourgeois world lost to war, revolution, mass culture, and modernism or to introduce, as cursory prelude, a twentieth century dominated by these forces—Hobsbawm explores the end-time of nineteenth-century capitalism and liberal bourgeois society in its own right, and in particular displays the various ways in which the Age of Empire celebrated the triumph of a civilization even as it presaged, and consciously anticipated, "a world different in kind from itself."[8] This historical juncture, where a future, potentially even a cataclysmic one, can be anticipated even as the present is celebrated as the triumphant culmination of the past, is an appropriate place from which to reread Sergei Witte and the industrialization of Russia.

Certainly, ever more loudly—and it might be added, ever more darkly—Witte in the last years of his life entertained a fascination for the apocalyptic, which at intervals, as was the case throughout late imperial high society, included revolution. Yet, subtextually in the memoirs he wrote then, and much more explicitly in earlier writing, Witte embraced the triumphant European civilization, which, at the end of the nineteenth century, he assumed to encompass the Russian Empire. Thus, one might ask quite rhetorically, was Witte, as Von Laue had it, the great industrializer—or might he better be understood simply as a Russian, and a European, of the later nineteenth century? Might it not be worthwhile to revisit Sergei Witte at the height of his public life in the 1880s, before politics and the imperatives of power intensified the need for him to mask himself, creating personalities that eventually complicated every reading of his memoirs? This paper seeks to contextualize Witte within place and time, in essence to historicize Sergei Witte, by reexamining aspects of his career experience as a railroad administrator and proto-technocrat in the 1870s and 1880s. Moreover, given the well-established linkage between Witte and the "industrialization of Russia," it also aims to historicize the great industrializer. This is not the place to reopen debates about modernization and the degree to which, as well as the ways in which, it contributed to the revolutionary crisis of the early twentieth century—although in light of new research this debate surely requires revisiting.[9] Instead, this examination of Witte as a railway man aims to interrogate some of the cultural assumptions about Russia and its place in Europe that were reflected in Witte's experience of the railroad. This most modern of European technologies, Witte understood, possessed the capacity to transform commercial–industrial (*torgovo-promyshlennaia*) culture and to intensify the benefits of an international economic order of which the Russian Empire, he assumed, was a component element.

By 1885, a year often used to date the "beginning" of Russian industrialization, Witte already had built a successful career as a railroad administrator in Ukraine, first in Odessa, and after a brief period in St. Petersburg, in the booming city of Kiev. As manager of operations (*nachal'nik eksploatatsii*) of the privately owned Society of Southwestern Railroads—or as he characterized himself in 1884, "a salaried employee (*sluzhashchie. . . . na opredelennom soderzhanii*) of the railroad,"[10] Witte oversaw the daily business of one of the empire's larger rail networks. Created in 1878 from three smaller lines, the Southwestern joined together commercial arteries stretching from the Black Sea port of Odessa in the south and Kiev in the east toward Brest-Litovsk in the northwest; lines through Kishinev led to the Rumanian border and the Danube River valley in the west. It extended over some 2,200 kilometers in 1878 and would more than triple in size by the turn of the century.[11] The Southwestern was a key component of a technological sector, the railroad industry, whose rapid growth in the 1870s and 1880s, even before the construction boom associated with the Trans-Siberian Railroad in the 1890s, was one of the startling features of the era (table 4.1).

Although passenger travel was still a novelty in the empire, moving people and goods more quickly across astoundingly larger expanses, of course, compressed, perhaps altogether altered time and space.[12] Shipping goods over longer distances and integrating regional and national markets, railroads also accelerated economic exchange and intensified commercial-industrial culture within the expanding zone of their "iron roads" (*zheleznye dorogi*). This latter feature, the impact of railroad technology on commercial-industrial culture, was in the Russian case even more striking than the overall extension of the network (see table 4.2). Or so Witte argued when he debuted as an author and a technological expert in 1883.

That year, he published a series of articles in the journal *Inzhener'*, which later appeared as a book in Kiev under the foreboding title *Principles of*

Table 4.1[13]   Kilometers of railroad track (thousands)

	United Kingdom	France	Austro-Hungary	Russian Empire
1867	19.8	15.0	4.1	5.0
1877	23.9	20.5	11.2	21.0
1887	27.2	31.4	14.1	28.2
1897	29.4	36.9	17.3	41.5

Table 4.2[14]   Total freight (millions of tons) and passengers (thousands) in transit on railroads annually

	United Kingdom		France		Austro-Hungary		Russian Empire	
1867	134.6	273.7	38.7	101.6	13.3	12.1	5.1	9.0
1877	211.6	532.3	61.6	138.8	43.8	32.8	36.6*	29.0*
1887	269.4	714.2	77.2	217.8	65.7	65.0	50.1	37.0
1897	375.2	1004.5	108.4	374.8	104.4	109.5	111.7	75.0

* 1876.

Railroad Freight Rates.[15] It examined the price structures utilized by railroads to transport freight and their relationship to a company's business volume and profits. A seemingly arcane technical problem, it bore sufficient fiscal, and thus political, import, to have become a subject of government concern several years earlier in the Ministry of Communications's Baranov Commission, where Witte had participated as an invited expert. Railroad construction in the 1860s and 1870s had occurred through state concessions. Government contracts created private companies that apportioned shareholdings between the treasury and investors. Guaranteed a minimum level of profit with the backing of the state treasury, such companies were intended to serve the imperial state as a means to mobilize both scarce investment capital and managerial expertise. By the early 1880s, however, such concessionary schemes more often than not had yielded high operating losses on many lines, an outpouring of treasury payments to investors as a result, and yet another strain on the chronically imbalanced state budget.[16] In this context, the expertise that Witte displayed in his writing, especially his technical analysis of the principles governing railroad price structures, as well as his evident knowledge of local commerce, industry, and markets was, it seemed, a very conscious step on the road that by 1888 would lead to his appointment as director of the Ministry of Finances's Department of Railroad Affairs. There, as scholars have indicated, he would implement one of the key arguments of the book: freight rates could be manipulated, and prices held artificially low, to encourage commerce, especially in grain, as well as the accompanying development of regional markets, business volume, and profit.[17] Indeed, a second section of *Principles*, entitled "Practical Section," amounted to a survey of his opinions for the as yet nonexistent post.[18]

Yet, besides marking both his growing technical expertise and careerist ambitions, *Principles* also reflected Witte's views of the railroad, the commercial-industrial culture of which it was a constituent element, and, if only as this, a set of assumptions, derived from his knowledge and practical experience, that the technology was altering that culture in a fundamental and potentially progressive way. Never one to dwell on the petty or arcane, Witte did not concern himself merely with prices. Rather, as he wrote in the book's introduction, he intended to examine systematically "the whole problem of railroad tariffs (*tarifnoe delo*), which flows from the entire totality of economic and commercial relationships and in turn exerts an influence upon them . . . ." What he called "the theoretical side" of the issue in part derived from his own reading in political economy, and in part from his own managerial practice. The latter rendered his views irrefutable, the inductively minded Witte believed, because they were "conclusions based on scientific data (*nauchnye dannye*)": the currency of his expertise and ambition, as well as the medium through which he understood and conceptualized experience. A theoretical exposition of freight rates, therefore, inevitably attended not only to the technology that the expert manager administered, but also the entire network of commercial and industrial relationships, the culture, with which it interacted. Any understanding of freight rates necessarily began from the axiomatic principle of classical political economy, "the economic law of supply and demand," Witte remarked. Yet, he continued,

> . . . when considered further, (it) also results from the interaction (*vzaimodeistvie*) among (all) elements of economic life, political life, and even the intellectual life of the nation (*zhizni naroda*). This interplay (*igra vliianiia*) is a quite interesting subject for study by the thinker (*myslitel'*) and the economist (*ekonomist*).

Readers would find, Witte concluded, that "we have tried to present, in as popularized a fashion as possible (and) taking into consideration contemporary conditions of time and place, all the basic principles upon which, in our deeply held conviction, the whole problem of railroad rates in our fatherland ought to be based."[19] A treatise on rate structures opened to readers Witte's observations of late-nineteenth-century commercial–industrial culture—what he called the interplay of the economic, political, and intellectual—as well as his thinking about the ways in which it should, and inevitably would, change.

His was, in the first instance, a view that was contextualized, as he had promised, in terms of time and place—although time incorporated more than the later nineteenth century, and place included all of Europe. The first section of *Principles*, a not altogether impartial rebuttal of the conservative agrarian argument against monopolistic railroads, reflected as well Witte's familiarity with commercial networks in Russia and throughout continental Europe: its roads, rivers, sea lanes, and railroads.[20] Railroads competed with other modes of transportation, he insisted, reminding his readers of what they and he encountered on a regular basis. "Railroads," he wrote, "always have been built, and still are, alongside existing pathways of communication, where enormous commercial interchange has been taking place over centuries." Certainly railroads were "more advanced" technologically than roads and waterways, but to think of them as monopolies was an untenable view, "contradicted at every turn," he charged, "by the most mundane circumstances of daily life." Crown officials "would frequently avoid" the train if their travel allowances were inadequate to pay the price of a rail ticket. The "mass of the poor population in Russia travels not only by horse, but simply on foot, even for great distances, parallel to the railroads . . . ." Throughout local Russia, the teamster hauling goods on Russian roads at prices far below those charged by the railroad was a fixture whose "competitive advantage . . . would decline significantly only after many years." Turning from land to sea, Witte noted the equally powerful competition of commercial sea lanes, which unified disparate regions of the European "peninsula." A "mass of products," he wrote, "moves among countries of the European continent and even among points within the same country by sea, not on the railroads that link them together . . . ." Traffic patterns on the Southwestern showed Ukrainian grain much more frequently shipped from a Black Sea port, via the Mediterranean and Baltic, to Hamburg, rather than exported overland by rail to Berlin. Much commerce between northern and southern Russia flowed from Odessa to St. Petersburg not by rail, but sea, despite the circumnavigation of Europe that it required. Finally, railroads confronted "the low prices of towage on the interior rivers and canals" of the country, especially for raw materials like lumber, salt, fuel, and grain. Indeed, Witte noted, river transport, a seasonal activity given the winter freeze, not only was increasing in volume, but had contributed to the development of commercial wholesale enterprises, which warehoused cheaply transported goods and supplied them to local markets during the long winter months.[21]

Familiar with the arterial networks interconnecting commercial–industrial culture, Witte was equally attuned to the complex, relational balance and flow of market exchange, which he knew to be the lifeblood of commerce and industry. Witte was well read in European political economy, and fully accepted its first principle.[22] The "antagonism of desires (*antagonizm zhelanii*) between producers and consumers . . .," he wrote in describing a nearly benthamite rational drive to maximize gain and minimize loss, eventually "led to one and the same end: an equilibrium between supply and demand." Witte thus could comment abstractly about unfettered competition (*konkurentsiia*) among producers, each seeking "to offer the consumer the most advantageous terms (*naivygodneishiia usloviia*)." Or, he could appraise the unequal confrontation between monopolies and impoverished consumers, the latters' lives inevitably entrapped in "an eternal struggle with deprivation" that obliged them "to weigh their needs against their means." Yet, even these scenarios, rather than the passivity of a near-subsistence agrarian world, instead naturally assumed that such consumers possessed a kind of power, albeit only that of their "own personal inertia." Reducing their demand, these chimerical consumers could influence the adroit producer, who after all could not "exist" without them, to conclude that "net income did not depend exclusively on the amount of earnings derived from each unit sold, but chiefly from the number of units sold, from extending consumption (*rasprostranenie potrebleniia*) through the masses of a population lacking significant resources."[23]

Although presented as if it were a theoretical postulate—a style that Witte often favored in his writing—this perception of intensifying market exchange rested upon, and derived from, his railroad career, in particular the experimentation with lowered freight rates that was the subject of *Principles*. Practice had allowed him to see that demand for railroad "services" was elastic (*kharakter otnositel'nosti*), since they were "not an absolute, irreversible requirement, but, on the contrary, a relative one . . . whose satisfaction depends on cost . . . ." Knowing, as he did, that a still novel technology competed with other modes of transportation, Witte also understood that the technology was unique, if not revolutionary, given its powerful capacity to intensify market exchange, the very essence of European commercial–industrial life. "The role of railroads," he wrote in a key passage where he justified a radical lowering of freight rates even at the cost of short-term losses,

> consists only in this, to eliminate the limitation of distance (*pregrad razstoianii*) and, in this manner, render products of any one particular kind competitive on

any number of commercial markets . . . Railroads (thus) . . . should seek freight out (*iskat' gruzy*), force it to begin moving, in short create it so that freight, which, so to speak, is concealed and useless, becomes accessible for consumption and thus, inevitably, itself consumed.

Experience was already showing, he concluded, that railroads operating in this manner "had increased the transport of goods to limits about which previously they had not dreamed . . . ." Statistics he produced from his own Southwestern Railroad emphasized the point; almost 70 percent of the 130 million *puds* of freight transported in 1881 had been shipped at low rates set to encourage long-distance commerce.[24]

This capacity of the railroad to generate commerce and wealth was a theme he returned to, and mulled over repeatedly, throughout *Principles*. The product of daily experience, these views of increasingly profitable commercial markets provoked Witte, whose propensity to think broadly and synthetically was his greatest intellectual strength, to consider the cultural topography that surrounded him, that is, the national and international context of railroad technology. In a section detailing the pricing strategies of the Southwestern, Witte defended its use of published rate structures (*preisku-ranty*), which, critics argued, violated the more traditional *laissez-faire* practice of individual contracts between the company and its customers. Witte, who himself had pioneered the innovation, explained this "apparent contradiction" by discounting its relevance to an increasingly complex commercial business world where "railroads ship thousands of commodities of varied type and ship them among thousands of stations and, moreover, . . . (at prices) that can fluctuate, sometimes daily. Moreover," he continued, in terms that conveyed a systemic understanding of late-nineteenth-century business and commerce,

all substantial concentrated commerce (*solidnaia krupnaia torgovlia*) requires a relatively stable framework. A representative of big industry (*obshirnaia promysh-lennost'*) or a wholesale merchant very often cannot transact business with thousands of clients, as does, for example, the owner of a small shop. . . . (A)lmost all large commercial firms, significant manufacturing enterprises and factories always sell the products they produce on the basis of rate structures. . . . These impart a level of stability to commercial transactions, systematize business management (*vedenie khoziastva*), and, by means of offering the selling price to a greater number of consumers, serve to energize demand (*sluzhat' k vozbuzh-deniiu energii sprosa*) and consequently enlarge consumption. That such rate structures are necessary for railroads of *general importance* (*obshchee znachenie*: italics in original) not only is predicated on their own interests as commercial enterprises, but also follows as well from their character as institutions that possess state and public significance. It is indisputable that railroads are summoned to serve the general good (*sluzhit' tseliam obshchago blaga*). And to do this they are obliged to afford, under identical circumstances, all consumers the same opportunity to utilize their services, which in turn is possible only if there exist published rates obligatory for railroads in their relations with every shipper.[25]

That railroad practice could be justified in terms of the technology's capacity to foster "the general good," a key conceptual category of tsarist political discourse, bespoke more than Witte's careerist and statist inclinations, although those certainly were in play.[26] The passage showed Witte justifying technological power and articulating its capacity to transform culture: to create the general good in ways that bore significance for both "state" and "society." That the railroad bore significance for the state bespoke the extent to which the tsarist government, like every other in Europe, had come to recognize, and invest in, the new technology's crucial role in economic and political development. That the railroad was significant in a public world of industrialists, wholesale merchants, entrepreneurs, consumers, and shippers, all increasingly integrated by the new technology, was a preeminent feature of national economies throughout Europe and the international order centered upon it in an age of empire.

The power of railroad technology entranced Witte and was fundamental to his thinking about the future of the Russian Empire and its place in this European order. In a subsequent passage, he explained why the Southwestern had moved away from a system of freight rates based only on distance traveled, and instead lowered prices charged for particular categories of goods shipped over long distances, most notably grain from the middle Volga and New Russia destined for export. Rebutting commentators who criticized an unwarranted departure from existing business practice, Witte offered an alternative vision and in so doing made explicit the connections between the commercial topography that surrounded him and the capacity of railroad technology to transform it. Because Witte had daily experienced this power, he easily projected the railroad's nearly talismanic potential to transcend the spatial and cultural limitations of a contemporary Russian imperial economy whose vast distances and commercial–industrial life the railroad was only beginning to alter. "Up until now, when the network of Russian roads is as yet still insufficiently extended," he declaimed, few commentators understood what, "after a bit of time, when iron ways (*zheleznye puti*) develop in Russia in the necessary quantity and extend into all the borderlands (*okrainy*), will stare them in the face." Small Western European countries, Witte wrote with characteristic specificity—England only occupied "3.21 percent of the European land mass, France 5.41 percent, Italy 3 percent"—could afford to pay less attention to long distances, but how was "it possible to do this in Russia, whose European part alone represents 55 percent of Europe's entire expanse?" His practical experience on the railroad, and the dreamwork that he indulged there as well, provided a ready answer to the rhetorical query:

> To impart the proper economic growth (*nadlezhashchii ekonomicheskii rost*) to our fatherland, we must make possible the easier distribution of natural resources throughout the broad expanse of our Empire. It is not acceptable that finished goods find only regional markets, in locales quite near the point of production; it is necessary to strive so that every producer has the broadest

possible market (*raion rasprostraneniia*) for his products, because the interests of consumers are advanced considerably through such an expansion of supply. A general expansion of domestic production is especially necessary in a country that maintains protectionist customs tariffs, the entire weight of which falls exclusively on consumers. If such in fact should be the objective, then how to attain it in an area of more than five million square versts, that of European Russia, and how to attain the same thing in the future in an area of over 18 million square versts, that of European Russia and Siberia together with the central Asian possessions?[27]

The specific answer to the proffered rhetorical query was straightforward: "Obviously, only via extremely low rates (charged) for long distances."[28] Yet, as was frequently the case with Witte, here too the particular and the general were intertwined. Revealed beneath the policy recommendation was a representation of a powerful imperial polity, set within the broad expanses of Eurasian space and increasingly transformed by the railroad, a communications technology of unparalleled import. Along its rails could circulate with increasing intensity, not only the plentiful mineral and natural resources upon which Russian wealth historically had depended, but also agricultural and produced goods of every kind. Whether these goods were produced at home or, as inevitably was the case in a country that still required high import tariffs to protect against more economically developed competitors, manufactured abroad, their circulation, that is, their movement from producer to consumer, through ever more extensive markets, generated wealth within all territories of the Russian empire. Certainly it can be said that by the 1880s, Witte, the great railway man, had found through his experience of the railroad the social and cultural context within which he could dream of a powerful Russian Empire and its place in the European order. The iron bonds of the railroad's communication network, the intensifying commercial exchange that it conducted, the culturally integrative technological power that was incorporating the diverse elements of a national economy, the vistas of further progress that it proffered, and the imperial space that it promised to strengthen, if not altogether create: the railroad, this quintessentially nineteenth-century European technology, was proving to be transformative for Witte as well.

NOTES

1. Theodore Von Laue, *Sergei Witte and the Industrialization of Russia* (NY: Columbia University Press, 1963 and Atheneum, 1969), ch. 1.
2. Ibid. "Sic et Non, and a Conclusion," 306 and 302–308.
3. Ibid., 70.
4. Ibid. 41–64, passim.
5. F.W. Wcislo, "Witte, Memory, and the 1905 Revolution: A Reinterpretation of the Witte Memoirs," *Revolutionary Russia*, 8, no.2 (December 1995): 166–178.
6. V. Naryshkina-Vitte, *Zapiski devochki* (Leipzig: Izdanie avtora, 1922), 5.
7. See Sergei Vitte, *Printsipy zheleznodorozhnykh tarifov po perevozke gruzov*, Tret'e dopolnennoe izdanie (St. Petersburg: Brokgauz and Efron, 1910) and Graf S. Iu.

Vitte, *Po povodu natsionalizma. Natsional'naia Ekonomiia i Fridrikh List*, 2-e izdanie (St. Petersburg: Brokgauz i Efron, 1912).

8. Eric Hobsbawm, *The Age of Empire 1875–1914* (New York: Vintage Books, 1987), 10–12.

9. Paul R. Gregory, *Before Command: An Economic History of Russia from Emancipation to the First Five-Year Plan* (Princeton, N.J.: Princeton University Press, 1994); Peter Gatrell, *The Tsarist Economy, 1850–1917* (New York: St. Martin's Press, 1986); Alexander Gerschenkron, "Problems and Patterns of Russian Economic Development," in Michael Cherniavsky ed., *The Structure of Russian History. Interpretive Essays* (New York: Random House, 1970); Arcadius Kahan, *Russian Economic History: The Nineteenth Century* (Chicago: University of Chicago Press, 1989), ed. Roger Weiss. A major departure that interrogates the cultural underpinnings and assumptions of development is Yanni Kotsonis, *Making Peasants Backward: Agricultural Cooperatives and the Agrarian Question in Russia, 1861–1914* (Basingstoke: Macmillan; New York: St. Martin's Press, 1999).

10. Vitte, *Printsipy*, iv.

11. Obshchestvo Iugo-Zapapnykh Zheleznykh Dorog, *Finansovoe polozhenie russkikh zheleznykh dorog k 1 Ianvaria 1880 goda* (St. Petersburg, 1881); *Bolshaia entsiklopediia*, 20 (St. Petersburg: Prosveshchenie, 1896); also Vitte, *Printsipy*, 44 and 35–69. The SWRR thus accounted for roughly 10% of the total mileage (2,200 km/21,000 km) of the empire's rail network in 1877 and 18% (7,600 km/28,200 km) by 1900 (see Table 4.1).

12. Stephen Kern, *The Culture of Time and Place* (Cambridge: Harvard University Press, 1983), especially ch. 1 and Michael Freeman, *Railways and the Victorian Imagination* (New Haven: Yale University Press, 1999).

13. B.R. Mitchell, *European Historical Statistics 1750–1970* (New York: Columbia University Press, 1978).

14. Ibid.

15. Sergei Vitte, *Printsipy*.

16. N.A. Kislinskii, *Nasha zheleznodorozhnaia politika po dokumentam arkhiva Komiteta Ministrov. Istoricheskii ocherk, sostavlennyi Nachal'nikom Otdeleniia Kantselarii Komiteta Ministrov*, 4 vols. (St. Petersburg, 1902), notes that the value of railroad company shares and bonds in circulation by 1881 totaled R1.6 billion; over 90% of this capital was in some fashion guaranteed by the state treasury. See ibid. vol. 3, 13–14. In the same year, the treasury had paid out over R205 million in guaranteed returns on these investments, ibid. 308–324.

17. T.M. Kitanina, *Khlebnaia torgovlia Rossii v 1875–1914 gg* (Leningrad: Nauka, 1978) and Thomas Fallows, *Forging the Zemstvo Movement*, Ph.D. diss. (Harvard University, 1981).

18. The suggestive trail of documents is A. Chuprov to S. Witte, February 17, 1884 (Bakhmetieff Archive, Witte Papers Box I, Witte Correspondence A–G), Vyshnegradskii to Witte, ca.1885, and "Vsepoddanneishie dokladnye zapisi ministra finansov za 1889 god po tarifnomu otdelu D-ta zheleznodorozhnykh del," RGIA f. 268, op. 6, d. 1.

19. Vitte, *Printsipy*, i–ii.

20. Ibid., 1–22.

21. Ibid., 10–12.

22. See Vitte, *Printsipy*, 107–133.

23. Ibid., 17–18.

24. Ibid., 20–21. One *pud* equals 36.06 pounds.
25. Vitte, *Printsipy*, 69–70.
26. See, in particular, Frank Wcislo, *Reforming Rural Russia: State, Local Society and National Politics, 1855–1914* (Princeton: Princeton University Press, 1990), chs. 2–4.
27. Vitte, *Printsipy*, 79–80. One verst equals 0.66 miles.
28. Ibid.

6

RELIGIOUS AND NATIONALIST ASPECTS OF ENTREPRENEURIALISM IN RUSSIA

Boris V. Anan'ich

In the development of capitalism in the Russian Empire, and in particular of bank structure and bank entrepreneurialism, representatives of various ethnic groups played a large role: not only Russians, but also Jews, Greeks, Armenians, Tatars and, finally, immigrants to Russia. The latter were either dissolved generally into Russian society or constituted as a particular ethnic group, such as the "Moscow Germans." A known exception among the foreign entrepreneurs working in Russia were the English. They were less subject to assimilation.[1]

In the characterizations of the entrepreneurial activity of various national or national-religious groups found in historical economic literature, we do not encounter such terms as, for example, "Russian capital," or "Armenian capital," or, correspondingly, "Russian entrepreneurialism" or "Armenian entrepreneurialism." At the same time, especially in American historiography, such formulations as "Jewish capital," or "Old Believer capital" and "Jewish entrepreneurialism" or "Old Believer entrepreneurialism" have wide currency. It seems to me that such expressions reflect an entrepreneurial ethic, or perhaps a strategy, based on fixed religious principles. In several cases these principles take the place of, or augment, laws regulating business relations.

Religion, economics, and social life are closely connected. Studying these phenomena in the aggregate, Max Weber pointed out the link between a "Protestant ethic" and the "spirit of capitalism."[2] Weber's ideas are extremely important also for understanding what happened in Russia, where various ethnic groups, religious communities, and adherents of various business ethics participated in the economic modernization of the country.

It is no accident that the ideas of Max Weber about the influence of religion on the entrepreneurial ethic were met with lively interest by such a well-known economist and philosopher as S.N. Bulgakov. As early as 1910, Bulgakov noted with regret that in Russia insufficient attention had been paid to "the study of the spiritual components of economic development."[3]

Bulgakov came to the conclusion that "the privileged inside position [of a state church] weakens the influence of religious factors on life, whatever the particular religion." He continued, "It would be interesting to clarify the particular economic potential of Orthodoxy . . . . Though in its fundamental character Orthodoxy is distinct from Puritanism and Protestantism in general, in the discipline of its aesthetic of 'obedience' and 'pacing before God,' Orthodoxy (as well as Old Belief, which is aesthetically and dogmatically identical to it), has powerful means for instilling individualism [*lichnost'*] and creating a feeling of personal responsibility and duty, which are equally as important for economic activity as for any other type of societal service. And if just now the influence of the religious discipline of Orthodoxy on the economic work of the Russian people can be characterized as weaker than that of the dissident faith, this only serves to underscore the regrettable decline of Orthodoxy at the current historical moment." For Bulgakov it was obvious that there was an "especially close connection between capitalism and Old Belief," to which belonged "representatives of a whole host of the large Russian firms."

Like Protestantism in Western Europe, Old Belief greatly influenced the development of capitalism in Russia. At the beginning of the nineteenth century, two large Moscow Old Believer communities, connected with the Rogozh and Preobrazhenskii cemeteries, became centers for the accumulation of capital. From its resources, the Preobrazhenskii community of Old Believer factory owners granted loans, often of very sizeable amounts. The community had significant funds available. It is known that in the 1840s, when the Preobrazhenskii community was subjected to governmental persecution, it saved its capital by passing to the factory-owning Guchkovs a trunk containing twelve million rubles in cash and securities. Moreover, Old Believer factory chiefs generally employed workers connected to the community. The factory owners accepted runaway peasants, procuring the necessary documents for them either legally or illegally, and drawing them into Old Belief. On holidays, the factories were converted into distinctive schools of Old Belief.[4]

Thus, Old Believer capital and Old Believer businessmen created a specific kind of entrepreneurial spirit and a specific kind of relationship between employer and employee. Old Believer entrepreneurialism developed most successfully in the early and mid-nineteenth century, at a relatively early stage in Russia's capital accumulation. Of great significance for the success of its business activities was the dissemination within the Old Believer community of ethical norms of behavior: temperance and asceticism in one's home life; sobriety; individual and mutual support; a readiness to come to the assistance of those suffering ruin for their beliefs; and, finally, a limit of 6 percent on all interest charges. These traditions preserved Old Believer businesses from disaster.

With the development of the economy, the industrial and banking concerns of the Old Believers gradually lost their uniqueness, although in many enterprises these features endured until the beginning of the twentieth century. This pattern can be seen, in part, in the example of the Riabushinskii Brothers Bank, originally linked to the Rogozh Cemetery community and occupying one of the premier positions in the Empire's business and financial system on the eve of World War I.[5]

The more their banking operations grew and strengthened, the more the nine Riabushinskii brothers gradually grew accustomed to empire-wide business practices, leaving behind the limits of pure Moscow Old Believer doctrine. At the same time, while being transformed into a huge enterprise, the Riabushinskiis did not desert the community and their coreligionists. Even on the eve of World War I, the Riabushinskiis "reluctantly brought people on board," and tried "to create a special cadre of employees," for which they took the very youngest, directly from the school bench, mainly from the graduates of the Moscow Practical Academy of Commerce, where they, themselves, had studied. To replenish "the younger ranks of the organization," they took on country and city youths "sending them to evening classes in their free time," and gradually bringing them into the firm. Young people aged 22 to 25 years often received responsible posts.[6]

The Riabushinskiis saw St. Petersburg as virtually a foreign city. To their St. Petersburg office, considered one of the most difficult posts, they sent specially trained employees from Moscow. To the Riabushinskii representatives, St. Petersburg was "a terrible city in terms of its temptations." Mikhail Pavlovich Riabushinskii later wrote, "The stock market bacchanals, the unprincipled brokers, mainly Jewish, and the women—all of this had a ruinous effect on the weaker of our young people. There many of our youth were thrown off the straight and narrow path and were lost. We sent them more and more new people as replacements" he recalled, "until finally the composition of the St. Petersburg department had become first class."[7]

At the beginning of the twentieth century, the Riabushinskiis adhered to the principle of maintaining a moderate level of dividends. Above all, they took pains to increase their production. However, by the beginning of the war, the Riabushinskiis were pursuing large-scale speculative transactions with an eye to creating a superbank through the purchase of packets of shares of the large joint-stock banks.[8]

The government viewed the representatives of Old Believer capital with mistrust, as schismatics and sectarians. Secret legislation, such as an order of June 10, 1853, established that honorary titles and other honors were to be conferred on sectarians only in exceptional cases. It was on this basis that the Senate refused the Riabushinskiis and their children the status of hereditary honored citizens in 1879. They received this title only in 1884, after lengthy petitioning.

Naturally, these Old Believer capitalists often found themselves in opposition to the government. As a rule their capital accumulation and business success was not dependent upon government orders, state railroad construction, or wine concessions. More often the Old Believers' capital grew simply as a result of their business activities. Such is the example of the Riabushinskiis. They began with small trade, then opened a modest shop. Thereafter, they purchased a small factory, increased its production and, finally, created a banking house that they nurtured into a huge joint-stock bank.

In American historiography there are various judgments about the charac-ter of Old Believer entrepreneurialism. James Billington, in his book devoted to the history of Russian culture, *The Icon and the Axe*, notes the "striking" similarities between the entrepreneurial ethic of West European Calvinists and Russian Old Believers.[9] However, another American scholar, Robert Crummey, challenges this view. In *Old Believers and the World of the Anti-Christ* he writes that the search for common ground between Protestants and Old Believers as entrepreneurs is completely unproductive. Further, Crummey believes there is no basis to speak of a "spirit of capitalism" in the religious ideology of the Old Believers. He stresses the fact that Old Belief adhered to a religious doctrine identical to that of official Orthodoxy and that the differences between them were limited to the area of church tradi-tions and ceremonies. Crummey does consider the Old Believers to consti-tute one of Max Weber's religious minorities, viewed with the kind of animosity most often associated with the Jews in Russia.[10] Like Bulgakov, Crummey sees Old Belief as a dissident movement within Orthodoxy. This is a reasonable view. Nonetheless, it is undoubtedly the case that whether or not it exhibits the "spirit of capitalism," Old Belief had much in common with Protestantism.[11]

How much do Old Believer and Jewish entrepreneurialism have in com-mon if we overlook the fact that both Jews and Old Believers were persecuted and limited in their legal rights? Is it not also the case, as Bulgakov puts it, that "Puritanism is often known as English Hebraism, having in view . . . their Old Testament spirit, with its self-righteousness and sober legalism. The characteristic messianic faith of the Jews was also strongly awakened in the Puritans, so that the Anglo-Saxons gathered Godly people, summoned to reign over others for the sake of their salvation and enlighten-ment."[12] Like Max Weber, Mariia Ossovskaia has also turned her attention to this question. She writes that the principal difference between the Puritan and the Jewish approach to increasing wealth is that the Jews adhered to traditional, "venture" capitalism, "while Puritan-capitalism was based on the rational organization of labor undertaken with a long-term perspective."[13]

Arcadius Kahan was seriously engaged in the study of Jewish entrepreneuri-alism in Russia for many years. Kahan properly extends his understanding of this phenomenon to all ethnically Jewish entrepreneurs, regardless of their actual religious affiliation.[14] However, the general understanding of Jewish entrepreneurialism quickly gave way to a focus on that part of the Jewish entrepreneurs who, like the Old Believers, had business ties to their religious community.

The isolation of the Jewish community, government persecutions, and the limitation of the community members' activities to the Pale of Settlement created rather distinctive conditions for the accumulation of capital. The Pale, in the western provinces, was home to a large concentration of Jewish-owned factories for the production of textiles, hats, glassware, leather goods, and candles in the middle of the nineteenth century. The overwhelm-ing majority of workers in these factories were also Jewish. Under these conditions, a special kind of relationship arose between workers and bosses who belonged to the same community. For some time these factories maintained relations with banking houses that provided enterprises in the Pale with financing. On the eve of the Great Reforms of the 1860s, for example, Berdichev was a large banking center, supplying the Kiev contract fair and discounting notes in St. Petersburg, Moscow, and Odessa. The Jewish banking houses and factories in the Pale were also often closely connected to the community. For example, rabbis could appear at these banks as arbitrators or mediators for the conclusion of deals and agreements. Jewish capitalists, then, like the Old Believers, labored under conditions of government persecution and restrictions.[15]

Did the authorities ever ask themselves whether the legal restrictions on religious minorities and sectarians were adversely affecting the economic development of the country? Undoubtedly. In government circles, there was ongoing debate on this subject. Particularly in the reform period, they initiated some departures from existing limitations that hindered the development of entrepreneurial activity. Thus, for example, in the 1860s, several changes were made in the existing laws that restricted the rights of the Jewish population.

In fact, as early as 1859, in connection with economic reorganization and the preparation of financial reforms, the tsarist government permitted Jewish merchants of the first guild to reside in the capitals. As a result of this legislation, several large Jewish banking houses opened up in St. Petersburg and Moscow. These banks played an increasing role in the development of several branches of industry and railroad construction, resulting, finally, in the creation of large joint-stock banks in Russia. In particular, two Jewish banking families, the Ginzburgs and the Poliakovs, assumed a significant role in the economic life of the two capital cities, as well as of the empire at large, at the turn of the twentieth century.

The law of 1859 created the conditions for sizeable groups of entrepreneurs from the southern and western provinces to settle in St. Petersburg. There, the nucleus of a new Jewish culture, a new Jewish community, took shape. It would seem likely that those leaving the Pale would bring with them their own traditions and the spirit of Jewish entrepreneurialism. However, the operations and activity of the Ginzburg and Poliakov banking houses does not support this proposition.

Ginzburg was the first large banking house established in the capital after the publication of the 1859 law. It took over the place of the extremely influential banking house of Baron Alexander Shtiglits, the last of the court bankers and head of the State Bank in the 1860s. As is well known, the Shtiglits family descended from German Jews, who had converted to Lutheranism. They played a most important role in the economy and finances of Russia from the 1830s to the 1850s. Shtiglits rendered great assistance to the Russian government, above all, in organizing foreign loans. It was through the Shtiglits Bank that the Russian government conducted relations with banks in Amsterdam, London, and Paris. Moreover, Alexander

Shtiglits served as president of the St. Petersburg Bourse for 13 years. The Shtiglits family acted as bearer of European entrepreneurial traditions to Russia. They owed their status in Russia in large part to their role as go-betweens in the international operations of the Finance Ministry.

From the time of its appearance in St. Petersburg, the Ginzburg Bank assumed a significant number of the functions that had formerly been taken care of by Shtiglits. The Ginzburgs had made their fortune on wine conces- sions in the western provinces. They earned millions, and the 1859 law allowed them to open not only the bank in St. Petersburg, but also a branch in Paris. Thus, the Ginzburg Bank had wide financial connections both inside Russia and abroad. It maintained close and friendly ties with Varburg in Hamburg, Mendel'son and Bleichröder in Berlin, de Gabor in Frankfurt-am- Main and Gosqué in Paris.

The Ginzburgs' close ties to the government grew not only out of their integral role in securing international backing for Russian state loans, but also from their role in the Russian gold mining industry. At the beginning of the twentieth century, the Ginzburgs had achieved a prominent place in the gold industry and were large shareholders in the infamous Lena Goldfields Company. Goratsii Ginzburg, his sons Alexander, Alfred, and David, as well as Goratsii's brothers, all played key roles in the economic and financial life of the Empire, especially in the creation of a host of large banks. The Ginzburgs were not court bankers, but this did not prevent them from conducting the financial affairs of the Duke of Hesse and maintaining the closest possible business contacts with the Finance Ministry and the state bank.

No less closely linked to government circles were the Poliakov brothers, Samuel, Lazar, and Iakov, who occupied a unique position in the world of Russian business from the 1870s to the 1890s, in railroads, banking, and other enterprises. The Poliakovs created their own kind of concern, which was virtually an entrepreneurial empire. Poliakov banks, with their branches, appeared in all the large cities of Russia: Moscow, St. Petersburg, Taganrog, Minsk, Iaroslavl, Orel. The Poliakov rail lines linked the Russian heartland with the south and the Donets Basin. Consequently, the Poliakovs had huge reserves of capital at their disposal. Upon his death, Samuel Poliakov's estate amounted to 30 million rubles, in immovable property, stocks, bonds, and cash. St. Petersburg was his headquarters. There, on the English Embankment, stood two separate residences: one belonged to Samuel, the other to Lazar. Lazar's main base of operations, however, was his bank in Moscow. The Poliakovs took a leading role in expanding the strategic railroad system to the ends of the Empire, an enterprise directed by the Finance Ministry, but closely linked to the War Ministry, as well.

The Poliakovs, like the Ginzburgs, in the final analysis served the interests of imperial policy in their entrepreneurial activities, which were not marked by clearly ethnic-religious characteristics. They did not break off relations with the Jewish community, but these relations had nothing to do with their businesses. Their support consisted of philanthropy, financial support of the community, and the construction of synagogues. Goratsii Ginzburg was president of the central committee of the Jewish Colonization Association at the same time that Iakov Poliakov was its vice-president. By family tradition, the Ginzburgs were notable defenders of the rights of the country's Jewish population. They had participated in the drafting of the 1860s legislation conferring upon certain segments of the Jewish population the right to live outside the Pale, and later strongly opposed the new chauvinistic legislation of the 1880s.

The Ginzburgs' philanthropy, however, was directed not only to the Jewish community, but had a more diverse character. Ginzburg played a big role in the cultural life of the capital. In his circle of acquaintances were such figures as V.V. Stasov, A.G. Rubinshtein, and I.S. Turgenev. M.E. Saltykov-Shchedrin was a banking client. In 1903, the 70-year-old actual state councilor and first-guild merchant, Baron Goratsii Ginzburg, was recognized in the Malyi Hall of the St. Petersburg Conservatory of the Imperial Musical Society. Such a scene was unusual, testifying to the remarkable service rendered by the Ginzburgs to Russian cultural life. The Poliakovs' philanthropy, also was not of an exclusively ethnic character. For example, they backed the Eletskii Railroad School, a classical gymnasium that was the first of its kind in Russia. They also provided financial support for students at St. Petersburg University and other schools.

Thus, in the realm of business activities, the Poliakov and Ginzburg banks were not marked by any kind of ethnic or religious specifications. Their taste for speculation and pursuit of high dividends were nothing out of the ordinary. It is hardly possible to identify any kind of significant distinction in the business activity of Shtiglits and Ginzburg, except, perhaps, for the international links to Jewish banks abroad and the general activity of Jews in the economic arena about which Werner Sombart wrote.[16]

At the very end of the 1850s, the advocates of financial reform in Russian government circles came under the influence of Western European economic theories, especially those of Henri Saint-Simon, about the fundamental role of credit in industrialization. In France, Saint-Simon's ideas found practical application in the business activities of the Périer brothers, founders of the French bank Crédit Mobilier, and in Russia, these ideas provided an impetus for the development of a private banking industry. It was in this atmosphere, also, that the Ginzburgs and the Poliakovs founded their banks. These men demonstrate the truth that large-scale capital, regardless of the ethnic origins of its masters, loses its national-religious characteristics and serves the interests of the Empire. Such an observation holds true not only for Russia, of course. In Prussia, for example, Gerson Bleichröder served as the personal banker of Otto von Bismarck and financed the unification of Germany.[17]

The business activities of the Ginzburgs and Poliakovs were not unique even for Russia. In the second half of the nineteenth century, there was a large group of Jewish entrepreneurs from Poland who were active in the banking and railroad industries, including Ivan Bloch, Leopold Kronenberg, V. Liaskii and A. Zak. They all served as bearers of European entrepreneurial traditions and facilitated the growth of the Empire's banking system and railroad network.

In Central Asia, a group of Bukhara Jews occupied a special place in business circles. These were the owners of cotton trading houses, who served as intermediaries in operations between the Moscow and St. Petersburg banks and local producers. To this group belonged Sion and Jacob Val'iaev, Rafael Poteliakhov, the Davydov brothers, the Kolontarov brothers, and others. Dushanbe scholar Namoz B. Khotamov considers this group of Central Asian entrepreneurs the most influential in the Khiva khannate and the Bukhara emirate, and offers as evidence of their influence the introduction of some of their characteristics into the Kokand department of the Moscow International Commercial Bank.[18]

Is it possible to consider the Bukhara Jews as representatives of a special group of Jewish entrepreneurs? Hardly. In Bukhara and Khiva, Moslem business traditions predominated. All-Russian legal jurisdiction was not in force there, and in the fulfillment of transactions, such as mortgages, for example, local entrepreneurs did not enter into the normal mortgage agreement with the capitals' banks, but undertook, "as it were, a sacred document, or 'Vasik.' " Khotamov points to two agreements between Bukhara businessmen and the Russo-Asian Bank, the Moscow Commercial Loan Bank and the Russian Foreign Trade Bank dated December 1912. One of these agreements began with the words, "I, having the legal authority of the *sharia* [Islamic law] . . ." while the other asserted that, "I sold in agreement with the *sharia*. . . ., and so on."[19] It is known that in 1912, there was a plan in the works to create a special Islamic bank in Russia, but apparently it came to nothing. Unfortunately, the influence of the Islamic religion on entrepreneurialism in various regions of the Russian Empire, and on the Moslem population itself, has not been investigated.

The study of entrepreneurialism in Russia, especially during the early stages of the country's economic modernization, underscores the importance of taking into consideration the complicated structure of the business community and the participation in this community of various national-religious groups. It is clear that a full understanding of Russia's business history requires much closer investigation not only of Jewish and Old Believer, but also of Islamic, entrepreneurialism. The asymmetrical development of the imperial economy, the national interests and the diverse religious cultures hindered the growth of a unified bourgeoisie even as entrepreneurial groups embraced similar strategies. The Empire's bourgeoisie developed within an atmosphere of internal contradictions. This was reflected in its relationship with tsarist authorities and in its conduct during the revolutionary events of 1905–06 and 1917.

NOTES

1. See William Blackwell, "The Russian Entrepreneur in the Tsarist Period: An Overview," in Gregory Guroff and Fred V. Carstensen, eds., *Entrepreneurship in Imperial Russia and the Soviet Union* (Princeton: Princeton University Press, 1983), 24.

2. See Max Weber, "Protestantskaia etika i dukh kapitalizma," in Max Weber, *Izbrannye proizvedeniia* (Moscow: Progress, 1990).

3. Sergei N. Bulgakov, *Dva grada. Issledovaniia o prirode obshchestvennykh idealov*, vol. 1 (Moscow, 1911), 198–199. The following quotations in this paragraph also come from these pages.

4. O. Rustik, "Staroobriadcheskoe Preobrazhenskoe kladbishche (kak nakapliali kapitaly v Moskve," *Bor'ba klassov* 1–8 (1934): 76.

5. See the detailed study by Iu.A. Petrov, *Dinastiia Riabushinskikh* (Moscow: Russkaia Kniga, 1997).

6. M.P. Riabushinskii, *Smutnye gody*. Manuscript Dept., New York Public Library. Riabushinskii Collection, 113–114.

7. Ibid. loc cit. See also, B.V. Anan'ich, *Bankirskie doma v Rossii, 1860–1914* (Leningrad: Nauka, Leningradskoe otd-nie, 1991).

8. M.P. Riabushinskii, "Tsel' nashei raboty, Noiabr'–dekabr' 1916" *Materialy po istorii SSSR* (Moscow: Institut istorii Akademiia nauk SSSR, 1959), vol. 6, 628–630.

9. James Billington, *The Icon and the Axe: An Interpretive Study of Russian Culture* (New York: Knopf, 1966), 193.

10. Robert Crummey, *The Old Believers and the World of the Anti-Christ. The Vyg Community and the Russian State, 1649–1855* (Madison, Milwaukee, London: University of Wiscorsin in Press, 1970), 136–137.

11. We should keep in mind the difficulty of the thesis concerning the links between the "spirit of capitalism" and the Puritan ethic. In the view of Mariia Ossovskaia, this thesis "is not clearly enough formulated and it is not altogether understood whether these two world views are similar or mutually dependent." See Mariia Ossovskaia, *Rytsar' i burzhua. Issledovaniia po istorii morali* (Moscow: Progress, 1987), 356.

12. Bulgakov, *Dva Grada*, vol. 1, 195.

13. Ossovskaia, *Rytsar' i burzhua*, 335.

14. See Arcadius Kahan, *Essays in Jewish Social and Economic History*, Roger Weiss, ed. (Chicago and London: University of Chicago Press, 1986), and Arcadius Kahan, "Notes on Jewish Entrepreneurialism in Tsarist Russia," Guroff and Carstensen, eds., *Entrepreneurship in Imperial Russia and the Soviet Union*, 104–124.

15. A.D. Iuditskii, "Evreiskaia burzhuaziia i evreiskie rabochie v tekstil'noi promyshlennosti pervoi poloviny XIX v.," *Istoricheskii sbornik*, 4 (1935): 116–117; S. Ia. Borovoi, *Kredit i banki v Rossii* (Moscow: Gosfinizdat, 1958), 237.

16. Werner Sombart, *Burzhua* (Moscow: Nauka, 1994), 334.

17. See Fritiz Stern, *Gold and Iron: Bismarck, Bleichroeder and the Building of the German Empire* (New York: Knopf, 1970).

18. Namoz B. Khotamov, *Rol' bankovskogo kapitala v sotsial'no-ekonomicheskom razvitii Srednei Azii* (Dushanbe, 1990), 106, 250.

19. Ibid., iii.

PART II

ENVISIONING A SOCIETY

7

The Role of "Europe" in Russian Nationalism: Reinterpreting the Relationship between Russia and the West in Slavophile Thought

Susanna Rabow-Edling

Western analysts have commonly found Russia to be exceptional and unlike the West. In fact, their arguments are quite similar to Russian nationalists' claims for national uniqueness. Both find the explanation for Russia's otherness in her own distinctive culture that has been formed in separation from the development of Western culture. In the standard account, there are primarily two historical factors that justify Russia's specific development: the reception of Christianity from Byzantium and the Mongol invasion. The impact of these events led Russia away from Western individualism toward an acceptance of Eastern absolutism. Samuel Huntington presents the most provocative argument for cultural difference based on religion. He argues that Russia is the core country of a separate civilization, "carrying and protecting a culture of Eastern Orthodoxy" and that "Europe ends where Western Christianity ends and . . . Orthodoxy begin[s]."[1] Richard Pipes employs a political argument for Russia's difference. He claims that what distinguishes Western types of government from non-Western ones, is the existence of a distinction between political power and private property. In Russia, these institutions were never clearly separated, something he claims accounts for the difficulties in restraining absolutism there.[2]

Western values and ideals have been used as a norm in assessments of Russia. Consequently, the lack of what are generally believed to be typically Western values is seen as an expression of a flaw in Russian culture. Western culture is defined in accordance with "positive" values, such as *civilization, progress, liberty, democracy, openness,* and *friendliness*. Russian culture is regarded as embracing opposite values. It therefore becomes *barbarian, backward, intolerant, authoritarian, secluded,* and *antagonistic*.[3] It is this essentialist view of Russian culture that forms the basis for many Western assessments of Russian nationalism. Since this culture is perceived as distinct from Western culture and thereby embodies a string of negative characteristics, it follows that Russian nationalism, basing itself on Russia's national character, must promote those values that are seen as destructive. Consequently, Russian nationalism has often been described as anti-Western, antagonistic, ethnic, and authoritarian in contrast to the liberal or civic nationalism, which allegedly characterizes most Western countries.[4] Hence, a dichotomy has been created between a good, liberal, rationalistic nationalism in the West and an evil, anti-Western deviation in the East. Hans Kohn made the classic and most influential distinction between these two forms, claiming that "[w]hile Western nationalism was, in its origin, connected with the concepts of individual liberty and rational cosmopolitanism current in the eighteenth century, the later nationalism in Central and Eastern Europe and in Asia easily tended towards a contrary development."[5] More recently, the ideology of Russian nationalism has been portrayed as "antagonistic to all the main principles on which modern democracy is based" and seen as a "malignant and monolithic force that is unreformable and tends inexorably towards extreme forms of racism and authoritarianism."[6] Its content is ethnic, collectivist, and authoritarian and infused with anti-Westernism.[7]

To explain this hostility to the West, scholars have long argued that Russians came to dislike the West since it served as the model. "The dependence of the West often wounded the pride of the native educated class, as soon as it began to develop its own nationalism, and ended in an opposition to the 'alien' example and its liberal and rational outlook."[8] Hence, scholars have seen Europe as the "Other" in relation to which the idea of Russia is defined.[9] Thus Liah Greenfeld claims that in Russia, *ressentiment* was the single most important factor in determining the terms in which national identity was defined.[10] Pointing at the role of Europe as the "Other" against which a Russian national identity must be formulated helps to uphold the dichotomy between a Russian and a Western culture.[11]

The main purpose of this article is to question the Russian–European dichotomy and the view of Russian nationalism as isolationistic or antagonistic to the West. This is not to say that there are not, nor have been, any forms of nationalism in Russia that fit this description. Neither do I want to argue for the existence of a "good" kind of Russian nationalism. However, through analyzing the formulation of the original idea of a unique Russian nation in its historical context, I want to present a more complex image of the role of Europe and the West in shaping a Russian national identity. The article proceeds through a discussion of the thought of Ivan Kireevskii and Aleksei Khomiakov, the so-called older Slavophiles, who formulated the first comprehensive notion of a distinctive Russian nation in the second quarter of the nineteenth century, which came to play a central role in the self-image and national identity of Russian intellectuals.[12] This notion of Russian distinctiveness, this "Russian idea," has continued to be articulated and reformulated by Russian artists and intellectuals to this day. It is a recurrent idea, which has appeared in different forms at times of ideological transformation and social unrest before, during, and after the Soviet period.[13] For every discussion of the "Russian idea," the ideas of Kireevskii and Khomiakov have constituted the necessary starting point. Nor has the impact of the Slavophiles on Russian intellectual life diminished over the years. They are still looked upon as authorities on issues of Russia's national idea.

Contrary to what is often presumed, the Slavophiles did not see Europe as "the . . . Other from which Russia must be saved."[14] They wanted Russia to be saved from the impasse European culture had reached, from the negative outcomes of European development, but not from Europe per se. Obviously, in making this claim, I do not deny that the Slavophiles disapproved of many aspects of Western culture and social life, especially what they saw as excessive rationalism and individualism. In their view, the extolling of reason in the West had destroyed the harmony and integrity of the human personality. As a consequence, the unity of social life was destroyed by individualism and fragmentation.[15]

Yet their critique of European conditions did not mean that they turned their backs on Europe. Indeed, by the 1840s, both radicals and conservatives in Russia believed it was their task to help Europe solve its social and political problems. Both agreed that a social consciousness had to be developed in order to curb unrestrained individualism, cultivated by unbridled liberalism. The Slavophiles presented the Russian peasant commune, the *obshchina*, as an alternative social and moral organization, destined to save humanity from the proletarianization they had seen developing in the West. Through its principle of land redistribution and the social obligation to help other members, the commune would eliminate poverty.[16] Moreover, the Slavophiles claimed that the development of a Russian philosophy, which united knowledge and faith, could give the West the solid spiritual foundation it was looking for.[17]

Although the Slavophile critique of the West may seem to corroborate Greenfeld's claim about the importance of *ressentiment* in the formulation of a national identity, the idea that Russia had a mission to solve Europe's problems shows that anti-Westernism does not exhaust the contents of the Slavophile ideology or the national identity it proposed.[18] Too much stress on anti-Westernism makes Slavophilism appear one-sided and antagonistic. In fact, a close reading of Slavophile writings shows that their ideas about Russia's relationship to the West were far more complex than merely an expression of *ressentiment*. Rather, they were an expression of an identity crisis experienced by members of the educated class.

The members of the educated Russian elite of the eighteenth and beginning of the nineteenth century saw themselves as European intellectuals, identifying with European culture and learning. Many of them spoke French, German, and sometimes English fluently, were brought up by French and German tutors, and traveled to Europe. They were familiar with the latest Western literary currents and philosophical ideas, which they discussed in salons, clubs, and philosophical circles.[19] These educated Russians saw it as their role to study, absorb, and disseminate European culture. Imitation was seen as a way of enlightening Russia. However, with the introduction of Romanticism in Russia in the early nineteenth century, this practice became unacceptable. Now, demands for a unique, national culture were raised. While in the eighteenth century educated Russians had to be European in order to be part of Europe, they now had to be Russian.

According to the new Romantic agenda, every nation had a unique, organic character that was expressed in its culture. It was the obligation of each nation to develop its national culture so that it could make a genuine contribution to the advancement of humanity. Progress was found solely in cultures that expressed their national spirit clearly and vividly. Consequently, the imitative Russian culture, which previously had represented enlightenment and advancement, became a sign of backwardness. Russia's lack of cultural originality showed that there was no progress in the Russian nation. It made her unworthy of being a member of the core European nations. Hence, it was the attachment to European culture and its prevailing ideas of Romanticism and Idealism that forced Russian intellectuals to develop a culture of their own and to formulate a specific Russian national character. Analyzing the problem of imitation in Russia, this paper argues that the aim of the Slavophile project was not to isolate or separate Russia from the West, but to make her a worthy member of Europe.

THE PROBLEM OF IMITATION

Signs of a reaction against imitation began to emerge in Russia already at the end of the eighteenth century itself. However, in the second quarter of the nineteenth century, the practice of imitation had become unacceptable and there was an outburst of criticism against the idolization of everything Western. The Slavophiles did not distinguish themselves from other articulate Russians in focusing on the problem of cultural imitation. Imitation was on everybody's mind, although, subsequently, different ideas of how to deal with it were developed. Peter Chaadaev offered the most pessimistic assessment, claiming that Russian culture was "based wholly on borrowing and imitation." "[W]here are our wise men, where are our thinkers," he asked. "We have nothing that is ours on which to base our thinking."[20] The literary critic and Westernizer Vissarion Belinskii declared that what was known as Russian literature was an imitative product without historical continuity or internal organic development. "Literary phenomena were not engendered by the national spirit."[21]

Imitation, which earlier had been a means to modernize Russia and to put her at the forefront, now caused her to lag behind Europe, since progress at this point depended on the development of the nation. Russian intellectuals of different opinions shared the concern for the lack of an original Russian culture and they agreed that without such a culture they would never be recognized as Europeans. However, to be of any significance, a Russian culture could not develop in isolation, that is, separated from universal history. It had to contribute to the advancement of history and of mankind. Belinskii neatly characterizes the uncertainty and feeling of backwardness in connection with this role among Russian intellectuals at the time: "We seem to have taken alarm for our life, for our significance, for our past and future, and are in a hurry to solve the great problem of to be or not to be? . . . we are now anxious to know whether any living organic idea runs through our history, and if it does, what exactly is it, what is our relation to our past from which we seem to have been sundered and to the West with which we seem to be related."[22]

Demands for a unique Russian contribution to European culture were raised in the first Russian philosophical circle, The Society of Lovers of Wisdom, 1824–25. The society's president, prince Vladimir Odoevskii, described Russia's predicament in his novel *Russian Nights* through the main character, Faust. "Every day we talk about German philosophy, about English industrialism, about European enlightenment, about the progress of reason, about the movement of humanity, and so on; but we have not yet thought of asking . . . : what kind of a wheel are we in this strange machine? . . . In a word: what are we?"[23] Dmitry Venevitinov, a fellow-member, was also concerned with the insignificance of Russian culture. He argued that it was not possible to build a national culture with external forms imported from the West. Without a genuine foundation, there could only be an illusory culture. Russian intellectuals had to ask themselves "which level of the movement or performance common to everyone [Russia] had attained in comparison with other nations?"[24]

Without a specific role in the universal progress of history, Russian culture would be insignificant, devoid of any common meaning and useless for the cause of progress. Slavophilism originated in an attempt to address this predicament. Ivan Kireevskii continued in the vein of the Society of the Lovers of Wisdom, where he himself had been a member. In an early article, he claimed that Russian works of literature could be of no interest to the rest of the world solely as reflections of European literature. Russian literature had to be regarded in relation to the literature of other nations, and in order to be of any significance to them, it had to reflect the Russian way of life. To Kireevskii, it was a cause of embarrassment not to have a literature of one's own. "If an enlightened European . . . asks us: Where is your literature? Which works can you be proud of before Europe? What are we to answer him?" The reason for the insignificance of Russian literature, Kireevskii wrote, was the Russian practice of imitation, which separated the educated elite and its specific culture from the inner source of the Russian way of life. In place of a Russian literature, there was "a strange chaos of undeveloped views and contradictory yearnings, there were discordant echoes of every possible movement in German, French, English, Italian, Polish, and Swedish literature, and a diverse imitation of every possible and impossible European tendency." It was not only writers who were accused of imitation. The critics were no less guilty. Their views were totally dependent on the influence of foreign literature. "One judges us according to the laws of French literature, the other takes German literature as his model, yet another takes English literature and praises everything that looks like this ideal."[25]

The principal arguments used by the Slavophiles to present this problem were based on the Romantic concepts of organism, and of the "degenerate West." But the intention of their critique was to counter the feeling of backwardness among Russian intellectuals by promoting the development of a genuine Russian culture of universal significance.

The Organic Argument

Like the German Romantics, the Slavophiles employed organic metaphors to justify their arguments. They compared the import of European ideas to the implantation of alien, or inorganic, elements into the body of Russia. On the surface of Russian life, Kireevskii stated, a borrowed culture prevailed, grown from another root.[26] Khomiakov described the state of Russian literature as "colorless words and colorless ideas," which revealed the foreign origin of the "engrafted plant."[27] The Westernizers, commonly seen as the ideological opponents of the Slavophiles, used a similar language. Belinskii, for example, maintained that an "alien, borrowed content" could never compensate, either in literature or in life, for the absence of "a national content," although it might, in time, be transformed into it. He described the "genius" of a nation as timid and subdued when it did not act originally and independently, maintaining that its produce in such cases would resemble artificial flowers.[28] We have come to take for granted that Europe should produce every truth and discovery by the sweat of her brow, Herzen argued. But there was one thing that had been overlooked: "the child [European culture] is not of our flesh and blood and there are no organic ties between it and us . . . Science can grow anywhere, but it will never produce a harvest where it has not been sown." It must germinate and mature in every nation.[29] Science, used here in the sense of learning, was a "living organism" and could thus not develop without an organic, that is, a national content.[30]

Hence, imported ideas, models, and systems were denounced because their foundations were derived from a culture and a history alien to Russian life. Whatever Russia acquired from the outside world had to be in harmony with the character and history of her own culture. It had to be the fruit of an inner organic development, based on Russia's own experiences. Consequently, the Romantic concept of organism turns imitation into a problem. In the article "Russians' opinions of foreigners," Khomiakov wrote that imported models or systems from foreign countries should not be understood as ready-made solutions, independent of "the spiritual historical movement" that had generated them. On the contrary, every system and institution in the West contained a solution to questions posed during earlier centuries. Khomiakov believed that transferring these systems to another people was dangerous and harmful, since the problems to which these systems constituted solutions had not had the possibility to arise under the conditions of this other society. If these questions could not reasonably have appeared in the new, receiving, society, the whole process, according to

Khomiakov, came to resemble that of trying to introduce inorganic elements into an organic body.[31]

This was also the view of Chaadaev, who held that Russia could not simply take over Western institutions or the Western way of life, since she did not enjoy the conditions out of which these institutions and this lifestyle developed.[32] In his view, the problem of imitation had to do with the absence of a natural, inward development in Russia. Thus, new ideas replaced old ones, instead of growing out of them. The fact that the Russian people were unable to connect their thinking with any succession of ideas, which had been progressively developed in society, influenced the mind of every individual. As a consequence, the best ideas were no more than "sterile visions," which remained "paralyzed in our brains" owing to precisely this lack of connection with earlier ideas.[33]

In nations that develop independently, Khomiakov held, the "richness of content" precedes the "perfection of form," but in Russia it was the other way around.[34] Kireevskii agreed, claiming that literature in Russia was only Western in form without any real, that is, Russian, content. Therefore, it was lifeless. In the Western nations, on the contrary, every movement in literature sprang from the inner movement of the culture, of which literature was a reflection. And in case this literature was subjected to foreign influence, it accepted this influence only when it corresponded to the requirements of the inner development of the nation's own culture.[35] Commenting on the same theme, Khomiakov stated that all remarkable artistic phenomena had so far carried a clear imprint of the nation or people in which they occurred. They were all full of that life that gave them a foundation and a content.[36] In Russia, on the other hand, the arts were not yet in harmony with Russian culture. They had, in Khomiakov's words, yet to become an expression of her contemporary soul. But in order to be so, both form and content had to be national. Forms taken from the outside world could not serve as expressions of the Russian soul. The spiritual personality of the nation could only be expressed in forms created by itself.[37] Lacking national forms of art meant lacking a national culture, the existence of which was a measure of enlightenment and progress.

The same argument was applied to philosophy. A specific Russian philosophy was needed in order to build a foundation for a Russian culture and way of life. "A philosophy is essential for us," Kireevskii wrote in 1830.[38] He criticized the universal claims of Western rationalism, or, as the Slavophiles frequently called it, the "Western Enlightenment." According to Kireevskii, its principles were not valid for the spiritual life of all human beings and of every people. Western thinking did not by itself give common meaning and truth to all external forms and individual ideas. If there was something essential in these forms and ideas, Russia could only incorporate it when it grew out of her roots, when it was a result of her own development and did not "descend on us from the outside in the form of a contradiction to the whole structure of our conscious and customary way of living,"[39] Khomiakov described the current state of the Russian imitated culture as "a ripe fruit, transferred as a formula from alien clime." The problem here was that this imported culture, which in itself was seen as a living force, had no connection to the life from which it arose, and on which it depended. Being cut off from its living foundation, it could not "feel sympathy" for *any* life or with anything living.[40]

Kireevskii argued that the foundation of Western thought and science had developed from the history of Western culture. This meant that in those states that shared a common European culture, the new rationalistic philosophy was not a fragment, but a continuation of the spiritual life of humanity. It built on the inheritance from earlier thinking. In those states, all elements of the "universal thinking" were joined with their nationalities, without any contradictions. In Russia, on the other hand, the imitated culture was not joined with the original development of the historical Russian culture. It had separated from its inner source.[41] The solution lay in the development of a Russian philosophy, where the highest development of thinking, or "true science," was in harmony with Russian life.

Khomiakov's views on the requirements of philosophy naturally influenced his theory of knowledge in line with the organic idea of the nation. He argued that every people must have a "living consciousness." This consciousness was not only necessary for every people; it was also broader and stronger than the formal and logical consciousness.[42] To Khomiakov, society was an organic being and, just as humans, it had a consciousness. However, in the same way as human beings were not conscious of themselves through logical reasoning, neither was society. Its consciousness was its life, which lay in the unity of habits, in the identity of the moral or spiritual motivation, in the continual organic exchange of ideas, in the founding of the people and its inner history. It belonged to the personality of the people. It was incomprehensible both to the foreigner and to such members who had isolated themselves from the rest of society. According to Khomiakov, philosophy was an outcome of the human spirit's striving for knowledge. In other words, it was a fruit of life. Consequently it needed a living basis, something that abstract logic did not provide. Russia's dilemma was that imitation had prevented scientific thinking from being a product of its local, historical life. Knowledge had become separated from the Russian way of life and was therefore weak and impotent.[43]

The theory of organicism, presented here by the Slavophiles, leads to a view of cultural development as unique and national. An imitative culture becomes a sign of backwardness, both with regard to the culture itself and to its articulators, since it was considered their duty to interpret and express the basis of the true national culture. To find a way out of this predicament, a national literature and philosophy had to be developed. However, there was more to the Slavophile critique of imitation. It was not just that the practice of imitation had become outmoded; the model that was being imitated was in itself deficient. It was only logical, as Liah Greenfeld claims in her theory of nationalism, that in order to demonstrate the nation's unique foundations, the earlier model had to be rejected, although it would not be correct to suggest that Slavophile criticism of the West was marked by *ressentiment*.[44] Another reason for turning against the Western model was that its founding ideas, such as rationalism, universalism, positivism, and materialism, were incompatible with the ideas of originality, uniqueness, sensitivity, and spontaneity, which were upheld by all Romantics regardless of home country. Hence, the Slavophiles' anti-Western arguments were part of a Western critique of European culture, and were not intended to separate Russia from Europe. Rather, the use of the concept of the degenerate West in Russian discourse reflects these intellectuals' involvement in and adherence to European culture.

The Degenerate West

The Slavophiles declared that the West had degenerated both morally and philosophically. They argued that with Hegel, not only German philosophy, but the whole Western philosophical tradition, had reached its impasse. The completeness of Hegel's system, providing a rationalistic explanation of all spheres of human life and understanding, was unsatisfactory to the deeply religious Slavophiles. German philosophy, represented by Kant and followed by Hegel, was considered the forefront of the rationalistic tradition of thought starting with Descartes. Its "fall," therefore, had vast implications for the whole of Western thinking. The result of Hegel's thinking was the decomposition of the whole development of "European reason" down to its last basis. There was nothing left to do. Reason had reached its limit and thus showed its inadequacy for philosophical development. In Kireevskii's view, the whole development of Western thought from Descartes to Schelling was joined in this Hegelian last system and in it found its final development and justification. Now, it seemed, the destiny of philosophy was determined, its goal was found, and its limits stretched to the impossible. For, as Kireevskii expressed it, "when the essence of reason and the laws for its necessary activity is understood, when the equivalent of these laws is determined as the laws for an unconditioned existence, when the same eternal reason recurs according to the same grounds for eternal necessity, whereto could the inquiring thought of human beings yet strive?" Not even Schelling's attempt to transcend logical reason was accepted by the Slavophiles. Kireevskii argued that, although aspiring to a new basis for science beyond logical reason, this philosophy nevertheless pursued the development of laws of intellectual necessity and thus could not transcend reason.[45]

Hegel had revealed the disastrous conclusion of Western thought, which in its turn exposed the plight of Western culture as it was based on this rationalistic thinking.[46] The life of its peoples had reached a final weakness, which was reflected in the unlimited dominance of the egoistic personality governed by reason. The Slavophiles were aware that Western Europe was considered degenerated and doomed even by Westerners, which of course did not make it a useful model for Russia. Khomiakov wrote that "we ought to be ashamed of ourselves chasing after the West. The English, French, or Germans do not have anything good for themselves. The further they look around, the worse and the more immoral their society appears to them." Instead, the "inner wavering" and "spiritual petrifaction" of the Western world, which, having lost belief in its earlier foundations, tried to create new ones artificially, by way of logic, should serve as a bad example for Russia.[47]

It was the Slavophiles' contention, clearly influenced by Romantic thought, that the dominance of England and Germany, currently at the fore-front of the European enlightenment, could not continue, for their inner life had already come to a close, making their culture suitable solely to them. It had lost its common significance and could therefore not contribute to uni-versal progress. As a result, Europe, marked by its old culture, appeared in a petrified form. Only two nations did not take part in the general degene-ration: the United States and Russia. However, due to "the one-sidedness of the United States' English culture," Russia was Europe's only hope.[48] Compared to the stale Western social life, Russia's spiritual forces were still vigorous. Her potential was great, because the development of her culture had been halted before it could yield any fruit.[49] Kireevskii noted that the prominent thinkers of Europe all complained about the contemporary situa-tion of moral apathy, about a lack of convictions, about a general egoism. According to him, these thinkers demanded a new spiritual force outside of reason. They demanded a new source of life outside of material advantage. In other words, they searched for faith and could not find it at home, for Christianity in the West was perverted by individualism.[50]

The West obviously constituted a poor model for Russia. Instead, Russia should turn to its indigenous foundations, which were not tainted by Western rationalism, and use those as a basis for its culture and society. However, Western thought was not to be totally discarded. Instead, it should be used as a seed to something new. What was needed was a Russian philos-ophy that could unite Western knowledge and Christian faith. In this way the development of a specific Russian philosophy would not only save Russia from falling into the same abyss as the West, but at the same time save the West from its own degeneration and decay. To the Slavophiles at least, that was an inevitable outcome of the logic of Western thought. Based on differ-ent foundations and developed by way of different paths, Russia had an important role to play in solving the predicament of Western philosophy.

Seen in the context of Romantic organicism, the idea of the degenerate West helped Russia to define her place in the progress of history. According to this thinking, all the cultures in the world are organisms, and they are tied together in a process of universal progress. Cultures live and grow old just like every other organic being, allowing new cultures to replace old and decaying ones in the continuous development of humanity. The concept of a decaying Western culture thus becomes not an argument for separation from the West, but for allowing Russia to make a genuine contribution to univer-sal progress. Combining the legacy of Western culture with her special way of life, Russia could save Europe. By declaring that Russian culture had a special role in universal history, the Slavophiles suggested a way out of the feeling of backwardness felt by members of the educated elite in their relation to the West.

The Universal Significance of the National Culture

The main disadvantage with imitation was that it prevented Russia from being part of the universal progress of humanity. Therefore, if like the Slavophiles you aspired to counter the feeling of cultural backwardness, it was not enough to denounce imitation as such, or to attack the Western model. The only way for Russian intellectuals to come to terms with their national identity was to present a national culture that could make a genuine contribution to the common cause of universal human enlightenment. The Slavophiles believed that enlightened Westerners were prepared to respect Russian thought when it was really genuine, and not just an imitation of foreign ideas.[51] On the other hand, any work, however great in artistic merit, which did not bear the sharp imprint of nationality, would lose its chief merit in the eyes of Europeans.[52] The central aim of the Slavophile criticism of imitation was therefore to show in what way Russia could make a contribution to universal progress.

An example of the importance that the Slavophiles attached to the role of Russian culture in a universal context is the way they expressed appreciation for the open lectures of Stepan Shevyrev on the history of the Russian literature and language. In a letter to a friend, Khomiakov wrote that the great interest in Shevyrev's lectures showed the heights of enlightenment to which Russia had arisen and how originally the nation could already think and speak.[53] The national contribution to, and participation in, a universal development was thus closely connected to the nation's originality and uniqueness. Russia had to be original precisely *in order to* make a contribution to humanity and in order to be part of universal progress. This also meant that the national culture had to be of universal significance. Without a genuine, national culture, Russia was left on the outside of universal history and of the progress of mankind. This was why Chaadaev's assertion that Russia had given nothing to the world was so devastating to the educated elite. Claiming that Russia had "not added a single idea to the mass of human ideas" nor contributed anything "to the progress of the human spirit" and that "nothing has emanated from us for the common good of men," he pointed precisely at the root of the problem of imitation.[54] Kireevskii stressed how important it was not to lose the universal meaning of Russian culture: "We have to be part of the common life of mankind or else the basis of our culture becomes one-sided, instead of being the basis of a complete, true, living enlightenment," he wrote.[55]

As we have seen above, the concepts of organism and of the degenerate West made it possible for the Slavophiles to argue that the time would come when Russia would be a cultural leader, because universal history would judge "the one-sided spiritual grounds," that is, the rationalistic principles that governed Western thinking, as irrevocable. As a consequence, looking for new principles to carry humanity forward, universal history would rouse to life and activity "the more complete and living foundations" contained in Russia.[56] Since Russian culture was born when other countries had already finished the circle of their spiritual development, it was Russia's task to begin where they had stopped. European culture could be seen as "the ripe fruit" of human development to be used as a stimulating means for the evolution of Russian intellectual and spiritual activity. Kireevskii compared the contemporary character of the European culture with that of the Roman-Greek culture, which, after having been developed to its own antithesis, was forced by natural necessity to adopt another, new, basis, that had been preserved in another people, and which before that time did not have any universal-historical meaning.

This historical analogy allowed Kireevskii to argue that Russia, in her Orthodox faith, had a firm basis for a national culture of universal significance. If the core principles of the Orthodox Slavic culture were true, he declared, then they should serve as a necessary complement to European culture, "cleaning it from its exclusive rationalistic character and penetrating it with new meaning." What was now inaccessible to the West was accessible to the Russian people, Khomiakov argued.[57] Only the Russian people could revive "the foundations of life itself," since they alone had preserved true Christianity, while the West had decided on a heretical path leading to rationalism and atheism. This made it possible for Russia to contribute to universal progress. Kireevskii held that the new demands of the European mind and Russian fundamental convictions in fact had the same meaning. At the root of European culture, there was one essential question about the relationship of the West to the hitherto undiscovered foundation of life, thought, and culture, which in fact lay at the basis of the Slavic-orthodox world.[58]

Hence, the possibility for saving Europe lay in the "living" enlightenment of the Russian culture. But in order for Russia to rise above other nations, her faith, which contained the basis of true social ideas, must penetrate social life. To do so, it had to be combined with reason and made universal. It had "to pass through science, that is, through the consciousness of all history and all the results of human intellectual activity," in order to be of common relevance.[59] That was the task the Slavophiles urged the educated Russian elite to take on. However, since the members of the educated elite had no knowledge of their nation and its past, there were no organs to express its founding principles. The Slavophiles urged Russian intellectuals and artists to get out of their state of "nonnational abstraction" and participate fully in the original life of the nation. A return to the national, or what the Slavophiles called "the foundations of life," was necessary in order for Russia to make an imprint on universal history and so become a worthy member of the cultural community of Europe.[60]

Conclusion

Looking at the purpose of the Slavophile nationalist project, this article concludes that a Russian national identity was formulated not in order to separate Russia from the West, as the common view argues, but to gain the respect of Europeans in order to counter the feeling of cultural backwardness among Russian intellectuals, triggered by the Romantic demands on a genuine contribution to the advancement of humanity. Obviously, neither isolationism, nor an antagonistic posture toward the West would remove these feelings. The only way Russian culture could be appreciated by others was for it to make a genuine contribution to universal progress. Hence, the Slavophiles used the Romantic concepts of organism and the decaying West to claim a place for Russia in universal history. By uniting the final results of Western culture with the unarticulated spiritual principles of the Russian way of life, a national culture would be regenerated that would be of common significance and thus could make an original contribution to humanity. Regardless of the impact of Slavophile ideas on Russian artistic creativity, it is a striking fact that within only a generation, Russia produced a literature that inhabits a place second to none in Europe's cultural heritage.

NOTES

1. Samuel Huntington, *The Clash of Civilizations and the Remaking of World Order* (New York: Simon and Schuster, 1996).
2. Richard Pipes, *The Russian Revolution* (New York: Knopf, 1990); *Russia under the Bolshevik Regime* (New York: Knopf, 1994); *Russia under the Old Regime*, 2nd ed. (London: Penguin, 1995).
3. See, e.g., Tibor Szamuely, *The Russian Tradition* (London: Secker and Warburg, 1974); Alexander Yanov, *The Russian Challenge and the Year 2000* (Oxford: Oxford University Press, 1987); Jonathan Steele, *Eternal Russia: Yeltsin, Gorbachev, and the Mirage of Democracy* (London: Faber, 1994); Pipes, *Russian Under the Old Regime*. For a more favorable view on Russia's distinctiveness, although with different emphasis, see N.O. Losskii, *History of Russian Philosophy* (New York: International Universities Press, 1951); J.M. Edie, J.P. Scanlan, M. Zeldin, eds., *Russian Philosophy*, vol. I (Chicago: Quadrangle Books, 1965); N. Berdiaev, *The Origin of Russian Communism* (London: G. Bles, 1937), *The Russian Idea* (London: G. Bles, 1947); James Billington, *The Icon and the Axe: An Interpretive History of Russian Culture* (New York: Vintage Books, 1966); P.K. Christoff, *An Introduction to Nineteenth-Century Slavophilism*, vol. I: *A.S. Xomjakov* (The Hague: Mouton, 1961); vol. II: *I. V. Kireevskij* (The Hague: Mouton, 1972); vol. III: *K.S. Aksakov* (Princeton: Princeton University Press, 1982); vol. IV: *Iu.F. Samarin* (Boulder: Westview Press, 1991); Iu.M. Lotman and B.A. Uspenskii, "Binary Models in the Dynamics of Russian Culture," in A.D. Nakhimovsky, and A.S. Nakhimovsky, eds., *The Semiotics of Russian Cultural History* (Ithaca: Cornell University Press, 1985). Tim McDaniel takes a more neutral position arguing for the uniqueness of the cultural pattern of social change in Russia in *The Agony of the Russian Idea* (Princeton: Princeton University Press, 1996).
4. Hans Kohn, *The Idea of Nationalism* (New York: Macmillan, 1946); Alexander Yanov, *Russian New Right: Right-wing Ideologies in the Contemporary USSR* (Berkeley: University of California Press, 1978); Yanov, *The Russian Challenge*; Pipes, *The Russian Revolution*; Stephen Carter, *Russian Nationalism. Yesterday,*

Today, Tomorrow (London: Pinter, 1990); Liah Greenfeld, *Nationalism. Five Roads to Modernity* (Cambridge, MA, 1993); Thomas Parland, *The Rejection in Russia of Totalitarian Socialism and Liberal Democracy. A Study of the Russian New Right* (Helsinki: Finnish Society of Sciences and Letters, 1993); Iver Neumann, *Russia and the Idea of Europe* (London: Routledge, 1996).

5. Kohn, *Idea*, 330. Friedrich Meinecke demonstrated this contrast long ago in his *Weltbürgertum und Nationalstaat* (Munich: R. Oldenbourg, 1908).

6. Yanov, *The Russian Challenge*, xii; D.G. Rowley, "Russian Nationalism and the Cold War," *American Historical Review* 99 (February 1994): 169–170.

7. Greenfeld, *Nationalism*, ch. 1.

8. Kohn, *Idea*, 330.

9. Neumann, *Russia and the Idea of Europe*, 1–2; Ilya Prizel, *National Identity and Foreign Policy. Nationalism and Leadership in Poland, Russia and Ukraine* (Cambridge: Cambridge University Press, 1998), 16–18, 23–29, 166–167.

10. Greenfeld, *Nationalism*, 15–17.

11. For scholars with a more favorable view of Russian nationalism, see John Dunlop, *The Faces of Contemporary Russian Nationalism* (Princeton: Princeton University Press, 1983), *New Russian Nationalism* (New York: Praeger, 1985); Carter, *Russian Nationalism*. They focus on the different strands of nationalism in the Soviet Union and their relationship to the Communist regime. In this context, nationalism appeared as a positive force fighting against a totalitarian regime.

12. The main works on the Slavophiles published in the West are F. Rouleau, *Ivan Kiréievski et la naissance du Slavophilisme* (Namur: Culture et vérité, 1990); Andrej Walicki, *The Slavophile Controversy* (Oxford: Oxford University Press, 1975); Abbot Gleason, *European and Muscovite: Ivan Kireevsky and the Origins of Slavophilism* (Cambridge: Harvard University Press, 1972); Christoff, *An Introduction*; N.V. Riasanovsky, *Russia and the West in the Teaching of the Slavophiles* (Cambridge: Harvard University Press, 1952). Notable works in Russian are E.A. Dudzinskaia, *Slavianofily v obshchestvennoi borbe* (Moscow: Mysl', 1983), *Slavianofily v poreformennoi Rossii* (Moscow: R.A.N., 1994); B.F. Egorov, V.A. Kotelnikov, and Iu.V. Stennik, *Slavianofilstvo i sovremennost'* (St. Petersburg: Nauka, 1994); N.I. Tsimbaev, *Slavianofilstvo: iz istorii russkoi obshchestvenno-politicheskoi mysli XIX veka* (Moscow: Izd. Moskovskogo Universiteta, 1986); Iu.Z. Iankovskii, *Patriarkhalno-dvorianskaia utopiia* (Moscow: Khudozh. Lit., 1981).

13. See Robin Aizlewood, "The Return of the 'Russian Idea' in Publications, 1988–91" *Slavonic and East European Review* 71, no.3, (1993) and S.B. Dzhimbinov, "The Return of Russian Philosophy" in James Scanlan, ed., *Russian Thought after Communism: The Recovery of a Philosophical Heritage* (Armonk, NY: Sharpe, 1994), for a review of the recent revival.

14. Neumann, *Russia and the Idea of Europe*, 33.

15. Christoff, *Xomjakov*, 245; *Kireevskij*, 326.

16. Christoff, *Xomjakov*, 45–46, 232–233; Losskii, *History of Russian Philosophy*, 47; Nicolas Zernov, *Three Russian Prophets, Khomiakov, Dostoevsky, Solovev* (London: S.C.M. Press, 1944), pp. 72–73; A.S. Khomiakov, *Polnoe sobranie sochinenii* 8 vols. (Moscow: Univ. Tip., 1900–1911) vol. III, 465–466. Baron Haxthausen discussed the Russian commune as early as 1843. See August von Haxthausen, *Studies on the Interior of Russia* (Chicago: University of Chicago Press, 1972).

17. I.V. Kireevskii, *Izbrannye stati* (Moscow: Sovremennik, 1984), 160.

18. Greenfeld, *Nationalism*.
19. Dominic Lieven, *The Aristocracy in Europe, 1815–1914* (Basingstoke: Macmillan, 1992), 179–180.
20. Peter Chaadaev, *Philosophical Letters & Apology of a Madman* (Knoxville: University of Tennessee Press, 1969), 36–41.
21. V.G. Belinsky, *Selected Philosophical Works* (Moscow: Foreign Languages Publishing House, 1956), 5–8, 44.
22. Ibid., 383.
23. V.F. Odoevskii, "Russkie nochi" in *Sochineniia kniazia V. F. Odoevskago* (St. Petersburg: Tip. E. Pratsa, 1844), vol. 1, 10.
24. D. Venevitinov, *Polnoe sobranie sochinenii* (Moscow: Academia, 1934), 216–217.
25. Kireevskii, *Izbrannye stati* 60, 146, 84.
26. Ibid., 276.
27. Khomiakov, *Polnoe sobranie*, vol. III, 111.
28. Belinsky, *Selected Philosophical Works*, 372, 29.
29. Alexander Herzen, *Selected Philosophical Works* (Moscow: Foreign Languages Publishing House, 1956), 18.
30. Herzen, "Dilettantism in Science," in W.J. Leatherbarrow and D.C. Offord, eds., *A Documentary History of Russian Thought* (Ann Arbor: University of Michigan Press, 1987), 140, 144.
31. Khomiakov, *Polnoe sobranie*, vol. I, 61.
32. There is a discussion of this idea by Raymond McNally in his introduction to *Philosophical works of Peter Chaadaev* (Dordrecht: Kluwer Academic Publishers, 1991), 15–16.
33. Chaadaev, *Philosophical Letters*, 39.
34. Ibid., 12.
35. Kireevskii, *Izbrannye stati*, 147, 276.
36. Khomiakov, *Polnoe sobranie*, vol. I, 74.
37. Ibid., vol. III, 117–118.
38. Kireevskii, *Izbrannye stati*, 51.
39. Ibid., 156–157.
40. Khomiakov, *Polnoe sobranie*, vol. I, 47.
41. Kireevskii, *Izbrannye stati*, 192–193, 76, 151.
42. Khomiakov, *Polnoe sobranie*, vol. I, 11, 28.
43. Ibid., 20–23.
44. Greenfeld, *Nationalism*.
45. Kireevskii, *Izbrannye stati*, 280, 67–68.
46. Ibid., 144–145.
47. Khomiakov, *Polnoe sobranie*, vol. III, 20; vol. I, 93, 66.
48. Kireevskii, *Izbrannye stati*, 61.
49. Khomiakov, *Polnoe sobranie*, vol. I, 93, 43; Kireevskii, *Izbrannye stati*, 276.
50. Kireevskii, *Izbrannye stati*, 120.
51. Khomiakov, *Polnoe sobranie*, vol. I, 33–34, 171; Kireevskii, *Izbrannye stati*, 151–152.
52. Belinsky, *Selected Philosophical Works*, 365.
53. A.S. Khomiakov, *Izbrannye sochineniia* (New York: Izd. im. Chekhova, 1955), 331.
54. Chaadaev, *Philosophical Letters*, 34, 41.
55. Kireevskii, *Izbrannye stati*, 155.

56. Khomiakov, *Polnoe sobranie*, vol. I, 174, 152, 156–157, 96.
57. Ibid., vol. I, 96.
58. Kireevskii, *Izbrannye stati*, 60, 160, 330, 151; Khomiakov, *Polnoe sobranie*, vol. I, 96.
59. Kireevskii, *Izbrannye stati*, 323, 330.
60. Khomiakov, *Polnoe sobranie*, vol. I, 98; Kireevskii, *Izbrannye stati*, 323.

8

STATISTICS, SOCIAL SCIENCE, AND SOCIAL JUSTICE: THE ZEMSTVO STATISTICIANS OF PRE-REVOLUTIONARY RUSSIA

Esther Kingston-Mann

THE EUROPEAN CONTEXT

The Quest for a Science of Humanity

Ever since the eighteenth century, the ideals of the Enlightenment inspired educated people the world over to believe not only that human beings could by their own efforts discover the universal laws and scientific principles that govern human and nonhuman behavior, but to assume as well that the pursuit of scientific knowledge would serve the cause of justice. That Enlightenment universals and scientific knowledge could be deployed to support unjust causes, or to reinforce a variety of despotisms and oppressions was inconceivable to the *philosophes*, and a vexed question for later proponents of radical and revolutionary change. On the other hand, there have always been plenty of scholars and policy-makers for whom Enlightenment universals and scientific knowledge provided a welcome promise of stability, order, and incremental change within quite undemocratic and economically polarized societies. So, from the outset, the "social sciences of humanity" occupied contested terrain.

This essay explores the emergence of modern statistics as a particularly contested and controversial social science. A brief discussion of Western European debates and dilemmas serves as the backdrop for the story of a group of late-nineteenth-century Russian statisticians, who (1) assumed—in keeping with their radical gloss on Enlightenment principles—that the most accurate, carefully presented, and rigorously analyzed statistical data invariably served the cause of social justice, (2) produced the largest database on a peasant population before the second half of the twentieth century, and (3) found their work dismissed as "unscientific" and "populist."

Universal Principles and Statistical Data

Statistics—a term derived from the German term *statistik*, or "state-istics"— originally referred to the systematization of data for the analysis and comparison of monarchical states.[1] It emerged as a category of knowledge in response to seventeenth- and eighteenth-century demands for reliable empirical figures, upon which modernizing rulers could base their fiscal and administrative policies. In the hands of German statisticians like Johan Sussmilch and English advocates of Political Arithmetic like William Petty, statistical data was produced to aid mercantilist governments concerned with policy issues of social control and the augmentation of tax revenues. Careful record-keeping—so the argument went—made for better surveillance, higher levels of stability, and greater economic prosperity. In its early stages, statistics did not refer solely to numbers or to the method used to analyze numbers. As late as the 1830s, many of its English practitioners continued to insist that the quantitative feature of statistics remained "subsidiary" to the main definition as "that department of political science which is concerned in collecting and arranging facts illustrative of the condition and resources of a state."[2]

In early-nineteenth-century England, modern statistics emerged within a social science context that was framed by the deductive precepts of liberal political economy—a "science of wealth" intended by scholar/policy-makers like David Ricardo, Thomas Malthus, Nassau Senior, and John Stuart Mill to fill out the master paradigm originally constructed by Adam Smith. Whether they were optimistic (Smith) or pessimistic (Malthus) about the operations of Smith's famous "Invisible Hand," liberal political economists believed that rational, abstract, and scientific laws governed the latter's operation.[3]

It is worth noting that neither the "Invisible Hand," nor liberalism's profit-maximizing, ideal yet typical "economic man" were in any sense the product of empirical research. Malthus did not consider statistics essential to prove his population theory, though he thought they were necessary "to illustrate it and to show its operations in a given context."[4] Nassau Senior declared, "I do not consider the truths of political economy as founded on Statistical facts";[5] and contended that "political economy is not greedy of facts, it is independent of them."[6] J.R. McCulloch, one of the leading statisticians of his day, contended that political economy "is to the statistician what the physical astronomer is to the mere observer."[7] As economic historian Mark Blaug has observed, there was a "curious separation between abstract theory and empirical work."[8] To early-nineteenth-century liberal economists, it was not self-evident that the validity of classical economics required testing against any systematically collected body of empirical evidence—statistical or otherwise.

In England, the effort to ground the principles of liberal political economy in empirical research gathered decisive force in the 1830s—a time of political unrest, exposés of massive poverty in the midst of English plenty, and Chartist labor demands for social justice. In this context, reform-minded noblemen and industrialists, Whig peers, and a number of the leading liberal scholars of the day began to recognize the need for what they called "moral statistics." By this term, they had in mind empirical data that would generate reforms to alleviate the ignorance and demoralization of the poor (caused, as liberals saw it, by urbanization, bad education, and inadequate health care but not by factory working conditions).[9]

Arguing that statistical data was superior to the "errors and ignorance" characteristic of the backward societies of the past, economists like Richard Jones conceived of statistics as the empirical arm of liberal political economy.[10] In his view, it was only through the systematic collection and analysis of relevant empirical data that the abstractions of liberalism's "economic man" could legitimately become the basis for rational and effective economic policy. One scientific society of the 1830s made a more benevolent case for the cause of statistics as a science that would "enable us to associate more immediate scientific and intellectual pursuits with works of benevolence and the rich luxury of doing good."[11] In general, early-nineteenth-century notions of social science were neither neutral nor dispassionate. They reflected instead a faith in the consonance of science and human progress with which the *philosophes* might easily have agreed.

In 1833, Jones, Thomas Malthus, the mathematician Charles Babbage, and the Belgian statistician Adolphe Quetelet proposed the creation of a new Statistics section within the British Association for the Advance of Science (BAAS). During the next two years, leading scholars and industrialists organized statistical societies in London, Manchester, Bristol, Glasgow, and Liverpool. However, despite what has been described as "an era of enthusiasm" for statistics on the part of England's liberal intellectual and industrial elites, the research they carried out was quite meager. Because most statistical investigations of English social life were privately funded, statistical research required—in addition to the requisite commitment to scholarship and reform—that the researcher possess great quantities of personal wealth. Although industrialist Henry Hallam could hire research assistants to carry out house-to-house surveys in the name of the London Statistical Society during the 1830s, others were either unable or unwilling to emulate his massive investment of personal income in the statistics enterprise. The experience of the Bristol Statistics Society was far more typical—after surveying 4,700 families, the Society ran out of money before its results could be published.[12] Among the men of leisure, knowledge, and political influence who joined the London Statistical Society in the course of the 1830s, it has been noted that "very few were willing to undertake the arduous labor necessary to prepare real statistical reports."[13] In stark contrast to both the level of commitment and social origins of the Russian statisticians discussed later in this essay, Whig peers discovered that "Statistical investigation . . . required more time and energy than busy people were willing to invest unless they had a real interest in the outcome."[14]

The cause of statistics was further plagued by controversy over the appropriate target population to be researched. In general, English statisticians sought to obtain data from "intelligent individuals," whose views could form the basis for the formulation of benevolent government policies. A typical 1835 survey on "the conditions of the People" prepared by the London Statistics Society was thus distributed to police, hospital and poor law administrators, school boards, factory commissioners, landlords, newspaper editors, magistrates and prison governors, but not to those who were supervised by any of the latter individuals. Statistical studies of strike activities generally tended to draw on the testimony of employers, journalists, legal experts, and economists (rather than strikers), while education statistics were based on interviews with schoolmasters but not with teachers or pupils. Although Richardson Porter's 1837 investigation carried out in several districts of London constituted an exception to the general tendency to avoid questioning factory workers, most pre-1850s surveys revealed a definite administrative bias.[15]

Statistics, "Politics," and the Search for Social Order

The general reluctance to engage in the drudgery and expense of gathering, classifying, arranging, and analyzing statistical materials was exacerbated as well by the specter of "politics" that haunted many proponents of the statistics enterprise.[16] Nineteenth-century researchers who departed from the "moral statistics" focus on urbanization, bad education, and inadequate health care were likely to be denounced as inciters of "class division and factionalism." BAAS member William Whewell warned that the social make-up of individuals that inclined to devote themselves to such research, could well politicize and discredit the cause of social science. In his words,

> Why sanction the activities of an ambulatory body, composed partly of men of reputation and partly of a miscellaneous crowd, to go round year by year from town to town and at each place, discuss the most inflammatory and agitating questions of the day?[17]

According to BAAS president Adam Sedgwick, the statistical section would have to follow strict rules, for

> if we transgress our proper boundaries, go into provinces not belonging to us, and open a door of communication to the dreary world of politics, that instant will the foul Daemon of discord find his way into our Eden of philosophy.[18]

The Association warned members of its new Statistics Section that if they did not refrain from dealing with larger political or economic generalizations, the section would be "dissevered from the objects of the association." Statisticians were directed to confine their activities to "matters of fact," and to avoid the "higher generalizations; of political economy and political philosophy."[19] Nevertheless, despite these precautions, the mathematician Charles Babbage continued to fear that

> all sorts of plans, speculations and schemes are afloat, and all sorts of people, proper and improper, are penetrated with the desire of wielding the sceptre of science.[20]

Comments of this sort suggested that in the English context, it was not only the legitimate scope of statistics as a social science, but the reliability and social status of its practitioners as well that were being called into question.

In the 1830s and 1840s, scholars like Babbage sought support and understanding from Adolphe Quetelet, a Belgian scholar widely recognized as the leading European statistician of his day. During the first half of the nineteenth century, Quetelet's efforts to discover in human communities the universal laws, regularities, and predictability characteristic of the natural sciences were particularly appealing to scholars and monarchs who hoped that the new social sciences would reinforce and support any duly constituted social order. Quetelet popularized the notion of statistics as a "social physics" that promoted equilibrium and harmony within society and the state.[21] In a language replete with antirevolutionary metaphors, Quetelet's writings revealed a commitment as deep as William Petty's to statistics as a kind of "scientific" line of defense against the threat of chaos and anarchy. In the wake of the Revolutions of 1848, Quetelet sought to demonstrate that statisticians were law-abiding professionals; to this end, he advised European rulers to use statistics as a way "to understand the factions that ordinarily divide a state, in order to judge the most appropriate means for combating and paralyzing them."[22]

In nineteenth-century Imperial Russia, government officials welcomed the teachings of Quetelet, but viewed statistical investigations of the Russian countryside with suspicion (particularly if they focused on the conditions of serfdom). Researchers who had to work under the constraints of an autocratic state risked sanctions that were similar—but far harsher—than those encountered by dissidents within the London Statistical Society. In the 1830s, the research of respected statisticians like Karl Hermann, D.P. Zhuravskii, and K.I. Arseniev was first censored and then suppressed because it contained evidence of the heavy material exactions imposed on the enserfed peasantry by serfowners and by the state. Hermann and Arseniev were dismissed from their posts at the University of St. Petersburg, and in 1848, all copies of Arseniev's *Statistical Sketches of Russia* were recalled by an enraged Tsar Nicholas I because the book's dedication expressed "grief over the existence (in Russia) of various obstacles to the free development of a new and better life for the common man." It was five years before government censors approved Zhuravskii's three-volume *Statistical Description of Kiev Guberniia*; the Holy Synod continued to prohibit the appearance of Zhuravskii's articles on the lands and profits of the clergy.[23]

Although neither Russia's church nor state was opposed to statistical research in principle, both were even more fearful than their English counterparts that statistics might be contaminated by the specter of "politics." To enhance the credibility of statistics as a discipline, Moscow University's Ivan Vernadskii, the leading economist and statistician of the 1850s, sought to define the statistician's role as a specialist who dispassionately served the leading institutions of society and the state. According to Vernadskii, the social sciences provided the authorities with a more secure foundation for government efforts to maintain order and stability. Like the officials of Britain's Association for the Advancement of Science who warned statisticians in the 1830s against excursions into "politics," Vernadskii welcomed Quetelet's notion of the social scientist as a trusted, "apolitical" professional, eminently worthy of recruitment into government service.

Vernadskii was a professor of economics and statistics first at Kiev and later at Moscow University, a delegate to the International Congress of Statisticians in Vienna (1857), London (1860), and Berlin (1863), an official of the Ministry of the Interior after 1856, and chair of the committee of political economy of the Imperial Free Economic Society. A dedicated Anglophile, he presented liberal statistics and economics to his Russian audience as a source of information, principles, and strategies intended to safeguard rather than threaten duly constituted socioeconomic and political institutions (including the institution of serfdom).[24] Opposed to the introduction of censorship to check the spread of Western ideas, Vernadskii contended that liberal social sciences served a fundamentally conservative function. If decisive steps were taken to prevent unsuitable, socially undesirable, and potentially disruptive students from gaining entrance to Russia's universities, there was in his view no danger that Western wisdom could play a radical or subversive role.[25]

The German Social Science Challenge

In the 1860s, liberal conceptions of the social sciences were challenged by a *methodenstreit* [dispute over method] that originated in the states of Germany. Drawing on Germany's statist traditions and on the work of legal scholars like Friedrich Savigny and the historian Leopold Ranke, German economists responded to the Revolutions of 1848 by challenging what they viewed as the universalist, deductivist, and "Anglocentric" features of classical liberalism. Led by the economist Wilhelm Roscher, a growing number of German social scientists of the 1850s and 1860s were willing to argue that the doctrines of classical liberalism were inadequately grounded in systematic empirical data. According to Roscher, Karl Knies, and Bruno Hildebrand, human economic behavior could best be understood by means of statistical and historical research. The massive statistical studies produced by Roscher and his colleagues suggested that the economic behavior of individuals was shaped not only by private interest, but also by the individual's participation in such collectivities as family, social class, and nation.[26]

Operating well within the statist traditions of their culture and history, German statistician–economists were convinced by the Revolutions of 1848 that genuine conflicts of interest—rather than the "harmonies" and equilibriums of Adam Smith—functioned to shape the economic behavior of different social groups and individuals in German society. In the mid-nineteenth century, these were not viewed as radical propositions. German historical economists were wholly in agreement with their English counterparts over the role of the social sciences as a key contributor to the maintenance of social order and domestic peace. Their researches were intended from the outset to aid government efforts to resolve socioeconomic conflicts.[27] But in contrast to the anti-statist English, economists like Roscher and Knies welcomed the government as an active and benevolent "third party" whose policies could—with the advice of statistician–economists like themselves—resolve fundamental social problems.

In 1872, a younger generation of German economists and statisticians founded a *Verein fur Sozialpolitik* that demanded government action to check "excessive" concentrations of wealth and property. In the wake of the Franco-Prussian War, leading social scientists like Gustav Schmoller, Adolf Wagner, and the noted statistician Ernst Engel argued that available statistical data revealed inequalities in the distribution of wealth in contemporary Germany that posed a dangerous threat to the survival of society and the state. As social science professionals, these scholars did not claim neutrality. They were proponents of stability and order, convinced that their expertise prepared them for the role of government advisers and policy-makers.

For the most part, the aspirations of Verein members were successfully realized in Bismarck's Germany. By the last decades of the nineteenth century, they were serving as members of the Reichstag, as government officials and advisers to labor associations, and they occupied every important chair of economics in Germany.[28] Labeled as "academic socialists," or *kathedersozialisten*, they were accused by conservatives of carrying out statistical research that legitimized Marxist critiques of German society. At the same time, Verein members were bitterly denounced by Marxists as the tools and agents of the Bismarckian state.[29] It should be noted that both contentions possessed a high degree of validity.

The "German" idea of economics as the statistical and historical investigation of diverse economic interactions and conflicts between social groups in varying contexts drew significantly upon empirical data from Russia and from Russian scholars. Ever since the early 1800s, the *Proceedings* of the Imperial Russian Free Economic Society had been available in German translation, and the *Landwirtschaftliches Centralblatt fur Deutschland* regularly printed excerpts from the *Proceedings* in its own publications. Baron Ludwig von Haxthausen's study of the Russian peasant commune was first published in German, and the economic writings of Russian scholars like B.N. Chicherin and K.D. Kavelin were also available in German translation.[30] Wilhelm Roscher devoted a whole chapter of his *Nationaloekonomie* to what he called the "German-Russian" school of economics, and enthusiastically welcomed the relativist implications of the work of Baltic German economist Johannes von Keussler, whose statistical data indicated that no universal rules or laws could be said to govern tenure relations in every part of the Russian Empire.[31]

Russia: A More Urgent Search for Order

Nowhere was the impact of German scholarship more profoundly felt than in Imperial Russia, where émigré German scholars and Baltic Germans had served Russian rulers as advisers and government officials ever since the eighteenth century. On the eve of a peasant emancipation reform powerfully influenced by Prussian models and examples, Roscher's student Ivan Babst replaced the Anglophile I.P. Vernadskii as professor of economics and statistics at Moscow University in 1860. In the decades to come, a younger generation of Roscher's students included A.I. Chuprov, who emerged as the leading Russian economist–statistician of his day.[32]

As a translator and popularizer of Roscher's work, Babst attempted to make the case that "German-style" statistical and historical research would not only provide solutions to contemporary socioeconomic problems, but could also reinforce the modernizing efforts of the Russian state. During the second third of the nineteenth century, the persistent threat of radical social upheaval made it exceedingly difficult for Russian government officials to be wholly convinced that domestic peace and stability would be enhanced by a wide-ranging program of statistical research into every aspect of the Russian economy. In the wake of the reforms that emancipated 23 million peasants from serfdom and created elective institutions called the zemstvo [pl. zemstva], the autocracy was confronted by a radical student movement that called for peasant revolution, engaged in political terrorism activity against a still repressive Russian autocracy, and produced an unprecedented body of "inflammatory" empirical data. In this context, Russian authorities were forced to weigh the need for more reliable data about the Empire's all-too-disparate inhabitants against a well-founded fear of the dangers that might be inherent in the data itself, the data-gatherers, and the data-gathering process.

Even within the traditionally staid environs of the government-sponsored Imperial Free Economic Society, troubling questions were raised. In 1865, with Vernadskii as chair of the Statistics Division of the Imperial Free Economic Society, one delegate asked:

> I have heard nothing here from peasants because they are not present. What kind of farmers are they? What do they themselves understand as their task?[33]

The government responded to such unwelcome queries by drastically curtailing the work of the Imperial Free Economic Society. In conservative circles, even the desire to consult with social scientists was viewed with alarm. When the Grand Duke Konstantin met with several economists and statisticians to discuss their research plans, future Minister of the Interior P.A. Valuev gloomily described these encounters as "a symptom of our [Russian Society's] disorganization."[34]

The early history of the Petrovskaia Agricultural Academy posed even more terrifying challenges to a government in dire need of statistical data. Created in 1865 with an unusual policy of open admissions, the institution's decidedly "nonelite" mission was to train local researchers and agricultural field workers, rather than future officials and diplomats. In many respects, the academy provided unprecedented educational opportunity for commoners of precisely the "undesirable" social origins that the liberal economist

Vernadskii had earlier warned against. In 1869, when one of the Academy's students was murdered by a group of radicals led by S.N. Nechaev, the institution became notorious among liberals and conservatives alike as a haven for "ragged, long-haired, heavy-booted revolutionaries." Demands for a purge of the Academy's radical elements soon brought an increase in admission fees to exclude the nondegree, economically disadvantaged students deemed particularly likely to engage in disruptive activity and particularly vulnerable to radical propaganda appeals.

In response to the raising of student fees, the future statisticians V.N. Grigoriev and K.A. Verner drew up a petition signed by 70 students that denounced political "collusion" between the academy's administration, faculty, and police (and were soon arrested and sent into exile). In later years, the statistician A.F. Fortunatov recalled the meetings of student liberals and radicals, who met in separate *skhodki* [assemblies] in the woods surrounding the Academy's model farm to debate over whether to join the revolutionary organization *Zemlia i volia [Land and Liberty]*. Fearing the impact of radical students upon the peasantry, the newspaper *Golos [The Voice]* vainly declared: "An agronomist is not a social activist, but a specialist" who carried out his professional duties and respected duly constituted authority.[35]

Outside of Russia's academic institutions, radicals found guilty of revolutionary activity carried out empirical and historical research in their places of exile. Political and economic tracts authored by A.S. Shchapov and N.S. Shelgunov cited statistical data published by English and German scholars, and contemptuously dismissed the "abstractions" of Quetelet and Ivan Vernadskii. The radical N. Bervi was eventually confined to a mental hospital for writing *The Condition of the Russian Working Class* (1869), a book that relied on Zhuravskii's earlier statistics about peasants and took its title from Engels' study of English factory workers.

For its part, the Russian government attempted to create a statistical enterprise capable of generating data more consistent with its fiscal priorities, and sent economists and statisticians like Vernadskii, P.S. Poroshin, and A.N. Kulomzin to participate in the international statistics conferences in the 1860s and 1870s. At the Brussels Congress of 1863 chaired by Adolphe Quetelet, Russians constituted the largest single foreign delegation. In 1872, St. Petersburg hosted the Eighth International Congress of Statisticians, where a welcoming speech to foreign and Russian statisticians by the Grand Duke Konstantin declared that the field of statistics was intended by Divine Providence to uncover the "sources of evil which halt humanity in its progress."

During the following year, the Russian government funded a new series of empirical studies of the Russian countryside. In 1873, a commission chaired by Minister of the Interior P.A. Valuev collected data from 900 provincial governors, chairs of agricultural societies, marshals of the nobility, and provincial zemstvo board chairmen. However, only 3 out of 133 who testified at its hearings were peasants.[36] Between 1878–80, the Imperial Free Economic Society and the Royal Geographic Society surveyed 816 communes in 24 provinces. Local officials, landlords, priests, and justices of the peace were interviewed, but peasants were not.[37] For reasons quite similar to those deployed by the London Statistical Society in the 1830s, these projects reflected the traditional view that local authorities could provide evidence more useful for the formulation of government policy than the direct testimony of peasants.

ZEMSTVO STATISTICIANS IN PRE-REVOLUTIONARY RUSSIA[38]

Just as for the Russian *muzhik* there was nowhere to go except "one beaten path—to the tavern," so too for every type of political "unreliable" there was "only one beaten path—to zemstvo statistics."

I.P. Belokonskii[39]

Even as the Russian government continued to survey the opinions of rural authorities, the increasingly pressing need for a reliable assessment of local land values for fiscal purposes triggered another, far more ambitious research project. During the last third of the nineteenth century, the government set in motion an investigative process through which field researchers hired by its newly created zemstvo organizations produced a body of evidence that came to be known as "zemstvo statistics." Although a significant proportion of the zemstvo data was relevant to the government's original directive, tsarist officials soon discovered that the zemstvo statisticians had far exceeded their research mandate. According to the statistician A.A. Kaufman, the narrowly fiscal concerns emphasized by the authorities turned out to be incompatible with the broader scientific objectives of the zemstvo researchers.[40]

The broader scientific objectives that Kaufman had in mind were first articulated by Alexander Chuprov, a student of Wilhelm Roscher who joined Moscow University's Department of Political Economy in 1874.[41] Imbued with the activist perspectives of Germany's *Verein fur Sozialpolitik*, Chuprov began his academic career in the midst of an Empire-wide "movement to go to the people" (*khozhdenie v narod*). Among his first students at Moscow University were veterans of the 1870s effort by thousands of radical dissidents to serve "the people's cause" by living and working alongside the peasantry. In this highly charged political context, Chuprov's declaration that the social sciences needed to be brought closer to life, which had "suffered so much from the separation" struck a responsive chord. Linking the aims of social science and social justice, Chuprov argued not only for statistical investigations to test the validity of commonsense economic notions and principles; he contended as well that the "best" science—and in particular, the social science of statistics—would foster changes that bettered the material conditions of the peasant majority of the Russian population. According to Chuprov, the zemstvo-sponsored research currently underway held out the promise of a more realistic and useful understanding of the workings of the Russian rural economy, and in particular the condition, behavior, and prospects of the peasantry and the communal institutions to which most of them belonged.[42]

In the 1870s, Chuprov organized Russia's first student seminar on the subject of statistics and introduced into Russian academic life the first university courses in applied political economy. His lectures were mimeographed by devoted students, and became the standard introduction to economics and statistics for university undergraduates during the second half of the nineteenth century.[43] Together with colleagues at prestigious institutions like Moscow University and field researchers from the "politically suspect" Petrovskaia Agricultural Academy, Chuprov attempted to devise strategies to coordinate and analyze the data emerging from the ongoing zemstvo statistical investigations of the Russian countryside.[44] In this process, Chuprov and his colleagues helped to create precisely the sort of activist social science that their radical students had demanded. However—in stark contrast to their German counterparts of the *Verein fur Sozialpolitik*— Russian statisticians discovered that their understanding of the statistical researcher's "mission" was quite incompatible with the Russian government's policy agenda.

From the government's point of view, one of the most troubling features of the zemstvo statistical enterprise was the political affiliation of the statisticians themselves. The still dissident veterans of "the movement to go to the people" turned out to be—if not the only applicants—then at least the ones most eager to take on the arduous, politically dangerous and financially unrewarding tasks of administering questionnaires to villagers across the length and breadth of the Russian Empire. Would-be field statisticians were exceedingly scarce. As a consequence, when radicals like V.N. Grigoriev and K.A. Verner returned from political exile, they were hired by provincial zemstvo organizations despite their arrest records, as were individuals of similarly "questionable" background and ideological commitments.

From the perspective of the newly hired radicals, rigorous social science research constituted service to the "people's cause." Quite willing to immerse themselves in the prosaic drudgery of the data collecting process, they tabulated tens of thousands of questionnaires without any sort of technological assistance beyond a pencil and a primitive hectographing machine.[45] Following the example first set by investigators in Moscow province, field workers frequently began by dividing each district (*uezd*) according to the form of land tenure (private or communal) and type of arable (hayfield, plowland, garden plot, etc.). They then interviewed individual landowners and commune peasants in order to determine soil type and average harvests. After considering the soil quality and characteristics of land use, they determined the value (in terms of income potential) of one *desiatina* (2.7 acres) of land.[46] In Moscow province, the statistician V.I. Orlov and his radical assistants were able to interview over 5,500 peasant households in Moscow province in less than three years. Convinced that the most rigorous research would vindicate their struggle for a fundamental restructuring of Russian society, they faced a government and a rural elite who shared their belief that research could threaten and destabilize society.

Data-Gathering as a Subversive Activity

Among local officials and landowners, the appearance of zemstvo statisticians in the Russian countryside aroused well-founded suspicions. Rural elites who feared the discovery of bribery and tax evasion tended to view investigators of dubious social origins as "anarchists" bent on nefarious and revolutionary agitation.[47] And in practice, the stark inequities of Russian rural life sometimes made it difficult to distinguish between "unreliable radicals" intent on exposing the corruption of the upper classes and "reliable social scientists" charged with the task of collecting data on rural economic activity. In 1867, the year after Karakozov's assassination attempt on the tsar, a government intent on defending its gentry constituency from the appearance of unwelcome statistical data issued a decree prohibiting the publication of zemstvo research without the express permission of the appropriate provincial governor.[48]

In the 1870s, the zemstvo bureau in Chernigov province was a particular flashpoint. Directed by the radical P.P. Chervinskii, (hired to direct provincial research investigations shortly after his return from political exile) field researchers compiled data that proved to be quite inflammatory. It turned out that approximately one-eighth of the privately owned lands in the province were omitted from the assessment rolls, and that landholders' properties were undervalued by as much as 50 percent.[49] The Chernigov authorities, enraged at the publication of massive evidence that the province's first families were benefiting from illicit privileges, closed down the provincial statistics bureau in 1877. The future liberal activist I.I. Petrunkevich was sent into exile as punishment for his defense of the statistics gathered by Chervinskii and his colleagues.[50] Elsewhere, government officials cut off funds to zemstvo organizations, prohibited the publication of zemstvo findings, and closed down statistical bureaus in Vladimir, Petersburg and Poltava.[51]

For very different reasons, peasants were also wary of information-seeking strangers in their midst. Suspecting that the information they supplied might result in higher taxes, peasants frequently protected their interests by reporting that each harvest was the worst one yet. To win the trust of their peasant informants, zemstvo statisticians sought therefore to distinguish themselves from government officials. Veteran researchers suggested to less experienced comrades that they (1) ask questions in informal settings (preferably out of doors), (2) tell respondents exactly what was being written down, and (3) record data with pencils rather than pens on a piece of paper that was torn, a bit smudged, and altogether unofficial-looking.[52] In important respects, their sensitivity to the factors that could affect the quality of the data provided by informants prefigured by well over half a century the work of social scientists—particularly in the fields of sociology and anthropology—who responded to the challenge of "negotiating entry" into unfamiliar group settings.[53]

*Acquiring Reliable Data: Challenge and Innovation in
Statistical Research Methods*
Zemstvo statistical bureaus were eventually able to attract enthusiastic, but not very efficient or knowledgeable university students, rural schoolteachers,

and village clerks as research staff. However, in order for research investigations to proceed, each zemstvo had to train them and in a sense, had to become its own school for statistical researchers. The results were sometimes good and sometimes discouraging. In 1872, the Kherson provincial zemstvo established a special statistical bureau, and recruited a trained supervisor and staff who in turn trained several hundred village clerks to carefully verify results, tabulate figures, and write up research results. But in St. Petersburg, where I.K. Pudovikov relied on elementary school teachers as assistants, he found that despite his detailed instructions, their work contained so many errors and omissions that much of the research initially carried out had to be repeated.

In other measures taken to enhance the reliability of the data obtained from peasant informants, the aforementioned Chervinskii, together with A.A. Rusov and V.E. Varvar attempted to ensure that no researcher in Chernigov province distributed questionnaires before acquiring a minimal knowledge of the land and people to be investigated. Staff were required as well to reside—at least briefly—in the area where questionnaires were to be distributed. By the 1880s, the "Chernigov" research model of residency-based research was being widely imitated by zemstvo organizations in neighboring provinces. Equally significant were the efforts of V.N. Pokrovskii, who was hired after being exiled to Tver province in the wave of arrests that followed Karakozov's assassination attempt of 1866. Appointed director of the Tver zemstvo statistical bureau, Pokrovskii devised a number of strategies in response to the possibility that peasants might provide superficial and misleading data if the statistician simply appeared, tabulated answers to their questionnaires, and then departed. Noting that the investigator's experience, prior knowledge of peasant life, and sensitivity to his or her status as "outsider" might significantly affect the quality of research data, Pokrovskii recommended that peasant testimony be treated with caution as well as respect. In Tver province, peasants were questioned in the company of neighbors who could comment and correct false statements and factual inaccuracies; afterward, oral testimony was checked against available official documents. In the course of a decade, the Tver statistical bureau published 20 volumes of statistical data. Pokrovskii was personally responsible for writing ten of them.[54]

In Voronezh province, F.A. Shcherbina pioneered the creation of peasant household inventories and budget studies that documented crop prices, wages, terms of tenancy, and other forms of communal and non-communal land use, as well as the role of such factors as family size and levels of indebtedness in shaping peasant decision-making about land use and other economic matters.[55] Like Shcherbina, N.F. Annenskii organized statistical investigations in Nizhnii Novgorod that included, but were not limited to, the assessment of land values. Arriving in Nizhnii after numerous arrests and years of political exile, Annenskii—like Chervinskii and Shcherbina—also required the investigators to be trained to live for a time in their "assigned" region so that they could provide guidance to the temporary assistants who interviewed peasant households in the various villages.

The research strategies of Chervinskii, Pokrovskii, Shcherbina, and Annenskii reflected an increasingly sophisticated grasp of the reaction to outsiders by illiterate or semiliterate research subjects who might be understandably wary of outsiders seeking detailed information about their economic lives. Using oral interviews as well as written questionnaires, they developed techniques of statistical sampling to deal with the large populations they were researching. With the aid and advice of academics like A.I. Chuprov, A.S. Posnikov, and A.A. Manuilov, these techniques were refined, revised, and revised again in the decades to come.

The "monographic" method of representative sampling that emerged in the course of zemstvo investigations required researchers to select a cluster of elements typical of a population, and deploy it as an adjunct to the complete enumeration used to determine the "typicality" of the elements to be sampled. Complete enumeration was the only method used to check the precision of the estimates obtained from such monographic samples. However, in cases where researchers were able to select reliable and useful "typical" elements, Chuprov proposed the use of monographic sampling as a useful independent means of investigation—not merely as an adjunct.[56]

The most influential and massive zemstvo statistical study of the post-Emancipation era was directed by V.I. Orlov, a priest's son, classmate of Chuprov at Moscow University, and teacher of statistics at the Alexandrovsk Military Academy until he was fired for his radical sympathies and arrested for his connection with the Balmashev affair. It was in Moscow province that Orlov embarked on the scholarly work to which he devoted his life. As bureau chief of the provincial zemstvo statistical board in 1876, he proved to be a gifted researcher, able to rapidly gather a wide range of statistical data and present them in comprehensible form. Among the men and women who became respected statistics researchers elsewhere after training with Orlov were the autodidact rural schoolteacher I.P. Bogolepov,[57] returned exile K.A. Verner, Chuprov's student N.A. Kablukov, as well as E.F. Fortunatov and A.A. Gorbunova.

Orlov and his assistants required field investigators to begin their work on a *volost* level by examining available documents on the conditions of agriculture and peasant life. They were directed to visit every village in the *volost* in order to gather an impression of the locality as a whole. In each village, the investigator asked peasants to call a meeting of the village *skhod* (an assembly comprised of the heads of all peasant households). Each of the householders present completed a two- to three-page questionnaire intended to gather a complex description of the village and its various households. In addition to questions about economic behavior, there were queries about education and medical care, and even—depending on the particular interests of the investigator—the books read and the names for land measurement in a particular locale.

Formy krestianskogo zemlevladeniia v moskovskoi gubernii [Forms of Peasant Landownership in Moscow Province] (1879), the landmark study that emerged from Orlov's investigations, became one of the most influential works of Russian economic research of the late nineteenth century.outside of Russia, it was praised by Karl Marx, and by the German economist–statistician Wilhelm Roscher; in a journal edited by the German *Verein* economist Adolf Wagner, Orlov's methodology and the richness of his data were described as "unequalled in Western literature."[58] Orlov's research methods became a model for investigators elsewhere in Russia. Zemstvo organizations in the provinces of Kursk, Voronezh, Samara, Tambov, and Orel turned to him for guidance and support in their efforts to establish statistical bureaus and research plans. In the 1880s, Orlov published the first data analyses for Kursk and Tambov, and helped Chuprov to establish a statistical section within the Moscow Juridical Society that became (1) a school for students interested in applied statistics, (2) an information clearing house, and (3) a source of guidelines for a comprehensive Empire-wide project for the statistical investigation of the agricultural economy.

By 1882, the government—torn between admiration for Orlov's work and hostility to his radicalism—decided to place research needs at the forefront, and invited him to direct the Central Statistical Committee of the Ministry of Internal Affairs. But Orlov refused to enter government service. Instead, he interceded with the governor of Samara in 1884 on behalf of K.E. Paprits, a statistician accused of "inciting" peasant rebellion.[59] In 1885, while participating in a Moscow regional meeting of zemstvo physicians, Orlov died of overwork at the age of 37. His successor was Chuprov's student N.A. Kablukov, who remained head of the Moscow zemstvo statistical bureau until 1907.

Zemstvo Statistical Findings: Poverty, Inequality,
and the Peasant Commune

A striking characteristic of late-nineteenth-century zemstvo statistics was the high priority given to the variations produced by particular social, economic, and institutional factors. Orlov, Chervinskii, and Shcherbina were particularly critical of the government's preference for the use of averages that lumped together the landed estates and peasant household allotments and treated all cultivators and owners as "profit-maximizers." Foreshadowing the major features of Chaianov's theory of a peasant economy that balanced production and consumption needs, they considered a wide range of economic issues— in addition to market factors—in their assessment of land values in the Russian countryside.[60]

An equally striking feature of late-nineteenth-century zemstvo statistics, and, as we shall see, a point of vulnerability in the eyes of their critics, was their general rejection of the notion that either class struggle or the development of capitalism were invariably the decisive factors in determining rural economic outcomes. In Voronezh province, the statistician F.A. Shcherbina contended that classifying peasants as rich or poor was difficult not because peasants enjoyed equal status, but because (1) definitions of wealth and poverty used by peasants and zemstvo statisticians differed so markedly, and (2) peasant definitions varied from region to region. To Shcherbina, it was not self-evident how a researcher was to weigh local assessments against his or her own assumptions about poverty and wealth.[61]

In some regions of the Empire, the amount of land per household was used to determine poverty levels, with investigators documenting the number of landless peasants, those with less than one *desiatina* of land, with one to three *desiatiny*, three to five *desiatiny*, and so on. At other times, the number of livestock owned by a peasant household was taken as the crucial index of material poverty or well-being—and as local inhabitants frequently pointed out, those who possessed larger allotments did not necessarily own larger numbers of livestock. In some areas, horse ownership served as the measure of wealth or poverty; in regions where oxen rather than horses generally pulled the plows, the ownership of oxen distinguished richer from poorer peasants. Those attempting to coordinate and compare zemstvo statistical findings noted with dismay that some bureaus recorded livestock ownership by counting sheep and pigs but not lambs and piglets and did not know that others were counting all livestock. Given the existence of such contradictory methods of categorizing data, it was difficult to assess the significance of the figures on livestock ownership.[62]

Clearly, zemstvo statisticians were in need of more consistent, Empire-wide categories for the assessment and evaluation of statistical findings. In 1882, when the government briefly relaxed its restrictions on mutual consultation by provincial zemstvo organizations, zemstvo statisticians attempted to render their strategies for data analysis more consistent with one another, so that a reliable basis for comparisons could be established. However, as more studies were completed, analytical challenges continued to multiply, as did the variety and scope of government constraints on zemstvo research efforts. N.A. Kablukov wrote of the Herculean labors of A.I. Chuprov, who began each morning at the Moscow Juridical Society by examining newly received statistical data, and spent the rest of the day and early evening analyzing its significance and writing summaries for the next day's discussion of ways to improve and systematize data collection and interpretation.[63]

In general, the zemstvo statistical data of the 1870s and 1880s revealed (1) mounting tax burdens and arrears in redemption payments that threatened the peasantry as a whole with economic disaster, (2) developing capitalism in the countryside, and (3) the survival of peasant communes. N. Romanov in Viatka, V.Ye. Postnikov in Ekaterinoslav and V.N. Grigoriev in Kursk documented in detail the plight of commune peasants whose poverty forced them to sell their land allotments. Romanov's study of three *uezdy* in Saratov province noted that peasant death rates were twice the level found among Swedish peasants of the 1870s. Zemstvo statistical studies documented the private ownership of tools and livestock within the commune framework, and demonstrated that the more prosperous could manipulate the decision-making process of village assemblies in order to exclude the poor and sometimes to deprive them of land. In a massive study that documented the record of rural innovation by peasants, the statistician V.V. Vorontsov noted the existence of economic inequalities within and outside the commune.[64]

Even the statistician Prugavin—whose conclusions were criticized by Orlov as excessively optimistic—did not claim that peasants as a whole were prospering.[65]

To many zemstvo statisticians, the most interesting research question was not whether inequality existed within the commune framework, but how to explain and analyze the origins of inequality and its implications for Russia's future development. N. Karyshev's research data indicated that the emergence of landless proletarians in the Russian countryside was a phenomenon of the 1850s, when serf owners, apprehensive about the terms of the approaching peasant emancipation, enlarged their properties by converting "possessional" into domestic, that is, landless serfs. F.A. Shcherbina documented the actions of wealthy serf owners who emancipated peasants with "beggarly" allotments of one-fourth *desiatina* per male, thus driving them into the ranks of the proletariat.[66] V.Ye. Postnikov emphasized the emergence of the kulak moneylender, who hired his indebted neighbors to work for him on rented land. Because Postnikov attributed rural inequality to the development of capitalism, Russia's Marxists considered his work particularly "scientific."[67] But it is worth noting that Postnikov himself did not believe that his data demonstrated the insuperable forward march of capitalism. His analysis of the data indicated instead that government policies disproportionately promoted and subsidized private entrepreneurs at the expense of other social groups and institutions in the Russian countryside.[68]

N.N. Chernenkov, a student of Orlov, drew from his investigations of Saratov province the conclusion that rural economic differences were a cyclical feature of commune life. His figures indicated that allotment size rose and fell with the various phases of a family's life cycle, particularly in the commune, which frequently distributed land according to family size. Thus, parents rich in land were those with many children, while the "wealthy" became land poor when their children married and claimed their own allotments. Chernenkov's statistical analysis suggested that inequalities were not signs of class formation; they were instead part of the cycle of growth and decline in the peasant household.[69]

The historical and statistical data analyses by Karyshev, Shcherbina, Postnikov, and Chernenkov during the last two decades of the nineteenth century each carried significantly different implications for Russia's future; but they were complicated as well by the continuing dilemmas posed by the data-gathering process itself. In most cases, reliable data had not been collected for a long enough time to permit meaningful generalizations about the dynamics and direction of change. Since statistical projects might last for as long as a decade, economic conditions could significantly alter before the research was completed. Data gathered at the outset might thus not be accurate by the time a project ended. Cycles of family growth and division, and the practice of periodic repartition also complicated the analysis of economic differences, since investigators who took a cross section of a village at a particular point in time might come away with a misleading or superficial picture of the actual socioeconomic relations of its members.

By the turn of the century, many of Russia's leading economists had concluded that zemstvo statistical research indicated (1) that capitalism was developing in the Russian countryside, and (2) that the peasantry's repartitional land communes were not dying out. Five out of seven professors of political economy and statistics at the University of St. Petersburg and four of Moscow University's economists believed that the data indicated that communes were capable of performing at least as well as private agricultural producers. However, like most zemstvo statisticians, they were far from certain that communes could continue to hold their own against government-subsidized entrepreneurs.[70]

"Terror" against the Data: The Danger of Inflammatory Numbers
Like every other aspect of zemstvo statistical research, the analysis of fieldwork data was exacerbated by a government fearful that both the statisticians and their findings might turn out to be revolutionary and subversive. Inconsistency in research methods and modes of tabulating results became increasingly unavoidable, as the government issued decrees that prohibited zemstvo bureaus from coordinating their activities or carrying out interprovincial research efforts. Statistical bureaus in Kursk, Kherson, and Riazan were repeatedly closed down during the 1870s. In 1879, when the Riazan bureau was closed, Grigoriev's four-volume collection of statistical data was confiscated and burned by the authorities. Not long afterward, complaints by conservative landowners resulted in the public burning of the research data carried out by K.A. Verner in Kursk province.[71] Fearing that their work might suffer a similar fate, zemstvo statisticians in Orel, Taurida, Tver, and Saratov provinces began to publish raw data before it could be destroyed by the authorities. With a zeal worthy of a character out of Nikolai Gogol's *Dead Souls*, provincial officials in Orel attempted to constrain their politically terrifying data collectors by issuing directives that expressly prohibited statisticians from communicating political opinions through "negative movements of the body" such as shrugs, winks, or facial expressions.[72]

Zemstvo statistical bureaus in Kherson, Chernigov, and Saratov—when they were not being closed down by government fiat—attempted to develop consistent standards for investigation, and formulas for the combination of economic variables that could permit the more systematic categorization of peasant households. But in 1888, government fears and prohibitions triumphed once more, as the Ministry of Internal Affairs disbanded the Samara statistical bureau and issued a circular requiring that all local studies be submitted to the Central Statistical Commission for prior approval. In addition, in order to forestall any discussion between statisticians and peasants of the national budget and its effects on the peasantry, the circular prohibited statistical bureaus from raising fiscal questions.[73] In 1893, a government commission staffed by government officials rather than statisticians was established to exercise greater supervision over *zemstvo* statistical research and researchers. Unable to endure restrictions that ranged from imprisonment, censorship, and destruction of data to prohibitions against negative "shrugs, winks and facial expressions," S.M. Bleklov and his entire staff resigned from the statistical bureau of Orel province in 1896.

Ideology Against the Data: "Populist" and Marxist Statistics
Ever since the late nineteenth century, a host of contemporary and later scholars, policy-makers, Marxist and non-Marxist activists and critics would argue that Russia's zemstvo statisticians were "populists" [*narodniki*]. This term has been deliberately omitted from the preceding discussion due to its peculiar history in the Russian context. The word "populist" was first intro-duced and popularized in the 1890s by Russian Marxists who were attempt-ing to position themselves as defenders of Science against a host of allegedly "subjective," "anti-Western," and "populist" zemstvo statisticians.[74]

Anti-populist arguments were quickly taken up by ideologues and policy-makers of both the Left and the Right, who were—for reasons that I have elsewhere described in detail[75]—equally happy to discover that the charge of "populism" could be used to dismiss the most unwelcome features of zem-stvo statistical data and data analysis. In the 1900s, a peculiar array of tsarist proponents of capitalism joined forces with Russia's Marxists to argue that capitalism and its promise for the future constituted the only factor worth examining in the Russian countryside. According to tsarist Finance Minister Witte and the Marxist V.I. Lenin, to doubt this single-factor explanation was to expose the doubter as a "subjectivist" committed to the Romantic propo-sition that Russia constituted an "exception" to the universal and scientific laws of development that governed the economic history of all other nations.[76]

While tsarist Minister of the Interior V.K. Plehve believed that the Russian peasant was at heart a capitalist *homo oeconomicus*,[77] Lenin marveled at

how far the main features of this general process in Western Europe and in Russia are identical, notwithstanding the tremendous peculiarities of the latter, in both the economic and non-economic spheres.[78]

Deploying what he judged to be the "best" of the zemstvo statistical data (and omitting those that contradicted his thesis), Lenin's book *The Development of Capitalism in Russia* (1899) advanced the quite dubious claim that Russia was already a wholly capitalist society where rural proletarians and kulaks were locked in a class struggle that would eventually produce a socialist revolution.[79] Although Lenin simply omitted the massive evidence that chal-lenged this shaky proposition from his book, his statistical analysis and con-clusions nevertheless garnered support among a wide range of readers predisposed to accept his capitalist economic determinism. On the other hand, the leading statisticians of his day criticized Lenin's superficial familiar-ity with relevant primary sources and his arbitrary selection of data to support a particular Marxist thesis.[80]

In 1905, when Russia's first twentieth-century revolution broke out and new political opportunities beckoned, Lenin's statistical analysis underwent a sudden transformation. Now convinced that the evidence demonstrated beyond question that Russian agriculture was predominantly precapitalist and "feudal," Lenin contended that a capitalist economic transformation was still in the offing.[81] When his newly minted categorical assertions were challenged by the statistician P.A.Vikhliaev's voluminous statistical data, Lenin triumphantly accused Vikhliaev of being "mired in detail."[82] Criticism of the zemstvo statisticians for a "fetishism of numbers"—together with the baseless claim that Lenin was in fact the founder of modern Russian and Soviet statistics—subsequently became a staple of twentieth-century Soviet scholarship.[83]

In considering the question of "subjectivism" levied against zemstvo statisticians by Lenin and by state capitalist reformers within the tsarist regime, one may easily establish that they—like other researchers—began their investigations with a particular set of prior values and assumptions. Investigators like Chernenkov, Orlov, and Postnikov possessed more or less hopeful, and quite humane attitudes toward peasants, and neutral to positive views of the ubiquitous peasant commune. However, it is useful to consider whether these predispositions rendered their statistical findings and analyses any more questionable than did the equally powerful predisposition of Marxists and state capitalists to believe that peasants and communes were destined for elimination by the ineluctable forces of advancing capitalism. The quite serious imperfections featured in many other historical, institutional, and economic data sources—those published by the tsarist regime's central administration, for example—have frequently been more easily tolerated than those that were categorized as "populist."

In my own scholarly experience,[84] the word "populist" has carried so much pejorative ideological baggage, that is, to be populist was to be sentimental, reactionary, irrational, anti-Western, and so forth—that it has served as a barrier rather than an aid to understanding or research. Unfortunately, the appeal of the "populist" stereotype has been quite successful in deflecting scholarly attention away from a massive body of statistical data and analysis that would in my view generously repay further study. The categorization of zemstvo statistics as "populist" data has in many instances been sufficient to deter scholars from undertaking a comprehensive and systematic survey of one of the largest databases ever compiled on a peasant population.

Once we set aside the populist stereotype, it becomes clear that the dominant research hypothesis deployed by most zemstvo statisticians was not the supposed "sanctity" of peasants or their communes, but, rather, the proposition that Russia's economic future was not predetermined. This argument recurs throughout the writings of Russia's zemstvo statisticians and professional economists (and surfaced as well in the final commentaries of Karl Marx on the complexities of the Russia case).[85] In the years to come, as zemstvo statistical findings became a bone of contention in a bitter debate on development, this agnostic stance became for Marxist and state capitalist critics the distinguishing mark of "subjective populism"—a proof that zemstvo statisticians were determined to deny the "laws of history."

A CONCLUSION AND COMPARATIVE NOTE

Although the terrorist government tactics used against zemstvo statisticians may have been peculiarly "Russian," the formidable methodological problems encountered by field investigators were not. Chuprov, Orlov, Kablukov, and their colleagues repeatedly expressed frustration about inconsistency and contradictoriness of questions, categories and modes of data analysis, and their nineteenth-century Western European contemporaries did the same. It was commonplace for European statisticians to complain that field researchers were woefully lacking in theoretical preparation, and to accuse academics of constructing elaborate theoretical models without benefit of empirical data.

Neither in England or Germany were the boundaries between the "professional" and the "activist" very clear-cut. In 1877, conflicts over the political motivations, inconsistent categories, and unreliable data of British statisticians became so heated that the president of the British Association for the Advancement of Science proposed that the entire Statistics Section be expelled from the association for being "insufficiently scientific."[86] Eventually, a number of more activist/social scientist/reformers created the London School of Economics as a venue for their more explicitly "engaged" scholarly research. In Germany, for reasons already indicated, the reception of scholar/activists was especially positive. In general, Bismarck and his successors were delighted with the notion that a benevolent and paternalistic government could best deploy the statistics produced by social scientists who were—in many instances—the government's most loyal supporters.

If we consider the Russian case in a broader context, it may be fair to say that during the post-Emancipation era, a host of "political undesirables" compiled a rich and massive body of empirical research on the Russian countryside, and devised research and methodological strategies that prefigured by half a century the methodological advances achieved by social scientists elsewhere who engaged in the study of nonelite populations. On the other hand, as their critics rightly pointed out, zemstvo statisticians failed utterly to develop a coherent and comprehensive framework for the analysis and prediction of the economic behavior that they researched. No system or general theory emerged from their empirical work. This failing, together with the appeal of Leninist polemics to educated Russians across the ideological spectrum, contributed to the long-term neglect of "populist" data and data analysis.

During the late nineteenth and early twentieth centuries, applied statistics was everywhere becoming a more systematic and regularized set of procedures. In this worldwide process, Russia's radical statisticians were leading participants, and among the foremost inheritors of the Enlightenment's double message with respect to the "Sciences of Humanity." Far from neutral in relation to their research subjects, their belief that scientific methods and analysis reinforced and accelerated the pursuit of social justice raised complex questions about the virtues and pitfalls of engaged scholarship. Although they have been described as "romantics" on the peasant question, it may be fairer to say that Russia's zemstvo statisticians were in fact "romantics" about the transformative power of the social sciences.

NOTES

1. Martin Shaw and Ian Miles, "The Social Roots of Statistical Knowledge," Martin Shaw and Ian Miles, eds., *Demystifying Social Statistics* (London: Pluto Press, 1979), 31.
2. M.J. Cullen, *The Statistical Movement in Early Victorian Britain: The Foundation of Empirical Social Research* (New York: Barnes & Noble, 1975), ll.
3. Philip Abrams, *The Origins of British Sociology: 1834–1914* (Chicago: University of Chicago Press, 1968), 9.
4. Quoted in Viktor Hilts, "Aliis exterendum, or the Origins of the Statistics Society of London," *Isis* 69, no.246 (March 1978): 27.
5. Quoted in Cullen, *Statistical Movement*, 84.
6. Quoted in Hilts, "Aliis exterendum," 24.
7. Ibid., 27.
8. Mark Blaug, *Ricardian Economics* (Westport, CT: Greenwood Press, 1973), 15 and Blaug, *Economic Theory in Retrospect* (New York: Cambridge University Press, 1968), 667.
9. Cullen, *Statistical Movement*, 135.
10. Theodore Porter, *Rise of Statistical Thinking 1820–1900* (Princeton: Princeton University Press, 1986), 27.
11. Abrams, *Origins*, 32.
12. It has been suggested that neither conscience nor a commitment to statistics would have resulted in Charles Booth's massive study, *The Life and Labor of the People in London*, if Booth had not been very rich. Abrams, *Origins*, 33–38.
13. Porter, *Rise*, 3–4.
14. Ibid., 35–36.
15. Abrams, *Origins*, 8–20.
16. In general, those troubled by this issue also feared that too great a focus on empirical data would lead to a devaluing of the crucial importance of scientific theory and theoretical understanding. Lawrence Goldman, "The Origins of British Social Science: Political Economy, Natural Science and Statistics, 1830–1835," *Historical Journal* 6 (1983): 609.
17. Gerard Koot, *English Historical Economics 1870–1926: The Rise of Economic History and Neomercantilism* (New York: Cambridge University Press, 1987), 20.
18. Cullen, *Statistical Movement*, 79.
19. Ibid., 83.
20. Goldman, "The Origins," 614.
21. Quetelet also devised the concept of the "average man" (derived by calculating the means and distribution of key physical and moral characteristics in particular social groups, regions, and nations). See David Landau and Paul Lazarsfeld, "Adolphe Quetelet," *International Encyclopedia of the Social Sciences*, vol. 13, 247–257.
22. Quoted in Porter, *Rise*, 46–47.
23. M.V. Ptukha, *Ocherki po istorii statistiki v SSSR* (Moscow: Izd. Akademii nauk, 1959), 111, and N.K. Karataev, *Russkaia ekonomicheskaia mysl' v period krizisa feodal'nogo khoziaistva* (Moscow: Izd. Moskovskogo Universiteta, 1957), 72–74.

24. Vernadskii is a significant but curiously neglected figure in Russian intellectual history. See *Politicheskoe ravnovesie i Angliia* (Moscow: Univ. Tip., 1855), and brief discussion in Esther Kingston-Mann, "In the Light and Shadow of the West: The Impact of Western Economics in Pre-Emancipation Russia," *Comparative Studies in Society and History* 33, no.1 (1991): 86–105, and Kingston-Mann, *In Search of the True West: Culture, Economics and Problems of Russian Development* (Princeton: Princeton University Press, 1999), 95–97.

25. N.K. Karataev, *Ekonomicheskie nauki v Moskovskom universitete, 1755–1955* (Moscow: Izd. Moskovskogo Universiteta, 1956), 93.

26. See general discussion in Ulla Schafer, *Historische Nationaloekonomie und Sozialstatistik als Gesellschaftswissenschaften* (Vienna: Bohlau, 1971), and G. Eisermann, *Die Grundlagen des Historismus in der deutschen Nationaloekonomie* (Stuttgart: F. Enke, 1956). Among the English-language scholarly works to address the economics *methodenstreit* in recent decades are D.C. Coleman, *History and the Economic Past: An Account of the Rise and Decline of Economic History* (Oxford: Oxford University Press, 1987), and Alon Kadish, *Historians, Economists and Economic History* (New York: Routledge, 1989).

27. English-language studies of German historical economics are rare. See William Cherin, "The German Historical School of Economics: A Study in Methodology of the Social Sciences." Ph.D. diss. (University of California at Berkeley, 1933) and Nicholas Balabkins, *Not By Theory Alone: The Economics of Gustav von Schmoller and his Legacy to America* (Berlin: Duncker and Humblot, 1988).

28. Although Verein economists shared a belief in the importance of what they called "the social question," they differed markedly in their proposed solutions. See Dieter Lindenlaub, *Richtungskampfe in Verein fur Sozialpolitik* (Wiesbaden: F. Steiner, 1967), Kenneth Barkin, *The Controversy over German Industrialization 1880–1902* (Chicago: University of Chicago Press, 1970), 138–147, and Woodruff Smith, *The Ideological Origins of Nazi Imperialism* (New York: Oxford University Press, 1986), 21–30.

29. Far more than is usually recognized, both the methods and content of classical Marxism were powerfully influenced by the *methodenstreit*, and particularly by the institutional and historical focus of Roscher, Hildebrand, and Knies. Marx's own challenge to classical liberalism economics is quite consistent with the broader historical traditions of German economic thought. See discussion of the intersections of Russian and German thought in Kingston-Mann, *In Search*, 117–118.

30. See B.N. Chicherin, "Die Leibeigenschaft in Russland," *Deutsche-Staats-worterbuch* 6 (Stuttgart, 1861): 393–411 and K.D. Kavelin "Einiges über die russische Dorfgemeinde," *Tübingen Zeitschrift*1, (1864): 1–53. Kavelin's essay "Obshchinnoe vladenie" (1876) was translated into German and published in book form as *Der bauerliche Gemeindebesitz in Russland* (Leipzig: F.A. Brockhaus, 1877).

31. Roscher was particularly impressed by Kavelin's article in the *Tubingen Zeitschrift*. See general discussion in Roscher "Die Deutsch-Russische Schule der Nationaloekonomik," *Berichte über die Verhandlungen der koniglich Sachsischen Gesellschaft der Wissenschaften zu Leipzig Philologisch-Historische Klasse* 22 (1870): 139–180.

32. Karataev, *Ekonomicheskie nauki*, 115–116.

33. I.I. Kudritskii *S"ezd sel'skikh khoziaev v Sankt Peterburge v 1865* (St. Petersburg: Tip. T-va "obshchestvennaia pol'za," 1866), 195–196, and *Trudy Imperatorskogo ekonomicheskogo obshchestva* 1 (February 1866): 316.

34. Quoted in S. Frederick Starr, *Decentralization and Self-Government in Russia, 1833–1870* (Princeton: Princeton University Press, 1972), 261.

35. S.M. Bleklov, *Travaux statistique des zemstvo russe* (Paris, 1893), 15.
36. Foreign observers like Emile de Laveleye, Paul Leroy-Beaulieu, the German scholar Christian Walcher, and the British journalist Donald Mackenzie Wallace criticized the Valuev Commission for the arbitrariness of its conclusions and its failure to invite direct peasant testimony. See discussion of Wallace's view in Kingston-Mann, *In Search* 169–170 and the careful analysis of the Valuev investigations in Steven Grant, *The Peasant Commune in Russian Thought, 1861–1905*, Ph.D. diss. (Harvard, 1973), 192–272.
37. L.I. Kuchumova, "Iz istoriia obsledovaniia sel'skoi pozemel'noi obshchiny v 1887–1880 godakh," *Istoriia SSSR* 3 (1978): 115–127.
38. I am indebted to Robert Johnson for his generous, long-ago sharing of biographical data on individual zemstvo statisticians. See Robert Johnson, "Liberal Professionals and Professional Liberals: The Zemstvo Statisticians and Their Work," W.S. Vucinich and T. Emmons, eds., *The Zemstvo in Russia: An Experiment in Local Self-government* (Cambridge: Cambridge University Press, 1982), 343–363. An extremely valuable discussion that illuminates the relationship between zemstvo statistical findings and the expectations of the tsarist regime is David Darrow, "The Politics of Numbers: Zemstvo Land Assessment and the Conceptualization of Russia's Rural Economy," *Russian Review* 59, no.1 (2000): 52–75. Useful surveys include N.A. Svavitskii, *Zemskie podvornye perepisi:Obzor metodologii* (Moscow: Gosstatizdat, 1961); A.A. Kaufman, "The History and Development of Official Russian Statistics," in John Koren, ed., *The History of Statistics: Their Development and Progress in Many Countries* (New York: Macmillan, 1918), 520–531; and A.A. Rusov, *Kratkii obzor razvitiia otsenochnoi statistiki* (Kiev, 1913).
39. Belokonskii was himself a zemstvo statistician exiled to Siberia for his connection with the revolutionary organization *Zemlia i Volia*. See I.P. Belokonskii, *V gody bespraviia* (Moscow: Izd. Vses. Ob-va Politkatorzhan i Ssyl'no-poselentsev, 1930), 43.
40. Kaufman made this argument in 1894 at the Ninth Congress of Naturalists and Physicians. See Z.M. Svavitskaia, "Moskovskii universitet i zemskaia statistika," *Ocherki po istorii statistiki SSSR*, 2 (Moscow: Izd. Akademii Nauk, 1957), 99, 101.
41. Like Ivan Vernadskii, Chuprov and the other Western-trained Russian social scientists responsible for the emergence of zemstvo statistics, are curiously neglected figures in Russian intellectual history. Kingston-Mann, *In Search*, 127–132 and the tendentious but useful Soviet account by Karataev, *Ekonomicheskie nauki*, 115–116.
42. In Russia, the practices traditionally associated with the English commons were far more pronounced in the peasantry's traditional, repartitional land communes. Although hereditary (*podvornoe*) tenure prevailed in the western regions of the Russian Empire and some parts of the south, the distinction between communal and *podvornoe* tenure was frequently problematic, because both usually featured the communal use of pasture and forest lands. See Steven Grant, "Obshchina i Mir," *Slavic Review* 35, no.4 (1976): 636–651.
43. Svavitskaia, "Moskovskii universitet," 61–77.
44. "Predislovie" by the influential statistician–economist N.A. Kablukov in Chuprov, *Rechi i stat'i* (Moscow: Izd. Sabashnikovykh, 1909), xxxvi–xxxvii.
45. It is useful to contrast the stance of Grigoriev and Verner with the English statisticians of the 1830s who were reluctant to take on such tasks.
46. Darrow, "The Politics of Numbers," 60.

47. V.V. Veselovskii and Z.G. Frenkel, *Iubileinyi zemskii sbornik* (St. Petersburg: Izd. Popovoi, 1914), 346–348.

48. Vera Romanova Leikina-Svirskaia, *Intelligentsiia v Rossii vo vtoroi polovine xix veka* (Moscow: Mysl', 1971), 209–210.

49. V.V. Veselovskii, *Istoriia zemstva za 40 let* (St. Petersburg: Izd. Popovoi, 1909–11), 1: 81–83.

50. I.P. Belokonskii, *Dan vremeni* (Moscow: Zadruga, 1918), 79–80.

51. Z. Tverdova-Svavitskaia, *Zemskie podvornye perepisi 1880–1913* (Moscow: Ts.SU SSSR, 1926), 117–118. In Kherson province, research was suspended after zemstvo statisticians revealed massive evidence of gentry tax evasion; see Robert Johnson, "Liberal Professionals," 345–346, 353–354.

52. See, e.g., the discussion of investigation methods in P.P. Chervinskii (Chernigovets), "Tri programmy dlia izucheniia obshchiny," *Nedelia* 36 (1878): cols 1164–1173; N.M. Astyrev, "K voprosu ob organizatsii tekushchei zemskoi statistiki," *Russkaia Mysl'* 5 (1887): 43–60; and Bleklov, *Travaux statistique*, 21–22.

53. See Chris Argyris, "Diagnosing Defenses against the Outsider," in G. McCall and J.L. Simmons, eds., *Issues in Participant Observation* (New York: Random House, 1969), 114–127, and L. Schatzman and Anselm Straus, eds., "Strategies for Seeing," *Field Research: Strategies for a Natural Sociology* (Englewood Cliffs, NJ: Prentice-Hall, 1973), 18–33.

54. Bleklov, *Travaux statistique*, 44.

55. Shcherbina was a particularly gifted researcher, whose investigation of Voronezh province made use of methods of representative sampling that did not become widespread elsewhere for more than a quarter of a century. Elvira Wilbur, commentary at First International Conference on the Peasantry of European Russia, Boston, 1986. See also discussion in Veselovskii and Frenkel, *Iubileinyi*, 62.

56. According to the statistician Eugene Seneta, writing in 1985 about Chuprov's approach to statistics: "This is a pioneering notion, but because of the last proviso, not a finalized concept, since the selection of typical elements may then be grounded on subjective considerations, and no measure of precision is possible." Seneta, "Sketch of the History of Survey Sampling in Russia," *Journal of the Royal Statistical Society* A (1985): 148, part 2, 120.

57. Bogolepov possessed little formal education, but eventually authored a highly praised monograph on one of the most poverty-stricken villages in Moscow province. Svavitskaia, *Zemskie podvornye*, p. 80.

58. N.A. Kablukov, "Russkie issledovaniia," *Russkaia Mysl'* (1881), 428–429.

59. In contrast, P.P. Chervinskii and I.P. Belokonskii would later attain prominent positions as statisticians within the tsarist bureaucracy. See discussion in R.A. Eidelman, "Russkii zemskii statistik V.I. Orlova," *Ocherki po istorii statistiki SSSR*, 4 (Moscow, 1961), 22.

60. See A.A. Rusov, *Kratkii obzor*, 5, and A.V. Chaianov, "On the Theory of Non-Capitalist Economic Systems" in Daniel Thorner, Basile Kerblay, and R.E.F. Smith, eds., *A.V. Chayanov on the Theory of Peasant Economy* (Madison, WI: University of Wisconsin Press, 1986), and especially Teodor Shanin, *The Awkward Class: Political Sociology of Peasantry in a Developing Society, Russia 1910–1925* (Oxford: Clarendon Press, 1974).

61. Elvira Wilbur's study of Shcherbina's work on Voronezh province highlights the contrast between poverty as defined by peasants and by Lenin and other Marxist commentators. See "The Faces of Poverty in Voronezh Province," Esther

Kingston-Mann and Timothy Mixter, *Peasant Economy, Culture and Politics* (Princeton: Princeton University Press, 1991), 101–127.

62. See general discussion in Kingston-Mann, "Peasant Communes," 40–45.

63. Kablukov, "Predislovie," xxvi.

64. See especially V.P. Vorontsov, *Progressivnye techeniia v krestianskom khoziaistve* (St. Petersburg, 1892), 25–27.

65. V.S. Prugavin, "Sel'skaia zemel'naia obshchina v povolzhskom krae," *Iuridicheskii Vestnik* no.5 (1885): 91–119, and *Russkaia zemel'naia obshchina v trudakh ee mestnykh issledovatelei* (Moscow, 1888), and V.P. Vorontsov, "Ocherki obshchinnago zemlevladeniia v Rossii," *Otechestvennye Zapiski*, 1 (1882): 211–250; 3 (1882): 83–111; 4 (1882): 331–364.

66. See N. Karyshev, "Krest'ianskoe zemledelie i obshchina v khersonskoi gubernii," *Russkoe Bogatstvo*, 2 (1895): 40 and Shcherbina, *Russkaia Mysl'*, 12 (1880): 58.

67. See discussion in Esther Kingston-Mann, *Lenin and the Problem of Marxist Peasant Revolution* (New York: Oxford University Press, 1983), 48.

68. V.E. Postnikov, *Iuzhno-russkoe krest'ianskoe khoziaistvo* (Moscow: I.N. Kushnerev, 1891).

69. N.N. Chernenkov, *K kharakteristike krest'ianskogo khoziaistva* (Moscow: Russkoe Tovarichestvo, 1905). According to the statistician K.R. Kachorovskii, Chernenkov was the first to focus on this cyclical process. See "The Russian Land Commune in History and Today," *Slavonic and East European Review* 7, no.21 (1929): 565–576. In the late nineteenth century, N.A. Kablukov and A.V. Peshekhonov published research and analysis along similar lines, which fore-shadowed the post-1905 work of A.V. Chaianov's "Organization and Production School." See N.A. Kablukov, *Lektsii po ekonomii sel'skago khoziaistva* (Moscow, 1897) and general discussion in Maureen Perrie, "A Worker in Disguise: A.V. Peshekhonov's Contribution to the Debate on the Peasantry at the Turn of the Century," Colloquium on Russian Social and Economic History 1860–1930, in honour of Olga Crisp (London, 1987).

70. See general discussion in the extraordinarily valuable but unpublished work of Steven Grant, "The Peasant Commune in Russian thought, 1861–1905," Ph.D. diss. (Harvard University, 1973), 334–336.

It is worth noting as well that after 1917, the former Marxist economist M.I. Tugan Baranovskii came to agree with this analysis of the zemstvo statistical data. *Osnovy politicheskoi ekonomii*, 5th edition (Petrograd: Pravo, 1918), 188–192.

71. Belokonskii, *V gody bespraviia*, 116.

72. Ibid., 51.

73. Veselovskii, *Istoriia*, vol. 3, 302, and Veselovskii and Frenkel, *Iubileinyi*, 273.

74. See Richard Pipes, "Russian Marxism and Its Populist Background: The Late Nineteenth Century," *The Russian Review* 19, no.4, (October, 1960): 316–377 and *Struve: Liberal on the Left* (Cambridge: Harvard University Press, 1970), 85. For a perspective quite sympathetic to Lenin's judgment on "populists" as anti-Western reactionaries, see the writings of Andrzej Walicki, and in particular, *The Controversy over Capitalism: Studies in the Social Philosophy of the Russian Populists* (Notre Dame: Notre Dame University Press, 1989), 2–3.

75. See Kingston-Mann, *Lenin*.

76. For tsarist Finance Minister Witte, capitalism represented the high point and culmination of Russia's economic development. To Lenin and his supporters, capitalism represented an essential prerequisite for proletarian socialist revolution. See discussion in Kingston-Mann, "Deconstructing the Romance of the

Bourgeoisie: A Russian Marxist Path Not Taken," *Review of International Political Economy* 10, no.1 (2003): 102–106.

77. David Macey, *Government and Peasant in Russia, 1861–1906: The Prehistory of the Stolypin Reforms* (DeKalb: Northern Illinois University Press, 1987), 37.

78. V.I. Lenin, *Polnoe sobranie sochinenii*, 5th edition (Moscow: Gos. Izd. Polit. Lit., 1971–1975), vol. 3, 7.

79. Kingston-Mann, *Lenin*, 49–50.

80. See, e.g., K.R. Kachorovskii, *Bor'ba za zemliu* (St. Petersburg: Tip. D. P. Veisborg, 1908), xlviii.

81. For a detailed discussion of Lenin's shifting analysis, see Kingston-Mann, *Lenin*, 48–54.

82. Ibid., 49–50.

83. Articles on Lenin's contribution to statistics made a yearly appearance in *Vestnik Statistiki*, the official monthly journal of the Soviet Central Statistical Administration (renamed in 1987 the State Committee on Statistics) usually in the April issue to coincide with Lenin's birthday. In 1958, it was even asserted that Lenin had established the foundations of contemporary statistical science. See E. Seneta "Lenin as a Statistician: a Non-Soviet View," *Journal of the Royal Statistical Society* A (1990), 153, Part 1, 73, and especially V. Ovsienko, "Sozdanie osnov sovremennoi statisticheskoi nauki y trudakh V.I. Lenina," *Nauch. Dokl. Vyss. Shk. Ekonom. Nauk*, no.2 (Moscow, 1958).

84. See, e.g., Kingston-Mann, "Marxism and Russian Rural Development: Problems of Evidence, Experience and Judgement," *American Historical Review*, 1981, 731–752. "Peasant Communes and Rural Innovation," and "Transforming Peasants: Dilemmas of Russian, Soviet and Post-Soviet Development, 1900–2000," *Cambridge Modern History of Russia*, ed., Ronald Suny, forthcoming, Cambridge University Press, 2005.

85. Kingston-Mann, *In Search* 137–138. As historian Richard Pipes long ago observed, "No prominent economist or even publicist of this era was so naïve as to believe that Russia was immune to capitalism, for signs of its penetration were visible everywhere . . . The prevailing view held that Russia had a mixed economy in which two systems—'capitalism' and 'popular production'—were locked in mortal combat. The outcome of the battle depended on the government." Pipes, *Struve: Liberal on the Left*, 39.

86. Koot, *The English Historical Economists*, 113.

9

"The Temple of Idleness": Associations and the Public Sphere in Provincial Russia

A Case Study of Saratov, 1800–1917

Lutz Häfner

In Russia, defined estates with corporate rights did not exist until the era of Catherine the Great. Even then, the autocracy had a deep abiding suspicion of corporative structures, not to mention social organizations, and acted to prevent their rise. By contrast, late-eighteenth-century German society simultaneously experienced a decline of corporative entities, a growth of individualism, and general emancipation. Associations filled the emerging organizational vacuum.[1] Three decades ago, the historian Dietrich Geyer pointed to these categorical differences between the social constitutions of old Europe and Russia. Russia lacked the West European dualism of state and society. In his view, state and society did not drift apart and consequently society [*obshchestvo*] was an artifact of the autocracy. The function of the collective of subjects ruled from above exhausted itself in the formation of the state. Nor did the local noble and urban societies created by Catherine II emancipate themselves.[2] Indeed, they possessed no political character. Geyer characterized this constellation as " 'society' as a state event."[3]

These peculiarities shaped the social development of the urban bourgeoisie and, for that matter, of the entire tsarist empire until the 1917 revolutions. Still, it would not do to exaggerate the phenomenon. The long nineteenth century witnessed significant change in Russia. Admittedly, until perhaps the early twentieth century few inhabitants of tsarist society professed the self-reflexive desire "to be a citizen," as Theodor Mommsen put it about many of the German Empire's inhabitants.[4] Yet, numerous examples evoked the ideal of the *obshchestvennyi deiatel'*—a socially active person committed to the common welfare.[5] This social actor, however, lacked citizen's rights and instead derived his identity from his ancestral living place. His experience and scope of action concerned the town and its "local society." Even so, toward the end of the nineteenth century a process of group formation among urban elites and, a few years later, other city dwellers occurred. This development allows us to assert with confidence the establishment of common European forms in Russia.[6] Russia's rapid advance in trans-regional communications notwithstanding, the final breakthrough to a bourgeois society either did not occur prior to 1917, or did so only weakly. Separate local societies had not yet combined into one nationally dominant society. What about local societies?

The advantage of focusing on "local societies," as opposed to utilizing current concepts of social change associated with bourgeois and civil society on a national level, lies in the fact that in Russia many phenomena existed in small-scale geographic units. Largely lacking trans-regional networks and platforms, these phenomena developed nationally only in a rudimentary form. This applies especially to oral communication and social interaction within associations. They were institutionalized in the local context, but hardly in a national one. The focus on smaller units of social self-organization brings into view the specifics of Russian history and facilitates analysis of important groups of social actors. "Local society" [*mestnoe obshchestvo*][7] is a term that occurs frequently in historical sources about the inhabitants of a specific area or town. Thus, as a category of analysis, it is less cumbersome than the term "bourgeoisie" and its compounds, which originate from a different linguistic, social, economic, and cultural framework. A further advantage lies in its ideological neutrality and its abandonment of normative concepts tied to Western societies.[8]

As regards Western and Central Europe, the German sociologist M. Rainer Lepsius urged research on the concrete processes of constitutionalization in relation to the bourgeoisie's heterogeneity and changes on the basis of intertemporal and intercultural comparisons. This approach makes possible precise statements about the bourgeoisie's impact on the shaping of structures. This essay transfers this approach to Russia,[9] while at the same time paying attention to Peter Kenez's caveat: "Our terms for describing social classes and groups come from Western European experience, and we apply these concepts to Russian history because we have no better ones. At the same time historians are aware that these terms only imperfectly fit the Russian situation."[10] In the presence of perceived shortcomings of bourgeois social formation in Russia, developmental tendencies of Western societies become implicit yardsticks. Commentators portray Russian history as a sequence of omissions, degenerative phenomena, and misguided developments, often in association with alleged insufficient reflection upon, imitation of, or derivation from Western institutions. This deprivation hypothesis of Russia's historical development argues from the negative. The lack of the Renaissance, of humanism and the Reformation, of Roman law and the estates, of municipal laws and the bourgeoisie all express "Russian deviation" from the "Western-occidental norm." Even a formulation such as "later than in Western Europe" (sometimes used in this essay) is an invidious comparison. Till now, however, the categories listed above have served as absolute norms. Against a positive self-image, Western authors employ a binary argumentative structure that posits Russia's deficient, alien, and backward historical development.[11]

How and to what extent did local units, functional equivalents of the bourgeois societies of Western Europe, take shape in a pre-political context in Russia during the second half of the nineteenth century? To answer this question, it is necessary to examine local individuals' involvement in processes of association [*Vergesellschaftung*] and communalization [*Vergemeinschaftung*]. Communalization "is based on a subjective feeling of belonging together." Association differs in referring to the forming of organizations, an activity that rests on shared values and on taking social actions motivated by common or complementary interests.[12] The category of sociability is central for this latter mode of social interaction. As Georg Simmel put it, sociability is "a mode of association" that suspends the social conditionality of the life world. It follows the constant anthropological factor to associate and is based mainly on communication.[13]

Examining life within associations has the advantage of being able to describe an ensemble of heterogeneous social formations in a concrete social space as a unit of actions and experiences. In Russia, the intermediate social sphere that we call associations, situated between the family on the one hand and state, municipality, and church on the other, gained considerable quantitative and qualitative importance during the long nineteenth century. The Moscow Businessmen's Club 1914 centennial commemorative volume explained: "In our time, clubs play such a significant role in Russian urban social life that their history is of a very great interest."[14] The historian Komissarenko has asserted that in Russia, too, the nineteenth century was the "century of clubs."[15]

This study's thesis is that associations, with all their social, political, and cultural implications, were central institutions in the formation of local society. The following examination is divided into five sections: (1) the legal determinants and historical development of the associations; (2) the social and ethnic structure of the members of the associations; (3) the daily life of the associations; (4) the politicization of the associations; and, finally, (5) the social significance of the associations.

LEGAL DETERMINANTS AND HISTORICAL DEVELOPMENT OF THE ASSOCIATIONS

Bourgeois society's associations display different characteristics than the older nonvoluntary estate corporations. They represent a basic institution of structural change in the public sphere.[16] The main characteristics of associations are: voluntary participation on the basis of shared (nonprofit) interests; a tendency toward nonexclusiveness; equality of members; and similarities and connections of the members in their joint socializing. Russian associations, as elsewhere, provided members space to spend free time together in a pleasant, useful, and "rational" way.[17] To this end, the associations opened their doors all year except for a few holidays. They offered games, balls, and masquerades, as well as musical evenings, dances, plays, readings, and lectures. They emphasized good conversation and, in connection with their stress on educational standards, purchased books and subscribed to periodicals.[18]

Most associations had charitable commitments.[19] Consequently, they collected money for local orphanages and schools and, in a broader framework, for war victims, natural catastrophes, and famines.[20] These social commitments reflected motivations of general charitableness and generosity, but also demonstrated that self-initiative could alleviate social grievances. Such activities originated in society's self-organization. Moreover, charity allowed women to step out of the family sphere into the public and thereby become important social actors. These developments opened a space for social initiative to fill functions neglected by the state.[21]

The organizations' claims to membership were not entirely accurate. First, no gender equality existed in the purely social associations. Except for balls and family evenings, these associations were masculine preserves.[22] Only shortly before World War I did women begin to penetrate the bastion of social associations.[23] Meanwhile, women had already entered certain charitable, artistic, and educational associations, whose functions differed somewhat from the social organizations.[24] Second, the social associations in effect excluded lower class members, who could hardly afford admission and membership fees and lacked the necessary leisure. The large Saratov social associations such as the Assembly of Nobles, the Society of the Friends of Horse Racing, the Aero-Club, and the Saratov Commercial Assembly charged a 15-ruble annual membership fee.[25] By 1905, only 400,000 people in the entire Russian Empire earned 1,000 rubles or more a year.[26] The Saratov physician A.E. Romanov regarded this income as a minimum to feed a family appropriately and live according to one's social standing, including membership in an association.[27] Furthermore, one could join an association only on the recommendation of the members. Admittedly, these modalities fortified the outer boundaries, but they also promoted the members' feeling of belonging together, itself an equalizing factor.

By defining their own goals and promoting them, the members participated in society's self-organization. The association movement also contained an unstated subproject of antimonarchical utopian liberalism. The associations' salient characteristics—equality, self-funding, majority decisions after rational discourse, election of leaders, external representation, rotation of offices, accountability to and control by members—evoke a *republic*. They were a new type of social organization that helped shape the bourgeois way of life. With reference to Alexis de Tocqueville, the associations functioned as nurseries of self-government and democracy.[28]

Foreigners, especially Germans and Englishmen, played an extraordinary role in the founding of associations during the late eighteenth and early nineteenth centuries. As in the case of the Saratov German Club (1840), foreigners served as a bridge by applying their ideas about associations to Russia.[29] Within the Russian Empire, Poland had a high density of associations. In their functions, the Russian associations did not differ from their Western equivalents. Only the reading society, typical of Germany, remained a marginal phenomenon due to high illiteracy rates, the low production of books, and rigid censorship. In Germany, sport and gymnastic societies, admittedly with national goals, emerged during the second decade of the nineteenth century, whereas they arose later in Russia.[30] The absence of codified rights for associations and assemblies meant that until the new post-1905 regulations, local authorities decided every request for an organizational permit individually, a process that hindered the rapid spread of associations. As in the area of the public press, numerous applications failed. *Quod licet Iovi, non licet bovi* (what was licit for elites was illicit for everyone else).[31] The ministries also promoted high membership fees as barriers against politically undesirable elements. Analogously, only elite associations normally got the right to establish libraries.[32]

One mid-nineteenth-century foreign visitor commented that, "in winter in the provincial cities, noble and businessmen's associations hold balls and assemblies . . . . A game of cards in the evening and a merry little dance every week . . ."[33] In Saratov, at least, the local Assembly of Nobles, plagued by declining membership, barely managed to stay afloat and, after the 1905 revolution, disappeared.[34] Meanwhile, the Commercial Assembly (1860) enjoyed much greater success, a telling comment on local social mores.[35] Both associations represented the estate principle, limiting membership respectively to noblemen and businessmen. Persons outside those categories could attend functions only with guest status.[36] During the early 1870s, both Saratov assemblies abandoned their former class exclusiveness in favor of equality. In accordance, both groups added the terms *vsesoslovnyi or obshchestvennyi* (all-estate or societal) to their titles.[37] As the *Saratovskii Listok* remarked in 1898, this alteration made the Commercial Assembly an "indispensable institution" for Saratov social life.[38] Not without sarcasm, however, a 1911 Saratov travel guide noted that the Commercial Assembly "was Saratov's . . . best institution, where rich people occupy themselves with the mental and physical work of cards and billiards."[39]

Although prior to 1850, Saratov had only 2 sociable associations, namely, the noble assembly and a brief-lived German Club, by 1881 the city had 24 associations, by 1899, 37, and by 1902, 47. Of the last, 17 were charitable, 11 were dedicated to scholarly purposes or the support of students, one was a temperance society, and five engaged in mutual support of the members. After the 1905 revolution, the number of associations in Russia grew exponentially, in part because new guidelines drastically simplified the application procedure.[40] By 1914, 68 new associations of quite differentiated character had arisen in Saratov.[41] A leading contemporary expert on Russian associations, Nikolai Anufriev, estimated that between 1906 and 1909 a total of 4,800 associations and societies had come into existence nationwide in big cities and even in sleepy provincial towns and rural areas.[42] The idea of associations had taken root in Russian society.[43] By 1900, Moscow and St. Petersburg, each with one million inhabitants, boasted perhaps two dozen associations each. By 1912, the old capital had roughly 600 associations and societies of all kinds.[44] By comparison, the much smaller Munich had 150 associations by 1850 and 3,000 at the turn of century, and Austria had 2,234 associations in 1856 and 85,000 in 1910.[45] Although delayed, the Russian association movement advanced rapidly.

SOCIAL AND ETHNIC STRUCTURE OF THE
MEMBERS OF THE ASSOCIATIONS

In 1911, a travel guide wrote about Saratov: "In a word, there are places to spend time and money. Those institutions are especially frequented by married, wealthy, well-educated and other such people . . . Only the employees and the lower civil servants cannot go anywhere, have nowhere to relax. Recently, Saratov society has increasingly felt the necessity of opening associations [*soedinenki*]."[46] In early 1914, Saratov had almost 240,000 inhabitants. Of these, about 3,000 were members of social associations, that is, less than five percent of the adult male urban population.[47] In terms of numbers, the Commercial Assembly proved to be the most popular. In 1861, it had 94 members and 101 guests.[48] By 1872, membership had increased to over 400 people and continued to grow, especially after the relocation to Saratov of the Riazan-Ural railway administration. In 1898, the association had 511 members, in 1907, 826, in 1912, 1,052, and in 1916, 1,568.[49] The Saratov Yacht Club had over 700 members just prior to World War I.[50] The Society of the Friends of the Performing Arts had 450 members by 1895.[51] Statutory limits capped the membership of some elite associations. For example, the Saratov Assembly of Persons of High Birth could accept only 100 persons.[52] This restriction existed elsewhere, for instance, in the St. Petersburg English Club and in German associations.[53] Eventually, the association model diffused itself downwards to new social strata. By the early 1900s, clerks,[54] craftsmen,[55] and even some workers entered certain associations that occupied places beside the noble, business, and professional clubs. Lower-class organizations, such as the Society for the People's Entertainment [*Obshchestvo narodnykh razvlechenii*][56] (1904), had the task of conveying local society's important values and cultural practices.[57] Nevertheless, the association movement remained on the whole socially exclusive.[58]

In one respect, the associations had a broader approach. They enjoyed a considerable mix in terms of ethno-religious background. Russian Orthodox and Old Believers, Catholic Poles, Lutheran and Reformed Germans, practicing Jews, and Muslim Tatars all assembled in certain associations, socialized there, and in a sense existed under a common roof, even though estate, professional, educational, ethnic, or religious boundaries otherwise segregated them.[59]

DAILY LIFE IN THE ASSOCIATIONS
Games and Gambling

A passage from *Anna Karenina* protrays the following scene: "Talking with one another and greeting their friends, Levin and the prince walked through all the rooms: the great room where the tables had already been set and the usual partners were playing for small stakes; the divan room, where people were playing chess . . .; the billiard room . . . . They peeped into the 'infernal regions,' where men were crowding around a table with Yashvin holding the bank."[60] As in Western Europe, games exercised a magnetic effect within urban associations. Merely sociable games, such as cards,[61] billiards, skittles, dice, dominoes, and lotto, coexisted with more or less professional gambling at very high stakes.[62] As regards the latter, one description went as follows: "Upon entering the club, the newcomer's eyes fix on a [prominently displayed] blackboard . . . covered with names and numbers in roughly this manner: 'Mikhail Mikhailovich Liboff, 2345 S. R.,' which means that said individual lost 2345 silver rubles while gambling at the club and [had] not paid the winner."[63] According to the statutes, gambling debts had to be paid in cash within three weeks or face suspension.[64]

Literary works such as Dostoevskii's *Gambler* or Pushkin's *Queen of Spades* reported on the spread of gambling in Russian society. In fact, many commentators noted that all too many people gambled their days away.[65] The passion for gambling recognized no gender. Women, too, indulged at the clubs on family days, as shown by travel descriptions and certain associations' debt and complaint books.[66] Why was gambling so popular? Why wasn't it forbidden in the clubs since it gave rise to vociferous disputes and scandals that undermined the clubs' ideals? First, games and gambling demanded techniques of communication easier to learn than conversation. Second, the cards were distributed anew before every game in a way that corresponded to the idea of equal opportunity. Third, the associations' leadership observed a kind of bourgeois double standard. On the one hand, the associations complained eloquently about the vice of gambling and, on the other, promoted and sustained it in their own clubs. Even associations concerned with physical fitness felt obliged to "subject themselves to the weaknesses characteristic of the highest cultural strata of society, [namely] playing cards and lotto . . . ." Thus the Saratov Cycling Club applied for a change of statutes for the purpose of allowing games and gambling. The leadership hoped thereby to attract financial resources that otherwise would go elsewhere.[67] For many associations, gambling was the greatest source of income. For example, gamblers often ignored club start-up times, for which they incurred heavy fines. Although the fines paled before the gains and losses of gambling, they helped fill the clubs' coffers.[68] Additionally, the games started every day with sealed packs of cards, which had to bought in the club. Despite the state monopoly on cards, the clubs sold every pack of cards to the players for double the purchase price.[69] Under those circumstances, club leaderships hardly contemplated calling a halt to their guests' and members' passion for gambling.[70] Of course, the associations had to keep watch against forbidden games. Still, even the prestigious Saratov Commercial Assembly felt unable, and probably unwilling, to guarantee this. According to the memoirs of I.Ia. Slavin, gamblers gathered at night in the ironically titled "children's room" for forbidden games of hazard. Unwilling to forgo the resulting income, the governing board tolerated this unseemly activity.[71]

Simmel emphasized that social games, whether of the harmless garden variety or gambling, carry a deep double meaning. Society indulges the games externally even as the members play at society in the games. Games constitute basic processes of socialization. Contradictorily, Kant's functional differentiation would suggest that a player's social status, occupation, station, or office does not count. Games have their own laws and regulations, to which all subject themselves regardless of social position. In a literally playful manner, games thus contribute to overcoming social differences.[72] One way or the other, sociable games have great societal significance.

The Reading Room

H. Barry, an English traveler, described Russian clubs as smoke-filled and resounding with an uproar from rows of card players. Books and newspapers were a "great rarity."[73] Perhaps selective perception hid books and newspapers from Barry's eyes but this may also have reflected Russia's relatively late reading revolution, roughly a century after Germany's. Reading exploded in Russia after the 1865 loosening of censorship laws and the subsequent spread of newspapers and magazines. High illiteracy rates and the consequent lack of a market for printed products also hindered reading and other forms of sociability. For instance, coffeehouses, where the public could consume coffee and the contents of periodicals, were a rarity,[74] as were reading societies.[75]

Regardless, the Saratov associations diverged from Barry's description. Perhaps tobacco smoke filled the rooms of its associations. Still, the Saratov associations' statutes reminded members of a prohibition on smoking and of fines for smoking in the hall during dances and other events.[76] The statutes also strictly prohibited smoking in the reading rooms. Saratov clubs attached great significance to their libraries. In part, this was because many provincial towns did not yet have public libraries. Additionally, periodical subscriptions and books were so expensive that many people entered associations to gain access to their libraries.[77] The Saratov Commercial Assembly, for instance, spent 3,000 rubles a year in 1900 and 10,000 in 1916 on its library, which eventually counted almost 47,000 volumes.[78]

Inventories of the associations' libraries suggest that they catered to a wide range of tastes. Commercial periodicals, Russian and foreign light literature, the standard works of literature, religion, philosophy, psychology, biology, medicine, art, geography, and history were all represented. Encyclopedias and law collections were also present. Modern works quickly made their way to the shelves of the associations' libraries. The novels of M. Gor'kii, H. Hesse, and H. Mann were in the libraries, as were the works of left-liberal authors such as P.N. Miliukov and even the socialist authors N.K. Mikhailovskii, Iu.O. Martov, and A.N. Potresov. Book orders and periodical subscriptions suggest the Saratov associations' democratic proclivities.[79] No significant differences in reading habits and tastes were discernable between members of associations in the capitals and in provincial towns. Both observed the same literary canon.[80] Furthermore, as we shall see in the following section, only short steps separated reading, discussion, and politics. An episode in *Anna Karenina* illustrates the matter: "Trying not to make any noise, they walked into the dimly lit reading room . . . They went too into what the prince called the 'intellectual room,' where three gentlemen engaged in a heated discussion of the latest political news."[81]

THE POLITICIZATION OF THE ASSOCIATIONS

Politicization within local associations primarily reflected their blending of various public spheres. At some clubs and their balls, social encounters formed a quite expansive public realm. Certain associations acted as public assemblies in other ways. Several participated in mass communication by publishing periodicals. Consequently, associations served as excellent public communicative junctions. The astounding spread of autonomous corporations after the reforms of the 1860s forced the state to cooperate with society. In this way, society contributed heavily to a subsurface democratization long before Russia's 1905 revolution. Many associations disdained the pre-political sphere assigned to them by the state, even as the latter proved less and less able to control the political dimensions of private charitable and sociable institutions.

The founding of the Saratov Society of the Friends of the Performing Arts (1889) contributed enormously to local cultural life. The literary section's lectures and discussions turned the association into "a kind of club for social questions, without cards and alcoholic beverages."[82] Discussions of socialist authors such as N.K. Mikhailovskii caught the attention of the authorities. Numerous former political exiles, not to mention currently "politically unreliable" persons,[83] entered the organization and even held office there, a circumstance that induced the authorities to demand "good behavior" under the threat of closure, which, predictably, occurred in 1894.[84] The Society for Literature, consisting primarily of editors and staff members of Saratov's liberal and socialist press, went one step further by publishing its own newspaper, *Nasha Gazeta* (*Our Newspaper*). The public spheres of assemblies and mass media thus blended potently together. Given the paper's obvious political orientation, its silencing by large fines was hardly a surprise, nor were repeated government threats of closure against the society.[85]

In Saratov and neighboring district towns, several associations openly promoted constitutional government, incurring closure orders from Governor Stolypin.[86] The progressive Sanitary Society (1897), founded with the goal of promoting hygiene among Saratov inhabitants, got into frequent conflicts with government administrators.[87] During one early 1905 discussion at the society, a speaker compared the sanitary conditions in Saratov to the overall political situation in Russia, which he called "a rotting swamp."[88] In a report on cholera, a lecturer demanded the formation of an urban militia instead of the police, called for a constitutional assembly, and urged the realization of civil rights such as freedom of speech and assembly and the right to strike.[89] Because of the "political unreliability" of some of its members and lecturers, the authorities shut down the Sanitary Society during early summer of 1905. The municipal duma protested and sent a telegram petitioning the Council of Ministers to annul the closing, which, surprisingly, the Minister of the Interior granted the following month (July 1905).[90] The society, however, remained under police observation and the authorities prohibited its public lectures.[91]

Associations jointly fulfilled important educational and political functions. The associations were places where many members first came in touch with democratic elements and engaged in self-organization. When they organized assemblies and public speeches, held elections, passed their budgets, and exercised administrative control, they operated outside estate-bound designations of social status. In addition, the associations' open lecture cycles contributed to general enlightenment. Educational lectures, averaging one a week in Saratov,[92] were the order of the day and dealt with history, philosophy, literature, medicine, and biology. In the Commercial Assembly, for instance, Moscow University's S.A. Kotliarevskii spoke on constitutionalism and parliaments and the lawyer M.A. Maslennikov lectured on "Our Political Parties" Such lecture topics, under relentless police surveillance, naturally placed the clubs at the center of scandal. After 1905, the police repeatedly shut down various organizations after lecturers spoke in a hostile manner toward the government.[93] Even the hiring of rooms by political parties and other such institutions became a "political" issue The Commercial Society let their premises to the Constitutional Democrats for a small fee and also cooperated closely with the Saratov Society of Adult Evening Classes.[94] Given its educational goals and high working class membership, the latter epitomized the association movement's ideal of overcoming social boundaries.[95] During its brief existence (September 1907–November 1908), no less than 32,000 people attended the Society of Adult Evening Classes' 76 lectures. The governor closed it on the grounds of political unreliability, alleged transgression of certain of its own statutes, and biased lecture topics. Examples cited were "The Decembrists in the Judgment of Contemporary Critics," "Central Moments in the History of the Russian Intelligentsia," and "The Political Ideas of John Locke."[96]

Indeed, the so-called days of freedom that followed the 1905 October Manifesto lasted hardly a month in Saratov. Thereafter, tsarist administrators quickly moved to control the activities of local associations. As of March 4, 1906, the new Provisionary Regulations formed the legal framework for the founding of associations. On the one hand, the authorities lost the right to impose high membership fees.[97] On the other, local administrators could still refuse licenses, especially on political grounds,[98] and close existing groups for infractions.[99] On the example of St. Petersburg, in 1909 a Society of Inhabitants and Constituents[100] opened its doors in Saratov. Its goal was to improve living conditions, inform the population about the municipal economy, and elect progressive candidates to the municipal duma, which lagged in the matter of addressing the needs of most Saratov inhabitants.[101] The new society's creed openly expressed its educational aims and political demands: "Using the power of education, we will transform city dwellers [*obyvatelei*] into citizens [*grazhdan*]."[102] Along with an Octobrist, a Progressist, and a Trudovik, six Constitutional Democrats constituted the society's officers.[103] During 1910, the Ministry of the Interior, on the basis of a Senate resolution, circulated a resolution calling for the prohibition of all organizations that addressed techniques of municipal economy. The motivation of this strange policy was that, by favoring alternative solutions to problems, such organizations undermined the competence of the municipal magistrates. A few months later, Saratov authorities closed the hapless Society of Inhabitants and Constituents.[104]

SUMMARY: THE SOCIAL SIGNIFICANCE
OF THE ASSOCIATIONS

Russian associations became the nursery of new culture, no longer exclusively shaped by the nobility. As noblemen, civil servants, industrialists, businessmen, members of the liberal professions, administrative employees, and *meshchane* took part in the life of the associations, they gave rise to a new sociability that rendered estate-bound and ethno-denominational discrepancies irrelevant. On an integrated basis, all of these groups entered the associations, where they built an "ensemble of cultural moments and ways of living." They formed a new aggregate: the "local society." The production and reproduction of culture proceeded hand in hand.[105] The association was *the* institution that shaped the conventions and rules of *civilized* behavior and exercised a normative effect on ways of life and manners. In viewing the associations as regulating institutions of social control,[106] two additional aspects require note. First, by suspending members on grounds of abnormal behavior, associations practiced social discipline and stigmatization. Behaviors such as actions harmful to the club, insults, drunkenness, unpaid debts, and the loss of citizen's rights all set in motion disciplinary measures.[107] Normally, those suspended from one association were barred from others.[108] Second, without adequate clothing, entry to the premises was barred.[109] The socializing nature of these phenomena is obvious. The societies had become the foundation and crystallizing point of local society.

The early German ideal of a classless bourgeois society had not yet found a full Russian equivalent before the 1917 revolutions. Rather, until quite late many associations utilized various mechanisms to fence their social groups off from below.[110] One gains a sense of this from Tolstoy's description, under the influence of his own experience in the prestigious Moscow English Club, founded in 1772. "As soon as he heard the mysterious ringing bell that preceded him as he ascended the shallow, carpeted staircase, and saw the statue on the landing . . . Levin felt the old impression of the club coming back in a rush, an impression of repose, comfort, and propriety . . . He walked past the tables, almost all full, and looked at the visitors. He saw people of all sorts, old and young. Some he knew a little, others were intimate friends. All . . . were calmly getting ready to enjoy the material blessings of life."[111] Comparisons of Russia's associations with those of other countries of Western and Central Europe suggest that obvious structural similarities accompanied somewhat later and lesser development, both of which in part reflected Russia's slower urbanization. These comparisons serve not to emphasize Russian uniqueness or backwardness, but rather to place Russia on a timeline that reveals its rapid, if tardy, development. Of special note about Russia's local societies was the failure of the Saratov Assembly of Nobles and the success of its Commercial Assembly. The regime carried out reforms and then obdurately refused to countenance many of the political and social consequences of the reforms, as suggested by its attitudes toward associations. Even so, if its local societies were the criterion, by the first decades of the twentieth century, Russia was on the brink of a breakthrough to a national bourgeois culture.

NOTES

1. Thomas Nipperdey, *Deutsche Geschichte 1800–1866: Bürgerwelt und starker Staat* (München: C.H. Beck, 1993), 266f.; also, Verein als soziale Struktur in Deutschland im späten 18. und frühen 19. Jahrhundert. Eine Fallstudie zur Modernisierung, Thomas Nipperdey, ed., *Gesellschaft, Kultur, Theorie. Gesammelte Aufsätze zur neueren Geschichte* (Göttingen: Vandenhoeck und Ruprecht, 1976), 180, 195.
2. A semantic correspondence exists between the double meaning of the words *obshchestvo* in Russian, society in English, société in French, and Gesellschaft in German. *Polnoe sobranie zakonov Rossiiskoi imperii*, sobr. 1-oe, 22, no.16187 (April 21, 1785), 349–352. August von Haxthausen, *Studien über die innern Zustände, das Volksleben und insbesondere die ländlichen Einrichtungen Rußlands*, vol. 1 (Hannover: Eulemann, 1847, reprint New York: G. Olms, 1973), 62, 66ff., noted the view that although corporations were alien to, "the Russian national character," Russian society disposed of a "strong inclination for associations."
3. Dietrich Geyer, " 'Gesellschaft' als staatliche Veranstaltung. Sozialgeschichtliche Aspekte des russischen Behördenstaats im 18. Jahrhundert," Dietrich Geyer, ed., *Wirtschaft und Gesellschaft im vorrevolutionären Rußland* (Köln: Kiepenheuer und Witsch, 1975), 20f., 34, 37, and 40.
4. L. Gall, " '. . . ich wünschte ein Bürger zu sein.' Zum Selbstverständnis des deutschen Bürgertums im 19. Jahrhundert," *Historische Zeitschrift* 245 (1987): 601–623, and especially 601.
5. *Izvestiia saratovskogo gorodskoi dumy* (September–December 1908), 129; *Saratovskii Dnevnik* (henceforth SD), no.74 (April 14, 1893); *Saratovskii Listok* (henceforth SL), no.27 (February 4, 1906); no.47 (March 1, 1906).
6. Geyer, " 'Gesellschaft'," 21; for 1905, see Max Weber, "Zur Russischen Revolution von 1905. Schriften und Reden 1905–1912," ed. Wolfgang Mommsen in cooperation with D. Dahlmann, in *Max Weber Gesamtausgabe* (Tübingen: J.C.B. Mohr, 1996), vol. 10, 101.
7. Rossiiskii Gosudarstvennyi Istoricheskii Arkhiv (henceforth RGIA), f. 1284, op. 187, d. 545 (1900 g.), l. 273; SD, no.277 (December 29, 1890); SL, no.212 (October 6, 1892); no.228 (October 25, 1892); no.256 (November 23, 1904); *Pravo*, no.10 (March 13, 1905).
8. K. Bönker, "Akteure der Zivilgesellschaft vor Ort? Presse, Lokalpolitik und die Konstruktion von 'Gesellschaft' im Gouvernement Saratov, 1890–1917," Arnd Bauerkämper, ed., *Die Praxis der Zivilgesellschaft. Akteure, Handeln und*

Strukturen im internationalen Vergleich (Frankfurt and New York: Campus Verlag 2003), 77–79.

9. M. Rainer Lepsius, "Bürgertum als Gegenstand der Sozialgeschichte," in Wolfgang Schieder and Volker Sellin, eds., *Soziale Gruppen in der Geschichte*, 4 vols. (Göttingen: Kleine Vandenhoeck-Reihe, 1987), vol. 4, *Sozialgeschichte in Deutschland. Entwicklungen und Perspektiven im internationalen Zusammenhang*, 67–71.

10. Peter Kenez, *A History of the Soviet Union from the Beginning to the End* (New York: Cambridge University Press, 1999), 3.

11. Edward L. Keenan, "Muscovite Political Folkways," *Russian Review* 45 (1986) 115–181, 130; Gabriele Scheidegger, *Perverses Abendland—barbarisches Rußland. Begegnungen des 16. und 17. Jahrhunderts im Schatten kultureller Mißverständnisse* (Zürich: Chrosos, 1993), 23, 33.

12. Max Weber, *Wirtschaft und Gesellschaft. Grundriß der verstehenden Soziologie* (Tübingen: J. C. B. Mohr [P. Siebeck], 1972), 21; Georg Simmel, "Soziologie. Untersuchungen über die Formen der Vergesellschaftung," in *Georg Simmel Gesamtausgabe*, 2 vols. (Frankfurt, 1995), vol. 2, 11, 19, 51; and his *Grundfragen der Soziologie (Individuum und Gesellschaft)* (Berlin and New York: Sammlug Göschenn, 1984), 13f.

13. Simmel, *Grundfragen*, 48–68, 53; his "Soziologie der Geselligkeit," *Verhandlungen des Ersten Deutschen Soziologentages vom 19–22. Oktober 1910 . . . G. Simmel, F. Tönnies, M. Weber, W. Sombart, A. Ploetz, E. Troeltsch, E. Gothein, A. Voigt, H. Kantorowicz und Debatten* (Tübingen: Mohr, 1911), 1–16.

14. I.G. Popov, *Moskovskoe kupecheskoe sobranie. Istoricheskii ocherk* (Moscow: Izd. Moskovskago kupecheskago sobraniia, 1914), 9. That the newspaper *Novoe Vremia* dedicated a daily column to associations also suggests their significance. See, e.g., *Novoe Vremia*, no.12893 (February 2 [15], 1912).

15. *Entsiklopedicheskii slovar' russkogo bibliograficheskogo instituta Granat*, 7th ed., (Moscow, 1910–1948) vol. 15, 427; S.S. Komissarenko, *Klub kak sotsial'-no-kul'turnoe iavlenie: Istoricheskie aspekty razvitiia* (St. Petersburg: St. Peterburgskaia gos. akademiia kultury, 1997), 117, 131f.

16. W. Hardtwig, "Verein–Gesellschaft, Geheimgesellschaft, Assoziation, Genossen-schaft, Gewerkschaft," Otto Brunner et al., eds., *Geschichtliche Grundbegriffe*, 8 vols. (Stuttgart: E. Klett, 1972–1997), 809; Nipperdey, "Verein," 195.

17. Gosudarstvennyi Arkhiv Saratovskoi Oblasti (henceforth GASO), f. 1, op. 1, d. 1473, l. 21; f. 2, op. 1, d. 7950, l. 5; d. 8866, l. 30, d. 8785, l. 12; f. 176, op. 1, d. 37, l. 25; *Ustav kluba Saratovskikh Podriadchikov Stroitel'nykh Rabot* (Saratov, 1908), 2, described it as "rational distractions" [*razumnyia razvlecheniia*]; GASO, f. 2, op. 1, d. 7971, l. 7ob; *Balashovskaia Gazeta*, no.22 (June 5, 1911).

18. GASO, f. 2, op. 1, d. 8378, ll. 2ob, 65–65ob; d. 8866, l. 31; f. 176, op. 1, d. 37, ll. 25–25ob; *Ustav Saratovskogo Kommercheskogo Sobraniia* (Saratov, 1872), 1; *Ustav Saratovskogo Obshchestvennogo Sobraniia (kruzhka-"kluba")* (Saratov, 1906) 1f.; *Ustav kluba Saratovskikh Podriadchikov*, 2f.

19. Moreover, the law on associations called for annual charitable events. See K.K. Il'inskii, *Chastnye obshchestva. Sbornik zakonov . . .* (Riga, 1912) 585 (this source refers to *Svod Zakonov*, vol. 14, art. 139).

20. GASO, f. 1, op. 1, d. 1473, l. 27ob; d. 2224, ll. 22, 47; f. 176, op. 1, d. 209, l. 23ob; d. 37, l. 32; f. 351, op. 1, ll. 1–3; f. 373, op. 1, d. 45, l. 1ob; f. 572, op. 2, d. 117, l. 1ob; *Privolzhskii Krai* (henceforth PK), no.68 (March 8, 1904); SD, no.237 (November 2, 1884); SL, no.37 (February 14, 1892); no.265

(December 3, 1904); no.259 (December 5, 1906); *Saratovskii Vestnik* (henceforth SV), no.255 (November 23, 1910).

21. Lutz Häfner: " 'Jetzt werden die Konstitutionalisten zu Feinden des Vaterlandes proklamiert': A.A. Tokarskij—liberale Biographie und liberales Handeln im Gouvernement Saratov," *Jahrbuch zur Liberalismus-Forschung* 15 (2003): 63.

22. *Spravochnaia knizhka ob obshchestvakh i soiuzakh. Sistematicheskii sbornik zakonov* . . . comp. by V.I. Charnoluskii (St. Petersburg: B.M. Vol. fa, 1912), 19; Il'inskii, *Chastnye obshchestva*, 31, 68f.; *V . . . m klube. Zapiski igroka Mortuusa* (Moscow, 1906), 57f.; on German associations, see K. Tenfelde, "Die Entfaltung des Vereinswesens während der Industriellen Revolution in Deutschland (1850–1873)," *Vereinswesen und bürgerliche Gesellschaft in Deutschland*, ed. Otto Dann (München: R. Oldenbourg, 1984), 76; U. Frevert, "Männergeschichte oder die Suche nach dem" ersten "Geschlecht," *Was ist Gesellschaftsgeschichte? Positionen, Themen, Analysen*, ed. Manfred Hettling et al. (München: Beck, 1991), 38–42.

23. The Saratov Yacht Club had its first female members in 1908, the Saratov Commercial Assembly in 1915. GASO, f. 373, op. 1, d. 58, l. 199.

24. RGIA, f. 1284, op. 223, d. 14 (1881 g.), l. 15ob; *Ustav Saratovskogo Obshchestva Esperantistov* (Saratov, 1914), 2.

25. RGIA, f. 1284, op. 223, d. 210 (1887 g.), l. 17; GASO, f. 1, op. 1, d. 1473, ll. 5ob, 21ob, 22ob; f. 2, op. 1, d. 7950, l. 8ob; d. 10839, l. 3; f. 176, op. 1, d. 204, l. 11; f. 373, op. 1, d. 30, ll. 12, 18; f. 572, op. 2, d. 3, l. 1ob; SL, no.1 (January 1, 1890); *Ves' Saratov 1900 na 1900 god. Adres-Kalendar', torgovo-promyshlennaia i spravochnaia kniga* (Saratov: Izd. A.I. Fridrikhson, 1899), 484, 486f. The Saratov Choir and the Saratov Yachtclub were cheaper, charging 10 rubles, as were the Saratov Society of the Friends of the Performing Arts, the German Club, and the Saratov Sport Club 8 rubles, the Sanitary Society 6, and the Saratov Russian Club 5. GASO, f. 1, op. 1, d. 5384, l. 18ob; f. 176, op. 1, op. 1, d. 96, l. 11ob; d. 281, l. 3aob; RGIA, f. 1284, op. 188, d. 272 (1902 g.), l. 4ob.

26. *Opyt priblizitel'nogo izchisleniia narodnogo dokhoda* . . . *v Rossii* (St. Petersburg, 1906), vii, xiv, xvii, xix, xxv, xxvii ff., 86–91.

27. SV, no.62 (March 18, 1909): 2.

28. Alexis de Tocqueville, *Über die Demokratie in Amerika* (Zürich, 1987), part 1, 279ff., 285; part 2, 160–164; Abram Gordon, *Nashi obshchestvennye sobraniia (kluby) s tochki zreniia iuridicheskoi i oblast' primeneiia grazhdanskogo iska* (St. Petersburg: Tip. Pravitelstvuiushchago Senata, 1883), 17; Joseph Bradley, "Voluntary Associations, Civic Culture, and Obshchestvennost' in Moscow," in Edith W. Clowes, Samuel D. Kassow and James L. West, eds., *Between Tsar and People: Educated Society and the Quest for Public Identity in Late Imperial Russia* (Princeton, NJ: Princeton University, 1991), 147.

29. N.F. Khovanskii, "Nemetskii i kommercheskii kluby v Saratove," *Saratovskii krai. Istoricheskie ocherki, vospominaniia, materialy*, Vyp. 1 (Saratov, 1893), 353; F.V. Dukhovnikov and N.F. Khovanskii, "Saratovskaia letopis'," *Saratovskii krai*, 80; Lutz Häfner, *Gesellschaft als lokale Veranstaltung. Kazan' und Saratov (1870–1914)* (Köln, Weimar, Wien: Böhlau, 2004), 176f. German clubs, too, fell victim to arbitrary government authorities. Fearing the ghost of "pan-Germanism" in 1908, the authorities in Saratov repeatedly refused to approve a "German Club" requested by reputable Germans. Only the fourth application, by limiting itself to cultural and economic goals, had success. GASO, f. 176, op. 1, d. 103, ll. 2a, 9ob–11, 26ob–28, 32ob, 44–45ob, 52, 58–58ob, 74ob–75; f. 59, op. 1,

d. 1417, ll. 6–6ob, 11, 12; SV, no.162 (September 11, 1907); no.217 (November 21, 1907), 3; J.W. Long, "The Volga Germans of Saratov Province between Reform and Revolution, 1861–1905," Rex A. Wade and Scott J. Seregny, eds., *Politics and Society in Provincial Russia: Saratov, 1590–1917* (Columbus, OH: Ohio State University, 1989), 159.

30. Military and veterans' societies had a very restricted role in Russia. German and English sport clubs heavily influenced Russian equivalents. For Saratov see RGIA, f. 1284, op. 187, d. 9 (1901 g.), ll. 1–3; GASO, f. 2, op. 1, d. 9771, ll. 12, 15, 19; f. 59, op. 1, d. 1678, l. 2; f. 176, op. 1, d. 281, ll. 1–1ob; d. 375, l. 18ob; f. 373, op. 1, d. 87, l. 3. On the elite Aero-Club, see GASO, f. 2, op. 1, d. 10839, ll. 1–3; f. 59, op. 1, d. 1528, l. 3; f. 176, op. 1, d. 204, ll. 2–3, 14, 20–21; d. 375, l. 16ob; SK, no.59 (November 21, 1910); no.828 (January 15, 1913), 3; no.43 (March 22, 1911); *Balashovskaia Gazeta*, no.36 (June 22, 1911).

31. Thus, the state rejected 1895, 1897, and 1904 applications for employee's clubs in Saratov. GASO, f. 2, op. 1, d. 7459, ll. 9, 33; d. 7684, ll. 3–3ob, 5; f. 53, op. 1, d. 15 (1905 g.), ll. 56ob, 58ob.

32. GASO, f. 1, op. 1, d. 5384, l. 10ob; f. 176, op. 1, d. 297, l. 4.

33. A. Zando, *Russische Zustände im Jahre 1850* (Hamburg: Nestler und Melle, 1851), 295f.

34. When the noble assembly finally closed, after close calls in the 1860s and in 1898, the fashionable Aero-Club took over its premises. SD, no.237 (November 2, 1884), 2; *Saratovskaia Zemskaia Nedelia*, nos. 42–43 (1898), 440; no.44 (1898), 455f.; N.P. Gusev, A. Khovanskii, *Saratovets. Ukazatel' i putevoditel' po Saratovu. God pervyi* (Saratov, 1881), 80; *Saratov. Sputnik-Ukazatel' na 1911 god* (Saratov, 1911), 21.

35. Dukhovnikov, Khovanskii, "Saratovskaia letopis'," 78.

36. GASO, f. 1, op. 1, d. 1473, ll. 1–2, 3–3ob, 19ob; f. 1283, op. 1, d. 19, ll. 46ob–47; Khovanskii, *Nemetskie i kommercheskie kluby*, 354f.; *Promyshlennyi Listok*, no.88 (November 1, 1858), 349; *Saratovskie Gubernskie Vedomosti*, no.2 (January 10, 1859); no.44 (October 29, 1860); SD, no.237 (November 2, 1884); SL, no.254 (November 23, 1910); SV, no.255 (November 23, 1910).

37. GASO, f. 176, op. 1, d. 375, ll. 43, 53; Khovanskii, *Nemetskie i kommercheskie kluby*, 359; *Izvestiia Saratovskoi Gorodskoi Dumy* (May–August 1908), 5; SV, no.219 (November 24, 1907), 3. The existence as late as 1904 of the local Society to Help Persons of Privileged Estates suggests a contradictory tendency. PK, no.129 (May 31, 1904).

38. SL, no.68 (March 25, 1898); GASO, f. 1283, op. 1, d. 19, l. 47ob.

39. *Saratov. Sputnik-Ukazatel'*, 21; GASO, f. 1283, op. 1, d. 19, l. 47.

40. *Polnoe sobranie zakonov Rossiiskoi imperii*, 3rd series, 26, no.27479 (March 4, 1906), 200–207; N.P. Anufriev, "Pravitel'stvennaia reglementatsiia obrazovaniia chastnykh obshchestv v Rossii," A.I. Elistratov, ed., *Voprosy administrativnogo prava* (Moscow, 1916), part 1: 15–44; Il'inskii, 5–53; Weber, "Revolution," 153–160.

41. GASO, f. 2, op. 1, d. 8015, ll. 9–9ob, 79ob; d. 8985, l. 136; f. 176, op. 1, d. 375, ll. 15–20ob, 126–129ob; *Adres-Kalendar' Saratovskoi gubernii na 1893 g.* (Saratov, 1893), 124–129; *Ves' Saratov na 1901 g.*, 334–340; *Pamiatnaia knizhka Saratovskoi gubernii na 1904 god* (Saratov, 1904), 118–127; I.N. Matveev, *Sanitarnye ocherki gorodskogo vracha g. Saratova I. N. Matveeva. Obshchestvennoe prizrenie v Saratove* (Saratov, 1898), 64–90, 151ff.

42. Häfner, *Lokale Gesellschaft*, 183.

43. Theodore von Laue, "The Prospects of Liberal Democracy in Tsarist Russia," Charles E. Timberlake, ed., *Essays on Russian Liberalism* (Columbia: University of Missouri Press, 1972), 164–181, 164; Anufriev, 37.

44. Bradley, "Associations," 132f.; Bianka Pietrow-Ennker, *Rußlands "neue Menschen": die Entwicklung der Frauenbewegung von den Anfängen bis zur Oktoberrevolution* (Frankfurt, New York: Canpus, 1999), 313; L.V. Belovinskii, ed., *Rossiiskii istoriko-bytovoi slovar'* (Moscow: Studia TriTe, 1999), 202.

45. *Novyi entsiklopedicheskii slovar'*, 29 vols. (St. Petersburg: Izd. Izdatel'skoe delo byvshee Brokgauz-Efron, 1911–1916), vol. 21, col. 917; Ingo Tornow, *Das Münchner Vereinswesen in der ersten Hälfte des 19. Jahrhunderts, mit einem Ausblick auf die zweite Jahrhunderthälfte.* (München: Kommissionsbuchhandlung R. Woelfle, 1977), 274; M. Sobania, "Vereinsleben. Regeln und Formen bürgerlicher Assoziationen im 19. Jahrhundert" Dieter Hein, Andreas Schulz, eds., *Bürgerkultur im 19. Jahrhundert. Bildung, Kunst und Lebenswelt*, (München: C.H. Beck, 1996), 170–190, 170; Tenfelde, 58.

46. *Saratov. Sputnik-Ukazatel'*, 22; GASO, f. 2, op. 1, d. 7684, l. 1.

47. Many people belonged to several associations. State Duma member A.M. Maslennikov belonged to at least 14, the lawyer B.A. Arapov 11, Count A. D. Nessel'rode, Mayors A.O. Nemirovskii and V.A. Korobkov 10, State Duma member A.A. Tokarskii and stock exchange head N.P. Kokuev 9, 1913 mayoral candidates V.I. Almazov and M.F. Volkov, and German "flour-kings" K.K. Reineke, E.E. Borel' and I.E. Borel' 6.

48. GASO, f. 572, op. 2, d. 3, l. 1ob; Khovanskii, "Nemestkie i kommercheskie kluby," 357f.

49. Khovanskii, "Nemestkie i kommercheskie kluby," 359; *Otchet Saratovskogo Kommercheskogo Sobraniia za 1898–99 god* (Saratov, 1899), 35; *Spisok chlenov Saratovskogo Kommercheskogo Sobraniia na 1911–12 g.* (Saratov, 1912), 25; *Spisok chlenov Saratovskogo Kommercheskogo Sobraniia na 1916–1917g* (Saratov, 1917), 40–44; SL, no.254 (November 23, 1910), 4; SV, no.255 (November 23, 1910), 4.

50. V. Tsybin, "Saratovskii iakht-klub" *Volga* (December 1993), 158–165, 161; *Saratov. Sputnik-Ukazatel'*, 20.

51. Häfner, *Lokale Gesellschaft*, 208.

52. GASO, f. 1, op. 1, d. 1473, l. 22; d. 1741, l. 2.

53. *Ustav Moskovskago Angliiskogo Kluba* (Moscow, 1859), 3, 13; "K istorii Moskovskogo Angliiskogo kluba" *Russkii Arkhiv* 27 (May 1889): 85–98, 86; *Moskovskoe kupecheskoe sobranie*, 11, 38f. See Margarete Busch, *Deutsche in St. Petersburg 1865–1914. Identität und Integration* (Essen: Klartext, 1995), 98; Otto Dann, "Die Anfänge politischer Vereinsbildung in Deutschland," *Soziale Bewegung und politische Verfassung. Beiträge zur Geschichte der modernen Welt* ed. Ulrich Engelhardt et al. (Stuttgart, 1976), 197–232, 200, note 10; Sobania, "Vereinsleben," 178.

54. RGIA, f. 1284, op. 187, d. 330 (1902 g.), l. 3; GASO, f. 176, op. 1, d. 375, l. 18; SL, no.279 (December 21, 1904).

55. GASO, f. 2, op. 1, d. 8378, l. 52.

56. The association was later renamed Society for Rational Entertainment (Obshchestvo razumnykh razvlechenii), RGIA, f. 1284, op. 187, d. 148 (1904), l. 2. This kind of association seems to be an adaptation of the English clubs of "rational recreation," see E.A. Svift, "Razvlekatel'naia kul'tura gorodskikh

rabochikh kontsa XIX—nachala XX veka," E.V. Dukov, ed., *Razvlekatel'naia kul'tura Rossii XVIII–XIX vekov. Ocherki istorii i teorii* (St. Petersburg: DB, 2000): 300–315, 306.

57. GASO, f. 2, op. 1, d. 8599, ll. 2–8; f. 2, op. 1, d. 8766, l. 1; PK (January 23, 1904); no.206 (September 2, 1904); no.241 (October 18, 1904); no.263 (November 15, 1904); SL, no.250 (November 16, 1904).

58. For a detailed analysis of the social structure of Kazan's largest sociable association, the "New Club," see Lutz Häfner, "Der 'Neue Club' in Kazan' 1900 bis 1913: Kristallisationspunkt lokaler 'Gesellschaft'," Guido Hausmann, ed., *Gesellschaft als lokale Veranstaltung. Selbstverwaltung, Assoziierung und Geselligkeit in den Städten des ausgehenden Zarenreiches* (Göttingen: Vandenhoeck & Ruprecht, 2002), 377–403, 383f.

59. Former head of the Saratov police and currently a print shop owner, F.Iu. Zatsvilikhovskii, of Polish noble descent, belonged to the Aero-Club, as did the Jewish tobacco factory owner, I.S. Levkovich.

60. L.N. Tolstoj, *Anna Karenina*, tr. F. Ottow, (München: Winkler Verlag, 1991), 825f.

61. On the significance of card games in Russian clubs, see *Moskovskoe kupecheskoe sobranie*, 87; *Novyi Entsiklopedicheskii slovar'*, vol. 21, column, 917; Zando, 292f.; a diametrically opposed view is in H. Barry, *Das neue Rußland. Following "Barrys' Russia in 1870" and "Ivan at home"* (Berlin 1873), 24. For Germany, see H. Freudenthal, *Vereine in Hamburg. Ein Beitrag zur Geschichte und Volkskunde der Geselligkeit* (Hamburg, 1968), 67; U. Jeggle, "Bemerkungen zur deutschen Geselligkeit," É. François, ed., *Geselligkeit, Vereinswesen und bürgerliche Gesellschaft in Frankreich, Deutschland und der Schweiz, 1750–1850* (Paris: Editions Recherche sur les civilizations, 1986), 230.

62. W. Giljarowski, *Kaschemmen, Klubs und Künstlerklausen. Sittenbilder aus dem alten Moskau* (Berlin, 1988), 219f.; E. Jerrmann, *Unpolitische Bilder aus St. Petersburg. Skizzen, nach dem Leben gezeichnet* (Berlin, 1851), 21; V.N. Semenov, N.N. Semenov, *Saratov kupecheskii* (Saratov, 1995), 197, 226.

63. Barry, *Das neue Russland*, 66; GASO, f. 1, op. 1, d. 1473, l. 15; d. 1741, l. 8; f. 2, op. 1, d. 8866, l. 36; f. 572, op. 1, d. 2, l. 10.

64. GASO, f. 176, op. 1, d. 37, l. 34ob; f. 2, op. 1, d. 7950, l. 18ob.

65. GASO, f. 572, op. 2, d. 130, l. 67; *Novosti i Birzhevaia Gazeta*, no.150 (June 3, 1897).

66. GASO, f. 572, op. 2, d. 4, l. 17ob; d. 60, l. 2; d. 74, ll. 1–187; d. 98, ll. 1–403ob; Barry, *Das neue Russland*, 67.

67. GASO, f. 176, op. 1, d. 69, ll. 2ob, 8ob; Gordon, *Nashi obshchestvennye sobraniia*, 25.

68. GASO, f. 572, op. 2, d. 33, ll. 10ob–112ob, ll. 43ob–92ob.

69. *Spravochnaia knizhka*, 80f.; C. v. Schwanebach, "Kaiserin Maria Feodorowna, die Begründerin der öffentlichen Fürsorge in Rußland," *Baltische Monatsschrift* 53 (1911): nos. 8/9, 4; Barry, *Das neue Russland*, 67; W.B. Steveni, *Things Seen in Russia* (London, 1914), 70–73; I.V. Golovina, "Igornye kluby Sankt-Peterburga v 1905–1907 gg.," *Peterburgskie chteniia* (St. Petersburg: Naidenov i kompan'eny, 1996), 419.

70. Cf. SL, no.273 (December 14, 1904), 2.

71. GASO, f. 1283, op. 1, d. 19, l. 47; d. 20, ll. 27ob–28; on gambling in the Saratov Commercial Assembly, see GASO, f. 572, op. 2, d. 19, ll. 1–12ob; d. 130, ll. 67–68, 72–72ob; d. 133, l. 105, 107.

72. Simmel, *Grundfragen*, p. 59.

73. Barry, *Das neue Russland*, 67.

74. Coffeehouses with thick journals were in big cities or on the periphery where foreign influences were strong, such as Riga, Warsaw, Kiev, and Odessa. By World War I, some district towns also had coffeehouses. K. Baedeker, *Russland nebst Teheran, Port Arthur, Peking. Handbuch für Reisende* (Leipzig: K. Baedeker, 1912), 52, 87, 378, 414; *Nash Krai*, no.16 (January 19, 1913); no.28 (February 2, 1913).

75. On the reading societies, see M. Aronson, S. Reiser, *Literaturnye kruzhki i salony* (Leningrad: Priboi, 1929), 241–247.

76. GASO, f. 1, op. 1, d. 1473, l. 27ob; f. 2, op. 1, d. 8866, l. 36; *Ustav SKS*, p. 19.

77. SL, no.254 (November 23, 1910); M. Turinskii, "Gazety v provintsii," *Istoricheskii Vestnik*, 128 (1912), no.4, 158; GASO, f. 572, op. 2, d. 4, ll. 1–48.

78. GASO, f. 572, op. 1, d. 2, ll. 1ob, 22; d. 62, l. 1ob; Khovanskii, "Nemestkie i kommercheskie kluby," 360ff.; SL, no.254 (November 23, 1910), 4; SV, no.255 (November 23, 1910), 4; *Otchet Saratovskogo Kommercheskago Sobraniia za 1912–1913 god* (Saratov, 1914), 14f.; . . . *za 1915–1916 god* (Saratov, 1917), 28, 30; Semenov, Semenov, *Saratov kupecheskii*, 271, 284.

79. GASO, f. 1, op. 1, d. 1473, l. 25ob; Ustav SKS, S. 23. Besides thick journals, the Society of Saratov Urban Employees also subscribed to two neo-populist periodicals, namely *Russkoe Bogatstvo (Russian Wealth) and Zavety (Legacy)*, the latter of which the Saratov Commercial Assembly also received. This implies progressive or radical political attitudes. *Otchet pravleniia Obshchestva sluzhashchikh v Saratovskom Gorodskom Upravlenii za vremia s 21-go noiabria 1912 g. po 1-e ianvaria 1914 g.* (Saratov, 1914), 1; Semenov, *Saratov kupecheskii*, 270.

80. *Novosti i Birzhevaia Gazeta*, no.127 (May 9, 1891).

81. Tolstoy, *Anna Karenina*, 825f.

82. GASO, f. 1, op. 1, d. 5384, l. 10; RGIA, f. 1284, op. 187, d. 112 (1900 g.), ll. 21–22; G. Ul'ianov, "Vospominaniia o M. A. Natansone," *Katorga i Ssylka* 89 (1932): no.4, 73; SL, no.1 (January 1, 1890); no.207 (September 29, 1892); *Ustav Saratovskogo obshchestva liubitelei iziashchnykh iskusstv* (Saratov, 1893), 1f.

83. Amongst others, the physician M.A. Natanson and the lawyer N.I. Rakitnikov, both later Socialist Revolutionary Central Committee members, belonged, as did liberals such as Count Nessel'rode.

84. After being shut down, the association reopened in late 1901. GASO, f. 1, op. 1, d. 5384, ll. 10, 18–20; d. 6322, ll. 1, 3, 38, 39–39ob; f. 53, op. 1, d. 7 (1895 g.), ll. 28ob–29ob; RGIA, f. 1284, op. 187, d. 217 (1902 g.), l. 90; SD, no.239 (November 6, 1901); *Saratovskaia Zemskaia Nedelia*, no.40 (October 11, 1898), 420; *Ocherki istorii Saratovskogo Povolzh'ia*, vol. 2, part 1: *1855–1894*. ed., I.V. Porokh (Saratov: Izd-va Saratovskogo Universiteta, 1995), 280; David R. Brower, *The Russian City Between Tradition and Modernity, 1850–1900* (Berkeley: University of California, 1990), 185; T.S. Fallows, "Forging the Zemstvo Movement: Liberation and Radicalism on the Volga, 1890–1905," Ph. D. diss. (Harvard University, 1981), 598.

85. RGIA, f. 776, op. 21, part 2, d. 241 (1907 g.), ll. 5, 8, 11; GASO, f. 176, op. 1, d. 80, ll. 86–101; SV, no.52 (April 15, 1907); SV, no.213 (November 16, 1907).

86. Gosudarstvennyi arkiv rossiskoi federatsii (hereafter GARF), f. 102, op. DOO 1905 g., d. 1350, part 20, ll. 17, 36.

87. RGIA, f. 1284, op. 188, d. 272 (1902 g.), l. 1.

88. GASO, f. 53, op. 1, d. 15 (1905 g.), l. 62.

89. GASO, f. 60, op. 1, d. 241, l. 80; Pravo, no.12 (March 27, 1905), 951; no.13 (April 3, 1905), 1026f.

90. GASO, f. 53, op. 1, d. 15 (1905 g.), ll. 85–85ob; *Obzor deiatel'nosti Saratovskogo Gorodskogo Obshchestvennogo Upravleniia za 1905–1908 gg.* (Saratov, 1909), 16; *Russkie vedomosti*, no.185 (July 11, 1905); no.194 (July 20, 1905); *Pravo*, no.29 (July 24, 1905), column 2400.

91. PK, no.74 (April 3, 1907); SV, no.29 (March 20, 1907); no.139 (August 10, 1907); no.172 (September 23, 1907); no.175 (September 28, 1907).

92. SV, no.195 (October 25, 1907).

93. SV, no.19 (December 31, 1906).

94. GASO, f. 572, op. 2, d. 10, ll. 1, 3, 13ob; PK, no.1 (January 1, 1907).

95. GASO, f. 176, op. 1, d. 99, l. 3; SV, no.194 (October 24, 1907); no.213 (November 16, 1907).

96. GASO, f. 176, op. 1, d. 99, ll. 4, 31–31ob, 35–36, 84ob, 87–88, 91–94a, 109–111ob, 130, 135, 148; NG, no.7 (November 19, 1907); SL, no.252 (November 19, 1908); no.254 (November 21, 1908); SV, no.261 (November 30, 1908); *Sovremennoe Slovo*, no.380 (November 29, 1908).

97. GASO, f. 1, op. 1, d. 5384, l. 10ob.

98. GASO, f. 176, op. 1, d. 28, ll. 3–3ob; d. 48, ll. 2, 4.

99. GASO, f. 176, op. 1, d. 99, ll. 109–111ob, 130, 138, 139; SL, no.247 (November 12, 1908); no.252 (November 19, 1908); no.254 (November 21, 1908); SV, no.261 (November 30, 1908); *Sovremennoe Slovo*, no.380 (November 29, 1908); GASO, f. 176, op. 1, d. 375, ll. 15ob, 122ob; GASO, f. 59, op. 1, d. 1415, ll. 2, 17–18.

100. "Ustav obshchestva obyvatelei i izbiratelei Liteinoi chasti," GD, no.16 (August 15, 1909), 821–825; A. Znosko-Borovskij, "Obshchestva obyvatelei i izbiratelei g. Peterburga," GD, no.2 (January 15, 1909), 69–72; *Otchet o deiatel'nosti Obshchestva obyvatelei i izbiratelei g. Saratova za vremia s 14 sentiabria 1909 g. po 1 ianvaria 1910 g.* (Saratov, 1910), 1f.

101. GASO, f. 60, op. 1, d. 277, ll. 50ob, 52; SL, no.197 (September 4, 1909); no.202 (September 11, 1909); SV, no.107 (May 21, 1909); *Volzhskaia Mysl'*, no.3 (July 27, 1909).

102. *Otchet o deiatel'nosti Obshchestva obyvatelei*, 4.

103. GASO, f. 60, op. 1, d. 277 (1909 g.), ll. 48–49ob, 56–59; SL, no.245 (November 3, 1909); SV, no.202 (September 16, 1909); no.241 (November 3, 1909); *Otchet o deiatel'nosti Obshchestva obyvatelei*, 3; PK, no.70 (March 29, 1907).

104. GASO, f. 176, op. 1, d. 116, ll. 3–4; *Russkie vedomosti*, no.59 (March 12, 1913); *Saratovskaia Kopeechka*, no.53 (November 15, 1910); "Ustav obshchestva obyvatelei i izbiratelei Liteinoi chasti," 821f.; *Spravochnaia knizhka*, 94f.

105. Bradley, "Associations," 132.

106. GASO, f. 1, op. 1, d. 1473, l. 24; f. 2, op. 1, d. 7950, l. 15ob; d. 8378, l. 72–72ob; d. 9581, l. 8; f. 176, op. 1, d. 37, l. 32ob; f. 572, op. 2, d. 4, ll. 42ob–43; *Ustav SKS*, 17.

107. GASO, f. 1, op. 1, d. 1473, ll. 15–17, 23ob; f. 2, op. 1, d. 7950, ll. 16–16ob; f. 572, op. 1, d. 1, l. 6ob; PK, no.76 (April 5, 1907); SL, no.257 (November 24, 1904); no.254 (November 23, 1910); *Ustav SKS*, 18f.; *Ustav Saratovskogo rechnogo Iakht-Kluba* (Saratov, 1877), 6; PK, no.79 (March 20, 1904).

108. GASO, op. 1, d. 1741, l. 8; f. 2, op. 1, d. 7950, l. 7ob; d. 8738, l. 4ob; f. 176, op. 1, d. 37, l. 27.

109. GASO, f. 176, op. 1, d. 37, l. 28; *Ustav Saratovskogo Obshchestvennogo Sobraniia*, 7.
110. GASO, f. 1, op. 1, d. 1473, l. 21; *Moskovskoe kupecheskoe sobranie*, 23ff., 28ff., 36ff., 157, 180–189.
111. Tolstoy, *Anna Karenina*, 821f.

10

RUSSIAN PUNISHMENTS IN THE
EUROPEAN MIRROR

Jonathan Daly

At the beginning of the nineteenth century, governments in Western and Eastern Europe gradually undertook to abolish the remaining forms of body mutilation and to lessen the use of other assorted physically violent punishments, such as burning people at the stake, for they appeared barbarous to modern sensibilities.[1] This reform movement was part of a broader effort to make punishment not only less inhumane but also more regular, efficient, and proportionate to the crime.[2] In some regards, the Imperial Russian government appears to have been at the forefront of this trend. A decade before the publication of Rousseau's *Contrat social* (1762) and Beccaria's *Dei delitti e delle pene* (1764), the Empress Elizabeth Petrovna strictly limited the legal scope of capital punishment. As the French legal historian Joseph Viaud has written, perhaps only a despot can do something so radical, so unpopular. For the next 70 years, only about a dozen people were executed on court orders in the Russian Empire (though a few times that number of people were summarily executed during the Pugachevshchina). Indeed, for several decades before 1845, capital punishment was considered an exceptional measure in Russia.[3] In England and Wales, by contrast, the *yearly* number of executions as late as the first decades of the nineteenth century was just under one hundred, before falling to roughly ten in the late 1830s. In France, the numbers were even higher in the late 1830s.[4] Similarly, the French penal code until 1832 prescribed the amputation of a parricide's right hand; such punishments in Russia had been abolished long before.[5] In other cases, Russia lagged behind some, but not all, Western European countries. Thus, public executions were abolished in England in 1868 and in Russia in 1881, but in France only in 1939.[6] Indeed, there seems to have been almost no major area of penal policy in which the Imperial Russian government was completely out of step with its Western European counterparts.[7] Even so, the Russian government has often been considered exceptionally repressive in the European context.

As one historian has recently argued, "there is no other way to determine whether there is exceptionalism in one's own national history than by doing comparative history and . . . therefore, anybody making the claim to national exceptionalism ought to probe the deep and troubled waters of comparative history first."[8] The present article, conceived as a modest contribution to exploring Russia's penological "exceptionalism" in the final century of the Imperial regime, compares the rates at which the four harshest forms of punishment—the death penalty, penal servitude, imprisonment, and punitive exile—were meted out to criminals in Russia and in the major Western European countries and also suggests what these rates might tell us about the nature of late Imperial Russian state and society.

Throughout the late Imperial period, capital punishment and sentences of hard labor and prison could be applied in Russia only by sentence of regular or military courts; a sentence of exile without hard labor could be imposed by administrative and other authorities as well as by the courts. In adjudicating alleged crimes, the regular and special courts complied with the penal code of 1845 and the criminal code of 1903, while military judges abided by the code of military statute of punishments of 1839 as well as some other laws, and nonjudicial authorities were guided by a disparate body of legislative acts.[9]

The penal code of 1845 classified three forms of punishment as "criminal" (*ugolovnye*), namely the death penalty, hard labor, and exile to Siberia or the Caucasus. All lesser punishments, including briefer periods (up to four years) of exile to Siberia (*na zhit'e*) and imprisonment, were termed "corrective" (*ispravitel'nye*).[10] It bears noting that the vast majority of all sentences were corrective and not criminal and that the proportion of criminal sentences declined from 13 percent in 1874 to 8.8 percent in 1894.[11]

Each of the three "criminal" punishments was accompanied, for the privileged social classes, by a further penalty termed "deprivation of all rights of status" (*lishenie vsekh prav sostoianiia*).[12] By this punishment nobles were stripped of their noble status, clergy were defrocked, and "honorable" (*pochetnye*) citizens and merchants lost their special privileges (Penal Code, arts. 24–32). Convicted members of these social categories relinquished their privileged access to educational institutions and to civil and military service. They also lost their exemption from corporal punishment, should they later be convicted of another crime. Deprivation of status was akin to civil death. The criminal forfeited all property, which was transferred immediately to his or her heirs, as was the right to inherit further property. All one's honors, patents, ranks, and titles were annulled or revoked. This state of deprivation did not extend to one's spouse or children, even if the latter voluntarily chose to adopt the person's life of exile. Members of the nonprivileged social categories, when sentenced to criminal punishments, were deprived of their "good name" and of the few social rights to which they were entitled, such as, in the case of peasants, membership in their commune or the right to vote for representatives to the zemstvos.[13] This loss of civil rights was akin to the French punishment called *mort civile*, which also accompanied capital punishment, a life sentence of hard labor, or exile to the colonies. This provision persisted in the French Penal Code fully until May 3, 1854 and partially thereafter.[14]

DEATH PENALTY

According to Russia's penal code of 1845, one could, strictly speaking, be put to death only for committing acts of violence against the sovereign, for conspiring to overthrow the existing state order, for high treason, or for breach of quarantine.[15] Unlike in most of Western Europe and in the United States, such grave crimes as murder, rape, armed robbery, and arson were not capital offenses. It is in this sense that the English diplomat and writer A.F. Heard, who was well acquainted with Russia, deemed the Russian penal code "one of the mildest in Europe."[16] This assessment may appear surprising to readers familiar with Russia's reputation for repressive government.[17]

In fact, the regular courts during Imperial Russia's final century condemned only a very small number of people to death. More active in this regard were the military courts, which were speedier, were more likely to convict than the regular courts, and issued harsher sentences.[18] The military statute of punishments allowed for the application of capital punishment to civilians only under exceptional circumstances. Most of the 50 death sentences issued in Russia from 1845 (when the knout was abolished) to 1875 were handed down by military courts.[19] Twenty of the sentences were carried out. Those executed had nearly all organized or sought to organize armed insurrections; seven of them were military personnel.[20] During the same interval, by contrast, 620 criminals in France, 271 in Prussia, 360 in England and Wales, and 1,325 in the United States were executed by sentence of the courts.[21] Adjusted for population differences (see table 10.1), courts in these three Central and Western European countries put as many as ten times more people to death during the interval than those in Russia. State and local authorities in the United States had perhaps 20 times more people executed than in Russia (see table 10.2).[22] The Russian government here appeared to be more lenient than its major Western counterparts.

Why were Russian government officials so reluctant to impose the death penalty in political-crime cases? On the one hand, throughout nearly the entire Imperial period, Russia's rulers regarded the people of their country as charges of the state for whose welfare the government bore responsibility. The government was to protect the subjects of the tsar because of its duty, not because of their right to protection. As the source of all social and public welfare, the emperor and the state were the only truly indispensable actors,

Table 10.1   Population in millions

	1860	1870	1880	1890	1900	1910	1913
USA	32	40	50	63	76	93	97
Russia	79	85	98	115	133	157	166
France	37	36	37	38	38	39	39
Prussia	18	25	27	30	34	40	43
England and Wales	20	23	26	29	32	36	36

Table 10.2   Executions per one million
population

	1845–75
Russia	2.1
England and Wales	20
France	16.9
Prussia	18
The United States	40[a]

[a] There were 2,453 executions in the United States
in 1800–65 and 825 executions in 1866–79—all
imposed by civil authorities (Schneider and
Smylka, "A Summary Analysis," 6).

which was why only attacks on them entailed capital punishment. This premodern, paternalistic notion contrasted with the Western European conception of citizens as possessing inherent rights to life, liberty, and property, which lay at the foundation of the existing political systems; an attack on an individual's life or property challenged the fundamental principles of the whole social system.[23] On the other hand, the Russian government's infrequent imposition of capital punishment almost surely stemmed in part from its commitment to "Europeanization," as paradoxical as that may sound. For, although many European governments continued to impose the death penalty relatively frequently during much of the nineteenth century, many of the most advanced penologists, beginning in the late eighteenth century, objected to its imposition on principle, and their arguments against capital punishment enjoyed a positive reception in the halls of government throughout Europe—including in Russia. For example, in the early 1880s, Russia's Ministry of Justice surveyed the views of government officials regarding capital punishment. The majority of officials surveyed recommended either its abolition or its redefinition as a strictly exceptional measure.[24]

In the mid-nineteenth century, the most dramatic example of the Imperial Russian government's commitment to Europeanizing and modernizing Russia was the creation on November 20, 1864 of an independent judiciary, which in one stroke hobbled administrative officialdom.[25] In the words of Richard Wortman, "For the Russian autocracy to accept an independent judiciary required that it betray its essence and cease to be the Russian autocracy."[26] Indeed, from November 20, 1864, Russia ceased to be an autocracy and became a species of semi-absolutist monarchy.[27] The judicial statutes not only limited the power of the monarch, they also fettered his administrative officials. Henceforth, the police could detain criminals for no more than 24 hours, military courts could try civilians in only narrowly defined cases,[28] and all persons accused of nonstate crimes had the right to a trial by jury.[29]

The Great Reform era also witnessed the elimination of the harsher forms of corporal punishment. The flogging of convicts with the lash (*pleti*), which had replaced the proverbial knout in 1845, was abolished by a law of

April 17, 1863 (whipping with birch branches, which succeeded it, was outlawed on August 11, 1904 for all but prisoners).[30] In this policy, Russia was following the United States and many European countries, where corporal punishment was abolished at mid-century or somewhat earlier,[31] and was outstripping England and Wales, where flogging remained a common form of punishment well into the twentieth century.[32] The law of April 17, 1863 also put an end to the branding of criminals. Until then, convicts sentenced to hard labor (*katorga*), in addition to whipping, had the letters "K-A-T" branded on their foreheads and cheeks. In this case, Russia seemed to be lagging just a few decades behind at least one of its European role models. Although the branding of criminals was abolished in 1779 in England, until 1832 criminals sentenced to penal servitude in France were branded with the letters "T-F" ("travaux forcés").[33]

The implementation of Alexander II's Great Reforms, which had failed to satisfy the demands of educated Russians for political representation at the highest level of government, in part gave rise to an activist radical intelligentsia and the outbreak of revolutionary terrorism. The widespread unwillingness of judges and juries to condemn defendants apparently guilty of criminal attacks against government officials and the impossibility of removing liberal judges provided the justification for selectively reabrogating the rights of Russian subjects and reasserting the powers of officialdom.[34] There followed from the 1870s to 1881 a series of emergency laws and statutes that marked a partial detour from the path toward constitutionalism.[35] In this connection, administrative officials began to send not only state-crime cases but also regular-crime cases to military courts. Ironically, one result of the campaign of political terror in the late 1870s was the return of capital punishment in regular criminal cases, a practice that had fallen into disuse in Russia in the late eighteenth century.[36]

Yet even with the more frequent use of military courts, the annual number of executions in Russia before 1906 remained quite modest, at least in comparison with similar figures for the European countries, and especially for the United States. Thus from 1876 to 1905, Russian military courts issued 484 death sentences, all of which were carried out. Most of those executed had committed regular crimes, like murder, banditry, and the like; 82 had been found guilty of political crimes, and 55 of military crimes. In addition, from 1879 to 1905 the Senate delivered 23 death sentences for political crimes; 12 of them were implemented. In all, from 1876 to 1905, roughly 500 people were executed in fulfillment of court-issued sentences. During the period 1875–1905, the English courts put as many as 405 people to death.[37] That is a figure roughly one-fourth lower than the comparable number for Russia, whose population was four times larger (120 versus 30 million). During the same years, 260 people were executed in Prussia with its population of roughly 30 million, and 620 were put to death in France with its population of 38 million.[38] These figures were still two to three times the Russian execution rate (see table 10.3). By far, the highest execution rate was in the United States. Between 1880 and 1905, there were as many as 2,743 executions in

Table 10.3   Executions per million population

	1876–1905
Russia	4
England and Wales	13.5
France	16.3
Prussia	8.7
The United States	36[a]

[a] Calculated for the period 1880–1905. There were 1,005 executions in 1880–90, 1,098 executions in 1890–00, and 1,280 executions in 1900–10 (Schneider and Smylka, "A Summary Analysis," 6).

the United States, a country with half the population of Russia (76 million in 1900 versus 126 million in 1897). In other words, five times more people were put to death in America than in Russia and during a briefer interval.[39]

Table 10.3, in comparison with table 10.2, reveals a second discrepancy among the countries in question: while the rate of capital punishment in Russia increased by 80 percent, it decreased in England and Wales by 38 percent, in France by 5 percent, and in Prussia by 48 percent (although the rate in the United States was also rising steadily).[40] Why was the rate increasing in Russia? First, toward the end of the century, Russia faced a far greater magnitude of social and political discontent and turmoil, brought on by rapid, state-driven industrialization, massive population migration, and agrarian reform, than anything the other countries (save perhaps the United States) experienced. Similarly, France had been shaken by political upheavals in 1848, 1851, and 1871, which had presumably exerted upward pressure on the rate of capital punishment during the earlier period. Second, the years from 1876 to 1905 were a period of nationalism and imperialism worldwide. The major European countries carved the African continent into colonial possessions, in the course of which they massacred thousands and thousands of people.[41] Russia was also an imperial power, albeit without overseas colonial possessions, and indeed a large proportion of the executions carried out in the Russian Empire took place in its borderlands. This was in part because the rate of criminality was highest in the borderlands. The murder and robbery rates, for example, were nearly three times higher in the Caucasus than in European Russia in the 1890s.[42] It might, therefore, seem appropriate to add to the various totals the incidence of capital punishment in the colonies of the major Western European powers. To take but one example, during the period from 1892 to 1906, nearly 500 people were sentenced to death each year in British India (or 26.2 per million population).[43]

The yearly number of executions might have increased even faster in Russia from 1845 to 1905, had many government officials not been opposed to the death penalty on principle. Jurists on an interdepartmental commission, chaired by Deputy Justice Minister E.V. Frisch, argued in 1881 against applying capital punishment to political and religious criminals, and the officials who drafted the criminal code of 1903 expressed their principled opposition to capital punishment in general, though the State Council preserved the death penalty in both cases.[44] In the courtroom itself, it seems that judges issued ever more mild sentences as the 1905 revolution approached. Even during turbulent 1905, the leniency of judges and prosecutors was striking: not a single person was executed in Russia from January 1 to October 6, 1905, when a soldier was put to death for attempting to kill an officer.[45]

Beginning in 1906, however, the number of executions in Russia rose dramatically. During the three years from 1906 through 1908, as many as 2,215 people were executed by military-court sentence (nonmilitary courts had put no one to death), or five per million population annually—a rate three times higher than for the same years in the USA.[46] To this figure, one must add the roughly 6,000 people killed by punitive expeditions from December 1905 into 1906 and the 1,000 people executed by military field courts.[47] This was terrible carnage, a shocking deviation from the path Russia had followed until those years. One would be remiss, however, not to compare this massive slaughter to the terrible repression of the Paris Commune in the final week of May 1871, when troops massacred as many as 20,000 *communards*.[48] France's population at that time was only about one-third of Russia's in 1905. Thus, the French government, in quashing the Commune, killed perhaps six times more people—and in a much shorter period—than Russia's did in suppressing the revolution of 1905. Actually, one must consider both episodes gross aberrations brought about by the desperation of governments struggling to survive in the face of broad-based popular disorder.[49] Indeed, the number of executions in Russia decreased to 129 in 1910 and to 25 in 1913.[50]

As shown in table 10.4, that figure compares very favorably with those of the major European countries (see table 10.4). In 1913 in Prussia, there were 22 executions with a population of 43 million; in England and Wales, roughly 13 with a population of 36 million; and in France, roughly 9 with a population of 39 million.[51]

Table 10.4 Annual executions per million population in 1896–1900 and 1913

	1896–1900[a]	1913[b]
Russia	0.11	0.15
England and Wales	0.4	0.36
France	0.13	0.23
Prussia	0.44	0.51
United States	1.6	1.02

[a] In the period 1896–1900 there were 15 executions per year in Russia, 13 in England and Wales, 5 in France, 15 in Prussia, and 122 in the United States (Gernet, "Smertnaia kazn'," 74, 97; Evans, "Rituals of Retribution," 919; Schneider and Smylka, "A Summary Analysis," 4).
[b] In the United States, 99 people were executed yearly from 1911 to 1915 (Schneider and Smylka, "A Summary Analysis," 4).

An important reason for the return to something like normality in the number of executions in Russia on the eve of the World War was that much of official and public opinion in that country was staunchly against capital punishment.[52] Most telling, on June 19, 1906, the First Duma voted without a single dissenting vote to abolish capital punishment entirely. The euphoria of the revolutionary changes then affecting Russia probably moved many conservatives and moderates not to oppose the bill (which in fact never became law, owing to the dissolution of the Duma on July 8).[53] Also influential in deciding the vote, however, must have been the immense authority wielded by educated public activists. In 1907, a host of Russian intellectuals, public figures, and clergymen contributed to a volume condemning capital punishment. Among the contributors were Vasilii Rozanov, Nikolai Berdiaev, Sergei Bulgakov, Petr Kropotkin, and Leo Tolstoy. Letters denouncing the death penalty by several well-known European intellectuals with an interest in Russia were also included in the book. This was but one of the more prominent salvos in a broader campaign against capital punishment conducted by Russian jurists, doctors, and writers.[54]

Moreover, as already noted, many government officials advocated only a limited use of the death penalty. In a speech to the First Duma on June 15, 1906, for example, Justice Minister I.G. Shcheglovitov agreed that capital punishment should not be used to punish regular crimes. His failure to denounce its application to political criminals prompted many deputies to shout him down from the rostrum.[55] As one critic objected three weeks later, "Trying to suppress political crimes with capital punishment is like pouring fuel oil on a fire." Political crimes, he argued, would disappear only after the abolition of capital punishment and the fundamental transformation of the political system.[56] Whatever the merits of this argument, it was remarkable that senior government officials should have advocated the abolition of capital punishment for regular crimes in a period when regular and political crime were blending together in something like an orgy of criminality.

HARD LABOR

The second harshest criminal punishment defined by the 1845 Penal Code was *katorga* (from *katerga*, the Greek plural for "galley, forced labor"), that is, exile or confinement under a regime of hard-labor, or penal servitude. This punishment was applicable to persons convicted of some acts threatening to state security, of forgery of state seals and currency, of willful and egregious disruption of public order, and of heinous crimes against person and property. (As already noted, many of the latter offenses were capital crimes in most of the major European countries.)

Penal servitude appeared throughout Europe during the early modern period as rulers sought to harness all available resources for state building and economic development: even criminals, it was argued, should help to fill the state's coffers.[57] *Katorga* developed in Russia most vigorously under Peter I, first on his galley fleet and later for his great building projects. By the second half of the nineteenth century, *katorga* as a regime of forced labor was retained only on Sakhalin Island in the Far East, on the Trans-Siberian Railroad, and in a few Siberian prisons, mines, and factories.[58]

A sentence of *katorga*, imposable only by a court of law, could range from 4 years to a life term, which in principle meant 20 years of hard labor or a harsh prison regime followed by penal exile for several years under a milder regime. Most convicted murderers were sentenced to no more than 10 years of *katorga*. Since 10 months of penal servitude counted as 1 year, a "ten-year" sentence lasted 8.3 years. During their term of sentence, most hard-labor convicts were allowed to live among the environing non-convict populations and could receive financial and other forms of support from friends and relatives. In practice, most penal exiles were released to simple exile after completing two-thirds of their sentence. Moreover, perhaps as few as 50 percent actually served as intended, that is, either at hard-labor or under a harsh prison regime.

The total *katorga* population in Imperial Russia reached 14,484 in 1892, with between 1,000 and 2,000 being sentenced each year; the total number fell to 10,688 in 1898 and climbed again to 11,066 in 1901. Most of the convicts serving terms of *katorga* in 1901 had committed heinous regular crimes, including murder (39 percent), armed robbery and other serious forms of theft (26.5 percent), the infliction of bodily injury (13.7 percent), and rape (2.9 percent). Only 180, that is, about 1.6 percent, had been convicted as political criminals.[59]

France was the one Western European country that continued to maintain a system of hard-labor exile as late as Imperial Russia did (i.e., at least until 1917). The practice arose there in the first half of the sixteenth century and persisted within the domestic territory until May 30, 1854. Thereafter, prisoners condemned by the courts to a regime of hard-labor were exiled to the French colonies.[60] The period of servitude varied from 5 to 40 years; one historian considered the system of penal servitude "as (perhaps more) inhuman than the system of galleys under Louis XIV."[61] This was especially true during the period from 1854 to 1880, when colonial administrators were left entirely to their own devices regarding their treatment of the convicts.[62] Those condemned to 8 years or fewer of penal servitude were, upon completing their sentence, obliged to remain exiled for an equal number of years. Those sentenced to more than 8 years were never allowed to return to France or even to leave the colony to which they had been sent. From 1864 to 1897, the French government sent most of its convicts of European origin to the pleasant climes of New Caledonia, whose use as a place of exile was discontinued in 1897 because the convicts' life there was considered too comfortable.[63]

Thereafter French Guiana, which had been established as a place of penal exile in 1852, received all the hard-labor convicts exiled from France. The highly insalubrious tropical climate in French Guiana was undoubtedly harsher than that of Siberia, which was not starkly different than that to which most Russian exiles were accustomed. In all, 43,582 convicts were exiled to French Guiana under sentence of hard-labor from 1854 to 1910.[64] Edmond Henri, a French colonial inspector writing in 1910, admitted that each year at least one-tenth of the exiles died, mostly of disease. One contemporary, therefore, dubbed this form of punishment "the bloodless guillotine."[65] Henri calculated, in fact, that between 1898 and 1910 as many as 7,500 hard-labor convicts, or 577 per year, died in French Guiana.[66] By contrast, between 1898 and 1904 only about 130 *katorzhniki* died each year, despite the fact that there were roughly twice as many hard-labor convicts in Russia.[67] Moreover, whereas almost no hard-labor convicts managed to evade captivity in French Guiana, each year about one-tenth of the Russian *katorzhniki* escaped to freedom.[68]

In 1882, there were 3,355 hard-labor convicts in French Guiana and 9,026 in New Caledonia, for a total of 12,381. In that same year, there were 8,520 *katorzhniki* in Siberia. These figures represented 34 and 9 per 100,000 of the population of France and Russia, respectively. By 1904, the *katorzhnik* population in Russia had risen to 10,680 (8 per 100,000 of the total population of roughly 140 million); after the amnesty of October 21, 1905, the number fell to 6,100, or 4 per 100,000.[69] On December 31, 1910 there remained 4,454 people, or 11 per 100,000 of population, under sentence of penal servitude in French Guiana (almost none remained in New Caledonia).[70] It is true that the number of penal convicts in the Russian Empire grew much larger in the immediate aftermath of the revolution of 1905–07. Between 9,000 and 11,000 people received sentences of *katorga* each year between 1908 and 1913; that figure declined to 8,500 in 1914. The average daily population of *katorzhniki* peaked in 1913 at 30,379.[71] Since the population of the Russian Empire was roughly 178 million in 1913, there were in principle 17 *katorzhniki* per million, that is, 65 percent more than those residing in French Guiana in 1910. In fact, however, over 6,000 hard-labor convicts in the Russian Empire in 1913 were being housed in regular prisons and a further 12,500 were residing in temporary *katorga* prisons for want of space in specially designed hard-labor prisons, so the actual ratio of hard-labor convicts to the population was probably closer to that in France.[72]

Late in the nineteenth century, the courts of England and Wales no longer exiled convicts abroad, yet they continued to sentence relatively large numbers of criminals to penal servitude. This form of punishment entailed 18 months of solitary confinement under harsh dietary and sleeping conditions with hard-labor performed in isolation, followed by a period of less stringent living conditions and labor under the "silent system." In 1880, roughly 10,000 convicts were completing sentences of penal servitude in England and Wales. Between 1881 and 1890, the courts sentenced 11,072 more people to terms of hard-labor, the vast majority of them from 5 to 10 years in length. The number of such convictions declined from 1,525 in 1881 to 729 in 1890. In 1893–94, there were just under 4,500 convicts at hard labor, or 16 per million of population, that is, nearly the same as Russia's rate at the point of its highest *katorzhnik* population.[73]

EXILE

Exile to Siberia and the Caucasus for periods longer than four years constituted Russia's third criminal punishment and was meted out for a wide range of crimes.[74] For Russia, as for several of the European powers, the exile of criminals helped to promote imperial expansion while costing far less than prisons did. Beginning with the exiles whom Christopher Columbus took with him on his third voyage to the West Indies (too few free men desired to make the trip), the European colonial powers shipped hundreds of thousands of politically and morally "undesirable" people to their far-flung territorial possessions. In England, the largest Western European exporter of convicts, exile was considered a humane alternative to capital punishment. Before the introduction of penal deportation in the early 1600s, the annual number of people executed was 600–1,200; by 1750 it had fallen to 80–100.[75] This decline was attributable in part to the fact that approximately 50,000 convicts were deported to North America from 1614 until 1775. In the final decade of British rule in the American colonies, over 500 felons were shipped each year for a variety of crimes, most prevalently for petty theft.[76] The English government then went on, during the 69 years between 1787 and 1855, to export 161,000 criminals—about nine-tenths for some form of theft—to Australia.[77] Although all of these criminals were sentenced to indentured servitude, and some even to short periods of hard-labor,[78] the overall conditions of their exile make a comparison with non-hard-labor exile in Russia appropriate. Most important, the exiles to North America and to Australia were tied to farms in somewhat the same way that most Russian exiles were tied to agricultural communes.

One might object that Australia was a more desirable place of exile than Siberia. In fact, however, Siberia as a destination of voluntary migration was proportionately far more popular than was Australia during their respective periods of state-imposed exile. Between 1893 and 1902, for example, over one million peasants freely migrated to Siberia (amid efforts by the Interior Ministry to keep the numbers down), while perhaps 100,000 exiles made the trip. In contrast, only 70,000 free migrants—compared to roughly 50,000 convicts—arrived in Australia from 1832 to 1842.[79]

Conditions in most places of Siberian exile were not as bad as one might think. For one thing, after ten years (or six years with good behavior), the exile could join any rural or town commune (with the latter's permission) nearly anywhere in Siberia, and the mobility of administrative exiles was even less restricted.[80] Moreover, by the 1890s, thanks to improved rail links, the trip out east was described by some as like a vacation, and many political exiles reported improved health.[81] By contrast, a relatively high number of convicts died during the four-to-six month voyage down under.[82] We now know that most of the exiles to Australia—and their descendants—were far luckier than their counterparts in Siberia. Without Russia's wars, revolutions, and civil wars, the contrast might not have been so stark.

In the Russian Empire, roughly 865,000 people were exiled during the 93 years from 1807 to 1899.[83] Between 1787 and 1855, as noted above, 161,000 people were deported from Great Britain. The latter's population in 1821, the midyear during the interval under consideration, was fourteen million. Russia's approximate population in 1853, the midpoint of the 93 years in question, was 70 million. The average number of exiles per year was 2,333 for Britain and 9,301 for Russia. Therefore, the rate was 17 per 10,000 for Britain and 13 per 10,000 for Russia. Yet, many of the exiles in the Russian aggregate were not being punished by the Russian government per se. About one-half were peasants excluded administratively by their own communities for disreputable behavior; such exiles were free to move about Siberia and did not suffer deprivation of rights, since theirs was not a court-imposed criminal punishment.[84] These numerical adjustments might lead one to conclude that it was as if three times more people were exiled by the British government than by its Russian counterpart during the periods in question. If one took into account that as many as half the above-mentioned Siberian exiles at any given time were fugitive, then it was as though the British government had succeeded in punishing six times more people with exile than its Russian counterpart during the periods under consideration.[85] Of course, the two periods in question were not entirely conterminous. Yet, the essential fact about penal exile in Russia was that it continued to be applied for several decades after its abolition in Britain—right down to the fall of the Imperial regime.

The reasons for the longevity of punitive exile in Russia in large part must be sought in Russia's backwardness. One of the most obvious indicators in this regard was the widespread use of society-based exile. In Russia, the legal basis for nonjudicial exile originated in the 1760s. Recourse to nonjudicial exile shows both that the regime lacked adequate institutional resources to govern the empire, and that local communities, and until 1861, landlords took the kind of active role in dealing with deviance in their midst that had not been seen in Western European countries for more than a century.[86] It bears noting that members of the elite, urban culture in Russia, like their counterparts in Western Europe and the United States, possessed no right to exile each other.

Many officials felt uncomfortable about such vestiges of "barbarism"— both judicial and administrative exile—in Russia. In 1840, Russia's ministers of justice and internal affairs submitted a plan for abolishing penal exile, arguing that it exerted a harmful impact upon the Siberian population.[87] In 1862, the emperor asked the Second Section of His Majesty's Own Chancery to consider the abolition of the administrative use of exile by peasant communities.[88] In 1880, K.P. Pobedonostsev, who had helped to evaluate the administrative exile process, told B.N. Chicherin that he and other members of the inspection commission had been "terrified by the unbelievable lawlessness they [had] discovered. In some cases they could find no reason for the exile; in others, the reasons were negligible and suspicions unproven."[89] The main problem seems to have been, as N.M. Baranov reported to M.T. Loris-Melikov in 1880, that there were no strict rules on whom to exile and not to exile, while the opinions of the relevant administrative officials regarding this matter diverged considerably.[90]

Even so, for nearly two decades the State Council and other decision-making institutions rejected all the recommendations in favor of eliminating or curtailing exile on the grounds that insufficient prison space was available to accommodate the criminal elements in the population. Indeed, alternative proposals remained the stumbling block of the penal- and administrative-exile system's critics. One notable example of this problem was illustrated by D.A. Dril', a jurist who traveled to Russian and French penal colonies in Sakhalin, Nerchinsk, and New Caledonia and in a book published in 1899 advocated their abolition. Although he praised one Russian prison, the Central Alexandrovskaia Hard-Labor Prison near Irkutsk, and in general advocated the imposition of hard-labor punishments, he advanced no concrete recommendations for replacing either form of exile. In opposition to Dril' and others, the celebrated criminologist and staunch opponent of capital punishment, N.S. Tagantsev, argued persuasively in favor of preserving penal exile in Russia (though he too opposed administrative exile). Penal exile, he wrote, was less expensive for the government and more humane for the convicts than prison and was especially appropriate in Russia, given the agricultural life-style of the population and the vast, relatively under-populated regions of the empire. Despite his support of penal exile in principle, Tagantsev did recommend abolishing non-colonizational exile outright and limiting the use of exile in general.[91]

By the turn of the century a consensus among penologists and government officials had been reached on the need to impose restrictions on exile, which then Justice Minister N.V. Murav'ev called "that aged and obsolete remnant." Thus, a law of June 12, 1900 put an end to judicial exile, except for political and religious crimes, and also curtailed administrative exile. Henceforth, rural communities were liable to pay an exile's way to Siberia and to compensate the exile for any land forfeited; societies of townspeople (*meshchanskie obshchestva*) lost their right to exile their members.[92] Even so, over 50,000 people were exiled between 1906 and 1910, nearly all by administrative process, in conjunction with the massive social unrest in those years. Thereafter, the yearly number of administrative exiles sank to 1,753 in 1912 and to 1,051 in 1913, while the number of court-sentenced exiles fell to 531 in 1910 and to 252 in 1912.[93]

IMPRISONMENT

Imprisonment was the most modern of the major forms of harsh punishment in Russia.[94] Although not one of the "criminal" (*ugolovnye*) punishments, it was arguably harsher than exile. Its development stemmed from the penal reform movement referred to at the beginning of this essay. Capital punishment and exile were the cheapest means of removing criminal elements from society. Yet capital punishment was viewed by most of educated society in nineteenth-century Europe as inhumane, or at least to be avoided in all but the most heinous criminal cases, while the exile of one's fellow countrymen in large numbers required having a suitable place to send them. Of the major European countries, only Russia, by the end of the nineteenth century, possessed an underpopulated territory sufficiently far away and inhospitable, yet at the same time sufficiently familiar, to which to send large numbers of exiles—Siberia. This fact helps to explain why Russia was slower to shift from the traditional forms of harsh punishment to imprisonment, despite the great interest of senior Russian officials in setting their country firmly on what they took to be the path of penal modernization.

The abolition of corporal punishment, coupled with social unrest in the 1870s and early 1880s, caused Russia's prison system to fill up well beyond its intended capacity. Thanks to relatively large prison-construction projects, however, by 1900 prison overcrowding had been eliminated. The building of 50 more prisons by 1905 permitted a modest per capita curtailment of the use of penal exile. Of course, the upheaval that began in 1905 overfilled even the new prisons. The Russian government responded to the crisis by imposing administrative exile with great frequency, a traditional impulse, and by instituting in 1909 a system of parole, a modernizing, reformist impulse.[95]

As indicated in table 10.5, between 1880 and 1910, the absolute number of prisoners in Russia was greater than that of any of the countries under consideration, though the number of prisoners in the United States in 1900, unfortunately not available, almost surely exceeded that of Russia. Likewise, the total number of prisoners in the United States in 1910, which, as given in the table, excludes juveniles, probably exceeded it in that year as well. A few other discrepancies need to be noted. Between 15 and 20 percent of the Russian prisoners were administrative, judicial, and hard-labor exiles en route to their place of exile.[96] The numbers given for France exclude hard-labor exiles and all prisoners in Algeria.

Table 10.5   Prison populations

	1880	1890	1900	1910
USA	69,228	95,480	a	111,498[b]
Russia	95,509[c]	106,478	85,857	168,864
France	47,289	42,639	29,437	27,241
Prussia	62,039[c]	52,058[d]	56,914	52,248
England and Wales	30,213	19,745	15,670	21,102[e]

[a] Not available.
[b] Excludes juveniles.
[c] 1882.
[d] 1889.
[e] 1909.

Sources: Cahalan and Parsons, *Historical Corrections Statistics*, 192; *Otchet po Glavnomu tiuremnomu upravleniiu* (St. Petersburg: Tip. Ministerstva vnutrennikh del, 1882, 1892, 1902, 1912); *Annuaire statistique de la France* (Paris: Imprimerie nationale, 1912); *Statistisches Handbuch für den Preussischen Staat*, vols. 1–12 (Berlin: Verlag des Königlichen Statistischen Bureau, 1893–1915); *Fourteenth Report of the Commissioners of Prisons* (London: Her Majesty's Stationery Office, 1891); *Report of the Commissioners of Prisons and the Directors of Convict Prisons* (London: Her Majesty's Stationery Office, 1900, 1909).

Table 10.6   Prisoners per 100,000 of population

	1880	1890	1900	1910
USA	138	153	a	121
Russia	97	93	65	109
France	128	112	77	70
Prussia	230	174	167	131
England and Wales	116	68	49	59

a Not available.

With these minor variations in mind, one can now examine table 10.6. It immediately becomes apparent that Russia's imprisonment rate was comparatively low for each of the four years in question. It had the lowest rate in 1880 and the second lowest in 1890 and 1900, and the third lowest in 1910. Imperial Russia's highest rate of imprisonment, 117 per 100,000, was reached in 1909.

Naturally, prison conditions varied in each of these countries. One recent student of Russia's prisons has argued that, toward the end of the Imperial period, they were being run according to the same standards as in Western Europe and the United States, although the situation in Russia deteriorated during the period of overcrowding that followed the massive social upheaval of 1905–07. If Russian prisons were perhaps less clean and orderly than many prisons in the West, the discipline in many of them was also less severe.[97] To take but one example, only three people escaped from English and Welsh prisons in 1890, whereas 612 did so in Russia.[98] Another recent study, by Stephen Wheatcroft, shows that Russia's prison mortality rate rose sharply from 30 percent above the adjusted rate for the civilian population in 1906 to 5 times that rate in 1911, which was probably caused in part by a threefold decrease in the area and volume of space available to each prisoner during that same period. The Russian prison mortality rate, at its highest pre–World War I level, hit 50 per 1,000 in 1911 (or 43 per 1,000 in 1910, according to Alan Barenberg), although on the eve of the war it had fallen back down to 36 per 1,000.[99] By contrast, the French prison mortality rate, excluding overseas hard-labor prisons hovered around 28 per 1,000 in 1900 and 28.8 per 1,000 in 1913.[100] Assuming the French civilian death rates (adjusted to exclude children, most women, and the elderly) were lower than those of Russia, and assuming also that the high prison mortality rates in Russia following the revolution of 1905–07 were aberrational, we may conclude that prison mortality in Russia was not wildly incongruent with that in at least one advanced Western European country.

One might object that the comparison is unfair, since the Russian figures do not reflect the full extent of the deprivation of liberty visited on Russian subjects. After all, in addition to prisoners, there were a huge number of exiles, too. Exile statistics are available for 1898. In that year, there were, on paper, 298,577 exiles in Siberia, that is, nearly all the exiles in the Russian Empire. As in the case of the statistics on exile for the entire century, fully one-half of the exiles in 1898 were peasants exiled on behalf of their communities. That leaves some 150,000 exiles sentenced by the courts. It also seems that in practice as many as half of all the exiles in 1898 were unaccounted for.[101] It may, therefore, be the case that only 70,000 to 80,000 people were actually completing government-imposed sentences of exile at the turn of the century. Were one to add, say, 80,000 to the number of prisoners in Russia for 1900, the number of prisoners plus exiles per 100,000 would be 124. That number is still lower than the figure for Prussia, almost certainly lower than the number for the United States, and about the same as for France.

To sum up, capital punishment was used less frequently in Russia than in France, England and Wales, Prussia, or the United States, except during the period during and immediately, after the 1905–07 revolution. France's system of penal exile, which still existed in 1917, was probably crueler than its Russian counterpart, at least in terms of convict mortality. In Imperial Russia, hundreds of thousands of people were exiled to Siberia and other inhospitable places in the nineteenth century, but their number represented a slightly lesser proportion of the population than did the exiles from Britain during almost the same period, despite Britain's being, at least in some respects, far more advanced culturally, politically, and socially than Russia. Both governments resorted to punitive exile as a method of colonization and for want of prison space. (Britain with less justification, given its greater available per capita monetary resources.) Finally, the rate of imprisonment in Russia was actually lower than the rates for the four other countries in table 10.6 for most of the four years in question. Moreover, in 1909, the Russian government adopted a system of parole, as usual, following the Western model. (In practice it seems that the majority of parolees vanished without trace.)[102]

CONCLUSION

If the late Imperial Russian penal system was as comparatively lenient as the foregoing evidence tends to suggest, why was this so? Part of the explanation is to be sought in Russia's economic and social backwardness, ethnic complexity, and geographical vastness, and in the government's socially destabilizing policy of rapidly industrializing the economy while striving to maintain the tiny landowning nobility in the face of a huge, land-hungry peasantry. In a word, it was harder to govern and to enforce the law in the Russian Empire than, say, on the English mainland. It is certain that these "logistical" problems played an important role in making Russia appear rather "liberal" in terms of its criminal justice system. Also, the very inefficiency of Russia's crime-fighting system may have played an important role in this regard. The police regularly bungled investigations, while the courts for that and other reasons often failed to find guilt.[103] The inefficiency of the administration in Russia probably contributed to the crime rate being higher in Russia than in the more developed Western European countries. The murder rate per

1,000,000 of population in the first half of the 1890s, for example, was 5 in England, 9 in Germany, 14 in France, and 25 in Russia. (The Russian figure excludes the Caucasus region, where the murder rate was four times higher than in European Russia.)[104] Thus, not only was the incidence of criminal punishment comparatively lower in Russia than in the major Western European countries, the incidence of crime, at least in terms of the murder rate, which is generally deemed by scholars to be the most reliable of all historical crime statistics, was actually higher.

Perhaps equally important in coming to terms with the comparative leniency of late Imperial Russia's penal system was the commitment of Russia's rulers and ruling elites to European-style penal reform. Since the time of Peter the Great, Russia's rulers had been committed to the project of rationalizing, modernizing, and, indeed, Europeanizing their country. This commitment was, as Richard Wortman has persuasively suggested, one of the key elements of the "imperial myth" that sustained Russia's absolutist political system.[105] One may further argue that only that commitment kept at least a portion of the nonofficial educated elites loyal to the Imperial Russian regime. Thus, in the realm of criminal punishment, the government instituted an independent judiciary, abolished corporal punishment, ended public executions, built modern prisons, instituted a system of parole, and sought repeatedly to limit or even to abolish outright the application of penal exile.[106]

This essay proceeded from the well-known observation that at the start of the early nineteenth century the Western European countries began to reform their penal systems, most notably by reducing the violently physical element in punishment. Spierenburg has argued that the commencement of the reform movement coincided in Western Europe with the transition from the early modern state to the nation-state. Beccaria's advocacy for more lenient, but also more predictable, punishment was actually "a plea for a stronger state, and in particular for a [modern] police force." As the European states grew more effective at maintaining public order, they could afford to treat lawbreakers more leniently.[107] Indeed, the regular police forces in some Western European countries, especially England, made great strides in professionalization during the nineteenth century. Peel's reform, for example, vastly increased the number of criminals apprehended; in the two years from 1828 to 1830, the number of convicts sent to Australia doubled.[108] Greater police efficiency, in time, helped reduce the incidence of crime and, therefore, opened the way to the low punishment rates achieved in England and Wales by the turn of the twentieth century. Even so, Spierenburg emphasizes that harsh forms of punishment were abolished, not primarily for utilitarian reasons, but because beginning in the mid-eighteenth century criminals "were increasingly perceived as fellow human beings." This shift coincided, according to Spierenburg, with the development of a "new sensitivity toward death."[109]

It is legitimate to wonder whether it was a "new sensitivity toward death" that drove Russia's rulers to abolish the harshest forms of punishment and to soften punishment regimes in general during the nineteenth century.

Addressing this issue directly lies beyond the scope of this essay. Yet Ben Eklof has discerned in Russia's schools at the turn of the century that a "growing repudiation of harsh discipline, and a new sensibility about the child . . . resulted in a redefinition of the notion of corporal punishment and a campaign to bring to public attention (and censure) all remnants of unacceptably harsh behaviour. In the process, as lurid examples surfaced, the impression was created that things were far worse than they actually were. This pattern . . . typifies the way Russians in general both overstated the degree of their own 'backwardness' in educational matters at the turn of the century and were misled about conditions in the West."[110] One presumes that it was, in large part, perceptions of Russia's backwardness that impelled government officials, and public activists seeking to influence them, to follow Western European and American penological theories and models.

If the Russian government was in a far weaker position to discipline and control society than were its Western European counterparts, nonofficial elites in Russia were by no means able to assume responsibility for disciplining society, as their counterparts in Western Europe had been doing throughout much of the nineteenth century.[111] Two examples come to mind. First, publicly funded and organized prison-aid societies (*patronaty*), modeled on Western European practice, achieved few results. Apparently too few people were interested in making them work.[112] Second, the Victorian sexual mores that were so important to building up a strong modern society in its early stages were already under attack by intellectuals in Western Europe at the time when Russian society was first ready to adopt them.[113] This dual impotence of state and society was a dangerous combination for a country in the throes of such wrenching social change—and in the face of repeated physical attacks on government officials—as was late Imperial Russia.

In many ways, official and nonofficial elites had a greater commonality of interests than either shared with the mass of Russians.[114] As the Kadet leader Ariadna Tyrkova-Villiams remarked, only in emigration did she and other Russian liberals grasp how much "we shared in our habits, in our upbringing, in our love for Russia [with government officials]. In the Duma, neither they nor we suspected any of these things, because of mutual prejudice."[115] Yet cooperation between the liberal opposition and even the most enlightened government officials would have been very difficult, not merely because of mutual prejudice but also because of concrete political disagreements. It would have been hard for many nonofficial educated elites to feel enthusiastic about Russia's relatively enlightened penal system when they were systematically excluded from political participation and when political self-expression was strictly regulated and in many cases a criminal offense. Here, in fact, one may find that aspect of penological and criminological practice where Russia was most out of step with the major Western European countries— the definition and punishment of "political crime," a topic I have explored elsewhere.[116]

NOTES

1. For comments and criticism on earlier drafts of this essay, I am grateful to Marc Raeff, Jörg Baberowski, John Bushnell, Ben Eklof, Richard John, Daniel Scott Smith, Karl Wood, Nicole Butz, Leonid Trofimov, Maria Villafuerte, and the participants in the University of Chicago Russian History Workshop. Thanks also to Leo Schelbert for pertinent bibliographical references. Support for this article was provided by the Institute for the Humanities Grants-in-Aid Program, with funding from the Office of the Vice Chancellor for Research at the University of Illinois at Chicago, and by the Kennan Institute for Advanced Russian Studies, Washington, D.C.

    In the late eighteenth century, the criminal punishment regimes in nearly every country of Europe were barbarous. See Max Grünhut, *Penal Reform: A Comparative Study* (Oxford: Clarendon Press, 1948), 33–34. In England, e.g., people were burned at the stake until 1789. See John Lawrence, *A History of Capital Punishment* (New York: The Citadel Press, 1960), 10.

2. On this broad trend, see Michel Foucault, *Discipline and Punish: The Birth of the Prison*, trans. Alan Sheridan (New York: Vintage Books, 1979); Richard J. Evans, *Rituals of Retribution: Capital Punishment in Germany, 1600–1987* (Oxford: Oxford University Press, 1996); Pieter Spierenburg, *The Spectacle of Suffering: Executions and the Evolution of Repression: From a Preindustrial Metropolis to the European Experience* (Cambridge: Cambridge University Press, 1984); David D. Cooper, *The Lesson of the Scaffold: The Public Execution Controversy in Victorian England* (Athens, OH: Ohio University Press, 1974); Patricia O'Brien, *The Promise of Punishment: Prisons in Nineteenth-Century France* (Princeton, NJ: Princeton University Press, 1982); Michael Ignatieff, *A Just Measure of Pain: The Penitentiary in the Industrial Revolution, 1750–1850* (New York: Pantheon Books, 1978); William James Forsythe, *The Reform of Prisoners, 1830–1900* (London and Sydney: Croom Helm, 1987); W.J. Forsythe, *Penal Discipline, Reformatory Projects and the English Prison Commission, 1895–1939* (Exeter: Exeter University Press, 1991).

3. Joseph Viaud, *La peine de mort en matière politique: Étude historique et critique* (Thèse pour le doctorat, University of Paris, 1902), 380; A.A. Piontkovskii, *Smertnaia kazn' v Evrope* (Kazan: Tip. Imperatorskogo Universiteta, 1908), 77. On the punishment of knouting, which replaced capital punishment in most cases after Elizabeth's reform, see Abby M. Schrader, "Containing the Spectacle of Punishment: The Russian Autocracy and the Abolition of the Knout, 1817–1845," *Slavic Review* 56 (Winter 1997): 613–644. It has been assumed that flogging with the knout often had occasioned death. See Peter Liessem, "Die Todesstrafe im späten Zarenreich: Rechtslage, Realität und öffentliche Diskussion," *Jahrbücher für Geschichte Osteuropas* 37 (1989): 492–523, here 394–395; a recent study argues that such occurrences were extremely rare: Cyril Bryner, "The Issue of Capital Punishment in the Reign of Elizabeth Petrovna," *Russian Review* 49 (October 1990): 390, 395–401.

4. M.N. Gernet, *Smertnaia kazn'* (Moscow: Ia. Dankin i Ia. Khomutov, 1913), 73, 82. Ironically, British penal reformers in the late eighteenth century often argued that the death penalty was "the natural offspring of monarchical governments" (Ignatieff, *A Just Measure of Pain*, 74).

5. Note to art. 13 of the Code pénal, in *Les codes français annotés, offrant sous chaque article l'état complet de la doctrine, de la jurisprudence et de la législation*

(Paris: Journal du Palais, 1843). Nineteenth-century Russia's most gruesome punishment, nostril slitting, was abolished in 1817: A. Lentin, "Beccaria, Shcherbatov, and the Question of Capital Punishment in Eighteenth Century Russia," *Canadian Slavonic Papers* 24 (June 1982): 128–137, here: 135–136.

6. Cooper, *Lesson of the Scaffold*, 170; *PSZ*, ser. 3, vol. 1, no.198 (May 26, 1881); Spierenburg, *Spectacle*, 198. In certain border regions (Caucasus, Turkestan, Omsk military districts), military commanders were granted the right to conduct public execution of indigenous peoples. Tagantsev, *Russkoe ugolovnoe pravo*, 2:108.

7. The major exception was "political" crime and punishment, on which subject see my "Political Crime in Late Imperial Russia," *Journal of Modern History* 74 (March 2002): 62–100.

8. Norbert Finzsch, " 'Comparing Apples and Oranges?' The History of Early Prisons in Germany and the United States, 1800–1860," in Norbert Finzsch and Robert Jütte, eds., *Institutions of Confinement: Hospitals, Asylums, and Prisons in Western Europe and North America, 1500–1950* (Cambridge: Cambridge University Press, 1996), 213–214.

9. John LeDonne, "Civilians under Military Justice during the Reign of Nicholas I," *Canadian-American Slavic Studies* 7 (Summer 1973): 171–187; Donald C. Rawson, "The Death Penalty in Late Tsarist Russia: An Investigation of Judicial Procedures," *Russian History* 11 (Spring 1984): 34–35. On the laws governing nonjudicial authorities, see Jonathan W. Daly, *Autocracy under Siege: Security Police and Opposition in Russia, 1866–1905* (DeKalb, IL: Northern Illinois University Press, 1998), ch.1.

10. *Ulozhenie o nakazaniiakh*, 1845 ed., arts. 9 and 34.

11. S.S. Ostroumov, *Prestupnost' i ee prichiny v dorevoliutsionnoi Rossii* (Moscow: Izd. Moskovskogo Universiteta, 1960), 123.

12. On the law's background, see S.V. Kodan, "Lishenie prav sostoianiia v sisteme karatel'nykh mer samoderzhaviia, konets XVIII–pervaia polovina XIX v.," *Pravovye problemy istorii gosudarstvennykh uchrezhdenii: Mezhvuzovskii sbornik nauchnykh trudov* (Sverdlovsk: Sverdlovskii iuridicheskii institut, 1983), 68–80. Military courts could choose to impose the death penalty without the deprivation of rights. See K.K., "Smertnaia kazn' po voenno-ugolovnym zakonam," *Entsiklopedicheskii slovar'*, 82 vols. (St. Petersburg: F.A. Brokgauz i I. A. Efron, 1890–1904) [hereafter: *ES*], 30A:499.

13. A. Ia., "Lishenie prav," *ES*, 27A:872–875. The emperor could restore a person's rights by executive fiat, as Alexander II did in 1862 with respect to the Decembrists and the Petrashevtsy (Kodan, "Lishenie prav," 79).

14. "Mort civile," in Block, ed., *Dictionnaire général de la politique*, 2:357–358; Eduoard Dalloz et al., eds., *Les codes annotés: Supplément au Code pénal* (Paris: Bureau de la Jurisprudence Générale, 1899), 24. The Bolshevik regime reserved a similar measure of repression for whole social categories: Elise Kimerling, "Civil Rights and Social Policy in Soviet Russia, 1918–1936," *Russian Review* 41 (January 1982): 24–46.

15. Rawson, "Death Penalty," 32. Apparently no one in Russia was executed for breach of quarantine: Piontkovskii, *Smertnaia kazn' v Evrope*, 79; M.N. Gernet, O.B. Gol'dovskii, and I.N. Sakharov, eds., *Protiv smertnoi kazni*, 2nd ed. (Moscow: Tip. I.D. Sytina, 1907), 385–423.

16. Viaud, *Peine de mort en matière politique*, 361–381; A.F. Heard, "Justice and Law in Russia," *Harper's Magazine* 76 (1888): 930. See also Jörg Baberowski, *Autokratie und Justiz: Zum Verhältnis von Rechtsstaatlichkeit und Rückständigkeit*

im ausgehenden Zarenreich, 1864–1914 (Frankfurt am Main: Vittorio Klostermann, 1996), 199–200, 694; G.B. Sliozberg, *Dorevoliutsionnyi stroi Rossii* (Paris, 1933), 295.

17. The reformism of the drafters of the code drove them to prescribe imprisonment, which was considered more humane and modern than exile or corporal punishment, for a wide range of crimes, despite the fact that for decades thereafter, adequate prison space was unavailable in Russia. See Bruce F. Adams, *The Politics of Punishment: Prison Reform in Russia, 1863–1917* (DeKalb, IL: Northern Illinois University Press, 1996), 10, 94–95.

18. Rawson, "Death Penalty," 38.

19. LeDonne, "Civilians under Military Justice," 173–177; Rawson, "Death Penalty," 34–38; Piontkovskii, *Smertnaia kazn' v Evrope*, 76–77.

20. These figures exclude the roughly 1,500 participants in the Polish rebellion who were executed without the benefit of a trial between 1862 and 1866 (Gernet, Gol'dovskii, and Sakharov, eds., *Protiv smertnoi kazni*, 394–395). Similarly, the figures cited below for France exclude summary executions occurring during the suppression of dissidence during the revolution of 1848, the coup of 1851, and the Commune of 1871.

21. Although most of the people executed in Western Europe had committed regular crimes, in England numerous Fenian Irish revolutionaries were executed for political murder; three Fenians were hanged on November 23, 1867; another was hanged on May 26, 1868 (Cooper, *Lesson of the Scaffold*, 148–149, 170).

22. Gernet, *Smertnaia kazn'*, 73, 96; Evans, *Rituals*, 933–934; Victoria Schneider and John Ortiz Smylka, "A Summary Analysis of *Executions in the United States, 1608–1987: The Espy File*," in *The Death Penalty in America: Current Research*, ed. Robert M. Bohm (Cincinnati: Anderson Publishing, 1991), 6–7.

23. Russia's rulers occasionally paid lip-service to similar principles, as when the government officially declared in 1878 that it was the government's "duty before every honest and good citizen (*grazhdanin*) of the Russian state to protect their life and property." See V.Ia. Bogucharskii, *Iz istorii politicheskoi bor'by v 70-x i 80-x gg. XIX veka: Partiia "Narodnaia volia", ee proiskhozhdenie, sud'by i gibel'* (Moscow: Russkaia mysl', 1912), 19.

24. S.N. Viktorskii, *Istoriia smertnoi kazni v Rossii i sovremennoe ee sostoianie* (Moscow: Tip. Imperatorskogo Moskovskogo Universiteta, 1912), 324. It is worth noting that several European governments in the 1860s and 1870s, beginning with those of Romania, Portugal, Holland, and Switzerland, abolished capital punishment outright. See Liessem, "Todesstrafe," 494.

25. On Russia's emulation of Western European judicial practice in general, see the magisterial study by Baberowski, *Autokratie und Justiz*.

26. Richard S. Wortman, *The Development of a Russian Legal Consciousness* (Chicago: University of Chicago Press, 1976), 270. See also Baberowski, *Autokratie und Justiz*, 57–58, 615–616.

27. For an elaboration of this argument, see Jonathan W. Daly, "On the Significance of Emergency Legislation in Late Imperial Russia," *Slavic Review* 54 (Fall 1995): 602–629.

28. William C. Fuller, Jr., "Civilians in Russian Military Courts, 1881–1904," *Russian Review* 41 (July 1982): 289–290.

29. In a few cases, most notably that of Vera Zasulich, senior officials chose to try political criminals in jury trials in the hope of turning public opinion against them (Baberowski, *Autokratie und Justiz*, 680).

30. *Polnoe sobranie zakonov Rossiiskoi Imperii*, 2nd series, 1825–1879 (St. Petersburg: Tip. 2-go Otdeleniia Ego Imperatorskago Velichestva Kantseliarii, 1885), vol. 38, pt. 1, nos.39504, 39505 (April 17, 1863); N. Evreinov, *Istoriia telesnykh nakazanii v Rossii* (St. Petersburg: V. K. Il'inchik, 1913), 10, 150, 153; A.Ia., "Knut," *ES*, 15:464–465; "Pleti," ibid., 23A:872–873; A. Timofeev, "Telesnye nakazaniia," ibid., 34:294; Adams, *Politics of Punishment*, 12–39. Abby Schrader argues that the knout was abolished largely for pragmatic reasons (Schrader, "Containing the Spectacle of Punishment," 617n, 644), yet the evidence she adduces suggests that the influence of Enlightenment ideas in Russia may have been as important a cause (ibid., 638). P.A. Kropotkin asserted that even before 1863, some governors refused to confirm corporal punishment sentences, while others demanded only a symbolic implementation of such sentences. By the early 1870s, it appears that exiles could almost always avoid flogging by paying a modest bribe to the flogger: P. Kropotkin, *V russkikh i frantsuzskikh tiur'makh*, trans. Batunskii, rev. ed. (St. Petersburg: Znanie, 1906), 26; S.A. Kovalenko, "Razbitaia zhizn': Rasskaz ssyl'nogo: K istorii brodiazhnichestva na Rusi," *Russkaia starina* (June 1900): 163–164. Stephen P. Frank shows that the *volost'* courts gradually issued fewer and fewer corporal punishment sentences in the years after 1863: "Emancipation and the Birch: The Perpetuation of Corporal Punishment in Rural Russia, 1861–1907," *Jarbücher für Geschichte Osteuropas* 45 (1997): 407–414.

31. Myra Glenn, *Campaigns against Corporal Punishment: Prisoners, Sailors, Women, and Children in Antebellum America* (Albany, NY: State University of New York Press, 1984).

32. J.J. Tobias, *Nineteenth-Century Crime: Prevention and Punishments* (New York: Barnes and Noble, 1972), 139. The British army abolished flogging only in 1889, although its use fell dramatically during the first decades of the century. See J.R. Dinwiddy, "The Early Nineteenth Century Campaign Against Flogging in the Army," *English Historical Review* 97 (April 1982): 308–331. An executive order of 1885 allowed governors in Russia to carry out mass floggings of peasants to quell popular unrest, but it was conceived as an exceptional measure and was applied relatively rarely: P.A. Zaionchkovskii, *Rossiiskoe samoderzhavie v kontse XIX stoletiia (Politicheskaia reaktsiia 80-x–nachala 90-x godov)* (Moscow: Mysl', 1970), 170–172; Frank, "Emancipation and the Birch," 415.

33. O.I. Chistiakov, ed., *Zakonodatel'stvo pervoi poloviny XIX veka*, vol. 6 of *Rossiiskoe zakonodatel'stvo X–XX vekov* (Moscow: Iuridicheskaia literatura, 1988), 170; A. Ia., "Kleimenie prestupnikov," *ES*, 15:346–348; V.A.C. Gatrell, *The Hanging Tree: Execution and the English People, 1770–1868* (Oxford: Oxford University Press, 1994), 16.

34. Baberowski demonstrates that juries tended furthermore to be dominated by illiterate peasants who did not share the Europeanized elite's conceptions of legality and justice (Baberowski, *Autokratie und Justiz*, ch. 3). Ironically, defense attorneys sometimes sought to exclude potential jurors from the lower middle class, whom they considered ill-disposed toward enemies of the regime (ibid. 682–683).

35. As I argue in "Emergency Legislation," 602–629.

36. Liessem, "Die Todesstrafe," 498. Gernet, *Smertnaia kazn'*, 96–97; Gernet, Gol'dovskii, and Sakharov, eds., *Protiv smertnoi kazni*, 396–398; Rawson, "Death Penalty," 33–37. See also *Smertnaia kazn': Sbornik statei N. S. Tagantseva* (St. Petersburg: Gos. tip., 1913), 89–90.

37. Evans, *Rituals of Retribution*, 934–935. Justice Minister N.V. Murav'ev petitioned the emperor for clemency on behalf of an average of 330 people per year from 1894 to 1904 (*Vsepoddanneishii doklad ministra iustitsii stats-sekretaria Murav'eva o deiatel'nosti Ministerstva iustitsii za istekshee desiatiletie, 1894–1904 gg.* [St. Petersburg: Senatskaia tip., 1904], 13, 34). From 1891 to 1902, not one person was sentenced to death in Russia by the civil courts: Tagantsev, *Russkoe ugolovnoe pravo*, 2:181.

38. Evans, *Rituals of Retribution*, 919–920. A rather high number of people were sentenced to death in Austria from 1877 to 1910 (2,552), but of these only 84, or 3.2 percent, were actually executed (Gernet, *Smertnaia kazn'*, 86–87). That was 5.9 executions per million population.

39. Gernet, *Smertnaia kazn'*, 83, 92, 94; Schneider and Smylka, "A Summary Analysis," 6.

40. The annual rate of executions per 100,000 in the United States rose from 0.24 in the 1890s, to 0.38 in the 1900s, to 0.69 in the 1910s: Margaret Werner Cahalan and Lee Anne Parsons, *Historical Corrections Statistics in the United States, 1850–1984* (Westat, Inc., Rockville, MD, for the Bureau of Justice Statistics, U.S. Department of Justice, 1986), 14.

41. See, e.g., Daniel R. Headrick, *The Tools of Empire: Technology and European Imperialism in the Nineteenth Century* (New York and Oxford: Oxford University Press, 1981), 115–119.

42. *Smertnaia kazn': Sbornik statei N. S. Tagantseva*, 90n; Gernet, Gol'dovskii, and Sakharov, eds., *Protiv smertnoi kazni*, 396–400; Liessem, "Todesstrafe," 500.

43. Gernet, *Smertnaia kazn'*, 94.

44. See Viktorskii, *Istoriia smertnoi kazni v Rossii*, 323–324; *Ugolovnoe ulozhenie*, 13–14; Titkova, "Razrabotka Ugolovnogo ulozheniia," 84.

45. Baberowski, *Autokratie und Justiz*, 742; reference to the execution in Viktor Obninskii, *Polgoda russkoi revoliutsii: Sbornik materialov k istorii russkoi revoliutsii, oktiabr' 1905–aprel' 1906* (Moscow: I. N. Kholchev, 1906), 47.

46. S.S. Ostroumov, "Repressii tsarskogo pravitel'stva protiv revoliutsionnogo dvizheniia v Rossii v period imperializma: Ugolovno-statistichekoe issledovanie," *Vestnik moskovskogo universiteta* Series 8, Pravo (1976), no.3:40. See also Gernet, *Smertnaia kazn'*, 98; *Sbornik statei N. S. Tagantseva*, 91–92.

47. V.M., ed., "K istorii karatel'nykh ekspeditsii v Sibiri," *KA* 1 (1922): 329–333; N.I. Faleev, "Shest' mesiatsev voenno-polevoi iustitsii," *Byloe* 2 (1907): 43–44, 69–70; Ostoumov, "Repressii tsarskogo pravitel'stva," 39. The military field courts wreaked by far their greatest havoc among the non-Russian periphery: only 104 out of the 629 people executed by the courts between August 31, 1906 and January 31, 1907 resided in European and Siberian Russia (Gernet, *Istoriia tsarskoi tiur'my*, 107–108). Similarly, the punitive expeditions of 1906 and 1907, whose death-toll was so terribly high, operated almost exclusively in the Baltic region, in Ukraine, and along the Trans-Siberian railroad (V. M., ed., "K istorii karatel'nykh ekspeditsii v Sibiri," 329–333).

48. Gordon Wright, *France in Modern Times*, 4th ed. (New York: W. W. Norton, 1987), 216–218.

49. The disorder in Russia was accompanied by an apparently huge increase in the murder rate. The number of murder investigations rose from 12,000 in 1904 to 30,000 in 1905 and 36,500 in 1906: E.N. Tarnovskii, "Dvizhenie prestupnosti v rossiiskoi imperii za 1899–1908 g.g.," *Zhurnal Ministerstva Iustitsii* 15, no.9 (1909): 66.

50. In 1911, there were 58 executions; in 1912, 108 (S.F., "Repressii: Iskliuchitel'noe polozhenie," in *Ezhegodnik gazety "Rech' " na 1914 god* [St. Petersburg: Rech', 1914], 41).

51. Evans, *Rituals of Retribution*, 920, 934–935.

52. In at least one part of the Russian Empire, Finland, capital punishment had fallen entirely into disuse: Piontkovskii, *Smertnaia kazn' v Evrope*, 99.

53. Viktorskii, *Istoriia smertnoi kazni v Rossii*, 367–369.

54. Gernet, Gol'dovskii, and Sakharov, eds., *Protiv smertnoi kazni*; Liessem, "Todesstrafe," 512–522. A public debate on capital punishment was also raging at that time in France. See Piontkovskii, *Smertnaia kazn' v Evrope*, 19.

55. B.S. Utevskii, *Vospominaniia iurista* (Moscow: Iuridicheskaia literatura, 1989), 33.

56. S.P. Makrinskii, "Smertnaia kazn' i bor'ba s politicheskimi prestupleniiami," *Pravo* (July 4, 1906), no.22:1989–92.

57. Ruth Pike, "Penal Servitude in Early Modern Spain: The Galleys," *Journal of European Economic History* 11 (1982): 198–200.

58. Tagantsev, *Russkoe ugolovnoe pravo*, 2:113; Adams, *Politics of Punishment*, 142–143. Some Russian penal reformers urged that *katorga* replace capital punishment entirely: Adams, *Politics of Punishment*, 101.

59. V.D. Zhizhin, "Ssylka v Rossii," *Zhurnal Ministerstva Iustitsii*, no.2 (Feb. 1900): 85–90; G.S., "Katorga, katorzhnye raboty" *ES*, 14A:759; Baberowski, *Autokratie und Justiz*, 199; Heard, "Justice and Law in Russia," 931; Adams, *Politics of Punishment*, 100. *Otchet po Glavnomu tiuremnomu upravleniiu za 1901 g.* (St. Petersburg: Tip. S-Peterburgskoi tiur'my, 1903), 33; S.V. Kodan, "Katorga," in *Otechestvennaia istoriia: Istoriia Rossii s drevneishikh vremen do 1917 goda: Entsiklopediia* (Moscow: Bol'shaia Rossiiskaia Entsiklopediia, 1994), 2:529–532; G.S., "Katorga," 759; Zaionchkovskii, *Rossiiskoe samoderzhavie*, 168; Adams, *Politics of Punishment*, 50, 100.

60. See André Zysberg, "Galley and Hard Labor Convicts in France, 1550–1850: From the Galleys to Hard Labor Camps: Essay on a Long-Lasting Penal Institution," in Pieter Spierenburg, ed., *The Emergence of Carceral Institutions: Prisons, Galleys and Lunatic Asylums, 1550–1900* 12 (1984): 78–124; André Zysberg, "Politiques du bagne, 1820–1850," in Perrot, ed., *L'impossible prison*, 165–205; "Déportation," in *Dictionnaire général de la politique*, ed. Maurice Block, new ed. (Paris: O. Lorenz, 1873), 647–648.

61. Zysberg, "Politiques du bagne," 200.

62. Edmond Henri, *Étude critique de la transportation en Guyane française: Réformes réalisables* (Paris: Librairie de la Société du Recueil Sirey, 1912), 16. The rules regulating the treatment of convicts, adopted on June 18, 1880, were subsequently considered too magnanimous and were replaced with harsher rules on September 4, 1891 (ibid., 17, 24–28).

63. "Relégation," *La grande encyclopédie: Inventaire raisonné des sciences, des letters et des arts* (Paris: Société anonyme de la grande encyclopédie, 1899), 28:333; "Transportation," in ibid. 31:309–310; "Travaux forcés," in ibid. 31:326; Mikhail Gubskii, "Ssylka," *ES*, 31:376; Henri, *Étude critique*, 5–6, 10, 14. There were in fact three kinds of exile in French law. *Transportation* was hard labor properly speaking; *relégation*, instituted in 1885, was exile without hard labor for recidivists; and *déportation* was exile without hard labor for political convicts. After 1880, *déportation* was scarcely used, but *relégation* was often resorted to for anarchists and other violent political activists (Gubskii, "Ssylka," 374).

64. Henri, *Étude critique*, 4–5.

65. Henri, *Étude critique*, 4–5; O'Brien, *The Promise of Punishment*, 26.

66. Henri, *Étude critique*, 55–56. To the numbers cited, one must add 10,549 convicts exiled from France without sentence of penal servitude between 1885 and 1910; by 1910, only 2,614 of these convicts were still alive (ibid. 5). Curiously, Henri suggests that adversaries and supporters of the practice of penal colonialization drew inspiration from both the Russian and British examples (ibid. 10).

67. *Otchet po Glavnomu tiuremnomu upravleniiu* (1898–1904).

68. Adams, *Politics of Punishment*, 100.

69. See *Annuaire statistique de la France* (1889), 109; *Otchet po Glavnomu tiuremnomu upravleniiu za 1882 god* (1884), 5; *Otchet po Glavnomu tiuremnomu upravleniiu za 1904 god* (1906), 18; Kodan, "Katorga," 531.

70. Henri, *Étude critique*, 18; Armand Mossé, *Les prisons et les institutions d'éducation corrective*, rev. ed. (Paris: Librairie du Recueil Sirey, 1929), 424. The last convicts were sent to French Guiana in 1938; between 1945 and 1954 the French government repatriated the last 2,020 exiles: Michel Devèse, *Cayenne: Déportés et bagnards* (Paris: Collection Archives, 1965), 276–277.

71. *Otchet po Glavnomu tiuremnomu upravleniiu za 1910 god* (St. Petersburg: Tip. S.-Peterburgskoi tiur'my, 1912), pt. 1:35; *Otchet po Glavnomu tiuremnomu upravleniiu za 1913 god* (St. Petersburg: Tip. Petrogradskoi tiur'my, 1915), pt. 2:30. The total number of *katorzhniki* rose to 9,700 in 1907, to 16,450 in 1908, to 23,095 in 1909, and up to 32,520 at the end of 1912, before declining to 28,742 by the end of 1913 (Kodan, "Katorga," 531; *Otchet po Glavnomu tiuremnomu upravleniiu za 1913 god* [1914]), 32.

72. *Otchet po glavnomu tiuremnomu upravleniiu* (1913), pt. 2:32.

73. Sidney and Beatrice Webb, *English Prisons under Local Government* (Hamden, CT: Archon Books, 1963), 181–182; *Report of the Directors of Convict Prisons for the Year 1890–91*, pt. 1:xviii; Christopher Harding et al., eds., *Imprisonment in England and Wales: A Concise History* (London: Croom Helm, 1885), 195.

74. On the complex classification of exiles, see Gubskii, "Ssylka," 379–380; Tagantsev, *Russkoe ugolovnoe pravo*, 2:115–125; Zhizhin, "Ssylka v Rossii," 91–93.

75. Philip Jenkins, "From Gallows to Prison? The Execution Rate in Early Modern England," *Criminal Justice History* 7 (1986): 66–67.

76. P.W. Coldham, *Emigrants in Chains: A Social History of Forced Emigration to the Americas of Felons, Destitute Children, Political and Religious Non-conformists, Vagabonds, Beggars, and other Undesirables, 1607–1776* (Baltimore: Genealogical Publishing Co., 1992), 1–3, 48.

77. Charles Bateson, *The Convict Ships, 1787–1868* (Glasgow: Brown, Son & Ferguson, 1959), 9; A.G.L. Shaw, *Convicts and the Colonies: A Study of Penal Transportation from Great Britain and Ireland to Australia and other Parts of the British Empire* (London: Faber and Faber, 1966), 153. Stealing an article worth a shilling or more from a person's pocket was a crime punishable by penal exile in the mid-nineteenth century (ibid. 226–228).

78. Bateson, *Convict Ships*, 5; Coldham, *Emigrants in Chains*, 3; Shaw, *Convicts and the Colonies*, ch. 10. The proportion of "assigned" servants to hard-labor convicts was probably about ten to one (Shaw, *Convicts and the Colonies*, 216, 351).

79. Edward H. Judge, "Peasant Resettlement and Social Control in Late Imperial Russia," in Edward H. Judge and James Y. Simms, Jr., eds., *Modernization and Revolution: Dilemmas of Progress in Late Imperial Russia: Essays in Honor of Arthur P. Mendel*, (New York: East European Monographs, 1992), 77; A.D. Margolis, *Tiur'ma i ssylka v imperatorskoi Rossii, issledovaniia i arkhivnye*

nakhodki (Moscow: Lanterna i Vita, 1995), 32; A.G.L. Shaw, *A Short History of Australia* (New York: Frederick A. Praeger, 1967), 94; idem, *Convicts and the Colonies*, 148. In 1846, Australia's European population was just under 190,000: A. Wyatt Tilby, *Australia*, vol. 5 of *The English People Overseas* (Boston and New York: Houghton Mifflin, 1916), 86.

80. Gubskii, "Ssylka," 379–380; Volker Rabe, *Der Widerspruch von Rechtsstaatlichkeit und strafender Verwaltung in Russland, 1881–1917: Motive, Handhabung und Auswirkungen der administrativen Verbannung von Revolutionären*, Wissenschaftliche Beiträge Karlsruhe, no.14 (Karlsruhe: Verlag M. Wahl, 1985), 40.

81. Rabe, *Widerspruch*, 178–179, 192.

82. Bateson, *Convict Ships*, 4; Shaw, *Convicts and the Colonies*, 116. Before the construction of rail lines to Siberia, the exiles had to walk much of the way there, but few died on the way. By the mid-1880s, they were transported by rail and steamer to Tomsk, whence the political prisoners were carried further by wagon and the regular convicts continued on foot. As the railroad was extended further, the exiles' travel was made still less arduous (A.S.L., "Etap," *ES*, 41:138).

83. For detailed statistics on penal exile in the nineteenth century, see Margolis, *Tiur'ma i ssylka*, 29–42. The yearly average of people exiled, interestingly, declined from 15,606 in the period 1864–83 to 13,224 from 1884 to 1893 (Ostroumov, *Prestupnost' i ee prichiny*, 125).

84. S.V. Kodan, "Administrativnaia ssylka," in *Otechestvennaia istoriia*, 1:28; Margolis, *Tiur'ma i ssylka*, 30–32; Tagantsev, *Russkoe ugolovnoe pravo*, 10.

85. Margolis, *Tiur'ma i ssylka*, 37; Gubskii, "Ssylka," 382; Alan Wood, "Russia's 'Wild East': Exile, Vagrancy, and Crime in Nineteenth-Century Siberia," in *The History of Siberia from Russian Conquest to Revolution*, ed. Alan Wood (London and New York: Routledge, 1991), 124.

86. Friedrich-Christian Schroeder, "Gesellschaftsgerichte und Administrativjustiz im vorrevolutionären Russland," *Osteuropa-Recht* 4 (1962): 297–300; Chistiakov, ed., *Zakonodatel'stvo*, 316n; Margolis, *Tiur'ma i ssylka*, 16–18; Tagantsev, *Russkoe ugolovnoe pravo*, 2:10. Until 1861, a portion of the exiles were serfs impressed into the military (see Elise Kimerling Wirtschafter, *From Serf to Russian Soldier* [Princeton: Princeton University Press, 1990], 21–22, 160n). Lev Deich, who spent 16 years in Siberian exile, reported that peasants exiled by their communes were generally treated harshly by the other exiles: Lev Deich, *Za polveka*, intro. Ezra Mendelsohn (Berlin: Grani, 1923; Cambridge: Oriental Research Partners, 1975), 1:57n.

87. On the deleterious effect that the exiles exerted on the Siberian population, see Alan Wood, "Crime and Punishment in the House of the Dead," in Olga Crisp and Linda Edmondson, eds., *Civil Rights in Imperial Russia* (Oxford: Clarendon Press, 1989), 226–227; idem, "Russia's 'Wild East,' " 118–134. Many reformers in the 1870s viewed *katorga*, since it was supposed to pay for itself, as a means by which to curtail the use of penal exile (Adams, *Politics of Punishment*, 92).

88. Rabe, *Widerspruch*, 47.

89. *Vospominaniia Borisa Nikolaevicha Chicherina*, 4 pts. (Moscow: Izd. M. i S. Sabashnikhovykh, 1929–34), pt. 4, 116. It goes without saying that many attorneys staunchly opposed administrative exile. See N. Karabchevskii, *Chto glaza moi videli*, 2 vols. (Berlin: Izd. Ol'gi D'iakovoi, 1921), 2:39; Baberowski, *Autokratie und Justiz*, chap. 7.

90. P.A. Zaionchkovskii, *Krizis samoderzhaviia na rubezhe 1870–1880-kh gg.* (Moscow: Izd. Moskovskogo Universiteta, 1964), 186.

91. Margolis, *Tiur'ma i ssylka*, 17–20, 24; Adams, *Politics of Punishment*, 50–51, 91–92, 101, 136–137, 162. Dmitrii Dril', *Ssylka vo Frantsii i Rossii: Iz lichnykh nabliudenii vo vremia poezdki v Novuiu Kaledoniiu, na o. Sakhalin, v Priamurskii krai i Sibir'* (St. Petersburg: Izd. L. F. Panteleeva, 1899), i–ii, 138–145, 168–173; Tagantsev, *Russkoe ugolovnoe pravo*, 2:113–115, 199, 201–204. Dril' was an official in the prison administration for 13 years, which may help to explain his preference for prisons over exile: *Otchet po Glavnomu tiuremnomu upravleniiu za 1910 god*, pt. 1:16.

92. Adams, *Politics of Punishment*, 135; *PSZ*, ser. 3, vol. 20, part 1, no.18839 (June 12, 1900); Margolis, *Tiur'ma i ssylka*, 23–25; Schroeder, "Gesellschaftsgerichte und Administrativjustiz," 301–303; Tagantsev, *Russkoe ugolovnoe pravo*, 2:10. Pointing to insufficient prison space, a majority of the members of the united departments of the State Council had opposed the law: "Iz dnevnika A.A. Polovtsova, 1895–1900" (diary entry for May 1, 1900), *Krasnyi Arkhiv* 46 (1931): 129.

93. See Rabe, *Widerspruch*, 149a, 151.

94. On the various types of imprisonment in Russia, see Tagantsev, *Russkoe ugolovnoe pravo*, 2:124–134.

95. Adams, *Politics of Punishment*, 133, 175, 183; Stephen G. Wheatcroft, "The Crisis of the Late Tsarist Penal System," in Stephen G. Wheatcroft, ed., *Challenging Traditional Views of Russian History* (New York: Palgrave Macmillan, 2002), 33–39.

96. *Otchet po Glavnomu tiuremnomu upravleniiu* (1880, 1890, 1900, 1910).

97. Adams, *Politics of Punishment*, 9, 133, 143. See also Kropotkin, *V russkikh i frantsuzskikh tiur'makh*, 24–25.

98. *Report of the Directors of Convict Prisons* (for the year 1890–91), xii; *Report of the Commissioners of Prisons* (for the year ended March 31, 1891), 10; *Otchet po Glavnomu tiuremnomu upravleniiu* (for 1890), 22.

99. Wheatcroft, "Crisis," 40–41; Alan Barenberg, " 'Among Prisoners': A Social History of Russian Prisons, 1879–1913" (unpublished seminar paper, University of Chicago, 2001), 46–49. For details on sickness and mortality in Russian prisons, see Barenberg, " 'Among Prisoners,' " 109–129.

100. *Annuaire statistique* (1902), 105; ibid. (1911), 123. The mortality rates are given by sex; I calculated from these data the gender-neutral rates.

101. Margolis, *Tiur'ma i ssylka*, 36–37.

102. Adams, *Politics of Punishment*, 183.

103. Daly, "Emergency Legislation," 624; Rabe, *Der Widerspruch*, 33; A.A. Loewenstimm, "Die Deportation nach Sibirien vor und nach dem Gesetz vom 12. Juni 1900," in *Zeitschrift für die gesamte Strafrechtswissenschaft* 24 (1904): 88–128.

104. E.N. Tarnovskii, "Dvizhenie prestupnosti v evropeiskoi Rossii za 1874–1894 gg.," *Zhurnal ministerstva iustitsii*, no.3 (1899): 139; Lombroso and Laschi, *Le crime politique*, 1:79; Baberowski, *Autokratie und Justiz*, 228–290.

105. Richard S. Wortman, *Scenarios of Power: Myth and Ceremony in Russian Monarchy*, 2 vols. (Princeton, NJ: Princeton University Press, 1995), 1:406–407.

106. These institutions and reforms had a harder time taking root in Russia than in Western Europe because, as Jörg Baberowski has eloquently argued with respect to the judicial reform of 1864, the European principles of the rule of law, of the separation of governmental power, of direct political participation, remained alien concepts to the vast majority of Russians (Baberowski, *Autokratie und*

Justiz, 783–789). On the conflict between the peasants' conception of criminality and justice and that of the Westernized reformers, see also Cathy A. Frierson, "Crime and Punishment in the Russian Village: Rural Concepts of Criminality at the End of the Nineteenth Century," *Slavic Review* 46 (Spring 1987): 55–69.

107. Spierenburg, *Spectacle*, 204–205.

108. Shaw, *Convicts and the Colonies*, 147.

109. Spierenburg, *Spectacle*, 184–185, 189–192. See also the references in note 3 above.

110. Ben Eklof, "Worlds in Conflict: Patriarchal Authority, Discipline, and the Russian School, 1861–1914," in *School and Society in Tsarist and Soviet Russia*, ed. Ben Eklof (New York: St. Martin's Press, 1993), 106–107.

111. On this issue see Foucault, *Discipline and Punish*; Ignatieff, *A Just Measure of Pain*, 211–214. Russian historians may consider Foucault's conception of disciplinary, "carceral" arrangements of social control more helpful for understanding Soviet Russia than nineteenth-century European countries, much less Imperial Russia. Only a highly authoritarian, centralized state could strive to bend the whole of society to social control in a manner at least relatively consonant with Foucault's vision. For a discussion of Foucault's relevance to European and Russian societies, see Laura Engelstein, "Combined Underdevelopment: Discipline and the Law in Imperial and Soviet Russia," as well as the comments and reply following it, in *American Historical Review* 98 (April 1993): 338–381.

112. Adams, *Politics of Punishment*, 172–174.

113. Laura Engelstein, *The Keys to Happiness: Sex and the Search for Modernity in Fin-de-Siècle Russia* (Ithaca and London: Cornell University Press, 1992), 3–9.

114. On this problem, see Leopold H. Haimson, "The Problem of Social Stability in Urban Russia, 1905–1917," in *The Structure of Russian History: Interpretative Essays*, ed. M. Cherniavsky (New York: Random House, 1970), 341–380; Daniel R. Brower, *The Russian City between Tradition and Modernity, 1850–1900* (Berkeley and Los Angeles: University of California Press, 1990), 221.

115. A. Tyrkova-Villiams, *Na putiakh k svobode* (New York: Izd. imeni Chekhova, 1952), 347–348.

116. Daly, "Political Crime in Late Imperial Russia."

11

St. Petersburg Workers and Implementation of the Social Insurance Law of 1912

Alice K. Pate

On June 23, 1912, the Russian Duma passed a "Law on Sickness Insurance." The law provided for *kassy* or benefit funds from worker and employer contributions managed by a board including worker representatives. Councils set up by the government, which included workers, would administer the law. Implemented first in St. Petersburg, the law provided for the election of representatives from eight metalworking factories, who would work with employers to draw up model rules. Afterwards, the law would be extended, industry-by-industry, to other factories covered by the law. The adoption and implementation of this law in Russia, a country described by modern historians and contemporary revolutionaries as politically and economically "backward," indicates that the tsarist bureaucracy, business elites, and worker activists had begun to develop a dialogue that had the potential to produce progressive change in late Imperial Russia. The tsarist government acted to protect child and female workers and provided factory inspectors and even worker representation in a series of reforms that addressed the problems specific to labor in a modernizing industrial state.

The Russian Ministry of Finance began a systematic study of social insurance in 1905. Before 1905, general consideration of the "workers' question" by the tsarist government focused on the workers' movement and its illegal activities, and most decisions impacting labor emerged from the Ministry of Internal Affairs. After the 1905 revolution, a decisive shift occurred within the bureaucracy that aligned economic growth and development with a resolution of the problems peculiar to the workplace and workers' lives and that placed the Ministry of Finance in control of the problem. A commission established under V.N. Kokovtsov studied tsarist social policies, such as the length of the workday, strike laws, social insurance, and medical assistance. Committee members included representatives of the Senate, industry leaders, manufacturers, wholesalers, stockbrokers, and representatives from manufacturing and trade societies. Such an extensive investigation of the social conditions of workers in large-scale industry indicates growing support for improving the lives of workers similar to the movements for reform that occurred in Europe and the United States after the turn of the century. The work of the commission resulted in an insurance law that was welcomed by workers in the major industries of St. Petersburg after 1912. In fact, the workers' involvement in the implementation of the law reflects the growing connection between labor organizers, intelligentsia, and manufacturing societies within Russia and far exceeded German workers' role in the famous Bismarckian legislation of 1883 and 1887.[1] Tsarist Russia, despite continued political oppression, was modernizing.

Labor response to the law and its implementation indicates a civic consciousness among workers that heralds an emergent civil society in late Imperial Russia. Before the turn of the century, workers voiced demands for political and social reform. Revolutionary activists, liberals, and legal activists addressed the workers' question and posited solutions in collaboration with legal and illegal workers' associations. After 1906, when "societies" became legal, workers organized libraries, educational societies, clubs, and cooperatives. Workers' associations engaged professors, doctors, teachers, and lawyers for courses and excursions. Legal congresses of women, factory inspectors, doctors, and cooperatives often included a workers' group and always examined workers' living and working conditions. Within this milieu, workers developed an awareness of citizenship and the rights and responsibilities that citizenship required. Intimately involved in the original demands for insurance protection and equally aware of the political consequences of the method of implementation, Russian workers sought not only the most favorable application of the law but demanded direct involvement in the control of insurance funds. Cooperating with doctors' groups and factory inspectors, workers communicated and collaborated with the revolutionary intelligentsia and industrialists to protect their own interests. Careful analysis of St. Petersburg workers' actions and voices in the implementation of the social insurance law from 1912 to 1914 finds a distinct worker identity. Workers as citizens of a modernizing European country demanded democratic political and social reforms to allow their full participation in Russian politics and society.

As noted in another study in this collection, the 1912 worker insurance campaign attracted the widest attention in Russian society. All political parties and movements, and certainly all socialists, including the Socialist Revolutionaries (SR) and Social Democrats (SD), addressed the matter at length, which also drew abundant press commentary. The response of the Social Democrats, one of the focuses of this study, to the insurance law and its implementation further augments our interpretation of these events. Historians, who have examined these years almost entirely within the context of factional debate, note the relative success of Bolshevik candidates in elections for governing boards of workers' associations, including insurance boards, and assert a Bolshevik predominance among workers or, at least, among radical workers during the period 1912–14.[2] Such bipolar thinking masks underlying support for a *united* workers' movement. A careful analysis of the language used in election campaigns refutes this simplistic factional interpretation. Throughout the revolutionary period, many rank-and-file activists openly promoted unity in the movement. The revolutionary intellectuals and workers, regardless of party or nonparty affiliation, cooperated on union boards and worker associations, in demonstrations, strikes, and election campaigns.[3] The elections for the newly created insurance boards in 1912 seemed an ideal opportunity for putting into practice the popular ideals of cooperation and unity. (Readers should be aware that the government tied the 1912 citywide insurance board elections to the Fourth Duma elections, a move that effectively excluded the Socialist Revolutionaries, who boycotted the Duma elections, and created an appearance of Social Democratic hegemony in the insurance movement.[4]) Just as the elections occurred, however, Social Democratic unity was in the process of being shattered by struggles between Bolshevik and Menshevik émigrés, an action that heavily impacted the entire revolutionary movement. Lenin's ongoing attempt to marginalize activists inside Russia and prevent SD Party reform hindered cooperation.[5] Separate SD conferences at Prague and Vienna presented activists with an official SD party schism realized in the Duma by the fall of 1913. Though activists and workers demanded unity in the revolutionary movement, Leninists had successfully seized the legitimizing labels—Marxist and unity— in a series of elections for the Duma and governing boards of trade unions and educational societies. The tactic of presenting a "Marxist" slate produced a "Bolshevik" majority within these institutions by 1914, although the "Marxist" slates also included Mensheviks, SRs, and Bolshevik conciliators. As Lenin moved against cooperation in other worker institutions, he saw the possibility of utilizing the insurance campaign to accomplish similar gains. Within this context, the workers' voice was often subordinated to the SD party struggle. However, while the party struggle provides the context, it does not inform the narrative of workers' developing civic consciousness. Specific demands made through the socialist press and throughout the implementation process indicate that Russian workers constructed their demands through a united socialist voice regardless of SD struggles or party affiliation.

In St. Petersburg, trade unionists had worked diligently on the insurance question for years. District and factory level meetings regularly heard reports on the legislative progress when discussion began in 1904.[6] In April 1909, workers' delegates to the Congress of Factory and Plant Doctors were determined to win passage of the "Theses on Insurance" that resulted from many months' work by trade unionists in St. Petersburg. The "Theses" were conceived in meetings of the St. Petersburg Metalworkers' Union and the Central Bureau of Trade Unions. Unions were legalized under provisions of the "Law on Societies" by the tsarist government in 1906. The Central Bureau, which had begin to function during the 1905 revolution, acted to coordinate the activities of trade union organizations in the capital. In 1908, the Bolshevik revolutionary, Roman Malinovskii, delivered a report on social insurance and organized a public hearing of legislation being considered by the government. Perhaps encouraged by those in the Ministry of Interior concerned primarily with political repression, the government banned the public hearing. In the absence of a broadly organized public meeting, the Metalworkers' Union formed a subcommittee, which composed the "Theses on Insurance" subsequently approved by the members.[7] Accepted by the Central Bureau of Trade Unions and published in the SD press, the unionists recommended workers' councils that were democratically elected in the district or at the factory to oversee the insurance program, which should be supported by the state and employers through taxation. They also demanded 100 percent pay in the case of total disability. Activists successfully included demands for free trade unions, a constituent assembly, and freedom of speech and assembly.[8] The workers' delegation to the congress adopted the "Theses" and asked the Duma Deputy, I. Pokrovskii, to present them to the entire delegation. When Pokrovskii was not granted the floor, the workers and about twenty doctors walked out in protest.[9] Perhaps the workers' obstinate defense of political, social, and economic aims, as well as the limited mandate of the Metalworkers' Union to represent workers in general, caused the congress leadership to reject the worker group's proposals. The proposals themselves indicate the high degree of civic consciousness that had become apparent in the majority of worker demands since 1905. Workers not only required full participation in civil government and extensive political reforms but also economic and social security financed by the state and the employers and administered by workers.

The question of insurance remained a topic of discussion among St. Petersburg trade unionists, especially the metalworkers. Vyborg and Vasileostrov districts passed the following resolution adopted by the Metalworkers' Union in September 1911:

> We think that government insurance for workers should cover without exclusion all wage workers and include all aspects of social insurance, that is, insurance in the case of illness, disability, old age, unemployment, pregnancy, maternity, widows and orphans.

Unionists wanted a single insurance body organized on a territorial basis completely controlled by workers to manage the fund. They argued that the government should finance the fund by taxing income, property, and inheritance.[10]

The legislative commission continued drafting social insurance rules and regulations and ultimately produced a more restrictive law than the "Theses." Once the law was promulgated, the revolutionary parties condemned it for excluding municipal and state workers, railway workers, postal workers, domestic servants, artisans, and agricultural workers. Socialists, active in the Metalworkers' Union, rejected the high contributions demanded from workers, the employer's control of the funds, and the absence of sufficient benefits.[11] Revolutionary activists, regardless of party affiliation, opposed a proposed boycott of elections to *kassy* boards and agreed fully with unionists' demands for workers' control and the widest possible application of benefits. A Bolshevik activist in the capital wrote, "There are no differences between the factions on this matter."[12] Indeed, both SD factions in the capital approved the establishment of an All Russian Labor Insurance Congress, a concept clearly linked to the earlier vision of a workers' congress.[13] In December 1912, Bolsheviks proposed a joint insurance commission, but before the plan could be carried out the police arrested the participants. In an attempt to prevent SD factionalism, the Bolsheviks Danskii and Malinovskii were invited to serve on the board of the Menshevik insurance organ, *Strakhovanie rabochikh*. Although they refused, *Pravda*, construed by many historians to be a Leninist publication, did not attack the editorial policy of the new journal until the spring of 1913, when factional strife had intensified. Initial cooperation and collaboration in the implementation of the insurance law paralleled conciliatory activities inside Russia in all aspects of the workers' movement involving all revolutionary parties and nonparty activists. However, Lenin and the émigrés began a struggle to gain control of the insurance campaign.

Mensheviks moved into the arena first. Boris S. Baturskii, a lawyer and legal activist, and Solomon M. Shvarts, who became a member of the Menshevik Central Initiative Group in 1913, led the Menshevik Insurance Commission and began publishing their journal *Strakhovanie rabochikh* in December 1912.[14] In *Luch*, the paper of the so-called Menshevik liquidators, V. Ezhov published model statutes later adopted in essence by the Bolshevik, Danskii.[15] Ezhov reiterated labor demands for workers' control of the *kassy* and the highest possible benefits. P. Garvi, using the pseudonym Chatskii, in *Nevskii golos*, proposed an All-Russian Labor Insurance Congress. N.N. Morozov, a Menshevik at the Semenov plant, encouraged the formation of a "Commission of Eight" in January 1913.[16] Legal activists' programs reflected the workers' demands and predicated future conflicts with the bureaucracy's plans for implementation of the law.

St. Petersburg trade unionists rejected many of the government's first steps at implementation and asserted political demands based upon their vision of their expanding role in Russia's emerging civil society. The first Insurance Council was appointed rather than elected from delegates who had elected the Leninist, A.E. Badaev, to the Fourth Duma. St. Petersburg legal activists had already condemned the indirect elections for the Fourth Duma. In these elections, the workers' curia had voted for unity candidates and had opposed factional lists. Before the election, Stalin's "Mandate to the St. Petersburg Deputy" called for SDs to "act in unity and with their ranks closed." However, in the elections, Stalin insisted only Leninists could hold this mandate and that Mensheviks should resign. After the government disqualified 20 workers' delegates from the workers' curia, a second urban curia presented three Mensheviks and two Bolsheviks for elections. The provincial electoral assembly chose the Leninist, Badaev, a decision that many trade unionists in the capital opposed.[17] Trade unions protested and urged the government's appointees to resign at the first meeting of the

Council on November 24, 1912.[18] New elections specific to the insurance campaign were necessary, they argued, to assure proper factory representation. St. Petersburg workers voiced opposition to indirect elections and supported equal representation with workers' control of insurance funds, indicative of their understanding of a democratic electoral process.

Instead of the government's Council, representatives elected from the eight pilot plants formed a Commission of Eight to draft model rules at a meeting in January 1913.[19] Elected chair of the Commission, the initiator of the proposal, N.K. Morozov, suggested to the 70 assembled delegates that a general fund be established rather than factory based funds.[20] However, the police prevented legal meetings of the Commission of Eight. In every case, police authorities opposed citywide organizations such as those proposed by Morozov. Malinovskii protested the government ban in the Duma and 20,000 workers joined a protest strike. Mass meetings held to defend the Commission continued to favor the general fund, but the Commission, after negotiations with employers, seemed to move away from this demand. In the end, only four of the eight factories continued to support the Commission. At this point, *Pravda* expressed support for the general fund and warned the Commission that their expectations for establishing satisfactory rules were overly optimistic, as they were working with "unreasonable men."[21]

The Bolshevik support for the concept of the "general fund" mirrored their tactic of seizing legitimizing labels to defeat political rivals. The "general fund" implied the widest possible application of benefits and for this reason remained consistent with earlier proposals voiced by St. Petersburg workers. Government opposition to the general fund further spurred its acceptance by the workers who were committed to ending tsarist autocracy.

As the time for adoption of model rules approached, SD factional conflict developed. On May 13, 1913, officials announced dates for industry adoption of model rules. The metalworkers were scheduled to be the last, which gave them an advantage over other industries in seeking alterations.[22] As activists came to the fore to assist the councils in making changes, the focus of the campaign quickly became the general fund. The Mensheviks did not provide an unequivocal alternative to the promotion of a general fund.[23] Pavel N. Kolokol'nikov and others supported a fund based upon profession. Many Mensheviks believed the general municipal fund could not realistically be administered.[24] Legal activists feared workers might boycott factory funds in favor of the general fund, or become disillusioned if they could not win its passage. Therefore, they maintained the general fund as a long-term aim, and in some cases, encouraged the establishment of an industrial fund in its place.[25] For the activists, the outcome of the law's implementation had to be continued worker participation in the administration of the fund even if the fund was not established in the most desirable manner. Small steps were favored over no steps at all. Disagreements over the type of fund disrupted the unity of the workers' movement. Legal activists always favored cooperation over conflict, a sentiment widely supported by workers in the capital. Reflecting the legal activists, support for the unity of legal and illegal work in the revolutionary movement, this policy preserved all arenas of activity, prevented failure of the law's implementation, and rejected party factionalism.

In the summer of 1913, the unity campaign was shattered by increased conflict within the SD faction of the State Duma, an expanding strike movement, and constant tactical and organizational disagreements within worker associations. Lenin continued to oppose conciliation although Stalin and *Pravda* warned that the workers disliked the increased factional squabbling. The reaction of SD party activists to the upsurge in strikes after the massacre of striking workers on the Lena also threatened the success of legal organizations. Bolsheviks, following the directives of the Prague conference, had actively moved into the legal arena and feared that the spontaneity of the masses would provoke increased government repression. Mensheviks initially feared "strike fever" as a "dangerous illness."[26] Although both SD party factions condemned the growing radicalism, Leninists moved to direct the striking workers and centralize control of the movement. Institutions and organizations were consistently failing to satisfy the workers' aspirations for unity.

By August 1913, the Commission of Eight was becoming ineffective and the Bolsheviks proposed formation of an insurance center from *kassy* delegates to oversee the growing strike movement.[27] In October, Bolsheviks began to publish *Voprosy strakhovaniia* with the slogan of the general fund. Initially, the Petersburg Metalworkers' Union voted financial support for the Bolshevik insurance journal. Then, after a confrontation between pro-Bolshevik members and those favoring unity, monies were granted to the Menshevik journal as well.[28]

The St. Petersburg Metalworkers' Union, like most trade unions, adopted the Bolshevik plan for a general fund. In September 1913, a mass meeting at Putilov voted for a citywide *kassa* and the highest benefits possible. Workers had been consistent in this stipulation since discussions of social insurance had begun. By the end of the month, 12 of the largest plants accepted the plan, four rejecting earlier more conservative resolutions. The 12 factories set up an Insurance Center and contacted 50 other factories to coordinate insurance work in the capital before being shut down by the police. In all, 36 metalworking plants adopted the proposal. The possibility of a conciliatory rather than a factional outcome remained real as *Pravda* agreed with legal activists that if the general fund was not permitted, factory funds should be approved.[29]

In the insurance campaign, activists of both SD factions utilized the slogan of "unity." *Pravdisti* continued to define this term as the unity of anti-liquidationist (Menshevik) elements in hopes of claiming center stage as the true revolutionaries. Legal activists and trade unionists still retained hope that workers in legal and illegal arenas could work together in a broad revolutionary movement free of factionalism. Menshevik insurance activists endorsed the unity platform asserting "divisiveness and fratricidal struggle among leading workers in the campaign is far worse, more senseless, than in political organizations embracing only the vanguard."[30] The call for unity was echoed among the electorate when the workers chose delegates to central insurance institutions in 1914.

The Bolshevik mandate for the election supported voting by slate and included a demand, known as Paragraph V, that the delegates inform the workers of their activities through the Bolshevik press. The Menshevik Baturskii rejected factionalism and Paragraph V.[31] On December 18, 23 representatives from *kassa* boards agreed there were "no differences between the mandates" except for Paragraph V, which was rejected. However, the Leninists declared the assembly an "accidental meeting" and ignored its findings.[32] Delegates from the *kassy* boards were arrested at a secret meeting three days later and electors chosen for the Petersburg Insurance Council refused to vote until those arrested were freed.[33] The postponement only led to more confusion.

Before the rescheduled elections on March 2, 1914, the Bolsheviks issued a revised mandate, which now stated in Paragraph VI "representatives of the workers must in all activity follow the decisions of the organized Marxists." With this revision, the Bolsheviks hoped to discredit groups considered outside the party according to the resolutions at Prague in 1912. Both Mensheviks and SRs opposed this, the Mensheviks reminding the Bolsheviks, "*kassy* are not party organs."[34] On March 2, 42 of 55 *kassy* sent representatives totaling 47 to the electoral assembly. The 24 delegates from Putilov who had previously made an agreement with the Bolshevik conciliator, Kiselev, and the rest of the metalworkers' governing board denounced factionalism, which, they asserted, overshadowed class interests. Ten other delegates joined the Putilov delegates in support of "mixed lists," that is, delegate lists composed through negotiations among socialist parties. They also voted to accept a "united mandate" that amended Paragraph VI to publish reports in all labor press organs.[35] Worker activists clearly rejected factionalism and sought to remove party squabbles entirely from the process. In a discursive struggle to assert the needs of the movement over those of any particular party, the metalworkers' resolutions demonstrated the strength of the call for unity. However, before unity won out, another representative suggested that labor delegates be "subordinated to the collective of the *kassy*." Since there was no such body, the proposal served once again to further complicate the discussion. Delegates rejected this proposal and in the resulting confusion voted instead for the original version of Paragraph VI. Although delegates had voted in favor of "mixed lists" earlier, a compromise list was not presented before the vote was taken. Therefore, the delegates elected the *Pravda* list. Nevertheless, Bolshevik hegemony was not established by the election of the *Pravdisti*. One of the two Mensheviks elected, P.I. Sudakov of the *kassa* board at St. Petersburg Metals, had received the most votes in elections to the workers' curia of the Fourth Duma.[36] Although five members and seven of ten alternates on the Insurance Council were Bolsheviks, the vote was the result of acquiescence due to exhaustion and confusion. Ten of the 15 delegates were metalworkers, which might indicate more support for trade union activists than for Bolsheviks and Mensheviks (not to mention the artificially excluded SRs).[37]

On March 30, 1914, elections were scheduled for the St. Petersburg Capital Insurance Board. In opposition to Paragraph VI, Mensheviks took up the idea of responsibility to the collective of *kassy*. Three days before the election, 17 *kassy* boards agreed in principle to a "mixed list" of candidates and "subordination to the collective." At the electoral assembly, on March 30, 53 *kassy* sent delegates. Among the delegates, 37 said they were *Pravdisti*, seven Menshevik, four SRs, and five nonparty, proportions that did not represent the actual make-up of much more equally divided factory level *kassy*. Of the 12 representatives who had directives from their *kassa* boards, 11 were to vote for non-fractional lists. When V.D. Rubstov, vice-chair of the Geisler *kassa* board, reported the vote from the meeting of the *kassy* boards, the changes to Paragraph VI were accepted by a vote of 31 to 22. However, when 31 voted to merge the Bolshevik and Menshevik slogans into "the collective of the *kassy* must be subordinated to the Marxist organization," the confusion resurfaced.[38] At this point, 28 delegates voted for the SR proposal of proportional representation. Though democratic in principle, such a policy dictated hegemony of parties, a principle most delegates had clearly rejected. Negotiations broke down, and the *Pravda* lists were accepted.[39]

On April 13, the elections to the Petersburg Provincial Board included electors from the capital, not from the provinces. In this election, Rubstov won the representatives' acceptance for a mixed list of candidates. Delegates approved another revision of the amendment to Paragraph VI that called for responsibility to the "representative body of sickness funds" to be subordinated to all-Marxist leadership.[40] Worker delegates interpreted this slogan as non-factional, democratic and pro-unity, since SDs, SRs, and even many nonparty socialists were Marxists in the broadest understanding of the term.

A simple count of affiliation among those elected to the insurance councils in 1914 gives the appearance of a Bolshevik victory among St. Petersburg activists. However, the Menshevik trade unionist V.V. Sher exaggerated the Bolshevik victory when he declared, "the preponderance in St. Petersburg of the *Pravdisti* is without doubt."[41] First of all, it must be noted that *Pravda* was quite conciliatory until 1914. Furthermore, many workers at large and small plants were excluded from participation in elections, along with employees of most state factories. *Kassa* boards, not general membership meetings, chose delegates. They also chose delegates who already had won previous elections and must have been well-known personalities. The fact that metalworkers were so dominant at the electoral assemblies and that a majority of those elected were metalworkers is more significant than their alleged affiliation with Bolshevism.[42] Since the delegates from the metalworking plants had openly rejected factionalism and called for unity in the insurance campaign, an interpretation of voter results based solely upon party affiliation ignores the complexities of worker identity and agency in the changing political culture.

While some historians have interpreted the election of a majority of Bolsheviks in the insurance campaign as an indication of increased worker radicalism, workers had rejected a simple Leninist majority. Bolshevism was hardly a unified ideology. A careful analysis of *Pravda* policies reveals conflict between activists inside Russia and Leninist émigrés until the summer of 1914. There was no Leninist Petersburg Committee after July 1914 and after the split of the Duma faction, circulation of *Pravda* began to drop precipitously. Throughout the campaign, St. Petersburg workers demanded mixed lists and voted for "Marxist slates," understood as signifying "socialist." During the elections, compromise had been reached with the rank-and-file leadership and with Mensheviks in the insurance campaign under the direction of the Bolshevik conciliator, Kiselev. Bolsheviks elected to governing boards and insurance organs were largely conciliators, not Leninists. Mensheviks and SRs remained on the governing boards of many workers' associations. Workers elected board members with long-term service in the legal arena, regardless of party affiliation.

Rather than a commitment to Bolshevism, examination of this incident demonstrates the growing civic consciousness of Russian labor. Although the workers in the capital did not identify with a particular political faction, their discourse was closely connected to Russian democratic socialism, which had consistently defined their common interests. Workers in the insurance campaign demanded control of insurance funds, drafted model statutes, and actively sought direct administration of *kassa* funds. Seeking to extend benefits as widely as possible, they elected the "Marxists" who sought to establish both the general fund and an insurance center. Working with government officials, doctors' groups, factory inspectors, and legal activists, workers sought to extend control over their own lives. However, the revolutionary intellectuals began a political battle for control of the workers' vote in the insurance campaign, subverting the central elements of the workers' vision. A major result of this conflict was the failure of the workers to fully realize their vision of an expanded role in Russian civil society. While the SD factionalist squabbles subordinated and attempted to marginalize workers' control, Russian workers remained agents of historical change and continued to seek a central role in Russia's emerging civil society. Without doubt, Russian workers believed the nation-state and their employers should provide economic security through pensions, health insurance, and disability insurance. In the worldview of the worker, industrialization implied modernity and must entail political, economic, and social reform.

Notes

1. See Clive Trebilcock, *The Industrialization of the Continental Powers, 1780–1914* (London and New York: Longman, 1981), 81–82.
2. See for example Leopold Haimson "The Problem of Social Stability in Urban Russia, 1905–1917," *Slavic Review* 23 (December 1964): 619–642, and 24 (March 1965): 1–22.
3. For discussions of this approach from varying viewpoints, see Alice Pate, "Liquidationist Controversy: Russian Social Democracy and the Quest for Unity" in Michael Melancon and Alice Pate, eds., *New Labor History: Worker Identity and Experience in Russia, 1840–1918* (Bloomington, IN: Slavica, 2002), 95–122, and Michael Melancon, " 'Marching Together!': Left Bloc Activities in the Russian Revolutionary Movement, 1900 to February 1917," *Slavic Review* 49 no.2 (Summer 1990): 239–252.

4. For discussion and sources, see Michael Melancon, " 'Stormy Petrels': The Socialist Revolutionaries in Russia's Labor Organizations, 1905–1914," *The Carl Beck Papers*, no. 703 (University of Pittsburgh Center for Russian and East European Studies, 1988), 40, 59–60, note 149.

5. For a complete study of these tactics, see Pate, "Liquidationist Controversy," *New Labor History*, 95–122.

6. The Ministry of Finance had considered introducing insurance legislation before the 1905 revolution.

7. "Po Rossii," *Golos sotsial demokrata*, no.8/9 (July/Sept 1908).

8. F.A. Bulkin, *Na zare profdvizhenniia. Istoriia Peterburgskogo soiuza metallistov, 1906–1914* (Leningrad: Izd. Tsentral'nogo komiteta i Leningradskogo raikoma Vserossiiskogo soiuza rabochikh metallistov, 1923), 208, 214; "Eshche o rabochem zakonodatel'stve," *Proletarii*, no.43 (March 1909); Theses published in same edition: "Tezisi o strakhovrabochikh priniata tsentral'nym biuro Petersburgskikh profsoiuzov i obsuzhdaiushchiesia v vsekh profsoiuzakh Peterburga"; N.I. Letunovskii, *Leninskaia taktika ispol'zovaniia legal'nikh vserossiiskikh s'ezdov v bor'be za massi v 1908–1911 gg.* (Moscow: Izd. Moskovskogo Universiteta, 1971), 26–35; R.V. Malinovskii, *Metallist*, no.23 (November 10, 1912).

9. "Pervyi s'ezd fabrichnykh vrachei" *Edinstvo* no. 2 (March 5, 1909); "Po Rossii" *Golos sotsial demokrata* no.14 (May 1909).

10. Bulkin, *Na zare*, 233–234.

11. *Luch*, 80 (December 20, 1912): 1; "Ptoses po strakhovaniiu rabochikh," *Nash put'* 16 (1911): 5; N. Aleksandrov (Dr. Semasko) "Gosudarstvennoe strakhovanie rabochikh," *Sotsial demokrat* 23 (14/1 September 1911): 1.

12. *Luch* 80 (December 20, 1912): 1; Robert McKean, *St. Petersburg between the Revolutions: Workers and Revolutionaries, June 1907–February 1917*, (New Haven, CT: Yale University Press, 1990), 164, citing A. Enukidze letter to S.S. Shaumin (February 1913), Gosudarstvennyi Arkhiv Rossisskoi Federatsii, f.102, DPOO 1913g. d.307.1.114.

13. Astrov, "Strakhovanie rabochikh i ocheredniia zadachi" *Nasha zaria* (1912), nos.7–8, 52; Iu. Chatskii (Garvi) "Strakhovyi s'ezd rabochikh," *Nevskii golos* 5 (June 28, 1912); *Pravda*, 116 (September 13, 1912).

14. *Strakhovanie rabochikh* was published until February 1917, then retitled *Strakhovanie rabochikh i sotsial'naia politka* until July 1918; *Strakhovanie rabochikh*, no.6 (1913): 31–32; nos.11/12 (1913): 45; no.8 (1913): 26.

15. "Liquidator" was a derogatory term applied by Lenin to party activists who hoped to combine both legal and illegal party work after 1907. Lenin opposed the "liquidation" of the underground party and condemned the legal activists as liquidators. For a complete study, see Pate, "Liquidationism and the Failure of Unity: Russian Social Democracy and the St. Petersburg Metalworkers' Union, 1906–1914," Ph.D. diss. (Ohio State University, 1995). For the Bolshevik proposal, see Danskii "Strakhovaia kampaniia" *Prosveshchenie*, no.4 (April 1913): 81. On Mensheviks and insurance councils, see G. Baturskii "Professional'nye soiuzy i strakhovye kampaniia," *Metallist*, no.1/25 (April 19, 1913): 4–6; M.K. Korbut "Strakhovye zakony 1912 goda i ikh provedenie v Peterburge," *Krasnaia letopis'*, no.1 (1928): 136–171.

16. It should also be noted that in April 1913, Morozov became secretary of the Metalworkers' Union. *Luch*, no.17/103 (January 22, 1913), 2; Ch. Gurskii (S.S. Danilov) "Strakhovaia kampaniia v Peterburge," *Prosveshchenie*, no.1

(January 1913), 76; Baturskii, "Professional'nye soiuzy i strakhovaia kampaniia" *Metallist*, no.1/25 (April 19, 1913), 4–6; For Menshevik statutes see E.Z. (Ezhov) "Ustav bol'nichnoi kassy," *Luch*, no. 42 (November 4, 1912); no. 49 (November 13, 1912); no.80 (December 20, 1912).

17. *Luch*, no.19 (October 7, 1912); no.28 (October 18, 1912); no.29 (October 19, 1912); *Pravda*, no.136 (October 6, 1912); no.146 (October 18, 1912); Joseph Stalin, *Works* 13 vols. (Moscow: Foreign Languages Publishing House, 1952–) vol. 2, 265–266.

18. *Luch*, no.79 (December 19, 1912); no.64 (December 1, 1912); *Pravda*, no.116 (September 13, 1912); no.177 (November 25, 1912); no.184 (December 4, 1912).

19. The eight factories were Erikson, Lessner, Nobel, Phoenix, St. Petersburg Metals, Semenov, Neva Stearine, and Russian-American Rubber.

20. K.A. Komarovskii (B.G. Danskii) "Strakhovaia kampaniia" *Prosveshchenie*, no.4 (1913): 77; "Khronika," *Strakhovanie rabochikh* (February 3, 1913) lists the seven factories as Semenov, Nobel, St. Petersburg Metals, Erikson, Neva Stearine, Feliks, and Lessner. On the meeting, see "Na ocheredi strakhovanie rabochikh," (February 3, 1913); "Obshchee sobranie upolnomochennykh," *Pravda*, nos.17, 18 (January 22 and 23, 1913).

21. "Khronika," *Strakhovanie rabochikh*, 4 (March 1913) "Strakhovaia kampaniia," *Strakhovanie rabochikh*, no.5 (April 1913); "Nekotorie itogi raboti upol-nomochennikh." *Pravda*, nos.66, 67 and 68 (March 20, 21, and 22, 1913); V.N. Morozov, "O deiatel'nosti strakhovoi komissii," *Novaia rabochaia gazeta*, no. 24 (September 5, 1913); On the conflict between *Pravda* and *Luch* in 1914, see Rossisskii Tsentr Khraneniia Dokumentov Noveishei Istorii, f. 450, op. 1, d. 48; op. 1, d. 50.

22. "Strakhovanie kampaniia," *Strakhovanie rabochikh*, nos. 7 and 8 (June 9 and July 1913).

23. This is the only difference between the proposals. See Danskii, "Strakhovanie kampanii," *Prosveshchenie*, no.6 (June 1913): 97 and *Voprosy strakhovaniia*, no. 1 (October 26, 1913): 2; no.2 (November 2, 1913): 2; *Pravda*, no.68/272 (March 22, 1913); Lenin, following the lead of local Bolsheviks, began to agitate for strengthening the Bolshevik position on the *kassy*. V.I. Lenin *Collected Works*, 45 vols. (Moscow: Foreign Languages Publishing House, 1960–70), vol. 19, 426–427.

24. B.S. Tseitlin "Rabochii ustav varshavskikh upolnomochennykh," *Strakhovanie rabochikh*, no.9 (August 9, 1913); Kolokolnikov, "Znachenie prof. kassy v strakhovoi kampanii" *Strakhovanie rabochikh*, no.1 (1914). See also Ezhov, "Bol'nichnye kassy," *Metallist*, no.24 (December 14, 1912); *Luch*, no.33/119 (February 9, 1913).

25. "Iz zhizni i deitel'nosti obshchestva," *Metallist*, no.1 (September 20, 1911); "Obshchegorodskaia i professional'naia kassa" *Strakhovanie rabochikh*, no.11/12 (November/December 1913).

26. *Luch*, no. 53 (November 17, 1912).

27. "O strakhovom tsentre," *Metallist*, no.10/34 (October 26, 1913); K.A. Komarovskii, "Strakhovaia kampaniia," *Prosveshchenie*, no.9 (1913), 98.

28. *Metallist*, no.8/32 (September 18, 1913), 10; no.11/35 (November 16, 1913), 14.

29. Korbut, 167; *Strakhovanie rabochikh*, no.10 (1913): 29; no.11/12 (1913): 18; K.A. Komarovskii (Danskii) "Obshchaia bol'nichnaia kassa," *Metallist*, no.9

(October 4, 1913): 10–12; Iv.Iv. "O strakhovom tsentre," *Metallist*, no.10/34 (October 25, 1913): 10; *Voprosy strakhovaniia*, no.2 (November 2, 1913): 5; "Strakhovanie" *Pravda* (September 1913).

30. *Strakhovanie rabochikh*, no.7(1914): 3.

31. *Novaia rabochikh gazeta* no.104 (December 11, 1913); no.106 (December 13, 1913); no.110 (December 18, 1913); *Voprosy strakhovaniia*, no. 9 (December 21, 1913), 2; Baturskii, "Vybory v sovet po delam strakhovaniia rabochikh," *Strakhovanie rabochikh*, no.5 (March 1914); "Proekt nakaza predstaviteliam rabochikh v strakovikh prisutstviiakh i strakhovom sovete," *Voprosy strakhovaniia*, no.8 (February 22, 1914).

32. *Voprosy strakhovaniia*, no.1/11 (January 4, 1914): 13.

33. A.K. Tsvetkov-Prosveshchenskii, *Mezhdu dvumia revoliutsiiami* (Moscow: Gos. izd-vo polit. lit-ry, 1957), 90.

34. *Voprosy strakhovaniia*, no.8/18 (February 22, 1914): 2.

35. "Vybory v strakhovoi sovet," *Voprosy strakhovaniia*, no.10 (March 8, 1914); "Vtoroi shag k raskolu," *Proletarskaia pravda*, no.30 (March 7, 1914); "Vpechatleniia ot vyborov v vyborov v strakhovoi sovet," *Proletarskaia pravda*, no.32 (March 9, 1914).

36. *Voprosy strakhovaniia*, no.19/20 (March 8, 1914), 5; Baturskii, "Vybory v sovet po delam strakhovaniia rabochikh," *Strakhovanie rabochikh*, no.5 (March 1914); *Nasha rabochaia gazeta*, no.13 (May 18, 1914). The *Pravda* list included 2 Mensheviks. *Put' Pravdy*, no.27 (March 4, 1914); no.30 (March 7, 1914).

37. These ten delegates were from Erikson, Koppel', Lessner, Neva Shipyards, Putilov, Russian Society, St. Petersburg Engineering, and St. Petersburg Nails. *Put' Pravdy*, no.27 (March 4, 1914); Baturskii, "Vybory v sovet po delam strakhovaniia rabochikh," *Strakhovanie rabochikh*, no.5 (March 1914); *Nasha rabochaia gazeta*, no.13 (May 18, 1914), 4.

38. N.A. Skrypnik (signed Asnik N.) "Vybory sotsial-vybory predstoiat," *Voprosy strakhovaniia*, nos.14–15 (April 3, 1914); "A." "Vybory v Peterburgskoe stolich-noe prisutstvie," *Voprosy strakhovaniia*, nos.14–15 (April 3, 1914).

39. *Strakhovanie rabochikh*, no.7 (April 1914), 22.

40. Rubstov was elected along with the Bolshevik, Iakovlev. *Voprosy strakhovaniia*, no.16/26 (April 19, 1914), 3; Rubstov was union secretary in 1910, and treas-urer in 1914. See "Iz zhizni soiuza," *Metallist*, no.4 (April 1, 1914); "Vybory v St. Peterburgskoe gubernskoe strakhovoe prisutstvie," *Put' Pravdy*, no.61 (April 15, 1914); Sher, "Vybory v strakhovie uchrezhdeniia v Peterburge i zadachi edin-stva," *Bor'ba*, no.6 (1914): 22–23.

41. Sher, "Vybory v strakhovie uchrezhdeniia v Peterburge i zadachi edinstva" *Bor'ba*, no.6 (1914): 20.

42. McKean argues that the main purpose of the general fund slogan was to split the factions on the issue of social insurance and therefore was not "a serious pro-posal." McKean, *St. Petersburg between the Revolutions*, 167. Alternatively, Geoffrey Swain, *Russian Social Democracy and the Legal Labour Movement, 1906–1914* (London, Basingstoke: Macmillan 1983), 167–170, argues the dis-pute was ideological. Sally Ewing, "Russian Social Insurance Movement. 1912–14: An Ideological Analysis," *Slavic Review*, 50, no.4 (Winter 1991): 914–926, on the basis of Shvarts' memoirs and the commentaries of Lenin, Zinoviev, and Kamenev, also insists on the ideological nature of the dispute. She does not discuss any proposals from the floor of the various electoral assemblies that indicate otherwise.

12

Russia's Outlooks on the Present and Future, 1910–1914: What the Press Tells Us

Michael Melancon

Russia's cataclysmic dual 1917 revolutions, her 70-year Communist experience, and the stunning events of the last two decades, taken as a whole, lay the basis for a complete reevaluation of modern Russian history, a virtual intellectual caesura between everything that went before and now. Mikhail Bakhtin once wrote, "the ultimate word . . . about the world has yet to be spoken, . . . the world is open and free, everything is still . . . and will always be in the future."[1] At no point during the saga of twentieth-century Russian development, stasis, and stunning revolutionary turnabouts have scholars provided analysis that bears the test of time. No one has had the last word and new words are badly needed, now that so many traditional interpretations of Russian and Soviet experience have gone awry. A good case in point is the topic chosen for this essay. Historians often view pre-1917 Russian society as hopelessly fragmented, with various social elements at odds both with the government and with one another. In this interpretation, the ultimate failure of the February 1917 revolution to bring about liberal constitutionalism rested squarely upon society's acute internal contradictions. A corollary was that only radical authoritarianism, such as imposed by the Bolsheviks, offered the prospect of maintaining the state intact in the face of powerful centrifugal forces allegedly unleashed by social strife.[2]

Research about the famous Lena Goldfields Massacre of April 4, 1912 has already called this predominant approach into question. Specifically, Russian society across the board responded to the Lena Goldfields strike and the shooting of April 1912 with consensus rather than strife. Society-wide animus was aimed at the government and the company responsible. Traditional interpretations are certainly correct about a widening gap between the government and society. Inspection of the prolonged press coverage of the strike, the shooting, and all related matters clearly suggests, however, a discrepancy between our historical judgments and reality as regards a society supposedly starkly riven by fault lines.[3] Of course, Russian society did not fully agree about everything. No society does. It is also true that most societies would register dismay at the wanton shooting of hundreds of unarmed workers. Russian society's consensual reaction to the Lena events, however, far exceeded the expected universal humane response. As described in detail elsewhere, the shooting provoked weeks of intense press scrutiny, with continued ongoing commentary into the next year. It kicked off a huge furor in the State Duma, replete with furious accusations against the government and accusatory interpellations to responsible ministers, all of which also received verbatim coverage in Russia's press, literally from Bielostok to Vladivostok. The events provoked an angry nationwide discussion within schools, workplaces, associations, clubs, and cultural institutions. Huge worker protest strikes beset the empire for weeks on end. Students at institutions of higher learning joined the strike movement. As the government noted with alarm, the socialist parties utilized the mass response to widen their organizations and activities.[4] Justifiably, commentators often credit the Lena events with launching the post-1905 revolutionary movement.

Even so, Russian society's reactions to the Lena shooting are not this essay's prime focus. Rather, this study examines attitudes that underlay and caused the empire-wide social dismay at the Lena tragedy. Aside from and predating the Lena events, Russia's press routinely reported and commented upon labor at home and abroad. This, too, was not surprising in a nation undergoing industrial expansion. Russia's severe 1905–07 strike movement and worker-oriented revolution also heightened awareness of labor. An unexpected twist arises from the fact that press commentary about strikes, the workers' plight, the rights of labor and labor unions, and even the socialist and liberal parties that spoke out for labor was quite pro-labor. The press across the board criticized government institutions and leaders who impeded workers' rights. These factors open up an even wider perspective.

This study analyzes Russian society's outlooks on politics, human rights, economic development, civic consciousness, and labor during the immediate pre–World War I years. It aims at a clearer vision than we currently have of where pre-1917 Russian society envisioned itself and where it thought it was going, as gauged by discussion of vital issues of the day. Russian language newspaper opinion during the 1910–14 pre-war era provides indelible impressions about societal attitudes on major issues.[5] The single most important of these regards government and politics. In this realm, Russia's press heavily reported the activities of the State Duma. Editorials and articles commonly addressed the parties, projects, and personalities of the Duma, as well as those of the upper house, the State Council. Transcripts of the two legislative houses' sessions also filled innumerable newspaper columns. The Russian press does not bear out the opinion of many histories that the Third and Fourth Dumas (1908–17) lacked centrality in Russian affairs because of their alleged status as governmental rubber stamps. Whatever problems society perceived in the State Duma's unequal electoral base and delimited power, people took an intense interest in what it was doing or not doing. Newspapers of the most varied tendency referred to the Duma as a "parliament" and its activities as "parliamentary," sometimes in irony and more often in a promotional way.[6] More importantly, newspapers commonly evinced belief in parliamentary or constitutional government. As *Sibirskaia Zhizn'* (*Siberian Life*, Tomsk) put the matter, "Whatever one says about [the Third] Duma, the great idea of popular government is not challenged."[7] This comment encapsulates widespread reservations about the existing Duma, conjoined with admiration for the principle of representative government, aspirations toward real representative government in the person of a transformed State Duma, and, as mentioned, close scrutiny of the present Duma.

Threatened by the prospect of censorship and closure, small local newspapers sometimes supported political progress elliptically. For example, in their 1911 inaugural issues the *Azovskii Vestnik* (*Azov Messenger*) promised to focus on the "best progressive aspects of our social and moral lives" and the *Akkermanskoe Obozrenie* (*Akkerman Review*, Bessarabia) believed in the "inevitable evolution of political and social life." Newspapers also adopted stances by reporting on certain events abroad, as when the Akkerman newspaper and others pointedly analyzed the recent British law that fully empowered the lower house of parliament. By late 1912, the somewhat emboldened *Akkermanskoe Obozrenie* espoused the "renewal of the October 1905 Manifesto [which had first created the elected Duma]" and noted "popular strivings and expectations toward promoting new effective public activists capable of taking upon themselves the burden of work in state and social realms."[8] Small newspapers sometimes restricted political reportage to such events as anniversary memorials for the death of Lev Tolstoy, a bitter critic of the tsarist government.[9] Russian society understood such "Aesopian" references as coded political commentary.

Bolder comments often occurred, as when the *Ural'skii Listok* (*Urals Leaflet*, Uralsk) noted the Constitutional Democrats' latest "struggle for parliamentary rights," any failure of support for which was "a big mistake." In its early 1913 founding issue, the *Astrakhanskii Kur'er* (*Astrakhan Courier*) pledged to "not talk about but shed light on politics." In its next issue, the Astrakhan paper quoted the new Minister of the Interior N.K. Maklakov as saying he "was an advocate of strong government but . . . without force." Two weeks later, the Astrakhan paper, under the sarcastic title, "V.N. Kokovtsev [the Prime Minister] and Parliamentarianism," reported an incident when the Constitutional Democratic Duma Deputy, A.I. Shingarev, complained about delays in applying a new pension law. Kokovtsev had curtly replied that it was "harder to work than to criticize," to which Shingarev answered that "as a member of the [not fully empowered] State Duma, [I] only have the right to criticize." Kokovtsev responded, "I hope never to live to see . . . Shingarev and his allies at the head of a government."[10]

In early 1912, the Irkutsk *Sibir'* angrily rebuked the State Duma for "trusting the government to deal with [the threat of] hunger." A month later, it scathingly criticized the State Council for sabotaging Duma legislation with frivolous amendments. For *Sibir'*, the lower house by right had sole legislative power. In early 1912, an editorial in *Arkhangel'sk* (*Arkhangel*) offered the opinion that, "Like any social phenomenon, reaction has its form and its content—repression, pressure, the closing of newspapers and meetings, limitations of inalienable rights, and an urge to return to the old order." As an antidote, the editors wanted "renewed State Duma powers." In a different vein, *Kommersant*, an influential Petersburg business-oriented newspaper, renounced the former political "fecklessness" of the business classes: "Fate has assigned a great political task to the business class, [which] should utilize its life experience for the great state affair of reconstructing our life."[11] Capitalism on the march to democracy was the implied slogan.

Most large newspapers, especially those in the capitals associated with State Duma factions, a status with some immunity from government harassment, expressed their political views with considerable openness and force. The January 1, 1912 issue of *Russkie Vedomosti* (Russian News, Moscow, Constitutional Democratic) discounted old pre-reform Russia in favor of today's Russia of "constitutional reform." Another article regretted society's growing cynicism at the dominating classes' continued power. Nevertheless, the writer believed that society maintained its "strong belief in constitutionalism" and urged "an active stance in upcoming [Duma] elections for further constitutional reforms."[12] In its 1912 New Year issue, the *Saratovskii Listok* (*Saratov Leaflet*, Progressist), a paper in its fiftieth year of publication, recalled earlier promises of governmental reforms and freedoms. In 1907, Prime Minister Petr Stolypin had wanted to transform Russia into "a government of rights, based on laws." Now, lamented the Saratov paper, "no hint of all that remains. 'Strong power' had become the [government's] slogan." In an editorial about the upcoming Duma elections, *Saratovskii Listok* commented, "despite poor conditions in the country, the progressive press has become a serious force, a fact that even [the far right] admits." Later that year, the paper complained, "if this were a real popular government, the Duma would be ahead of society and the press. This is not the case."[13]

The most outspoken of all was *Russkoe Slovo* (*Russian Word*, Moscow), the newspaper of the Progressists (a centrist movement that wished to quicken the pace of reform). In its 1912 New Year issue, the paper noted that during the preceding year "for the first time in Russian history both houses joined in coordinated battle against the . . . government" over its blatant abuses of "constitutionalism" and "parliamentarianism." A few days later, the editors again slammed government practices toward the "parliament." During February, the paper condemned the upper house's tendency to water down State Duma legislation and recommended the English example of constitutional reforms beginning in 1832. On April 1, *Russkoe Slovo* regretted that "compared to Western Europe, the Duma confronts huge barriers." In a February 9, 1912 editorial, the Progressist newspaper offered a simple solution. The government should "follow the English example and fully empower the lower house."[14] The Octobrist *Golos Moskvy* (Voice of Moscow), whose line was somewhat softer, editorialized about the new principle in Russia of "popular representation that would powerfully penetrate bureaucratic strongholds." *Golos Moskvy* cautioned, "only reforms carried out carefully really work. Don't try to carry out in five years in Russia what took centuries in Western Europe. Be sober and realistic." Regardless, the Octobrist newspaper made clear its stance when it noted, "we often hear from people not hostile to the government that the government does not want to deal with the new political conditions." Elsewhere it wrote, "sober people who value the development of Russia . . . still insist that the entire Russian people without consideration of class be represented in the government."[15]

The normally quite conservative *Novoe Vremia* (*New Times*, St. Petersburg, Nationalist) showed clear signs of internalizing reformist and constitutional values. In a March 1912 discussion of the State Duma, the paper accused "our liberals" of often referring to Western constitutional standards in their arguments. "Of course," conceded *Novoe Vremia*, "the experience of older Western constitutions can be quite important for us . . . Our government itself constantly refers to . . . Western constitutions. The English constitution [sic] is more convincing . . . about parliamentary free speech than some other examples," concluded the Nationalists. When the Third State Duma ended its final session in June 1912, *Novoe Vremia* intoned, "*La Douma est morte! Vive la Douma!*" and detailed the past Duma's accomplishments and shortfalls. "It was not radical, not conservative, not untalented, . . . it showed a rather Slavic softness of soul . . . [and] had grey, October-like weather" (a play on words for the cautious Octobrists). Elsewhere, *Novoe Vremia* again proffered the English model: "The English Parliament won the sympathy of the nation and considerable power not by force but rather by its exemplary behavior . . . [It is] a good criterion for parliamentary elections and for people who wish to make laws for the nation." A few weeks later, the Nationalist reprised recent Russian politics under the title "Russian Popular Government." Prior to 1904–05, "Russian politics had been silent [*sic*]." During the revolution, "many dissatisfied voices spoke out. . . . When the bloody conflict was over, it became possible to settle issues within the Duma framework." But, regretted the newspaper, the still inexperienced population had elected many radicals, forcing the government "to admit that the country was not yet ready for fully representative government." Elsewhere, the Nationalist newspaper analyzed the nature of political parties: "In countries where popular government has a past behind it, a party is a natural phenomenon arising from the fabric of popular institutions. Here our recently established parties are [still] somewhat artificial."[16] Regardless, *Novoe Vremia* commentary invariably premised Russia's path to representative, popular government.

With reluctance and anguish, even the reactionary Union of the Russian People and other such groups adjusted to political reality. *Tverskoe Povolzh'e* (*Tver-Volga*, Monarchist) made the traditional complaint about bureaucrats deceiving tsar and people and regretted the tendency in a republic for people to be distracted by "party affairs." Putting an interesting twist on the idea of elected government, it hoped that the Fourth Duma's role would be to "destroy the gap between tsar and people." The arch-conservative Odessa newspaper *Russkii Golos* noted the "constitutional" character of the supposedly rightist Nationalists of *Novoe Vremia*, whose aim was to attract (and presumably corrupt) "trusting monarchists, non-party people, and Octobrists." As a consequence, the monarchists had decided in 1909 to "stay away from the Nationalists as an extremely unreliable and dangerous group."[17] Their dismay aside, the monarchists had little choice but to play by the new rules of Russian politics. As the progressive *Saratovskii Listok (Saratov Leaflet)* described the situation, "Now even the rightists recognize that they can't get by without the Duma but maneuver so that the Duma serves their interests and not those of a majority of the Russian people." In another issue, the Saratov newspaper remarked that "the right now understands that it must campaign [and that] it needs its own press." The Progressist *Russkoe Slovo* played on the same theme when it stated that the right "clearly understands the significance of the 3 June law [Prime Minister Peter Stolypin's 1907 decree that manipulated voting participation] which placed the elections in the hands of the gentry (*pomeshchiki*)." The monarchist newspaper *Volga* (Saratov) described its approach in its masthead slogan, "Unity of Russia, the Tsar, and the Duma [for] Freedom, Order, and Peaceful Labor." *Volga* editorialized that for the upcoming Fourth Duma elections, all rightists "should come out as a [single] party" to promote the "slogans of Orthodoxy, Autocracy, and Nationality." The editors opposed cooperation with Nationalists and Octobrists, whose "constitutionalism" had rendered them unreliable and dangerous.[18] In the new political conditions, even the far right, with miniscule popular support and starkly reactionary views, entered the fray of Duma elections and politics, thereby conceding a principal point of constitutional government.

Press support for parliamentary government across the political spectrum implies additional progressive attitudes. Indeed, the Russian press staked out liberal territory on a range of issues. As one would expect, the Constitutional Democratic *Russkie Vedomosti (Russian News)* and *Rech' (Speech)* and the Progressist *Novoe Slovo* unstintingly supported economic, social, and political progress. For example, *Russkie Vedomosti* raised sharp questions about women's rights and progress in education. It supported the Duma project for free compulsory education and praised the development of free schools for workers funded by local government. The Constitutional Democratic paper also lined up behind a government project to enhance funding for city dumas and zemstvos (elected land councils), institutions responsible for local services, and recommended freeing them from ancillary tasks imposed by the government.[19]

The Russian press everywhere displayed much the same characteristics. Only the extreme right displayed limited interest in (indeed, as regards Jews, outright opposition to) the advancement of human rights. On many economic and social issues, even right wing newspapers promoted development over stasis, as for instance, on the matter of education. As the Nationalist *Novoe Vremia* put the matter, "The role of the . . . Duma in the area of popular education cannot be denied . . . The Third Duma did everything it could, especially in [the matter of] primary schools."[20] The entire Russian press reported and commented widely on educational issues. Educational opportunities for workers, women, Jews, and for all children (general, compulsory, and free) received support and praise. The newspaper *Arkhangel'sk* identified the question of general education (*vse-obshchee obuchenie*) as "the most important problem in contemporary life," the principal obstacle to which was financial. *Sibir'* (Irkutsk) deplored the obstructionism of the State Council in the matter of general education and saw this as a chief issue for the Fourth Duma. During early 1914, the *Kurskaia Gazeta* (*Kursk Gazette*) praised the recent national educational congress's resolution in favor of special schools for non-Russian ethnic groups, including Jews. Two years earlier, the *Khar'kovskaia Vecherniaia Gazeta* (*Khirkov Evening Gazette*) scorned the "bureaucracy for not sharing the intelligentsia's [dedication] to general education. Not for nothing did Count [S.Iu.] Witte," continued the Khirkov newspaper, "call the proposal for general education the first national duty." The Octobrist *Golos Moskvy* (Voice of Moscow) recommended a compromise between the State Council's and the Duma's legislative proposals on general education and criticized the liberals for "playing politics" with the issue. The *Kazanskaia Gazeta (Kazan Gazette)* noted the increasing number of educational institutions opening in regional cities and praised the idea of "decentralization," which allowed schools to cater to the needs of local populations. The *Vostochnoe Pomor'e* (*The Eastern Seaboard*, Nikolaevsk-on-the-Amur) praised the proposed legislation on general education.[21] The Russian press lined up squarely behind education for the entire population.

   Other matters of rights and status received similar coverage and commentary. One early 1912 analysis in the Progressist *Russkoe Slovo* might serve as a template of human rights press coverage and commentary. "Those interested in freedom of conscience, general education, [and] workers' insurance must take an active stance," insisted the Progressist paper. On the one hand, *Russkoe Slovo* wanted to "end violations of personal rights and press freedom" and, on the other, demanded "equality of all citizens before the law [within] a system based upon the law."[22] On the women's question, the conservative *Novoe Vremia* reported favorably on a proposed law for opening the legal profession to women. The *Ufimskii Vestnik (Ufa Messenger)* criticized current legislative failures as regards "women's rights." The *Saratovskii Listok* called for the "expansion of women's rights" and drew an invidious comparison on this issue between "civilized Europe" and Russia. During 1910, the *Altaiskaia Gazeta* (*Altai Gazette*, Barnaul) discussed the role of the Moscow branch of the League of Equal Rights for Women in the formation of the local Society for the Struggle Against Child Mortality. "Our summons and hopes," stated the paper, "have been fulfilled."[23] No opposition to reform on the women's or related questions reached the press.

   The local press, itself vulnerable to government reprisals, constantly reported and deplored government censorship and closure of newspapers. The 1910 inaugural issue of *Belorusskii Golos* (*Voice of Belorus*, Gomel) noted bitterly that "we have grown used to newspapers without news." The analogous 1910 issue of the *Bakinskie Novosti* (*Baku News*) asserted its "sacred dedication to freedom of the press" and pledged to "serve society faithfully with the truth." In an early 1914 editorial about economic growth, the *Ural'skii Listok* described the press as a "powerful motor for enlivening social mechanisms and for hearing various ideas. The press is the necessary moving force of creative life." The *Astrakhanskii Kur'er* noted with alarm certain 1913 changes in the law on press censorship. Under the old law, censorship (and penalties) occurred after distribution, whereas the new law required each issue to be delivered to the censors' office three hours before printing.[24] (This obviously raised the prospect of confiscated issues and suppressed articles, as in fact became common practice.) As with most human rights issues, differing opinions did not surface in the press. The press, of course, would hardly espouse limitations upon its freedom of expression and right to exist. An aspect of press freedom that reached the widest imaginable application was reportage of, commentary about, and polemics with the stances of other newspapers, both local and national. Access to almost any newspaper in Russia of virtually any tendency would have familiarized the reader with reportage and stances of the press in general. Although hardly inviolable, press freedom in Russia had come a long way, with the clear support of much of Russian society.

Among human rights issues, only the Jewish question witnessed significant differences in the press. All right wing newspapers engaged in constant Jew-baiting. Even the Nationalist *Novoe Vremia*, which on some issues shared a growing civic consciousness with the progressive press, displayed an obnoxious tendency to make disparaging comments about Jews. The rightist press reiterated *ad nauseam* such expressions as "Jews—the enemies of peace," "the Kike-(*Zhido-*)Octobrist Block," "Kike-Masonry," and so forth. *Russkoe Znamia* (*Russian Banner*, St. Petersburg, Union of the Russian People) provided an abysmal standard in its incessant anti-Semitic ravings. On one occasion, it proclaimed the "international Yiddish Sanhedrin a threat to the world." On another, it analyzed the international strike movement as a "kike-mason plot to enslave the world." Other reactionary newspapers, such as *Volga* (Saratov), *Tverskoe Povolzh'e* (Tver), and *Russkii Golos* (Odessa), followed suit.[25] One has the impression that for arch-conservatives in Russia, anti-Semitism had become, variously, the mother's milk of the movement, a handy whipping boy for any problem, a ritualistic exercise to distract from real issues, and perhaps even a rite of passage. It was part of right-wing identity, hatemongering standing in for real analysis. The reactionary parties' artificially swollen Duma fractions, based upon flagrantly manipulated election laws, increased the matter's significance. In addition, the tsarist regime itself, in the person of Nicholas II and others, gave moral and real support to the reactionaries.

Still, if newspapers are a measure, anti-Semitism had little hold on Russia's population. Between 1910 and 1914, of all human rights issues, aside from labor, the Jewish question surfaced most often in the Russian press. From one end of the empire to the other, the press condemned manifestations of anti-Jewish sentiment. The *Azovskii Vestnik* pointedly noted the resolution of the recent Congress of the Nobility (February 1911) aimed at "delimiting the rights of Jews, as exerting a harmful influence in all walks of life." In early 1912, the *Akkermanskoe Obozrenie* characterized as "obscurantists" (*mrakobesov*, literally "dark demons") those responsible for the recent appearance of a leaflet that "pit one part of the population against another in violation of [the law]." The occasion was an article that had appeared about an alleged "ritual murder" in Kiev (evidently the infamous Beilis case). The Petersburg *Kommersant* criticized laws that restricted residence rights for Jews and quoted the Constitutional Democratic *Rech'* about lifting the limitations. Elsewhere, the paper noted that many stock exchange officials complained about how existing residence laws hindered business. The Barnaul exchange, according to *Kommersant*, was demanding temporary passes for Jewish merchants to attend an upcoming Omsk trade fair. The *Saratovskii Listok* sharply criticized the Nationalist Congress (February 1912) for passing resolutions against the widening of Jewish rights. According to the Saratov newspaper, the Nationalists wanted ownership of "all state resources in Russian and not in non-Russian (*inorodets*) hands," to which *Saratovskii Listok* added caustically "for non-Russian read Jewish." The *Khar'kovskaia Vecherniaia Gazeta (Khirkov Evening Gazette)* noted that visa problems for English Jews, when they tried to come to Russia, violated the Russian–English Treaty of 1895. The progressive Moscow paper, *Utro Rossii (Morning of Russia)*, criticized alleged anti-Semitism among Polish liberals.[26]

An especially interesting case was the *Kurskaia Gazeta (Kursk Gazette)*, which from its inaugural January 1, 1914 issue hammered away about the Jewish question. In one editorial, it contrasted Russian practices with that of other European countries where Jews held high political positions. It commented on problems Jews had in Russian universities and, as noted earlier, advocated special schools for Jewish and other ethnic minorities. Finally, on February 12, 1914, the Kursk paper drew aim on the recent circular of the Education Minister, A.L. Kasso, on Jews in institutions of higher learning. This circular, accused the *Kurskaia Gazeta*, "has as its goal to retain existing limitations." The local authorities promptly shut down the newspaper. When it finally reappeared on June 1, its opening issue renewed its promise to "strive to promote the development of society . . . and the interests of Kursk citizens without consideration of party, nationality, position, or status."[27] With this, the unusually intolerant local authorities shut down the newspaper once and for all. *Kurskaia Gazeta*'s defiance of the government reflected pure civic courage since small provincial Russian cities such as Kursk had few Jewish citizens.

The Russian press's position on the Jewish question was part of a broader stance about ethnic minorities. *Saratovskii Vestnik* criticized the "zoological nationalism" of the Nationalists for their tendency to "delimit the rights of other ethnic groups [*inorodtsy*]." The paper wanted "basic reform" on the nationalities: "Russia should be the motherland, not the step-mother land of these nationalities." *Utro Rossii* published and praised a letter from a person who identified himself as "Not a Russian [*russkii*] but whole-heartedly a citizen of Russia [*rossiian*]." The newspaper then lauded the Constitutional Democrats' and Octobrists' "progressive" stance on this issue.[28] Many newspapers had begun to draw a distinction between "*rossiian*" and "*russkii*" when discussing the population.

Across the board, newspapers also recognized, advocated, and presumed economic progress. Even rightist newspapers had outlived opposition to industrial and agricultural transformation. A common mode of commentary singled out one or another industry, such as coal mining, gold mining, or agricultural machinery, for analysis and praise for technological innovation and growth. The newspapers also endlessly scrutinized industrial and commercial congresses, such as those of the Urals mining industry, the Siberian gold mining industry, Moscow heavy industry, national trade and industry, small business, cooperatives, and so forth. The *Arkhangel'sk* discussed improvements in local administrative organizations dealing with trade and industry, such as the local stock exchange. The *Akkermanskoe Obozrenie* analyzed a new type of shares' company recently introduced in Russia on the example of other European countries. One issue of the *Astrakanskaia Gazeta* reported on a local agricultural congress's outlook on agronomical improvements and discussed an artisanal congress with professional organization as one of its topics. In 1914, the *Ural'skii Listok* discussed a recent congress of small business and trade that sought State Bank financing for small business.[29]

The rightist *Volga* noted the business-like approach of various professional and technical congresses. One *Volga* editorial attributed "growth in the industrial sector and of the economy as a whole" to the phenomenon of "social organizations—stock market committees, congresses, commercial societies, and numerous other public institutions." The *Volga* editors regretted the absence of such a well-developed institutional network in the agricultural sphere. They warned that, "life does not wait. The government and society would provide Russian agriculturalists an enormous service if they would devote their attention and aide to helping them coordinate their interests." On another occasion, the paper spoke of the peasants' emancipation from serfdom in 1861 and from the commune (*obshchina*) in 1907 (by the Stolypin land reform) and then analyzed the positives and negatives of the individual farm (*khutor*) as opposed to the commune.[30] Under the title "Industrialists against the Third Duma," the liberal *Kazanskaia Gazeta* (*Kazan Gazette*) analyzed a recent commercial and industrial congress, whose representatives had criticized the Duma for not paying sufficient attention to the financial needs of industry and trade. In another issue, the newspaper noted that the government was financially subsidizing the agricultural machinery industry and reported the laying down of telephone lines in rural regions, matters positively noted by other newspapers as well. *Utro Rossii* reported on the second annual Air Ship (*Vozdushno-plavatel'nyi*) Congress in April 1912, which reminds us of Russia's rapid technological transformation.[31]

Within the realm of economic commentary, the expanding cooperative movement received universal support. The Constitutional Democratic paper

Russkie Vedomosti noted the heady growth of the cooperatives, which in 1911 alone had increased from 16,900 to 21,000 organizations. Still, in terms of cooperative legislation, complained the newspaper, "Russia lagged far behind the countries of the West. In England, France, Belgium [etc.] legislation met the needs of the cooperative movements . . . [whereas] in Russia everything was in the hands of local administrators."[32] In an early 1911 issue, the *Astrakhanskaia Gazeta* reported the rapid growth of cooperatives both in cities and the villages since 1908. "People patronize hundreds of cooperatives in all their forms, whose usefulness is so obvious that, if only they are not hindered by certain political and technical conditions," they will continue to "multiply like mushrooms." There is no use, continued the Astrakhan newspaper, "talking of the political conditions, they are well-known [the government closing of some cooperatives for political activities]." The technical problem, a lack of trained cooperative personnel, could be solved by "opening schools to train cooperative activists." The *Belorusskii Golos* wrote in 1910 about people's attraction to rapidly growing cooperatives in Mogilev Province. "Energetic, experienced people are needed in [these] social organizations," concluded the Gomel newspaper. The *Kazanskaia Gazeta* produced statistics about the hectic growth of the cooperatives, especially during 1910–11. The editors expressed the opinion that agricultural cooperatives "help modernize Russian agriculture" by promoting the use of farm machinery. The rightist Saratov newspaper, *Volga*, described huge agricultural plantations in the United States and foresaw a Russian future in which cooperatives united small individual peasant farmers on a similar scale.[33] Like women's and educational issues, the cooperative movement found nothing but praise in the Russian press.

Although most of the Russian press shared a conceptual framework about economic development, some nuances merit further examination. In March 1912, *Birzhevye Vedomosti* (*Stock Market News*, St. Petersburg) critiqued the nobles in association with their recent congress. "They differ sharply from the intelligentsia in that productivity factors do not enter their economic considerations—not benefits from the cooperatives, not the strengthening of credit, not improvements in agricultural methods, industry or commerce . . . What else can one expect from our wild medieval land owners." Although too harsh in view of noble-oriented parties' recent rapid adjustment to economic development, this view focuses attention on the business class's orientation. *Kommersant* (St. Petersburg) worried that most of the profits from agriculture were winding up in the hands of "middlemen." "Between the peasant's barn and the exporter's elevator line up rows of speculators who warm their hands on fluctuations in grain prices," remarked the business paper. Elsewhere, *Kommersant* lauded the role of "fairs in developing the economy in Russia's peripheries" by connecting outlying areas with the center and with world markets. Trade fairs, the editors pointed out, had until recently played a crucial role in Western economies. In another editorial, the newspaper again recommended the West as a model for "mobilization of the consumer." According to *Kommersant*, in the West "factories produce the goods, banks finance them, and syndicates distribute them." The potential for Russia, with its 150,000,000 population, was enormous, concluded the editors.

During the winter of 1912, *Kommersant* recalled a series of economic discussions (*ekonomicheskie besedy*) three years ago, summoned at the initiative of "progressive merchants and industrialists." The meetings had "attracted academic economists and representatives from various government ministries," as well as "rightist and leftist" deputies from the State Council and Duma. The lively exchange of ideas had provided the professors and government figures with direct knowledge about conditions in the nation's largest industries. Unfortunately, noted *Kommersant*, few such conversations had taken place recently. Lack of government familiarity with business problems might, the editors feared, lead to a new economic crisis. Regardless, a few months later, the newspaper expressed remarkable confidence in Russia's business classes. At the May 1912 trade and industry congress, some speakers had used the saying, "clear the road, the merchants are coming!" Newspapers of various tendencies had found this threatening, to which the *Kommersant* editors replied caustically, "for the noble landowners and the intelligentsia the commercial class is a bunch of petty traders at fairs." The bourgeoisie does not fear the slogan, claimed the business newspaper. The business classes had the task of using their experience to "reconstruct our way of life."[34]

Kommersant's preference for the exchange of ideas over confrontation introduces a related topic, the spread of socially responsible economic attitudes. For example, under the rubric "Trade and Industry," the *Azovskii Vestnik* reported heavily on general economic questions and on Azov's port facilities. Nevertheless, the paper's 1911 inaugural issue regretted the "tendency of many newspapers to serve chiefly the . . . financial interests of wealthy entrepreneurs." As a counterweight to "entrepreneurial greed," the editors pledged to bring to the "awareness of society moral and socially responsible views." An example occurred when the newspaper criticized the trading syndicate *Rost* (Growth) for raising the price of matches. The *Kurskaia Gazeta* recommended a "struggle against the fuel and metallurgical syndicates if they are criminal, [whereas] if they represent a healthy evolution in economic life," then data to this effect should be brought to the public attention. The business-oriented *Kommersant* again criticized grain speculators for reaping profits at the expense of peasant farmers and backed a state grain monopoly as a solution. "Russia produces," continued *Kommersant*, "1/2 of the world's rye, 1/3 of its barley, 1/4 of its oats, and 1/5 of its wheat [on the basis of which she] should dictate world grain prices, instead of [remaining] completely dependent on foreign buyers, who often engage in dumping." Here high moral purpose intersected with national economic assertiveness. In a somewhat different vein, the *Torgovo-Promyshlennaia Gazeta* (*Trade and Industry Gazette*, St. Petersburg) disliked the tendency of entrepreneurs to shunt off onto sub-contractors the costs of workers' health insurance. This preeminent entrepreneurial paper asserted "the entrepreneurs' responsibility for workers' insurance." The

Constitutional Democratic *Russkie Vedomosti* (Russian News) accused the Octobrist Duma fraction of "maneuvering on certain statutes in favor of industrialists."[35] The *Azovskii Vestnik's* complaint notwithstanding, blatant acquisition of profit at the expense of the laboring classes was not popular in Russian public discourse.

The topic of civic consciousness, that is, outlooks that transcend class, religious, ethnic, or personal boundaries in favor of a broadly conceived public good, arises naturally from the entire preceding analysis. When *Russkie Vedomosti* wanted improved financing for local government, this marks an example of civic consciousness. So do attitudes on parliamentarianism, mass education, press freedom, the women's and Jewish question, and so forth. During early 1912, the *Arkhangel'sk* praised "a new development" in which congresses of city government officials in Kiev, Khirkov, Maikop, and elsewhere occurred for the purpose of "working out general ideas of city governance and organization." The *Vostochnoe Pomor'e* urged local city administrators to take part in an upcoming city government congress on "city welfare." On a related matter, the *Azovskii Vestnik* commented on the "unexpected liberal turn" in the State Council vote on a proposed law to limit the juridical competency of land captains (*zemskie nachal'niki*, local state-appointed officials with dictatorial powers). Many newspapers wanted to eliminate all juridical functions for land captains. The *Astrakhanskii Kur'er* called for police reform on the basis of "raises in salaries," a still familiar theme in present-day Russia and elsewhere. During 1910, the *Bakinskie Novosti* demanded the immediate creation of local courts that extended full equal rights to peasants, as did the *Kurskaia Gazeta* in 1914. The Octobrist *Golos Moskvy* praised the zemstvo (elected rural councils) movement in the realm of "cultural endeavors." It had been a "great mistake to have identified zemstvo teachers and doctors as secret revolutionaries," a critical reference to the post-1907 government crackdown on zemstvo activists said.[36]

What positions did conservative groups take in respect to this new civic consciousness? Indisputably, rightist parties and even the right-centrist Nationalists and Octobrists impeded the pace of reform and, in some instances, the kind of reforms desired by the Progressists, the Constitutional Democrats, and the socialists. Even so, reformist values and a new tolerance were penetrating the Russian conservative consciousness. For example, one prominent monarchist urged the upcoming Fourth Duma "to concentrate on the affairs of the lower-middle class (*meshchane*) and the peasantry," groups allegedly "completely forgotten" by the last Duma. As regards the Third Duma's unfinished legislative agenda, the Nationalist *Novoe Vremia* urged passage of laws on religious toleration for non-Orthodox and non-Christian religions, the inviolability of the individual, a state income tax, using state lands for poor peasants, and providing full citizenship for Old Believers (a persecuted Orthodox sect). Less positively, *Novoe Vremia* also edged close to curbs on speech when it proposed laws aimed at punishing revolutionary propaganda in the press and in schools (e.g., "criminal responsibility for praising criminals or criminal activity in speech or print").[37]

In its report of a recent agricultural congress, the right-wing *Volga* calmly noted that the "majority of our 'academic' and everyday agronomists [farmers] belong to the liberal and radical intelligentsia and do not trust the government about the land question." On another occasion, the monarchist newspaper scorned "our dead three-field Russia," which would be replaced by the new agricultural Russia. The "peasantry working the land makes up three quarters of our population," who will now be working under the new "higher cultural conditions in the village." Elsewhere, *Volga* editors urged political figures to "occupy themselves with real problems, and not 'politicking' (*politikanstvo*)," a common conservative refrain. At the beginning of 1912, *Volga* noted that the "debates of recent congresses of geologists, chemists, machine-building entrepreneurs, linguists of ancient languages, did not fulfill the hopes of our Russian friends of 'freedom' [the liberals and socialists]. Not one incendiary speech, not one saying against the government [was heard]. There was a time when even cement producers gathering in Petersburg began their sessions with anti-government declarations," recalled the editors.[38] *Volga* spoke a little too soon, since the Lena shooting soon revived the era of "anti-government declarations."

Meanwhile, the progressive Moscow newspaper, *Russkoe Slovo*, spoke out on the issue of "freedom of association" with respect to the wave of public congresses. The government allowed the recent mining industry congress to meet, because that group was "reliable," whereas it had cut off a congress of bicyclists! "Why not let them all meet?" queried the newspaper. On another occasion, it remarked that in the past, the alleged "backwardness of the peasantry served as an excuse for not carrying out a full range of reforms." The "darkness" of the peasantry, accused the editors, is prolonged by tactics of the "old regime" (a startling insult to the still existing tsarist regime). The truth is, continued the progressive newspaper, that the "peasants have already fully matured, to the level of [participation in the local] . . . zemstvo's and many other reforms." The government always delays reforms for a "better time." On another occasion, *Russkoe Slovo* wrote that "the Russian worker is already playing an historical role. Workers and student youth are the most aware [of all Russian groups]."[39]

These comments raise questions about the widespread belief that Russia's political and intellectual elites viewed the people as dark and unenlightened (*temnyi narod*). Only with utter rarity did anything equivalent to the idea of the "dark masses" appear in the newspapers inspected for this study. At one point, the Nationalist *Novoe Vremia* regretted that population's "inability" to participate in fully representative government. The Octobrist *Golos Moskvy* worried that some workers "may be too dark and downtrodden to state their own case without help." The New Year issue of the Constitutional Democratic *Russkie Vedomosti* attributed poor Russian productivity to the "low cultural level of the people [*narod*] and the weak juridical position of labor."[40] A far more common refrain, however, was that the Russian population was ready for participation in elections, in constitutional government, and in any other tasks laid to them in a modern society. Most commentators attributed low productivity solely to low pay and the "lack of civil rights in Russia."[41] Public discourse located Russia's problems in the laws, the administration of the laws, and "entrepreneurial greed," rather than in the people.

The parameters of civic thinking shifted, depending on any group's general political position. Even so, the new civic consciousness permeated the thinking even of the extreme right and thoroughly dominated public discourse in the rest of Russian society. Aside from stances on government, the labor question best tests the nature and limits of the new civic consciousness. This is the case because interpretations of late tsarist history commonly posit specially sharp worker–bourgeois hostility, within a society intricately dissected into worker, peasant, intelligentsia, bourgeois, and noble segments. (These and other social groups had their own identities and interests, but press reportage discloses no fault lines dividing them into irreconcilably hostile camps.) The workers' significance also reflects their adherence to radical parties and the sharpness of their dissent during the 1905–07 revolution. Also, it so happens that, of all the social questions, the labor issue received by far the widest and most sympathetic attention in the press during this period. In other words, society heard the pleas of the workers and peasants. As mentioned above, analysis of Russian society's responses to the April 1912 Lena massacre has already called into question the social fragmentation thesis.[42] The consensual social response was too sweeping and prolonged to have been accidental or situational. It reflected deep-seated, broadly held assumptions about labor's place in a developing Russia. A general discursive framework, a civic consciousness, therefore predated and formed a specific context for social responses to the famous massacre. What did the press say about labor in light of the new civic consciousness?

The following section examines press coverage of the workers' movement abroad and within Russia. The Russian press's supportive reportage of labor and even socialism abroad immediately strikes the eye. That this was not mere "Aesopian" commentary on affairs at home is suggested by the fact that the same newspapers constantly deployed specific invidious comparisons between Russia and "the West." A comparative framework, inevitably to the detriment of the Russian government's stances, was a hallmark of press commentary on labor, even in business-oriented and, on occasions, conservative newspapers.

During early 1912, *Russkie Vedomosti* published an article about the English coal-miners' strike entitled, "How they deal with the workers' question in the West." Just two months before the Lena shooting, it successfully forecast an "enlivenment of the workers' question here" and wanted the Fourth Duma to "place the workers' question on its agenda . . . on the English example." Toward the end of March 1912, the Constitutional Democratic *Rech'* admired the "peaceful end" of the English coal-miners' strike, as did many newspapers. In a regularly featured column, "The Workers' Question," the St. Petersburg *Torgovo-Promyshlennaia Gazeta* (*Trade and Industry Gazette*) detailed all aspects of the English strike, including its vast scale and potential economic costs. Regardless, noted the business newspaper, it has been characterized by "ongoing negotiations [and] support in government circles for the workers' demands for minimum pay rates." The conduct of the strike so far, guessed the editors presciently, "suggests that it will be settled in the nearest future." The business paper characterized the recently ended German strike as "unsuccessful" in winning anything but minor pay raises. The editors then directly praised the new minimum wage law for English coal-miners, which, until "now exists only in Belgium, Austrialia, and New Zealand." The editors suggested a "legally guaranteed wage" as the proper method for avoiding strikes and recommended laws that "protect both sides in the great struggle between labor and capital and defend society from the economic losses of these devastating [strikes]."

Birzhevye Vedomosti remarked, barely a month prior to the Lena shooting, that "when a Russian reader hears of millions of striking English workers, his head fills with questions about how many police and soldiers have been summoned. How many workers have been beaten, arrested, and brought to court? The answer," claimed the paper too rosily about strikes abroad, "is not one soldier, not one person." As regards the new English minimum wage law for miners, the Octobrist *Golos Moskvy* commented that "for the first time in 150 years of industrial development, [the new law] gives a minimum wage to the important category of mining workers. No one doubts for a moment," continued the Octobrist newspaper, "that this marks a new era in English worker legislation." During May 1912, *Kommersant* recommended the English Shop Act's regulation of hours for commercial workers as a proper criterion for settling the Russian commercial and office clerks' lengthy struggle for shorter working hours. Many newspapers supported the clerks on the matter of hours.[43]

During 1912, local newspapers reported widely, and always without criticism of the workers, on coal-miners' strikes in England, Germany, America, Japan, and elsewhere. *Sibir'* characterized the English coal-miners' demands as "very modest." *Arkhangel'sk* noted that "in the struggle between labor and capital [a phrase that seems to have captured the Russian imagination] both sides have perfected their weapons. The strike is the workers' sharpest weapon . . . [and it] has great significance for all capitalist nations." The *Saratovskii Vestnik* urged the English government to "exercise great tact" in its approach to the striking coal-miners. The rightist *Volga* commented reservedly about "interesting data in the English newspapers on the spread of ideas about strikes among English workers." *Russkoe Znamia* asked provocatively "who needs the English and German coal strikes?" which it then blamed on a "kike-mason plot," a formula that, for all its absurdity, eschewed criticism of the workers. Newspapers sometimes reported the forceful repression of strikes abroad or worker violence. *Volga* posed the plaintive question, "don't they struggle against strikes in England, even with troops?" The more common tendency was to emphasize and even exaggerate, presumably for the government's ears, the "peaceful" nature of strike transactions in other countries.

Newspapers raised other worker-oriented questions. *Vostochnoe Pomor'e* noted that in America, "industrialists don't get by without the intervention of various government bodies that mediate between entrepreneurs and workers . . . We don't have this." The editors promoted government regulatory bodies as the "most vital link in the chain between industrialists and workers." The Octobrist *Golos Moskvy* described "the success of socialism in various European countries." In Germany, claimed the Octobrists, the "socialists live according to the strict rules of Karl Marx [*sic*]," whereas in France, the socialists have compromised class ideology by "allying themselves with the [bourgeois] masons." The *Akkermanskoe Obozrenie* compared the recent "German Social Democratic victories" in parliamentary elections with the "boring politics in France." The *Saratovskii Vestnik* urged the German liberals and big bourgeoisie to "extend a hand toward . . . the German Social Democrats."[44] The even-handed remarks, friendly in tone toward workers and socialists abroad, indisputably expressed advocacy for the home front.

What about at home? Along with the 1912 Lena shooting, several labor-oriented issues attracted great attention. The government's incessant attacks on labor unions struck a deep note in Russian society and in the press. In a 1910 issue, *Altaiskaia Gazeta* (Barnaul) reported on a recent labor conflict (quite rare that year) that led to the closing of a metalworkers' union. During 1911, *Astrakhanskaia Gazeta* discussed the Social Democratic Duma interpellation about the closing of labor unions and the *Bakinskie Novosti* stated in its first 1911 issue that "the closing of labor unions was continuing as throughout 1910." By May 1912, even *Moskovskie Gubernskie Vedomosti* (*Moscow Province News*), a government publication, reported, without comment of course, the closing of labor unions in several localities. In its 1912 New Year issue, the progressive *Russkie Vedomosti* insisted that most labor unions "have been closed for reasons having nothing to do with [their activities]." Many unions, asserted *Russkie Vedomosti*, exist "purely formally and carry out no activities. Repression, pressure, and liquidation continue." The real reason for the strikes, which the government blamed on the unions, was "very low wages and poor conditions." *Birzhevye Vedomosti* complained that first the new 1906 law had allowed hundreds of unions to open and now the government was closing them down by the hundreds. The entire attempt to "follow the cultural example of the West" by allowing workers to unite to defend their interests was collapsing in the wave of repressions. According to the business newspaper, the government's activities were "in complete violation of the [1906] law of association that is the main guarantee of cultural development."

Only *Kommersant* and the rightist *Volga* approached a note of criticism about the labor unions. The former agreed that many unions "have been closed or are leading a pitiful existence," but attributed this to "the unions' refusal to live within their statutory framework." *Kommersant* noted attempts (presumably by moderate socialists) to refocus the labor union movement on "the workers' material conditions" rather than on politics. The editors praised the numerous cooperatives that "catered to the workers' economic needs." The conservative *Volga* reported that the "left" wanted a "cultured country where a whole range of professional unions existed [whereas, according to the left] the Russian government is preventing this." *Volga* countered with the observation that "in Russia 2000 societies [cooperatives] serve the needs of the agricultural population." Even these newspapers did not oppose the principle of workers' unions but only their extracurricular political activities. Russia's conservatives promoted cooperatives as a supposedly non-politicized alternative to labor unions, although cooperatives too often engaged in politics and were closed.[45]

The workers' insurance movement and the insurance law that eventually passed in the Third Duma attracted prolonged reportage and favorable commentary. Differences arose only about methods and amounts. The Duma debates reported in *Novoe Vremia* elucidate the question. One speaker from the left complained that "the position of the . . . workers is very heavy. Help is long overdue. But the government regrets spending a kopeck on them. This legislation provides insufficient help for injuries and excludes representatives from [some categories of workers] from the main [insurance] committee." Another speaker also argued "this project does not suffice" and urged the "inclusion of aid for people suffering from work-related illnesses [*professional'nye bolezni*]." The government spokesperson insisted that "this law provides aid for all injuries. If the amount is insufficient, then individuals can turn to the courts without canceling their benefits. This is not ideal but a step forward." One politician close to the government agreed that "this Duma has [not] fulfilled all the demands of the working class. But we do have to deal with reality and soften those demands somewhat. I am convinced that when the Third Duma's workers' legislation goes into effect, it will lay a firm basis [for improving workers' conditions]." The principle of ameliorative legislation was a given on all sides. When the workers' insurance law passed, the Nationalist *Novoe Vremia* commented about a celebratory dinner attended by Duma and State Council members. "This was the first friendly meeting [of the two houses] since 1907. It represents a new atmosphere of cooperation, the main result [of which] is the workers' insurance law."[46]

Torgovo-Promyshlennaia Gazeta remarked that "the government [workers' insurance] project has attracted broad sympathy from the public . . . much of the press favors it." This important entrepreneurial newspaper then insisted on "grant[ing] medical compensation to workers at the owners' expense." During June 1912, *Kommersant* discussed Moscow area business owners' plans to form an association to deal with the new insurance obligations. By 1913, newspapers reported such associations in other industrial centers. *Russkoe Slovo*, a newspaper with deep ties to entrepreneurial circles, noted former Prime Minister Witte's support for the insurance law in the State Council. "The cost of insurance for the owners," the newspaper continued, "will be reasonable and just in view of the profits of Russian industry." *Russkoe Slovo* even promoted insurance for hired agricultural workers. The Octobrist *Golos Moskvy* philosophized that "at the heart of worker legislation is the principle that conflict between workers and their employers cannot be left to the free sphere of negotiations. The law must intervene . . . On the Western example, the state must struggle against [socialism] only if it threatens to deepen class divisions."[47]

The *Akkermanskoe Obozrenie* characterized the insurance law as the "first major example of the new Russian social legislation." Although, continued the newspaper, it has "some inadequacies, we should not just criticize it but bring it into practice and improve it." During early 1914, the *Kurskaia Gazeta*, soon to be closed for its coverage of the Jewish question, commented on the enormous growth of the factory insurance funds. In the capital, there were 422 funds with 342,000 members, in Moscow 504 with 635,000 members, in Warsaw 330 with 193,000 members, and so forth. In total, these "provided huge compensations." On a more ominous note, other issues of this newspaper reported the closing down of factory insurance funds because of their political activities.[48]

The Russian press coverage of all these and other worker-related issues operated within a framework of recognition of the workers' plight and support for their cause. Of special note were the responses even of the rightist parties, whose positions on basic economic progress, the improvement of laborers' conditions through cooperatives and other organizations, and the necessity of state intervention did not differ from the rest of the political spectrum. A good case in point was the rightist *Volga*'s response to the Lena shooting. The editors insisted that the "worker's demands had definitely been just . . . The[ir] conditions . . . were like [imprisonment] at hard labor . . . The workers were not a threat [and their] demands were modest." *Russkoe Znamia*, the reactionary press leader, agreed. "Earning millions, [Lenzoto] paid the lowest wages. If our Russian government was as active and broadly aware of its tasks [as it should be], it would have managed to find a solution to the conflict." The fly in the ointment of *Russkoe Znamia*'s civic position was that, predictably, it blamed everything on "kike-mason control of the Russian economy, . . . a grave threat to the Russian worker."[49] During July 1912, *Novoe Vremia* published a communication about a linen factory in Vladimir Province. When the roughly 1,000 workers, all local peasants, tried to complain about low pay and horrendous conditions, the owners dismissed the complaints as "silliness." When peasants from a nearby village informed the owners that the factory's drainage of bleach polluted their land, the owners threatened to "fire all the workers from your village. The men," remarked *Novoe Vremia*, "had to bite their tongues." Russian society's response to the Lena Massacre makes sense against the background of general outlooks on labor, just as society's outlooks on labor become explicable in terms of shared approaches to the Russian polity, society, and economy.

During the years before the outbreak of World War I, Russian newspapers displayed little that suggested social fragmentation. Quite the contrary, many past fractures were in the process of healing. Russia's main social groups were reaching agreement about what kind of government Russia would have, about the nature of the society and economy, and about major issues of concern for workers and peasants. The monarchist parties were adjusting to the fact of constitutional monarchy with its concomitants. Parties to the right of center such as the Nationalists and Octobrists accepted constitutional monarchy for the time being on the expectation of ultimate parliamentary rule.

Progressists, Constitutional Democrats, and the socialist parties aimed at a constitutional republic. The agreements did not cover everything. Russian socialists, as elsewhere, wanted socialism and others did not. Political conflicts and normal polemics summoned by these differences did not represent social fragmentation.

Further undercutting the concept of fragmentation was a genuine convergence on issues of human rights, economic development, and labor. These fit very well under the heading of civic consciousness. Only the extreme right and, to a much lesser degree, the Nationalists sometimes offered less than full support for progressive initiatives in these realms. Even here, care is required since the conservatives were also edging toward enlightened positions on the society and the economy, with anti-Semitism as the exception. If one were to extract the anti-Semitic slurs from the Nationalist *Novoe Vremia*, an unwary reader might imagine the newspaper to be representative of the moderate Russian intelligentsia. As regards the socialists, whose press is not featured here because of its special nature (some papers appeared abroad, others from inside Russia were repressed, censored, and short-lived), we should recall that on all these major questions, they shared outlooks with the progressive center. They were for constitutional government, for human rights, against anti-Semitism, for economic growth, and, of course, desired full workers' and peasants' rights. The emerging consensus was, therefore, quite broad indeed. It was against the government, which bode ill for that institution. It was for a broad range of social, political, and economic developments, with emphasis both on private initiative and state intervention, a factor that places Russia squarely within the European norm. Extreme inter-social strife at the level of public discussion was not part of the picture. The business-oriented press displayed a distinct willingness for entrepreneurs to share the social burdens and supported costly state initiatives as well. Laissez-faire was not a popular concept in Russian discourse. Indeed, no one used it.

The press everywhere both reflects and helps form public opinion. Russia's newspapers could not operate for long completely outside the realm of existing predominant public opinion. The opinions expressed in the newspapers reflected social reality. Russian society viewed itself on a path of development in all realms of human endeavor in alignment with Western and European models. All sides constantly deployed comparisons with other European countries and with industrialized, constitutional non-European nations as appropriate frameworks for Russian development. A "special Russian path" and a "Russian idea" simply did not appear. Likewise, press and other public discourses showed little sign of historical analysis's autocratic culture, dark masses, and social fragmentation. Were not these all figments of imagination? Is it not possible that we have confuted epiphenomenal philosophizing with reality, thereby thoroughly confusing major issues of early-twentieth-century Russian development?[50] In any case, we should examine Russia's new civic consciousness before formulating any more theories about pre-revolutionary Russia. This study's findings refocus attention on World War I, the breaker of nations and empires, and on the vagaries of the 1917 revolution as explanations of the rise to power of the Bolsheviks. Retroactive arguments that ignore masses of evidence no longer suffice.

NOTES

1. Quoted in David Danow, *The Thought of Mikhail Bakhtin: From Word to Culture* (New York: St. Martin's Press, 1991), 21.
2. For the basic interpretation of social fragmentation, see Leopold Haimson, "The Problem of Social Stability in Urban Russia, 1905–1917" (parts 1 & 2) *Slavic Review*, no.4 (December 1964): 619–642; no.1 (March 1965): 1–22. For a more recent use of this approach, see Tim McDaniels, *Autocracy, Capitalism, and Revolution in Russia* (Berkeley: University of California Press, 1988). A useful summary of the social fragmentation question is Arthur Mendel's "On Interpreting the Fate of Imperial Russia," in *Russia under the Last Tsar*, Theofanis George Stavrou, ed. (Minneapolis: University of Minnesota Press, 1969), 12–41. See also Mendel's "Peasant and Worker on the Eve of the First World War," and Theodore von Laue, "The Chances for Liberal Constitutionalism," *Slavic Review*, vol.XXV (1966): 23–46. For an updated version of the original thesis, see Leopold Haimson," 'The Problem of Political and Social Stability in Urban Russia on the Eve of War and Revolution' Revisited," *Slavic Review*, no.4 (Winter 2000), 849–850. For summaries and my critical commentary see "Unexpected Consensus: Russian Society and the Lena Massacre, April 1912," *Revolutionary Russia* 15 no.2 (December 2002): 3–5, 47–50.
3. My research about the massacre and responses to it can be found in "The Ninth Circle: The Lena Goldfields Workers and the Massacre of 4 April 1912," *Slavic Review* 53 no.3 (Fall 1994): 766–795; and "Unexpected Consensus," 1–52.
4. All of this is recounted in "Unexpected Consensus," *Revolutionary Russia*, as cited in the previous note.
5. Data for this study came from over 100 Russian-language newspapers of every tendency and from many parts of the Russian Empire. Several newspapers represent major political parties or movements: the Constitutional Democratic *Rech'* (*Speech*, St. Petersburg) and *Russkie Vedmosti* (*Russian News*, Moscow), the Nationalist *Novoe Vremia* (*New Times*, St. Petersburg), the Progressist *Russkoe Slovo* (*Russian Word*, Moscow), the Octobrist *Golos Moskvy* (*Voice of Moscow*, Moscow), and the Monarchist *Russkoe Znamia* (*Russian Banner*, Moscow) and *Volga* (Saratov). Most newspapers used in this study reflect random selection. These papers commonly designated themselves as "independent," "progressive," "non-aligned," "social," "political" and/or "cultural." Socialist newspapers, which existed under the threat of censorship and usually for short runs, although consulted, are not part of the database used here.
6. *Golos Moskvy*, no.73 (March 29, 1912); *Russkoe Slovo*, no.6 (January 8, 1912), no.9 (January 12, 1912); *Azovskii Vestnik*, no.48 (March 3, 1914); *Astrakhanskaia Gazeta*, no.21 (February 5, 1911); *Astrakhanskii Kur'er*, no.14 (March 20, 1913); *Ural'skii Listok*, no.90 (April 29, 1914).
7. *Sibirskaia Zhizn'*, no.55 (March 8, 1912).
8. *Azovskii Vestnik*, no.1 (January 22, 1911); *Akkermanskoe Obozrenie*, no.1 (December 31, 1911), no.3 (January 3, 1912), no.215 (November 29, 1912).
9. *Azovskii Vestnik*, no.9 (February 11, 1911); *Astrakhanskaia Gazeta*, no.7 (January 11, 1914); *Bakinskie Novosti*, no.1 (November 29, 1910), no.1 (January 3, 1911); *Belorusskii Golos*, no.9 (February 28, 1910).

10. *Ural'skii Listok*, no.90 (April 29, 1914); *Astrakhanskii Kur'er*, no.1 (March 5, 1913), no.2 (March 6, 1913), no.14 (March 20, 1913).

11. *Sibir'*, no.2 (January 3, 1912), no.31 (February 7, 1912); *Arkhangel'sk*, no.8 (January 11, 1912); *Kommersant*, no.802 (May 15, 1912).

12. *Russkie Vedomosti*, no.1 (January 1, 1912).

13. *Saratovskii Listok*, no.1 (January 1, 1912), no.64 (March 2, 1912), no.91 (April 27, 1912).

14. *Russkoe Slovo*, no.1 (January 1, 1912), no.6 (January 8, 1912), no.7 (January 10, 1912), no.41 (February 19, 1912), no.48 (February 28, 1912), no.76 (April 1, 1912).

15. *Golos Moskvy*, no.76 (April 1, 1912), no.79 (April 5, 1912), no.86 (April 13, 1912).

16. *Novoe Vremia*, no.12946 (March 29, 1912), no.12947 (March 30, 1912), no.13018 (June 10, 1912), no.13020 (June 12, 1912), no.13024 (June 16, 1912), no.13052 (July 14, 1912), no.12999 (May 22, 1912).

17. *Tverskoe Povolzh'e*, no.472 (January 15, 1912), no.473 (January 22, 1912); *Russkii Golos*, no.1 (February 12, 1912).

18. *Saratovskii Listok*, no.5 (January 6, 1912), no.64 (March 2, 1912); *Russkoe Slovo*, no.2 (January 3, 1912); *Volga*, nos.1–3 (January 1–4, 1912), no.51 (March 11, 1912).

19. *Russkie Vedomosti*, no.4 (January 5, 1912), no.21 (January 23, 1912), no.22 (January 27, 1912), no.78 (April 4, 1912).

20. *Novoe Vremia*, no.13022 (June 14, 1912).

21. *Arkhangel'sk*, no.62 (March 16, 1912); *Sibir'*, no.31 (February 7, 1912); *Kursksaia Gazeta*, no.1 (January 1, 1914); *Khar'kovskaia Vecherniaia Gazeta*, no.306 (January 7, 1912); *Golos Moskvy*, no.67 (March 21, 1912), no.79 (April 5, 1912); *Kazanskaia Gazeta*, no.2 (January 8, 1912), no.5 (January 29, 1912); *Vostochnoe Pomor'e*, no.2 (January 25, 1911); *Azovskii Vestnik*, no.2 (January 25, 1911).

22. *Novoe Slovo*, no.48 (February 28, 1912).

23. *Novoe Vremia*, no.13002 (May 25, 1912); *Ufimskii Vestnik*, no.64 (March 18, 1912); *Saratovskii Listok*, no.36 (February 14, 1912); *Altaiskaia Gazeta*, no.52 (April 13, 1910).

24. See, e.g., *Astrakhanskii Kur'er*, issues from March and April 1913, and *Kurskaia Gazeta*, issue from winter 1914. *Belorusskii Golos*, no.1 (January 24, 1910); *Ural'skii Listok*, no.1 (January 1, 1914); *Bakinskie Novosti*, no.1 (November 29, 1910); *Astrakhanksii Kur'er*, no.3 (March 7, 1913).

25. *Russkoe Znamia*, no.8 (January 11, 1912).

26. *Azovskii Vestnik*, no.15 (February 18, 1911); *Akkermanskoe Obozrenie*, no.6 (January 6, 1912); *Kommersant*, no.709 (January 13, 1912), no.717 (January 23, 1912); *Saratovskii Listok*, no.42 (February 21, 1912); *Khar'kovskaia Vechernaia Gazeta*, no.347 (February 27, 1912).

27. *Kurskaia Gazeta*, no.1 (January 1, 1914), no.2 (January 3, 1914), no.8 (January 17, 1914), no.17 (February 12, 1914), no.19 (June 1, 1914).

28. *Saratovskii Vestnik*, no.42 (February 21, 1912); *Utro Rossii*, no.53 (March 4, 1912).

29. *Russkoe Slovo*, nos.43–47 (February 21–25, 1912); *Torgovo-Promyshlennaia Gazeta*, no.68 (March 21, 1912); *Rech'*, no.64 (March 6, 1912); *Sibirskaia Zhizn'*, no.56 (March 9, 1912); *Arkhangel'sk*, no.8 (January 11, 1912); *Akkermanskoe Obozrenie*, no.216 (November 30, 1912); *Astrakhanskaia Gazeta*,

no.3 (January 5, 1911), no.8 (January 12, 1911), no.13 (January 26, 1911); *Vostochnoe Pomor'e*, no.28 (March 6, 1912).

30. *Volga*, no.5 (January 6, 1912), no.8 (January 11, 1912), no.21 (January 26, 1912), no.49 (March 1, 1912), no.65 (March 2, 1912).

31. *Kazanskaia Gazeta*, no.7 (February 12, 1912), no.12 (March 18, 1912); *Utro Rossii*, no.74 (March 30, 1912).

32. *Russkie Vedomosti*, no.58 (April 4, 1912).

33. *Astrakhanskaia Gazeta*, no.3 (January 5, 1911); *Belorusskii Golos*, no.4 (February 7, 1910); *Kazanskaia Gazeta*, no.2 (January 8, 1912), no.4 (January 22, 1912), no.7 (February 12, 1912); *Volga*, no.21 (January 26, 1912), no.60 (March 14, 1912).

34. *Birzhevye Vedomosti*, no.12823 (March 7, 1912); *Kommersant*, no.700 (January 2, 1912), no.702 (January 4, 1912), no.711 (January 16, 1912), no.743 (February 25, 1912), no.802 (May 15, 1912).

35. *Azovskii Vestnik*, no.1 (January 23, 1911), no.3 (January 27, 1911); *Kommersant*, no.774 (April 9, 1912); *Kurskaia Gazeta*, no.6 (January 12, 1914); *Torgovo-Promyshlennaia Gazeta*, no.93 (April 21, 1912).

36. *Arkhangel'sk*, no.3 (January 3, 1912); *Vostochnoe Pomor'e*, no.2 (January 25, 1911); *Azovskii Vestnik*, no.2 (January 25, 1911); *Astrakhanskii Kur'er*, no.3 (March 7, 1913); *Golos Moskvy*, no.72 (March 28, 1912); *Bakinskie Novosti*, no.4 (December 20, 1910), *Kurskaia Gazeta*, no.1 (January 1, 1914).

37. *Russkie Vedomosti*, no.73 (March 29, 1912); *Novoe Vremia*, no.13020 (June 12, 1912); *Russkoe Slovo* no.5 (January 6, 1912).

38. *Volga*, no.36 (February 15, 1912), no.5 (January 6, 1912), no.60 (March 14, 1912).

39. *Russkoe Slovo*, no.5 (January 6, 1912), no.6 (January 8, 1912), no.88 (April 15, 1912).

40. *Golos Moskvy*, no.53 (March 4, 1912); *Russkie Vedomosti*, no.1 (January 1, 1912).

41. *Volga*, no.77 (April 10, 1912).

42. See note 3 earlier.

43. *Russkie Vedomosti*, no.48 (February 29, 1912); *Torgovo-Promyshlennaia Gazeta*, no.52 (March 2, 1912), no.53 (March 3, 1912), no.67 (March 20, 1912), no.73 (March 29, 1912), no.102 (May 2, 1912); *Kommersant*, no.805 (May 18, 1912); *Golos Moskvy* no.69 (March 23, 1912); *Birzhevye Vedomosti*, no.12829 (March 10, 1912).

44. *Sibirskaia Zhizn'*, nos.56–58 (March 9–12, 1912); *Arkhangel'sk*, no.43 (February 23, 1912), no.57 (March 10, 1912); *Russkoe Slovo*, no.1 (January 1, 1912); *Vostochnoe Pomor'e*, no.57 (May 24, 1912); *Sibir'*, no.52 (March 2, 1912); *Saratovskii Vestnik*, no.2 (January 3, 1912), no.40 (February 18, 1912); *Saratovskii Listok*, no.42 (February 21, 1912); *Volga*, no.25 (January 31, 1912), no.77 (April 10, 1912); *Russkoe Znamia*, no.54 (March 7, 1912); *Golos Moskvy*, no.50 (March 1, 1912), no.71 (March 25, 1912); *Akkermanskoe Obozrenie*, no.3 (December 31, 1911); *Astrakhanskii Kur'er*, no.1 (March 5, 1913).

45. *Altaiskaia Gazeta*, no.53 (April 14, 1910); *Astrakhanskaia Gazeta*, no.5 (January 8, 1911); *Bakinskie Novosti*, no.1 (January 3, 1911); *Russkie Vedomosti*, no.1 (January 1, 1912), this article included materials from *Torgovo-Promyshlennaia Gazeta*, no.51 (March 2, 1912); *Birzhevye Vedomosti*, no.12819 (March 4, 1912); *Kommersant*, no.829 (June 15, 1912); *Volga*, no.77 (April 10, 1912).

46. *Novoe Vremia*, no.12977 (April 29, 1912), no.12961 (April 13, 1912), no.13017 (June 9, 1912).

47. *Torgovo-Promyshlennaia Gazeta*, no.84 (April 11, 1912), no.93 (April 21, 1912); *Kommersant*, no.820 (June 5, 1912); *Astrakhanskii Kur'er*, no.39 (April 26, 1913); *Russkoe Slovo*, no.72 (March 28, 1912), no.91 (April 19, 1912); *Golos Moskvy*, no.86 (April 13, 1912), no.67 (March 21, 1912).

48. *Akkermanskoe Obozrenie*, no.218 (December 2, 1912); *Kurskaia Gazeta*, no.13 (January 31, 1914).

49. *Volga*, no.79 (April 12, 1912); *Russkoe Znamia*, no.78 (April 7, 1912), no.99 (May 2, 1912).

50. For analysis of the Russian press over a broader time period that supports this study's interpretation, see Louise McReynolds, *The News under Russia's Old Regime: The Development of a Mass Circulation Press* (Princeton, NJ: Princeton University Press, 1991).

INDEX